1. INTRODUCTION

Egypt and Mesopotamia, the cradle(s) of civilizati
This study takes another approach and focuses on
river-based civilizations. Contacts between Egypt
already in the late fourth millennium BCE (when both lands transitioned from prehistory to history) as well as in the Amarna period (when the rulers of Egypt, Babylonia, and Assyria interacted in the diplomatic arena). These contacts intensified in the seventh century BCE when the Neo-Assyrian empire fought with the Sudan-based kings of Kush and conquered Libyan-dominated Egypt. This study deals with this period, during which Assyria (centred in today's north-eastern Iraq) was the dominant power of the Near East (Figs. 1-2).[1]

1.1 Aims and questions

The overarching aim of this work is to discuss relations between Africa and Mesopotamia. The preciser aims of this study are to identify Africans (Egyptians, Kushites, Libyans) in Neo-Assyrian texts, and to discuss the presence of Africans in the Neo-Assyrian empire from the viewpoints of individual-biographic and collective-demographic levels and perspectives.

The following research questions (centred on five interrogative words) are posed. *Who* were these Africans (in terms of ethnicity, gender/sex, age, and class)? *What* did these people do (in terms of profession)? *When* did they live (in terms of reign or time period)? *Where* did they live (in terms of the Assyrian heartland and provinces, the vassal states, or Africa)? *How* were they incorporated into the Assyrian realm (in terms of forced/voluntary, etc.)?

1.2 Previous research

Most previous research on Africa in the Neo-Assyrian empire tends to focus on Mesopotamia in Egypt (rather than on Egypt in Mesopotamia) and on Assyrian royal inscriptions (rather than on Assyrian letters and documents), and it also tends to have either a philological or historical-political perspective (rather than a socio-cultural perspective).

Regarding the philological perspective, Egyptologists have often used the writing of Egyptian names and words in cuneiform to reconstruct the vowel system in the Egyptian language (the hieroglyphic script renders only consonants and semi-vowels) (see e.g. Steindorff 1890; Ranke 1910; Edel 1980; Leahy 1993). Concerning the historical-political perspective, studies have often had the aim of

[1] For an overview of African-Mesopotamian relations (with references), see section 1.5.

reconstructing historical events related to the conquest of Egypt by the Neo-Assyrian state (see e.g. Kitchen 1973; Spalinger 1974; Onasch 1994; Kahn 2006). To a lesser extent, economic and ideological perspectives have been applied to describe the interaction between Egypt, Kush, Libya and the Neo-Assyrian empire (see e.g. Elat 1978; Fales 1981).

Studies based on the socio-cultural perspective are relatively uncommon. K. Radner (2009; 2012a) has written two papers on the African prisoners of war in the battle at Eltekeh in 701 BCE and on Egyptian scholars at the Assyrian court, and the present writer has written a paper about the representation of Egypt(ians) and Kush(ites) in Neo-Assyrian state letters and documents (Karlsson 2018). However, the former papers are limited in scope, and the latter paper is centred on ideology. The paper by I. Huber (2006) on Egyptians in later Mesopotamia merely gives a survey.[2] There are also some dated and very brief articles concerning Egypt in Assyria, such as the article by L.W. King (1914) on examples of Egyptian influence in Nineveh, and the article by W. Struve (1927) on a Libyan-Egyptian prince referred to as a son-in-law of the Assyrian king Sennacherib. A note on archaeological evidence of Egyptians in Nineveh has been written by O. Pedersén and L. Troy (1993). An "archive of Egyptians" (termed N31) in Assur has attracted some scholarly attention, but mostly by way of archival classification and text publication rather than content-based discussions (see e.g. Pedersén 1986: 125-129; Donbaz and Parpola 2001: 117-154; Faist 2007: 125-149).[3]

1.3 Material and method

This study builds upon two kinds of textual sources. Firstly, there are compilations of personal names from which to proceed. First and foremost, there are the six volumes of the work "The Prosopography of the Neo-Assyrian Empire" (PNA). This work lists all personal names attested in texts from the Neo-Assyrian empire, and contains etymological comments for each name and biographic data for each individual. Around 8 000 names and 30 000 individuals are attested in Neo-Assyrian texts (Radner 1998: xii). The online database "The Prosopography of the Neo-Assyrian Empire online" (PNAo) complements the printed volumes, and covers names and individuals appearing from 1998 onwards. The most recent

---

[2] It should be noted here that Africans are attested textually also in southern Mesopotamia. For the phenomenon of Egyptians in Babylonia, see Wiseman 1966; Hackl and Jursa 2015.

[3] That said, there are two MA-theses written on the subject, namely R. Mattila's "Egyptian Personal Names in Cuneiform Documents" from 1983 and Helsinki University and C. Draper's "The Egyptian Diaspora in Assyria: A Study of the Cuneiform Evidence, c. 1074-612 BC" from 2014 and Cambridge University. The former work is in Finnish (and has therefore been unavailable to me), and the latter work came to my attention only in the final stages of the preparation of the present study. In her book on everyday texts from Assur, B. Faist (2007: 126) announces that she (in collaboration with H.-U. Onasch) will present a study on the N31-archive some time in the future, but such a work does not seem to have appeared, as of December 2021.

PUBLICATIONS OF THE
FOUNDATION FOR FINNISH ASSYRIOLOGICAL RESEARCH
NO. 25

STATE ARCHIVES OF ASSYRIA STUDIES
VOLUME XXXI

STATE ARCHIVES OF ASSYRIA STUDIES

Published by the Neo-Assyrian Text Corpus Project, Helsinki
in association with the
Foundation for Finnish Assyriological Research

Project Director
Simo Parpola

VOLUME XXXI
Mattias Karlsson

FROM THE NILE TO THE TIGRIS

AFRICAN INDIVIDUALS AND GROUPS IN TEXTS FROM THE NEO-ASSYRIAN EMPIRE

THE NEO-ASSYRIAN TEXT CORPUS PROJECT

State Archives of Assyria Studies is a series of monographic studies relating to and supplementing the text editions published in the SAA series. Manuscripts are accepted in English, French and German. The responsibility for the contents of the volumes rests entirely with the authors.

Published with the support of the
Foundation for
Finnish Assyriological Research

FAR

Set in Times
The Assyrian Royal Seal emblem drawn by Dominique Collon from original
Seventh Century B.C. impressions (BM 84672 and 84677) in the British Museum
Cover: Detail from the victory stele of Esarhaddon showing the Kushite crown prince
Uš-Anaḫuru on his knees at the feet of the Assyrian king (VA 2708)
© Vorderasiatisches Museum / Staatliche Museen zu Berlin
Typesetting by Mattias Karlsson
Cover typography by Teemu Lipasti and Mikko Heikkinen

Printed in the USA

ISBN-13 978-952-10-9510-8 (Volume 31)
ISSN 1235-1032 (SAAS)
ISSN 1798-7431 (PFFAR)

FROM THE NILE TO THE TIGRIS

African Individuals and Groups in Texts from the Neo-Assyrian Empire

By

Mattias Karlsson

THE NEO-ASSYRIAN TEXT CORPUS PROJECT

2022

ACKNOWLEDGEMENTS

This book is a part of my own long-term project which focuses on interactions between ancient Egypt and Mesopotamia. At the completion of this study on Africans in Neo-Assyrian texts, I would like to thank Simo Parpola for accepting my work in the series State Archives of Assyria Studies, the Department of Linguistics and Philology at Uppsala University for granting me valuable staff access, and Sara Karlsson for commenting on my English.

CONTENTS

LIST OF ILLUSTRATIONS

ABBREVIATIONS

Bibliographical abbreviations

ADD	see Johns 1898-1923
ATAE	Archival Texts of the Assyrian Empire
BagM 16	see Deller 1985
BATSH 6	see Radner 2002
CAD	see Gelb et al. 1956-2010
CT 53	see Parpola 1979
CTN 3	see Dalley and Postgate 1984
CTN 6	see Herbordt et al. 2019
CTNMC	see Jacobsen 1939
Edubba 10	see Ahmad and Postgate 2007
FNLD	see Postgate 1976
Iraq 41	see Fales 1979
KAN 4	see Faist 2010
KAV	see Schroeder 1920
MZL	see Borger 2003
NWL	see Kinnier Wilson 1972
OLZ 8	see Peiser 1905
PEF	see Macalister 1912
PNA	Prosopography of the Neo-Assyrian Empire
PNA 1/I	see Radner (ed.) 1998
PNA 1/II	see Radner (ed.) 1999
PNA 2/I	see Baker (ed.) 2000
PNA 2/II	see Baker (ed.) 2001
PNA 3/I	see Baker (ed.) 2002
PNA 3/II	see Baker (ed.) 2011
PNA 4/I	see Baker (ed.) 2016
PNAo	Prosopography of the Neo-Assyrian Empire online
Rfdn 17	see Ahmad 1996
RGTC 7/1	see Bagg 2007
RGTC 7/2	see Bagg 2017
RIAo	Royal Inscriptions of Assyria online
RIMA	Royal Inscriptions of Mesopotomia, Assyrian Periods
RIMA 3	see Grayson 1996
RINAP	Royal Inscriptions of the Neo-Assyrian Period
RINAP 2	see Frame 2021
RINAP 3	see Grayson and Novotny 2012, 2014
RINAP 4	see Leichty 2011
RINAP 5/1	see Novotny and Jeffers 2018
RINAPo	Royal Inscriptions of the Neo-Assyrian Period online
SAA	State Archives of Assyria
SAA 1	see Parpola 1987

SAA 3	see Livingstone 1989
SAA 4	see Starr 1990
SAA 6	see Kwasman and Parpola 1991
SAA 7	see Fales and Postgate 1992
SAA 10	see Parpola 1993
SAA 11	see Fales and Postgate 1995
SAA 13	see Cole and Machinist 1998
SAA 14	see Mattila 2002
SAA 16	see Luukko and Van Buylaere 2002
SAA 19	see Luukko 2012
SAA 21	see Parpola 2018
SAAB 5	see Fales and Jakob-Rost 1991
SAAB 9	see Deller et al. 1995
SAAo	State Archives of Assyria online
SAAS 5	see Jas 1996
StAT	Studien zu den Assur-Texten
StAT 1	see Radner 1999
StAT 2	see Donbaz and Parpola 2001
StAT 3	see Faist 2007
TH	see Friedrich et al. 1940
T. Hadid	see Na'aman and Zadok 2000
TIM 11	see Ismail and Postgate 1993
VS 1	see Delitzsch 1907
Wb	see Erman and Grapow 1926-1961
WVDOG 152	see Miglus, Radner, and Stępniowski 2016
ZA 73	see Fales 1983
ZA 105	see Radner 2015

Symbols and other abbreviations

*	marking inclusions (see 7.1.5)
▪	marking certain African names
▫	marking likely/possibly African names
A	siglum of Istanbul Museum of Archaeology (Ashur collection)
Ada	Adad-narari III
Akk.	Akkadian
(Ar)	Arbela
(As)	Assur
Ash	Ashurbanipal
ass	Assyrian
Ass.	Assur / Assyria
AssU	siglum for Old Aramaic documents from Assur
Assur 52b	name for an "archive of Egyptians"
Bab(yl).	Babylon(ia)
DN	divine name
EA	El-Amarna (tablets)

Eg.	Egyptian
Esa	Esarhaddon
fig(s).	figure(s), external reference
Fig(s).	Figure(s), internal reference
(K)	Kalhu
Lib.	Libyan
mb	Middle Babylonian
(N)	Nineveh
N31	name for an "archive of Egyptians"
nb	Neo-Babylonian
ND	prefix of excav. nos. from the British excavations at Nimrud
NN	unknown (*nomen nescio*)
p612	post-612 (BCE)
pAsh	post-Ashurbanipal (period)
PN	personal name
RN	royal name
Sar	Sargon II
Sen	Sennacherib
Sha	Shalmaneser III
Shal	Shalmaneser V
Tig	Tiglath-pileser III
VAT	siglum of the Vorderasiatisches Museum (Tontafeln)
v. state	vassal state
YBC	tablet siglum, Yale Babylonian Collection

version of the database contains 2 657 entries and was last updated in August 2018.[4] The PNA-volumes are partly built upon the work "Assyrian Personal Names" by K. Tallqvist (1914) and to a lesser extent upon works on Mesopotamian and Egyptian personal names (Stamm 1939; Ranke 1935, 1952).

Secondly, the present study relies on various compilations of Neo-Assyrian texts, notably those of the "State Archives of Assyria" (SAA) series and those of the "Royal Inscriptions of Mesopotamia, Assyrian periods" (RIMA) and "Royal Inscriptions of the Neo-Assyrian Period" (RINAP) series. Texts not included in these text corpora are (for example) accessible in the "Studien zu den Assur-Texten" (StAT) series and in the online database "Archival Texts of the Assyrian Empire" (ATAE).[5] The narrations in Assyrian royal inscriptions about military campaigns to Egypt and some archives of Egyptians from Assyrian cities (notably from the city of Assur) are especially informative with regard to this study. These Egyptian archives from Assyria are particularly relevant, as they are focused on the ordinary citizen rather than on the elite.

In his work of identifying archives and libraries from tablets discovered at the German excavations 1903-1914 on the site of ancient Assur, O. Pedersén (1986: 125-129) identified an archive of Egyptians, which he named N31. This archive consists of around 100 tablets. The majority of these is kept in the Istanbul Archaeological Museum.[6] A substantial minority of the tablets is housed in the Vorderasiatisches Museum Berlin.[7] Two tablets from the archive in question are stored in London and Copenhagen.[8] The N31-archive derives from the western settlement area near the Nabu temple (Fig. 3), and its texts date to 675-612 BCE (with most texts dated to the latter half of the seventh century). The contents of the tablets are focused on loans, purchases, and legal settlements. *Kiṣir-Aššur* (45.), *Lā-turammanni-Aššur* (3.-4.), and *Urdu-Aššur* (5.) are the main protagonists in this archive of Egyptians (Donbaz and Parpola 2001: xvi; Faist 2007: 125-129).

A second archive of Egyptians was discovered from the tablets found during the renewed German excavations in Assur (the western settlement area) in 1989-1990 and 2000-2001. O. Pedersén (1998: 143) refers to it as Assur 52 in his survey of archives and libraries in the ancient Near East. In her publication of the archive, K. Radner subdivides these texts into the archive of *Dūrī-Aššur* (Assur 52a) and the archive of a group of Egyptians (Assur 52b).[9] The 15 tablets of Assur 52b (which can be dated) date to 658-632 BCE (that is, to the reign of Ashurbanipal), and they are all concerned with legal matters (Radner 2016: 79, 121).

---

[4] See http://oracc.museum.upenn.edu/pnao (last checked 2021-12-28).
[5] See http://oracc.org/atae/corpus/ (last checked 2021-12-28).
[6] Published by V. Donbaz and S. Parpola in StAT 2, pp. 117-154, nos. 164-233.
[7] Published by B. Faist in StAT 3, pp. 125-149, nos. 78-101, 114.
[8] BM 103956, published by F.M. Fales in *ZA* 73, no. 11, and Copenhagen National Museum 8612, published by T. Jacobsen in *CTNMC*, no. 68 (and then by J.N. Postgate in *FNLD*, no. 18).
[9] See Radner 2016: 82-121, nos. I.0-I-72 (Assur 52a), and 121-126, nos. II.1-II.15 (Assur 52b).

A third archive that can be referred to as an archive of Egyptians is the one of *Inurta-šarru-uṣur* (and a few related individuals) from Nineveh. The said main owner of the archive can be identified as an Egyptian, as the texts of the archive include numerous Egyptian names. The archive was discovered through Iraqi excavations in the eastern and western parts of Nineveh in 1967-1968. A broken pottery jar containing around 33 clay tablets was excavated from a site near the Shamash gate in eastern Nineveh.[10] *Inurta-šarru-uṣur* is defined as a "son of the palace" (*mār ekalli*) and in a leading position in relation to some Egyptians in Nineveh. The tablets can be dated to 669-612 BCE (with most texts dated late), and they consist of documents (dealing with loans, purchases, legal settlements) and other types of writing, including a letter (Pedersén and Troy 1993: no. 48).

Methodologically, Africans in Neo-Assyrian texts are identified on the grounds of etymology, ethnonyms, family relations, and institutional affiliations. In other words, personal names in African languages,[11] references to someone as "the Egyptian/Kushite/Libyan", references to someone as closely related to an identified African, and references to someone as tied to an African political or cultural institution are pivotal to the process of identifying Africans. Naturally, identifications are based on qualified assumptions. The problematic term ethnicity aside, it is not self-evident that an individual with an African name really was African, that an individual referred to as "the Kushite" was Kushite, that someone married to an identified Libyan was Libyan, or that someone tied to an Egyptian temple was Egyptian. Nevertheless, it is reasonable to assume all this, unless evidence to the contrary exists.

The following principles are applied with regard to etymology. Personal names considered safely African (whether on contextual and/or etymological grounds) in the PNA-volumes are accepted as African also in the present study.[12] Critical analysis is undertaken with regard to names that are classified as likely or possibly African in the PNA-volumes as well as concerning names that are etymologically unclassified in the PNA-volumes. Critical analysis is also undertaken regarding the names in PNAo (of which all are unclassified) as well as concerning names in texts not considered in the PNA-volumes or in PNAo.

There are five components integral to the above-mentioned critical analysis. To begin with, the reading or interpretation of Akkadian and Egyptian, aided by the standard dictionaries CAD and Wb, is essential. Secondly, earlier research (e.g.

---

[10] Published by K. Ismail and J.N. Postgate in TIM 11, nos. 3-30e (and then by R. Mattila in SAA 14, pp. 271-292, nos. 426-457, 459-460).

[11] It should be noted here that the definition of an African name in this study is that at least one component of the name can be identified as expressing an African language. For example, there are examples of personal names that have one Egyptian element and one Akkadian element, such as *Amān-išme*, meaning "Amun has heard".

[12] Regarding the former (contextual) identification ground (relevant e.g. in the enumeration of names belonging to Egyptian vassals), it may not always be clear what African linguistic elements the name consist of.

Yoyotte 1952; Edel 1980; Zeidler 1993) on African names and words in Mesopotamian cuneiform is valuable. The lists in the study by H. Ranke (1910) on Egyptian names and words in Mesopotamian cuneiform are crucial in this respect.[13] Thirdly, textual contexts are also pivotal. For example, the likelihood that an unclassified, clearly non-Akkadian name in an archive of Egyptians is Egyptian and refers to an Egyptian is high. Likewise, the presence of clearly African names close to an unclassified, clearly non-Akkadian name makes it likely that the latter is African as well. Fourthly, the compilation by H. Ranke (1935) of Egyptian personal names is a vital tool. Finally, the naming traditions in ancient Egypt and Mesopotamia play a role in the interpretation of names.

The last-mentioned component of critical analysis requires some discussion. In his comparison of Egyptian and Mesopotamian naming traditions (making use of the study by J.J. Stamm (1939) on Mesopotamian names), H. Ranke (1952: 250-256) concludes that the similarities far outweigh the differences.[14] He lists 14 names which have exact counterparts and 21 names which are very similar in content.

Examples of similarities include the common tradition of giving names to newborns, the common option of changing names (either by the parents or by the name bearer), the circumstance that Egyptian and Mesopotamian names were meaningful (adapted along with language development), the bipartion of Egyptian and Mesopotamian names into profane and religious names (with the latter growing in importance throughout history), the custom of having short forms of names in both cultures, the tradition of referring to individuals as "the servant of DN" or the like in both cultures, and the circumstance that "word names" in both cultures can be grouped in the same way, namely in those involving animal or plant names, names indicating descent or professions, names for adornments, names referring to various parts of the body, names pointing to the day or month of an individual's birth, and names expressing the belief in resurrection.

Examples of differences include the Egyptian custom (not found in Mesopotamia) of having the same name for several family members (who are then distinguished by the attributives elder/younger, etc.), the circumstance that men and women could have the same name in Egypt (as opposed to Mesopotamia), and the fact that "clause names" which contain imperatives (often with requests of a deity intervening) were very rare in Egypt, but not in Mesopotamia.

Regarding African individuals identifiable in other ways than through etymology, ethnonyms, family relations, or institutional affiliations, there may be instances in which individuals (even if they bear perfectly Akkadian names) can be

---

[13] A revised version of his "Verzeichnis der in keilschriftlicher Umschreibung erhaltenen ägyptischen Worte und Eigennamen" (Ranke 1910: 43-62) is presented below (table 7.1.5), serving as a methodological tool.

[14] Ranke (1952: 253, 255) here summarizes that "gegenüber diesen Zahlreichen Ähnlichkeiten zwischen ägyptischen und akkadischen Namen treten die Verschiedenheiten zurück", and "aber alle diese Unterschiede sind, den Zahlreichen und das Grundsätzliche betreffenden Ähnlichkeiten gegenüber, fast belanglos".

linked to African ethnicity in that they are embedded in textual contexts where identified Africans dominate. For example, these individuals may act as witnesses for (or with) Egyptians, they may be business partners with Egyptians, and they may be part of the same labour force as Egyptians. Such circumstances increase the probability that these individuals were Egyptians. As a rule of thumb in this study, individuals who can not be identified as Africans by means of etymology, ethnonyms, family relations, or institutional affiliations but who appear in African textual contexts at least three times and among several groups of Africans are classified as "indirectly identifiable as Africans".

Africans are not always named in texts from the Neo-Assyrian empire. Sometimes, African individuals and groups may be referred to simply as "the Egyptian" or as "15 Kushite women". These people are, of course, also relevant for the present study. Anonymous Africans can be detected through the search-words *Muṣur(āiu)* "(Lower) Egypt(ian)", *Paturisu/Uriṣṣu* "Upper Egypt",[15] *Magan/Makan* (another name for Egypt),[16] *Kūs(āiu)* "Kush(ite)", and *Meluḫḫa* (another name for Kush) in the online databases ATAE, RIAo, RINAPo, and SAAo.[17] When the search-words alone or in combination with another/other (directly connected) word(s) refer to individuals or groups, there are attestations of anonymous Africans.

The collection and analysis of biographic and demographic data are central for this study. Certain interrogative words (mirroring the research questions stated above) are highlighted in this process. Data on *who* (in terms of ethnicity, gender/sex, age, and class) the Africans in Neo-Assyrian texts were, *what* these people did (in terms of profession), *when* they lived (in terms of time period or reign), *where* they lived (inside or outside Assyria, etc.), and *how* these Africans were incorporated into the Assyrian realm are central to the discussion.

More concretely, biographic data are first gathered on the basis of what the individual PNA-entries say, and then on the grounds of what the texts in which the person in question appear can tell, as well as on what the contexts (historical, religious, ideological, archival, etc.) of the texts in which the person in question appear suggest. The demographic data are processed in several steps. First, the collected biographic data of every African individual are sorted under headings related to identities, properties, and settings (responding to who, what, when, and where).[18] Then, statistics based on this material, showing, for example, the

---

[15] For the distinction between Lower and Upper Egypt in Assyrian texts, see Karlsson 2020a.

[16] The twin terms Magan and Meluhha originally (i.e. in the third millennium BCE) referred to Oman and the Indus valley respectively but pointed to Egypt and Kush respectively in the first millennium BCE (Heimpel 1997).

[17] See http://oracc.org/atae/corpus/; http://oracc.org/riao/corpus/; http://oracc.org/rinap/corpus/; http://oracc.org/saao/corpus (last searched 2021-12-28).

[18] Due to the complex nature of the issue of mode of integration (speaking of circumstances and the interrogative word how), this issue is treated only in the discussion sections (notably in subsection 3.2.3) and not through demographic statistics (which require relative unambiguity).

proportion of Egyptian Africans compared to Kushite Africans or the proportion of African women in relation to African men, are compiled. Finally, conclusions based on these statistical data about African demographic structures in the Mesopotamian-Assyrian context are drawn.

Regarding the afore-mentioned headings on identities, properties, and settings, the following (admittedly rather coarse) distinctions are made.[19] Concerning ethnicity, data are sorted into Egyptian, Kushite, or Libyan. The dichotomies male/female and adult/child, and the differentiations upper/lower/slave are pivotal with regard to sex/gender, age, and class.[20] Regarding time, data are sorted into reign or time period, depending on how informative the sources are.[21] Additionally, the terms *pre*-conquest era and *post*-conquest era (related to the first Assyrian conquest of Egypt in 671 BCE) are employed. Concerning place, distinctions are based on whether the person lived in Africa, in other vassal states, in Babylonia, or in Assyria. A distinction between Assyria proper/the Assyrian heartland and Assyria is made in the discussion.[22] Of course, the incomplete nature of the sources may lead to situations where full classifications can not be made.

Focusing especially on ethnicity, references to "Kushites" or "Libyans" in this book are made principally from a linguistic standpoint, meaning that they are realized when the sources mention an individual with a Kushite or Libyan name, or an individual qualified by such an ethnonym, or an individual closely tied to an identified Kushite or Libyan. Some scholars question the distinctions between Kushites and Egyptians or between Libyans and Egyptians in this time period (see e.g. Baines 1996; Morkot 2000). Other scholars maintain that there are cultural markers (other than language) that differentiate Libyans and Kushites from

---

[19] The coarse nature of the distinctions are due to the incomplete nature of the sources. As a way of compensating, nuances will be identified and discussed.

[20] The distinction male/female is usually made on the basis of the DIŠ-sign which indicates male personal names (*MZL*, sign 748) and the MUNUS-sign which indicates female personal names (*MZL*, sign 883). By "upper class", people defined as political (rulers), religious (priests), military (officers), and administrative (officials) leaders, people who belong to the intelligensia (scholars, scribes), people who are closely related (in terms of kinship) to individuals of the afore-mentioned groups, and people who are mentioned frequently and prominently in the sources (but without their having labels which indicate social rank) are meant. By "lower class", people not defined as above or as slaves are meant. By "slaves", people who feature as objects of business transactions are meant. The terms *ardu* and *amtu* are too broad and complex to be used as bases for classification.

[21] Ideally, the tablet in question carries a date. Without a date, texts must be dated on the basis of other pieces of evidence, such as archaeological context. As for time periods, the term "post-Ashurbanipal period" refers to the time span 630-612 BCE, and the term "post-imperial period" points to the time from 611 BCE to the end of the earliest phase of the Neo-Babylonian empire.

[22] While Assyria proper/the Assyrian heartland refers to the land delineated (roughly) by Nineveh in the west, Arbela in the east, and Assur in the south, Assyria points to (broadly) the land between the Euphrates and the Tigris in northern Mesopotamia (Figs. 1-2). Justifying the inclusion of non-exiled (and relatively free-standing) Africans in this study, rulers like Taharqa and Mentuemhat still belonged to the *sphere* of the Neo-Assyrian empire. The movement from the Nile to the Tigris does not just refer to people migrating but also to transfer of authority.

Egyptians even in this period of intense contact (see e.g. Leahy 1985; O'Connor 1990; Török 1997; Ritner 2009). The term "Africa(ns)" corresponds to the modern, geographic notion of the term, employed here in a practical, pragmatic sense. Having said that, it is possible that the mutual dependence on the Nile might have lead to a sense of shared identity, triggered for example by the interaction with people beyond the easternmost Nile branch and Sinai.

1.4 Theory

In terms of theory, the concept of ethnicity is pivotal in this study. Ethnicity points to a group of people that share certain attributes (such as a common ancestry, language, customs, and religion) that differentiate them from other groups of people. This concept is generally understood in a constructivist sense, pointing to the idea that ethnicity is fluid and dynamic rather than fixed and static. Consequently, ethnic groups are seen as results of social processes, implying that ethnicity is constantly negotiated. Although ethnicity can be used interchangeably with the term nation, it is distinct from the concept race, in that ethnicity is not a biological given (Barth 1969; Smith 1986).[23]

The transition from a belief in primordial and essentialist ethnicity, where ethnicity is regarded as fixed and static and as a basic human condition (virtually a biological given), to a belief in ethnicity as socially constructed is detectable in the disciplines of Assyriology and Egyptology. Previously, the concept of race was widely used, leading to an emphasis on differences between Sumerians and Akkadians and claims of a uniqueness and isolation of ancient Egypt in relation to its African neighbours (see e.g. Bilabel and Grohmann 1927; Petrie 1939). Nowadays, it is commonplace to recognize the complexity of the concept of ethnicity in Egypt and Mesopotamia (see e.g. Kalvelagen et al. 2005; Matić 2020).

Concepts regarding ethnic minorities in empires, such as assimilation, acculturation, integration, and multiculturalism, are also crucial in this study. The concepts of assimilation and acculturation point to a strict policy on the part of the majority ethnic group in relation to the minority ethnic group, while the terms of integration and multiculturalism indicate a less strict policy, according to which the ethnic minority can co-exist with the ethnic majority without having to give up its cultural identity. At the same time, both the attitude of the majority ethnic group as well as that of the minority ethnic group play a part in this dynamic. In other words, responses (surrender/resistance) to the demands of the majority group also matter (see e.g. Chandra 2012).

---

[23] Drawing from the anthropologist F. Barth, the sociologist A.D. Smith outlines six characteristic features of ethnicity: the use of a common name for the group, a myth of common descent, shared histories of a (perceived) common past, one or more distinctive cultural elements (often language or religion), a sense of having a territorial homeland (either ancestral or current), and a self-aware sense of membership among the group.

Regarding the attitude on the part of the majority group, earlier research diverges with regard to the strategy of the Neo-Assyrian empire in relation to conquered peoples. Some scholars argue that the strategy in question was centred on political and economic goals and carried no real aim of "Assyrianizing" the local population but implied a policy of (loose) integration and multiculturalism (see e.g. Machinist 1993; Bagg 2011). Other scholars claim that the strategy indeed was to Assyrianize the local population, that it aimed at acculturating and assimilating the other, and that it proceeded from an ethnocentrism and a dichotomy Assyrians vs. foreigners (see e.g. Spieckermann 1982; Zaccagnini 1982). It may be relevant to refer to minimalist and maximalist interpretations in this context.

The relative status of the minority in the eyes of the majority matters as well. Some scholars have identified an "Egyptomania" in Assyria (Feldman 2004; Karmel Thomason 2004: 157-161). This Egyptomania could, for example, occur by way of an influx of Egyptian or Egyptianized objects, such as ivories with Egyptian motifs and cylinder seals illustrating Mesopotamian cuneiform and Egyptian deities (Figs. 11-12). It could also be expressed through the import of Egyptian scholars (Radner 2009). It has also been suggested that Assyrian relief sculpture and "obelisks" were inspired by Egyptian art (Kaelin 1999; Reade 2002: 189; Frahm 2011: 73-75). Such a sentiment (Egyptomania) could have affected the way the Assyrian state treated its Egyptian subjects.[24]

Concerning the attitude of the minority group, earlier research also diverges regarding the self-perception of the ancient Egyptians on ethnicity. Some works, often proceeding from official sources, detect an idealistic (Egyptians vs. foreigners, Order vs. Chaos, etc.), inward-looking, and self-sufficient (even xenophobic) attitude on the part of the Egyptians (see e.g. Loprieno 1988; Assmann 1990). Other works identify a more pragmatic approach, according to which not everything foreign was automatically alien and inferior, recognizing that Egyptians too may be subjected to acculturation and assimilation. Official sources present a biased picture and hide the fact that ethnicity in Egypt was a complex issue (see e.g. Baines 1996; Matić 2020).[25]

Bringing Kushites and Libyans into the debate on ethnicity in Egypt, official Egyptian sources tend to convey ethnic stereotypes (see e.g. Helck 1977; Gordon 2001) while other sources often indicate blurred ethnic boundaries (see e.g. Cohen 1992; Baines 1996). Regarding the stereotypes, visual representations of Libyans

---

24 The Assyrian kings distinguished between Egypt and Kush, and there is a tendency that the latter was not as esteemed as the former (Karlsson 2019). On his victory stele, Esarhaddon proclaims that he "tore out (*nasāḫu*) the roots (*šuršu*) of Kush from Egypt" (RINAP 4 98, r 45-46), and the image on the stele displays a Kushite captive much smaller than Esarhaddon and clearly smaller than the accompanying (Levantine) captive (Fig. 4).

25 The self-perception of the Kushites on ethnicity seems similar to that of the Egyptians. Although it is unfair to say that Kush was fully Egyptianized (Török 1997), the Kushite kings adopted much of the Egyptian worldview (Morkot 2000), and e.g. borrowed the topos of the "miserable Asiatic" in their inscriptions (Karlsson 2021c).

and Kushites (and Asiatics) smited by the mace of the Egyptian king or trampled on by the feet of the Egyptian king come to mind. Libyans and Kushites (and Asiatics), being part of the hostile and generic "Nine Bows" (*psḏt-pḏwt*), are pictured as the eternal enemies of an ethnically homogenous Egyptian state (Helck 1977). As noted, these perceptions belong to the fictive, ideological sphere and to the foreigner *topos* rather than to perceptions rooted in the "real" world expressing *mimesis* (Loprieno 1988). As concluded by C. Riggs and J. Baines (2012: 9) in their entry on ethnicity in Egypt in which the presence of "Nubians" and "Libyans" (among others) in Egypt is highlighted, "any notion that the ancient Egyptian population was ethnically uniform in any period should be abandoned as a fiction projected by the dominant ideology and often largely accepted by Egyptologists".

1.5 Historical background

In order to put the following presentations and discussions in context, an outline of African-Mesopotamian relations will now be given. Prior to the Greek-Persian era, there are four periods in which African-Mesopotamian contacts were especially frequent, namely the late prehistoric period, the Amarna period, and the Neo-Assyrian and Neo-Babylonian periods.[26]

Starting with the late prehistoric period, there is archaeological evidence of contacts between the Uruk-based Mesopotamian culture and the late Naqada culture in Egypt. Cylinder seals, motifs in the visual arts (such as juxtaposed mythical animals), and elements of palace architecture (such as niched facades) all typical of Mesopotamia appear in early Egypt, and the art of writing has been counted among the cultural impulses from Mesopotamia (see e.g. Kantor 1952; Moorey 1987; Budka 2000). Even though the latter in particular has been questioned in recent years (see e.g. Wengrow 2011), cultural exchanges between Egypt and Mesopotamia certainly took place in this period.[27]

Moving on to the Amarna period, that is, to the 14th century BCE, there is textual evidence of contacts between the kings of Egypt on the one hand and the kings of Assyria and Babylonia on the other. Letters written by the rulers of Assyria and Babylonia to the Egyptian kings have been found in the remains of the royal archive of the short-lived Egyptian capital city Akhetaton (modern el-Amarna). This high-level correspondence shows that envoys travelled between the two regions and that there was a custom of exchanging gifts between Egypt and Assyria and between Egypt and Babylonia. The individual representatives of the great

---

[26] See also the bibliographic online resource "A Bibliography of Studies on Egyptian-Mesopotamian Relations", downloadable at (permanent link) http://urn.kb.se/resolve?urn=urn:nbn:se:uu:diva-334908 (last updated 2021-07-06).

[27] That said, the notion of a "dynastic race" that invaded Egypt from the north-east and introduced civilization in Egypt (see e.g. Petrie 1939; Derry 1956; Emery 1961) is generally disregarded in modern scholarly literature.

powers greet each other as "brothers" (*aḫu*) (see e.g. Moran 1992; Cohen and Westbrook 2000; Liverani 2001).[28]

Continuing to the Neo-Assyrian period, a clash between an alliance (led by Damascus and Hamath) in which Egypt (at this period dominated by kings with Libyan names) was a part and the troops of the Neo-Assyrian empire under Shalmaneser III (858-824) took place in the mid-ninth century BCE and early Neo-Assyrian period (934-745). It resulted in (according to Assyrian sources) an Assyrian victory. The "black obelisk" of the same ruler includes images and texts about Egyptian tribute to Assyria (Dietrich 1975a; Röllig 1997; Helck 2005).[29]

During the late Neo-Assyrian period (744-612), Tiglath-pileser III (744-727) established the western limit of the Neo-Assyrian empire at the doorstep to Egypt. Hanunu, ruler of Gaza and a foe of Assyria, fled to Egypt. In the reign of Sargon II (721-705), Egyptian-Assyrian relations were complex. Sargon II, in some sources, claims that he encouraged trade between Egyptians and Assyrians and that he received tribute from Egyptian rulers. Nevertheless, a battle between Egyptian troops, supporting the ruler of Gaza, and Assyrian forces is recorded in Assyrian royal inscriptions. The sources claim that the Egyptians were defeated and that the ruler of Gaza was captured. Another Levantine ruler, Yamani of Ashdod, sought refuge in Egypt, but was eventually extradited to Assyria by the Kushite ruler controlling much of Egypt. During the reign of Sennacherib (704-681) there was a battle between a Levantine coalition including troops from Egypt and Kush and Assyrian troops. According to Assyrian texts, the Assyrian forces defeated the African troops. However, Egypt escaped conquest at this time (Dietrich 1975a; Röllig 1997; Helck 2005).

During the reign of Esarhaddon (680-669), the Kushite state, controlling the whole of Egypt, became an arch-enemy to Assyria. After an initial failed conquest attempt in 674 BCE, the Assyrian army managed to conquer (northern) Egypt in 671 BCE, defeating the forces of Taharqa (690-664), king of Kush. The conquest is commemorated in texts and on stelae and glazed tiles (Figs. 4, 9-10). Uprisings followed, and a new campaign to Egypt was initiated in 669 BCE, but it was halted by the death of Esarhaddon. The army of his son, Ashurbanipal (668-c. 631), marched to Africa in 667 BCE and re-conquered Egypt, making Taharqa flee to the south once again. The victory is commemorated in texts and through wall reliefs (Fig. 8). The new ruler in Kush, Tanutamon (664-656), successfully re-conquered

[28] 14 letters (EA 1-14) between Babylon and Egypt and two letters (EA 15-16) from the Assyrian king have been preserved. While the Babylonian-Egyptian relations were well-established, the Assyrian-Egyptian relations were relatively novel. The Babylonian king complains to his Egyptian "brother" about him having direct contact with the Assyrians whom the Babylonian ruler saw as his subjects. In the inscriptions of the later Assyrian king Ashur-bel-kala (1073-1056), Egypt is the sender of exotic tribute (Kuhrt 1997: 350-352, 361).

[29] That said, there is no consensus regarding the identification of Egypt here. For detecting Egypt, see e.g. Grayson 1996: 23, 150; Karlsson 2016: 200-202. For sceptical approaches, see e.g. Garelli 1971: 38-40; Collon 1995: 161.

northern Egypt in 664 BCE. This caused the Assyrian army to return and victoriously re-enter Egypt, sacking Thebes in the process. Necho I (672-664), the main Assyrian vassal in Egypt, was succeeded by his son and heir Psammetichus I (664-610) as Assyria's man in Egypt, the latter even granted an Akkadian name. Gradually, Psammetichus I managed to diminish Assyrian and Kushite influence in Egypt and establish a native Egyptian state independent of Assyria. During the civil war in Assyria in 652-648 BCE, Psammetichus I was allied to the Babylonian ruler Shamash-shuma-ukin (668-648). Later on, however, Egypt, first under Psammetichus I and then under Necho II (610-595), aided Assyria in its fight for survival against a coalition of the Medes and the Babylonians around 610 BCE, probably for geo-political reasons (Dietrich 1975a; Röllig 1997; Helck 2005).

Concluding with the Neo-Babylonian period, relations between Egypt (initially ruled by Psammetichus I and later by Necho II) and the Neo-Babylonian empire (which had taken over from the Neo-Assyrian empire) were generally conflict-ridden. In a decisive battle at Carchemish in 605 BCE, the Assyrian-Egyptian coalition was defeated, leading to the final blow to Assyria and to Babylonian dominion over the Levant. Egyptian kings repeatedly encouraged Levantine rulers to rebel against Babylonia, resulting for example in the fall of Judah. At one stage, Babylonian forces under their ruler Nebuchadnezzar II (605-562) took advantage of an internal conflict between Apries (589-570) and Amasis II (570-526) to attack Egypt in 567 BCE. Although the effects of this attack are partly unclear, the fact is that Amasis II (who opposed Babylon) remained on the Egyptian throne. A period of stalemate and relative peace followed. Eventually, both Egypt and Babylonia were incorporated into the Persian empire, whose troops seized Babylon in 539 BCE and Egypt in 525 BCE (Dietrich 1975b; Spalinger 1977; Röllig 1997).[30]

[30] For details of this period, see e.g. Vogt 1957; Spalinger 1977; Kahn 2018. Notably, Egypt proper was threatened by Babylonian forces already in 601 BCE, a few years after the battle at Carchemish. According to a Babylonian chronicle, the battle ended in a stalemate, and the Babylonian army retreated (Lipiński 1972).

2. THE EVIDENCE: THE INDIVIDUAL LEVEL AND THE BIOGRAPHIC PERSPECTIVE

This chapter focuses on the gathered evidence with regard to the individual level and biographic perspective, meaning that every identifiable African person in Neo-Assyrian texts is presented and discussed on the basis of the interrogative words who, what, when, where, and how, giving biographic details for each individual. The chapter has three sections, centred on identified Africans (2.1), likely and possible Africans (2.2), and anonymous Africans (2.3). The data on the individual level and biographic perspective are also presented through tables 7.1.1-3.

2.1 Identified Africans

The first section brings up identified Africans and their biographic details. Its subsections are structured according to the above-mentioned four identification grounds, namely etymology (2.1.1), ethnonyms (2.1.2), family relations (2.1.3), and institutional affiliations (2.1.4). Totally 257 individuals will be presented and discussed in this section.

2.1.1 People with clearly African names

The first subsection centres on Africans identifiable on the identification ground etymology, meaning that the language with which a name is written identifies someone as African. 177 individuals will be presented and discussed in this subsection.

Abdi-Mūnu

The first individual of this category is *Abdi-Mūnu*. The name of this individual means "servant of Amun" and expresses masculine gender. Its first part is West Semitic and its second part is Egyptian, referring to the Egyptian god Amun. *Abdi-Mūnu* is mentioned in a text (*Rfdn* 17 17) from Assur and 612 BCE as engaged in commercial activities, where he, along with *Iaḫunu*, both qualified as "commercial agents" (*bēl ḫarrāni*), owe two shekels of silver to *Aššur-ukallanni*, *Mannu-kī-ilī*, and *Ilā-ēdiš*.[31]

On the basis of the above data, the interrogative words who, what, when, and where can be responded to. *Abdi-Mūnu* seems to have been an Egyptian, a male, an adult, and a commoner. He lived in the post-Ashurbanipal period, and he seems to have been a resident of the city of Assur. The question of how this individual ended

[31] Drawing from the text publication and the PNA-entry of K. Radner (PNA 1/I, p. 7).

up in Assyria is difficult to answer, but it is likely that he or older relatives of his came to Assyria forcibly by means of deportation.[32]

Abī-Ḫūru 1.

The second individual of this category is *Abī-Ḫūru* 1. The name of this individual means "Horus is (my) father" and conveys masculine gender. Its first part is West Semitic and its second part is Egyptian, referring to the Egyptian god Horus. *Abī-Ḫūru* 1. is mentioned in a broken text (ND 2306) from Kalhu and 687 BCE as a witness (*šību*) concerning the sale of land and people (names and details are missing). He is presented as a gate guard (*etû*) in the document.[33]

On the basis of the above data, identities, properties, and settings can be identified. *Abī-Ḫūru* 1. seems to have been an Egyptian, a male, an adult, and a commoner. He lived in the reign of Sennacherib, and he seems to have been a resident of the city of Kalhu. The circumstances leading to this individual being in Assyria are difficult to pin down, but it is likely that he or older relatives of his came to Assyria forcibly through deportation.[34]

Abī-Ḫūru 2.

The third individual of this category is *Abī-Ḫūru* 2. This man appears in a text (SAA 14 436) from the archive of *Inurta-šarru-uṣur*, Nineveh, and the seventh century BCE (probably the post-Ashurbanipal period) as one of the witnesses when the archive owner *Inurta-šarru-uṣur* 2. lends barley to *Ēdu-šal[lim]*.[35]

On the basis of the above data, the interrogative words who, what, when, and where can be responded to. *Abī-Ḫūru* 2. seems to have been an Egyptian, a male, an adult, and a commoner. He probably lived at the end of the seventh century BCE,

---

[32] Regarding etymology, Radner notes that the divine name has been subjected to an *aphaeresis* whereby the initial vowel has disappeared. A.Y. Ahmad (1996: 249), the publisher of the archive (of *Aššur-mātu-taqqin*) to which this text belongs, suggests (without elaborating) that the personal name may be Phoenician. Supposedly, he centres on the first element of the name. The name "servant of Amun" speaks of the name bearer as a loyal devotee of the god Amun. Amun(-Ra) was one of the most important gods in Egypt, having his main cult centre in Thebes and the Karnak temple (Shaw and Nicholson 1995: 31-32). Concerning textual content and context, the document has six witnesses, all of them bearing Akkadian names.

[33] Drawing from the description of this text by B. Parker (1954: 37) and the PNA-entry of R. Mattila (PNA 1/I, p. 10).

[34] Regarding etymology, Mattila refers to a study by A. Leahy (1993: 57). The name in question is brought up also in Tallqvist 1914: 4. Leahy does not identify the first element of the name with certainty and adds that it is not impossible that the name points to the Egyptian goddess Hathor. The name "Horus is (my) father" points to the notion of Horus as protective with regard to *Abī-Ḫūru* 1. (and 2.). The falcon-headed god Horus was an important god in Egypt and was closely linked to kingship (Shaw and Nicholson 1995: 133-134). Concerning textual content and context, the document does not clarify which institution or household *Abī-Ḫūru* 1. served.

[35] Drawing from the text publication and the PNA-entry of R. Mattila (PNA 1/I, p. 10).

and he seems to have been a resident of the city of Nineveh. The question of how this individual ended up in Assyria is difficult to answer, but it is likely that he or older relatives of his came to Assyria forcibly via deportation.[36]

Abši-Ešu

The fourth individual of this category is *Abši-Ešu*. The exact meaning of the name of this individual is unknown, although it probably contains the theophoric element Isis, referring to the Egyptian goddess so named. *Abši-Ešu* appears in a text (SAA 6 311) from Nineveh and 666 BCE as "the Egyptian" (*Muṣurāiu*) and as the father of *Issar-dūrī* 26. and *Lū-šakin* 14., who sell their house in Bet-Eriba-ilu to *Rēmanni-Adad* for four minas of silver by the mina of Carchemish.[37]

On the basis of the above data, identities, properties, and settings can be identified. *Abši-Ešu* seems to have been an Egyptian, a male, an adult, and a commoner. He lived in the reign of Ashurbanipal, and he seems to have been a resident of the city of Bet-Eriba-ilu. The circumstances leading to this individual being in this part of Assyria are difficult to pin down, but it is likely that he or older relatives of his came to Assyria forcibly through deportation.[38]

Aḫūru

The fifth individual of this category is *Aḫūru*. The name of this individual seems to be shortened and an Assyrianized form of the name *Ḫūru*, pointing to the name of the Egyptian god Horus employed as a personal name. *Aḫūru* features in a text (StAT 2 177) from the N31-archive, Assur, and 617 BCE as a witness when *Kiṣir-Aššur* 45. and *Urdu-Aššur* 5. lend silver to *Pūnašti*▪. Probably the same person appears in a text (StAT 2 175) from the N31-archive, Assur, and 635 BCE as a witness when *Urdu-Aššur* 5. lends fish to *Bibî*. Probably the same person appears in a text (StAT 3 82) from the N31-archive, Assur, and 617 BCE as a witness when *Kiṣir-Aššur* 45. lends silver to *Unabi*, *Mušallim-Adad*, and *Kapī[ru]*.[39]

On the basis of the above data, the interrogative words who, what, when, and where can be responded to. *Aḫūru* seems to have been an Egyptian, a male, an adult,

---

36 *Abī-Ḫūru* 2. appears as the fourth of eight witnesses. Three of the other (seven) witnesses have African (two Egyptian, one Libyan) personal names.

37 Drawing from the text publication and the PNA-entry of R. Mattila (PNA 1/I, p. 15).

38 Regarding etymology, the name is brought up (as *Ab-ši-e-ku*) also in Tallqvist 1914: 6. The name *Abši-Ešu* tells of a relationship between the name bearer and the goddess Isis, who was a central deity in Egypt, being the sister-wife of Osiris and the mother of Horus (Shaw and Nicholson 1995: 142-143). Concerning textual content and context, none of the preserved names of the witnesses seem to be African. The said *Rēmanni-Adad* is presented as the "chief chariot driver of Assurbanipal, king of Assyria". Bet-Eriba-ilu was a town in the western part of Assyria, judging by its association with (the mina of) Carchemish.

39 Drawing from the text publications, the PNA-entry of A. Berlejung and R. Zadok (PNA 1/I, p. 87), and two PNAo-entries of H.D. Baker.

and a commoner. He lived in the reign of Ashurbanipal and later, and he appears to have been a resident of the city of Assur. The question of how this individual ended up in Assyria is difficult to answer, but it is likely that he or older relatives of his came to Assyria forcibly by means of deportation.[40]

Al-ḫapi-mepi

The sixth individual of this category is *Al-ḫapi-mepi*. The name of this individual is fully Egyptian, meaning "the Apis bull has been brought to Memphis" (Eg. *ʿr-Ḥp-(r)-mn-nfr*). *Al-ḫapi-mepi* is sold by her father, *Puṭu-Meḫēši*▪ 2., for half a mina of silver as a wife to *Puṭi-Eše*▪ in a text (SAA 14 443) from the archive of *Inurta-šarru-uṣur*, Nineveh, and (probably) the post-Ashurbanipal period. The document stipulates that if *Puṭi-Eše* would divorce her, she can pay ten shekels to him and be free to leave. However, as long as *Puṭi-Eše* is alive, she and her sons are obliged to serve as "votaries" (*šēlūtu*) of the Assyrian goddess Ishtar of Arbela.[41]

On the basis of the above data, identities, properties, and settings can be identified. *Al-ḫapi-mepi* appears to be an Egyptian, a female, an adult, and a commoner. She probably lived in the post-Ashurbanipal period, and she seems to have been a resident of the city of Nineveh. The circumstances leading to this individual being in Assyria are difficult to pin down, but it is likely that she or older relatives of her came to Assyria forcibly through deportation.[42]

Amān-išme

The seventh individual of this category is *Amān-išme*. The name of this individual means "Amun has heard" and conveys masculine gender. Its first part is Egyptian, referring to the Egyptian god Amun, and its second part is Akkadian. *Amān-išme* is

---

[40] Regarding etymology, Berlejung and Zadok link this name form to a name form found in a Phoenician text. For *Ḥr(w)* in Egyptian texts, see Ranke 1935: 245:18. Concerning textual content and context, *Aḫūru* appears on first place in the list of (three) witnesses in text StAT 2 175. There are (two) further African names in the lists of witnesses of StAT 2 177 and StAT 3 82. Also, the prominent Egyptian *Lā-turammanni-Aššur* 3. acts as a witness in StAT 2 177 and StAT 3 82.

[41] Drawing from the text publication and the PNA-entry of R. Mattila (PNA 1/I, p. 97).

[42] Regarding etymology, Mattila refers to a study by A. Leahy (1993: 56). For this name in Egyptian texts, see Ranke 1935: 70:16. Leahy notes that the name is masculine in Egypt. The naming tradition, attested in Egypt by contrast to Mesopotamia, of having men and women sharing names may be expressed here (Ranke 1952: 254). Leahy (1993: 62) also concludes that this name identifies the name bearer as coming from Lower Egypt. The Apis bull was a manifestation of the Egyptian, Memphite god Ptah (Shaw and Nicholson 1995: 35-36). The name "the Apis bull has been brought to Memphis" tells of a blessed event in the earthly sphere. Concerning textual content and context, it is interesting to note that an Egyptian woman could be associated with an Assyrian goddess (Ishtar) in this way (being a votaress). The section in which the witnesses would have been listed is almost completely destroyed. Only the name of one witness (with an Egyptian name) remains.

mentioned in a text (*Rfdn* 17 19) from Assur and 612 BCE as a witness when the owner of the archive, *Aššur-mātu-taqqin*, lends silver to *Aššur-ballussu-iqbi*.[43]

On the basis of the above data, the interrogative words who, what, when, and where can be responded to. *Amān-išme* seems to have been an Egyptian, a male, an adult, and a commoner. He lived in the post-Ashurbanipal period, and he seems to have been a resident of the city of Assur. The question of how this individual ended up in Assyria is difficult to answer, but it is likely that he or older relatives of his came to Assyria forcibly by means of deportation.[44]

Amat-Emūni

The eighth individual of this category is *Amat-Emūni*. The name of this individual means "female servant of Amun" and expresses feminine gender. Its first element is Akkadian, and its second part is Egyptian, referring to the Egyptian god Amun. *Amat-Emūni* is brought up, along with three unnamed slave women, in a text (SAA 7 24) from Nineveh and the reign of Esarhaddon or Ashurbanipal which lists all the female personnel of the palace in Nineveh.[45]

On the basis of the above data, identities, properties, and settings can be identified. *Amat-Emūni* seems to have been an Egyptian, a female, an adult, and a member of the elite. She lived in the reign of Esarhaddon or Ashurbanipal, and she seems to have been a resident of the city of Nineveh. The circumstances leading to this individual being in Assyria are difficult to pin down, but it is likely that she or older relatives of her came to Assyria forcibly via deportation.[46]

Ameḫi

The ninth individual of this category is *Ameḫi*. The meaning of the name of this individual of masculine gender is unknown but probably includes the name of the Egyptian god Amun. *Ameḫi* appears in a text (StAT 2 167) from the N31-archive, Assur, and 646 BCE where he is one of ten men (most of them bearing Egyptian names) who divide an inheritance.[47]

---

43 Drawing from the text publication and the PNA-entry of K. Radner (PNA 1/I, p. 98).

44 Regarding etymology, Radner notes that the name has been subjected to *sandhi*, with the name written *a-ma-a-niš-me*. The name "Amun has heard" conveys the idea of the god Amun as listening to prayers. Concerning textual content and context, none of the other five witnesses, nor the contract parties, bear African names. *Amān-išme* is listed last.

45 Drawing from the text publication and the PNA-entry of F.M. Fales (PNA 1/I, p. 99).

46 Regarding etymology, Fales refers to a study by R. Zadok (1997: 212). The name in question points to the status of a loyal devotee in relation to the god Amun. Concerning textual content and context, *Amat-Emūni* is, along with a *Šīti-tabni*, the only one named in the list. This circumstance, together with the fact that she has three "maids" (*amtu*) at her disposal, suggest that *Amat-Emūni* belonged to the palace elite. Anonymous women from various corners of the empire (including Kush) are enumerated elsewhere in the document.

47 Drawing from the text publication and the PNA-entry of R. Mattila (PNA 1/I, p. 100).

On the basis of the above data, the interrogative words who, what, when, and where can be responded to. *Ameḫi* seems to have been an Egyptian, a male, an adult, and a commoner. He lived in the reign of Ashurbanipal, and he seems to have been a resident of the city of Assur. The question of how this individual ended up in Assyria is difficult to answer, but it is likely that he or older relatives of his came to Assyria forcibly by means of deportation.[48]

***Amman-tanaḫti* 1.**

The tenth individual of this category is *Amman-tanaḫti* 1. The name of this individual of masculine gender is fully Egyptian and means "Amun is my strength" (Eg. *Imn-tꜣy.i-nḫtt*), referring to the Egyptian god Amun. *Amman-tanaḫti* 1. appears in a text (StAT 2 167) from the N31-archive, Assur, and 646 BCE where he is one of ten men (most of them bearing Egyptian names) who divide an inheritance.[49]

On the basis of the above data, identities, properties, and settings can be identified. *Amman-tanaḫti* 1. seems to have been an Egyptian, a male, an adult, and a commoner. He lived in the reign of Ashurbanipal, and he seems to have been a resident of the city of Assur. The circumstances leading to this individual being in Assyria are difficult to pin down, but it is likely that he or older relatives of his came to Assyria forcibly through deportation.[50]

***Amman-tanaḫti* 2.**

The eleventh individual of this category is *Amman-tanaḫti* 2. This man is mentioned in a text (*FNLD* 18) from the N31-archive, Assur, and 625 BCE as one of the three slaves (the others being the woman *Bēlet-issē'a* 2. and the girl *Apî*▪ 1.) whom *Puṭi-Mūnu*▪ 2. inherits from his father *Lā-turammanni-Aššur* 3.[51]

On the basis of the above data, the interrogative words who, what, when, and where can be responded to. *Amman-tanaḫti* 2. seems to have been an Egyptian, a male, an adult, and a slave. He lived in the post-Ashurbanipal period, and he seems to have been a resident of the city of Assur. The question of how this individual

---

[48] *Ameḫi*, who is enumerated on third place, and the other nine people give a house of six seahs to the Egyptian *Tap-naḫte* 3. in lieu of his share of the inheritance. The prominent Egyptians *Urdu-Aššur* 5. and *Lā-turammanni-Aššur* 3. head the list of (six) witnesses.

[49] Drawing from the text publication and the PNA-entry of R. Mattila (PNA 1/I, p. 102).

[50] Regarding etymology, Mattila refers to studies by R. Zadok (1977b: 63) and J. Zeidler (1994: 37-38). The name in question is brought up also in Ranke 1910: 38; 1935: 31:7. It speaks of Amun as a source of personal strength. Concerning textual content and context, *Amman-tanaḫti* 1., who is listed on fourth place, and the other nine people give a house to the Egyptian *Tap-naḫte* 3. in lieu of his share of the inheritance. The prominent Egyptians *Urdu-Aššur* 5. and *Lā-turammanni-Aššur* 3. head the list of (six) witnesses.

[51] Drawing from the text publication and the PNA-entry of R. Mattila (PNA 1/I, p. 102).

ended up in Assyria is difficult to answer, but it is likely that he or older relatives of his came to Assyria forcibly by means of deportation.[52]

Amu-rṭēše 1.

The twelfth individual of this category is *Amu-rṭēše* 1. The name of this individual of masculine gender is fully Egyptian and conveys the statement "it is Amun who has given him" (Eg. *Imn-ir-di-sw*), referring to the Egyptian god Amun. He appears in a text (ND 2315) from Kalhu and 663 BCE in which he sells his slave woman (whose name is destroyed) to the free woman *Attâ-ḫāṣi*▫ for 30 shekels of silver. All the names of the twelve witnesses of the text are broken.[53]

On the basis of the above data, identities, properties, and settings can be identified. *Amu-rṭēše* 1. seems to have been an Egyptian, a male, an adult, and a commoner. He lived in the reign of Ashurbanipal, and he seems to have been a resident of the city of Kalhu. The circumstances leading to this individual being in Assyria are difficult to pin down, but it is likely that he or older relatives of his came to Assyria forcibly through deportation.[54]

Amu-rṭēše 2.

The 13th individual of this category is *Amu-rṭēše* 2. This man is mentioned in a text (SAA 14 161) from Nineveh and 623 BCE as the father of *Nabû-rēḫtu-uṣur* 17., who sells his daughter *Mullissu-ḫāṣinat* to the woman *Niḫti-Eša-rau*▪, who then gives *Mullissu-ḫāṣinat* to her son *Ṣi-ḫû*▪ 4. as a wife. *Amu-rṭēše* 2. also features as the first witness in the document.[55]

On the basis of the above data, the interrogative words who, what, when, and where can be responded to. *Amu-rṭēše* 2. seems to have been an Egyptian, a male, an adult, and a commoner. He lived in the post-Ashurbanipal period, and he seems to have been a resident of the city of Nineveh. The question of how this individual ended up in Assyria is difficult to answer, but it is likely that he or older relatives of his came to Assyria forcibly by means of deportation.[56]

---

52 The social stratification of the Egyptian group is apparent in this context, with one Egyptian (*Puṭi-Mūnu* 2.) owning another (*Amman-tanaḫti* 2.). Several of the 17 witnesses have Egyptian names.

53 Drawing from the description of this text by B. Parker (1954: 40) and the PNA-entry of R. Mattila (PNA 1/I, p. 109).

54 Mattila refers to studies by H. Ranke (1910: 27), K. Tallqvist (1914: 14), and R. Zadok (1977b: 67) concerning the etymology of the name. For this name in the Egyptian onomasticon, see Ranke 1935: 26:24. The name bearer is pictured as a gift from the god Amun.

55 Drawing from the text publication and the PNA-entry of R. Mattila (PNA 1/I, p. 109).

56 There are 15 witnesses listed in the document. Several of these have Egyptian names. Also, one of the three guarantors of the transaction has an Egyptian name. The transaction in question clearly took place within the Egyptian community of Nineveh. *Nabû-rēḫtu-uṣur* 17. seems to have had the profession of fuller (*ašlāku*), possibly inherited from his father *Amu-rṭēše* 2.

Amu-rṭēše 3.

The 14th individual of this category is *Amu-rṭēše* 3. This man appears in several texts from the N31-archive, Assur, and the time range of 644-620 BCE. *Amu-rṭēše* 3. buys the woman *Tatašīri*▫ from her husband *Saḫarpunḫu*▫ for half a mina of silver (StAT 2 180), acts as a witness when *[...]-ilu* borrows silver from someone whose name is lost (StAT 2 204), acts as a witness in a broken text whose content is unclear (KAV 189), and is one of six men who owe three horses, *iškaru*-tax of the king, to *Urdu-Aššur* 5. (StAT 2 213). Outside of the N31-archive, *Amu-rṭēše* 3. is a witness when *Ṭāb-Bēl* 7. redeems his sister *Apî*▪ 2. and her son *Pašî*▫ 9. from *Bīšâ* in a text (KAN 4 7) from Assur and 624 BCE. *Amu-rṭēše* 3. seems to have been in some position of authority, being a "chief [...]" (*rab [...]*).[57]

On the basis of the above data, identities, properties, and settings can be identified. *Amu-rṭēše* 3. seems to have been an Egyptian, a male, an adult, and a member of the elite. He lived in the reign of Ashurbanipal and later, and he seems to have been a resident of the city of Assur. The circumstances leading to this individual being in Assyria are difficult to pin down, but it is likely that he or older relatives of his came to Assyria forcibly through deportation.[58]

Apî 1.

The 15th individual of this category is *Apî* 1. The meaning of the name of this individual of feminine gender is unknown but is believed to correspond to the Egyptian name *Ipy*. *Apî* 1. appears in a text (*FNLD* 18) from the N31-archive, Assur, and 625 BCE as a slave girl and the daughter of a slave family of three (with the man *Amman-tanaḫti*▪ 2. and the woman *Bēlet-issē'a* 2.) which *Puṭi-Mūnu*▪ 2. inherits from his father *Lā-turammanni-Aššur* 3.[59]

On the basis of the above data, the interrogative words who, what, when, and where can be responded to. *Apî* 1. seems to have been an Egyptian, a female, a child, and a slave. She lived in the post-Ashurbanipal period, and she seems to have been a resident of the city of Assur. The question of how this individual ended up in Assyria is difficult to answer, but it is likely that she or older relatives of her came to Assyria forcibly by means of deportation.[60]

---

[57] Drawing from the text publications and the PNA-entry of R. Mattila (PNA 1/I, p. 109).

[58] Regarding etymology, the reconstruction of the name *Amu-rṭēše* in text StAT 2 213 is not made by V. Donbaz and S. Parpola (2001: 144-145) but by Mattila. Concerning textual content and context, the position of *Amu-rṭēše* 3. in the lists is not consistent. StAT 2 180 presents seven witnesses, one with a possibly Egyptian name. At least one more of the six witnesses in StAT 2 204 has an Egyptian name. Several of the contract parties of StAT 2 213 appear with (certain or likely/possibly) Egyptian personal names. By contrast to Donbaz and Parpola (2001: 127-128), Mattila speaks of 629 BCE and *Tatabarri* with regard to text StAT 2 180.

[59] Drawing from the text publication and the PNA-entry of R. Mattila (PNA 1/I, p. 112).

[60] Regarding etymology, Mattila refers to studies by H. Ranke (1935: 22:21-23; 23:3; 23:23), R. Zadok (1977b: 63), and J. Osing (1978: 37). The name is brought up also in Tallqvist 1914: 24.

Apî 2.

The 16th individual of this category is *Apî* 2. This woman is mentioned in a text (KAN 4 7) from Assur and 624 BCE as being redeemed (together with her son *Pašî*□ 9.) by her brother *Ṭāb-Bēl* 7. from *Bīšâ* through the sum of 30 shekels of silver, thus (re-)establishing her status as a free woman.[61]

On the basis of the above data, identities, properties, and settings can be identified. *Apî* 2. seems to have been an Egyptian, a female, an adult, and a commoner. She lived in the post-Ashurbanipal period, and she seems to have been a resident of the city of Assur. The circumstances leading to this individual being in Assyria are difficult to pin down, but it is likely that she or older relatives of her came to Assyria forcibly through deportation.[62]

Apiḫuniawa

The 17th individual of this category is *Apiḫuniawa*. The name of this individual of masculine gender was formerly read *Apiḫuniṣi[...]* and its exact meaning is unknown, but it has been identified as safely Egyptian. *Apiḫuniawa* appears in a text (StAT 2 216-217) from the N31-archive, Assur, and the seventh century BCE as the father of *Apâ*▪, who borrows 15 shekels of silver from *Urdu-Aššur* 5.[63]

On the basis of the above data, the interrogative words who, what, when, and where can be responded to. *Apiḫuniawa* seems to have been an Egyptian, a male, an adult, and a commoner. He lived some time in the seventh century BCE, and he seems to have been a resident of the city of Assur. The question of how this individual ended up in Assyria is difficult to answer, but it is likely that he or older relatives of his came to Assyria forcibly by means of deportation.[64]

Aṣê

The 18th individual of this category is *Aṣê*. The name of this individual of masculine gender is Egyptian and means "prosperous" (Eg. *Wḏꜣ*). *Aṣê* is mentioned

---

Concerning textual content and context, the social stratification of the Egyptian group is apparent in this context, with one Egyptian (*Puṭi-Mūnu* 2.) owning another (*Apî* 1.). Several of the 17 witnesses have Egyptian names.

61 Drawing from the text publication and the PNA-entry of R. Mattila (PNA 1/I, p. 112).

62 As remarked also by B. Faist (2010), it is not clear how *Apî* 2. became subservient to *Bīšâ*. Perhaps her time under the patronage of *Bīšâ* could have been part of a debt repayment plan.

63 Drawing from the text publication and the PNA-entry of R. Mattila (PNA 1/I, p. 112).

64 Regarding etymology, Mattila supposedly focuses on the Egyptian textual context. For the revised reading of this personal name, see the relevant PNAo-entry (made by H.D. Baker). It is possible that this name is related to *Apî*/*Ipy*. Concerning textual content and context, four people, of which three have clearly or likely Egyptian names, are listed as witnesses in the document(s). The prominent Egyptian *Kiṣir-Aššur* 45. heads the list of witnesses. The document is dated to 613 BCE in the publication by V. Donbaz and S. Parpola (2001: 146-147).

in a text (SAA 14 446) from the archive of *Inurta-šarru-uṣur*, Nineveh, and 612 BCE as the son of *Taḫ-arṭiše*▪ 2. and as owing somebody (whose name is lost) ten(?) shekels of silver, and in another text (SAA 14 443) from the same archive and city as a witness for *Puṭi-Eši*▪, who purchases *Al-ḫapi-mepi*▪ from *Puṭu-Meḫēši*▪ 2. as a wife.[65]

On the basis of the above data, identities, properties, and settings can be identified. *Aṣê* seems to have been an Egyptian, a male, an adult, and a commoner. He lived in the post-Ashurbanipal period, and he seems to have been a resident of the city of Nineveh. The circumstances leading to this individual being in Assyria are difficult to pin down, but it is likely that he or older relatives of his came to Assyria forcibly through deportation.[66]

Ati'

The 19th individual of this category is *Ati'*. The meaning of the name of this individual of masculine gender is unknown but is believed to correspond to Egyptian *Iti/ꜣti*. *Ati'* is mentioned in a text (SAA 14 161) from Nineveh and 623 BCE as a witness and as the father of the fuller *Ubru-Mullissu*, who is one of the guarantors when the woman *Niḫti-Eša-rau*▪ buys *Mullissu-hāṣinat* as a wife for her son *Ṣi-ḫû*▪ 4. from *Nabû-rēḫtu-uṣur* 17.[67]

On the basis of the above data, the interrogative words who, what, when, and where can be responded to. *Ati'* seems to have been an Egyptian, a male, an adult, and a commoner. He lived in the post-Ashurbanipal period, and he seems to have been a resident of the city of Nineveh. The question of how this individual ended up in Assyria is difficult to answer, but it is likely that he or older relatives of his came to Assyria forcibly by means of deportation.[68]

Aṭû

The 20th individual of this category is *Aṭû*. The name of this individual of masculine gender is Egyptian and means "the deaf one" (Eg. *Id*). *Aṭû* appears in texts (StAT 2

---

[65] Drawing from the text publication and the PNA-entry of R. Mattila (PNA 1/I, p. 139).

[66] Regarding etymology, Mattila refers to a study by A. Leahy (1993: 56). For names composed of or beginning with *wḏꜣ* in Egypt, see Ranke 1935: 88:14-89:7. The name of this individual, meaning "prosperous", naturally tells of a desire for well-being throughout life. Concerning textual content and context and the former document, one of the two preserved names of witnesses is Egyptian. As for the latter document, *Aṣê* appears as the only witness whose name has been preserved.

[67] Drawing from the text publication and the PNA-entry of R. Mattila (PNA 1/I, p. 233).

[68] Regarding etymology, Mattila refers to studies by R. Zadok (1977b: 63) and J. Osing (1978: 38). The name is brought up also in Ranke 1910: 36-37; 1935: 49:12-21, and Tallqvist 1914: 47. Concerning textual content and context and the former document, *Ati'* features as number 14 of 15 witnesses, of which several bear Egyptian names. Also, one of the three guarantors has an Egyptian name. In other words, the transaction in question took place in the Egyptian community of Nineveh. It is possible that *Ati'* (just like his son *Ubru-Mullissu*) was a fuller (*ašlāku*).

216-217) on a tablet and its envelope from the N31-archive, Assur, and the seventh century BCE as a witness when *Apâ*▪ borrows silver from *Urdu-Aššur* 5.[69]

On the basis of the above data, identities, properties, and settings can be identified. *Aṭû* seems to have been an Egyptian, a male, an adult, and a commoner. He lived some time in the seventh century BCE, and he seems to have been a resident of the city of Assur. The circumstances leading to this individual being in Assyria are difficult to pin down, but it is likely that he or older relatives of his came to Assyria forcibly through deportation.[70]

Bakkî

The 21st individual of this category is *Bakkî*. The meaning of the name of this individual of masculine gender is uncertain but may be found in the Egyptian form *bꜣky*. *Bakkî* appears in a text (*FNLD* 18) from the N31-archive, Assur, and 625 BCE as a witness when *Ḫuṭ-naḫti*▪ and *Puṭi-Mūnu*▪ 2. share the inheritance of their father *Lā-turammanni-Aššur* 3.[71]

On the basis of the above data, the interrogative words who, what, when, and where can be responded to. *Bakkî* seems to have been an Egyptian, a male, an adult, and a commoner. He lived in the post-Ashurbanipal period, and he seems to have been a resident of the city of Assur. The question of how this individual ended up in Assyria is difficult to answer, but it is likely that he or older relatives of his came to Assyria forcibly by means of deportation.[72]

Batu-naḫti

The 22nd individual of this category is *Batu-naḫti*. The name of this individual of masculine gender is not completely understood but is believed to contain the Egyptian word *nḫtw*, meaning "strength". *Batu-naḫti* is mentioned in a text (StAT

---

69 Drawing from the text publication and the PNA-entry of R. Mattila (PNA 1/I, p. 237).

70 Regarding etymology, this name appears in the Egyptian onomasticon (Ranke 1935: 53:12). The name "the deaf one" supposedly refer to a specific body malfunction that the bearer of the name had. Concerning textual content and context, four people, of which three have clearly or likely Egyptian names, are listed as witnesses in the document(s). The prominent Egyptian *Kiṣir-Aššur* 45. heads the list of witnesses, while *Aṭû* appears on third place. The document is dated to 613 BCE in the publication by V. Donbaz and S. Parpola (2001: 146-147).

71 Drawing from the text publication and the PNA-entry of R. Mattila (PNA 1/II, p. 254).

72 Regarding etymology, Mattila refers to studies by R. Zadok (1977b: 64) and J. Osing (1978: 37). For this name in Egyptian texts, see Ranke 1935: 90:13. By contrast, Osing argues that there are too many options to determine that this name should be read *Bꜣky*. The word *bꜣky* means "Diener" (Wb I, pp. 429-430). Concerning textual content and context, *Bakkî* appears as number 13 of 17 witnesses. There are numerous Egyptian names in the list. Obviously, this affair took place in the Egyptian community of Assur.

2 167) from the N31-archive, Assur, and 646 BCE where he counts as one of ten men (most of them bearing Egyptian names) who divide an inheritance.[73]

On the basis of the above data, identities, properties, and settings can be identified. *Batu-naḫti* seems to have been an Egyptian, a male, an adult, and a commoner. He lived in the reign of Ashurbanipal, and he seems to have been a resident of the city of Assur. The circumstances leading to this individual being in Assyria are difficult to pin down, but it is likely that he or older relatives of his came to Assyria forcibly through deportation.[74]

Bukunanni'pi 1.

The 23rd individual of this category is *Bukunanni'pi* 1. The name of this individual of masculine gender is Egyptian and means "servant of the wind" (Eg. *Bȝk-n-nfy*). *Bukunanni'pi* 1. appears in a text (RINAP 5/1 11) from Nineveh and 644-642 BCE as the ruler of the Egyptian city of Ahni, a ruler appointed as vassal by Esarhaddon and re-appointed by Ashurbanipal after the revolt by Taharqa, king of Kush.[75]

On the basis of the above data, the interrogative words who, what, when, and where can be responded to. *Bukunanni'pi* 1. was an Egyptian, a male, an adult, and a member of the elite. He lived in the reigns of Esarhaddon and Ashurbanipal, and he resided in the Egyptian city of Ahni. The question of how he became a part of the Neo-Assyrian empire is difficult to answer, but it was voluntary in the sense that he (as far as is known) chose not to resist but forced in the sense that he surrendered in light of the threat of Assyrian arms.[76]

Bukunanni'pi 2.

The 24th individual of this category is *Bukunanni'pi* 2. This man is mentioned in a text (RINAP 5/1 11) from Nineveh and 644-642 BCE as the ruler of the Egyptian

---

[73] Drawing from the text publication and the PNA-entry of R. Mattila (PNA 1/II, pp. 277-278).

[74] *Batu-naḫti*, who is listed on seventh place, and the other nine people give a house to the Egyptian *Tap-naḫte* 3. in lieu of his share. The prominent Egyptians *Urdu-Aššur* 5. and *Lā-turammanni-Aššur* 3. are among the six witnesses, and so are two people with possibly/likely Egyptian names.

[75] Drawing from the text publication and the PNA-entry of R. Mattila (PNA 1/II, p. 350).

[76] Regarding etymology, Mattila refers to a study by H. Ranke (1910: 27). The name is brought up also in Steindorff 1890: 348, Tallqvist 1914: 65, and Ranke 1935: 91:10. The meaning of the name is unclear, but the status of servant in relation to the divine sphere is implied. Concerning textual content and context, *Bukunanni'pi* 1. is referred to (on 13th place) in a list of (20) Assyrian vassals in Egypt. The city of Ahni (Eg. *Iḫnw*) was situated somewhere in Lower Egypt (RGTC 7/2-1, p. 11). The terms voluntary and forced in the context of the integration of these vassals are relative and depend on what Assyrian royal inscriptions convey. It may be noted here that in a minority of these royal inscriptions (see notably RINAP 5/1 11), all 20 vassals (and not just *Nikkû*, *Šarru-lū-dāri* 13., and *Pa-qruru*) are portrayed as rebelling against Assyria.

city of Athribis, a ruler appointed as vassal by Esarhaddon and re-appointed by Ashurbanipal.[77]

On the basis of the above data, identities, properties, and settings can be identified. *Bukunanni'pi* 2. was an Egyptian, a male, an adult, and a member of the elite. He lived in the reigns of Esarhaddon and Ashurbanipal, and he resided in the Egyptian city of Athribis. The question of how he became a part of the Neo-Assyrian empire is difficult to answer, but it was voluntary in the sense that he chose not to resist but forced in the sense that he surrendered in light of the threat of Assyrian arms.[78]

Bukurninip

The 25th individual of this category is *Bukurninip*. The name of this individual of masculine gender is Egyptian and means "servant of his name" (Eg. *Bꜣk-n-rn.f*). *Bukurninip* appears in a text (RINAP 5/1 11) from Nineveh and 644-642 BCE as the ruler of the Egyptian city of Pahnutu, a ruler appointed as vassal by Esarhaddon and re-appointed by Ashurbanipal.[79]

On the basis of the above data, the interrogative words who, what, when, and where can be responded to. *Bukurninip* was an Egyptian, a male, an adult, and a member of the elite. He lived in the reigns of Esarhaddon and Ashurbanipal, and he resided in the Egyptian city of Pahnutu. The question of how he became a part of the Neo-Assyrian empire is difficult to answer, but it was voluntary in the sense that he chose not to resist but forced in the sense that he surrendered in light of the threat of Assyrian arms.[80]

Butanaḫte

The 26th individual of this category is *Butanaḫte*. The name of this individual of masculine gender is partly unclear but probably contains the Egyptian word *nḫtw*, meaning "strength". *Butanaḫte* appears in a text (StAT 2 167) from the N31-

[77] Drawing from the text publication and the PNA-entry of R. Mattila (PNA 1/II, p. 350).
[78] *Bukunanni'pi* 2. is referred to (on fifth place) in a list of (20) Assyrian vassals in Egypt. The city of Athribis (Akk. *Ḫatḫariba*, Eg. *Ḥwt-tꜣ-ḥry-ib*) was situated in Lower Egypt and was given the Akkadian name *Limmer-iššak-Aššur* by the Assyrian kings (RGTC 7/2-1, p. 221).
[79] Drawing from the text publication and the PNA-entry of R. Mattila (PNA 1/II, p. 350).
[80] Regarding etymology, Mattila refers to a study by H. Ranke (1910: 27). The name is brought up also in Steindorff 1890: 353, Tallqvist 1914: 65, and Ranke 1935: 91:11. The meaning of the name is unclear, but the status of servant in relation to the divine sphere is implied. Concerning textual content and context, *Bukurninip* is referred to (on 16th place) in a list of (20) Assyrian vassals in Egypt. The city of Pahnutu was situated in Upper Egypt, probably somewhere between Memphis and Hermopolis (RGTC 7/2-2, p. 473).

archive, Assur, and 646 BCE as one of ten men (most of them bearing Egyptian names) who share an inheritance.[81]

On the basis of the above data, identities, properties, and settings can be identified. *Butanaḫte* seems to have been an Egyptian, a male, an adult, and a commoner. He lived in the reign of Ashurbanipal, and he seems to have been a resident of the city of Assur. The circumstances leading to this individual being in Assyria are difficult to pin down, but it is likely that he or older relatives of his came to Assyria forcibly through deportation.[82]

Butinaḫ

The 27th individual of this category is *Butinaḫ*. The name of this individual of masculine gender is partly unclear but probably contains the Egyptian word *nḫtw*, meaning "strength". *Butinaḫ* is mentioned in a text (StAT 2 207) from the N31-archive, Assur, and 618 BCE as a witness when *Bābilāiu* buys a house from *Urdu-Aššur*, son of *Puṭi-ḫutapiša*▪. The "ditto" following his name refers to him as "the Egyptian" (*Muṣurāiu*).[83]

On the basis of the above data, the interrogative words who, what, when, and where can be responded to. *Butinaḫ* seems to have been an Egyptian, a male, an adult, and a commoner. He lived in the post-Ashurbanipal period, and he seems to have been a resident of the city of Assur. The question of how this individual ended up in Assyria is difficult to answer, but it is likely that he or older relatives of his came to Assyria forcibly by means of deportation.[84]

Dān-Ešu

The 28th individual of this category is *Dān-Ešu*. The name of this individual of masculine gender means "Isis is strong". Its first element is Akkadian and its second element is Egyptian, conveying the name of the Egyptian goddess Isis. *Dān-Ešu* features in a text (SAA 21 58) from Nineveh and the reign of Ashurbanipal. The text in question is a letter sent by the king of Assyria to the king of Elam in which

---

[81] Drawing from the text publication and the PNAo-entry of H.D. Baker (the name and/or individual in question is not listed in PNA).

[82] *Butanaḫte*, who is listed on eighth place, and the other nine people give a house of six seahs to the Egyptian *Tap-naḫte* 3. in lieu of his share of the inheritance. The prominent Egyptians *Urdu-Aššur* 5. and *Lā-turammanni-Aššur* 3. are among the six witnesses.

[83] Drawing from the text publication and the PNAo-entry of H.D. Baker (the name and/or individual in question is not listed in PNA).

[84] Regarding etymology, the similarity to *Butanaḫte* and the Egyptian textual context make it very likely that *nḫtw* is expressed, even though a final *t* is lacking. Last but not least, *Butinaḫ* is qualified by an Egyptian ethnonym. Concerning textual content and context, this man appears as number seven of 15 witnesses, of whom several are soldiers and guards. One witness is referred to as "superintendent of the crown prince". *Butinaḫ* is one of five men called "the Egyptian".

a statement made by *Dān-Ešu* concerning *Šamaš-šumu-ukīn* (Assyrian king of Babylon) to an individual named *Sîn-šarra-ibni* is quoted.[85]

On the basis of the above data, identities, properties, and settings can be identified. *Dān-Ešu* seems to have been an Egyptian, a male, an adult, and a member of the elite. He lived in the reign of Ashurbanipal, and he may have been a resident of Babylonia. The circumstances leading to this individual being in Babylonia are difficult to pin down, but it is likely that he or older relatives of his came to southern Mesopotamia forcibly through deportation.[86]

Eptimu-rṭešu

The 29th individual of this category is *Eptimu-rṭešu*. The name of this individual of masculine gender is fully Egyptian and means "it is Nefertem who has given him" (Eg. *Nfrtm-ir-di-sw*). *Eptimu-rṭešu* is mentioned in a text (RINAP 5/1 11) from Nineveh and 644-642 BCE as the ruler of the Egyptian city of Trenuthis, a ruler appointed as vassal by Esarhaddon and re-appointed by Ashurbanipal.[87]

On the basis of the above data, the interrogative words who, what, when, and where can be responded to. *Eptimu-rṭešu* was an Egyptian, a male, an adult, and a member of the elite. He lived in the reigns of Esarhaddon and Ashurbanipal, and he resided in the Egyptian city of Trenuthis. The question of how he became a part of the Neo-Assyrian empire is difficult to answer, but it was voluntary in the sense that he chose not to resist but forced in the sense that he surrendered in light of the threat of Assyrian arms.[88]

---

[85] Drawing from the text publication and the PNA-entry made by S. Parpola and K. Radner (PNA 1/II, p. 376).

[86] Regarding etymology, Parpola and Radner note that the writing *da-né-e-šu* tells of *sandhi*. The name "Isis is strong" naturally centres on the power of the goddess. Isis was one of the main deities in Egypt, tied to Osiris (as wife) and Horus (as mother) (Shaw and Nicholson 1995: 142-143). Concerning texual content and context, the Assyrian king writes that *Dān-Ešu*, after he had been kept in fetters (as a detained messenger?), made a correct observation on Babylonian and Elamite kings to *Sîn-šarra-ibni*, saying "Šamaš-šumu-ukin gave me a gift, and for this reason I did everything. Instead of your supporting the old man Menanu against Ummanigaš, you should have given the office in Elam to me. See, now Menanu is yours, and what has he ever done and given to you?". *Dān-Ešu* must have been an individual of high rank, in his being involved in important state matters like that of foreign policy. Judging by his direct contact with *Šamaš-šumu-ukīn*, he may have been a resident of Babylonia.

[87] Drawing from the text publication and the PNA-entry of R. Mattila (PNA 1/II, p. 398).

[88] Regarding etymology, Mattila refers to studies by H. Ranke (1910: 29) and G. Fecht (1958: 113-114). For this name in Egyptian texts, see Ranke 1935: 200:25. Ranke (1910: 29) identifies the divine name Ptah, while Fecht offers the reading Nefertem. The name "it is Nefertem who has given him" defines the name bearer as god-given. Nefertem was an Egyptian god, associated with the sun-god and Memphis (Shaw and Nicholson 1995: 199). Concerning textual content and context, *Eptimu-rṭešu* is referred to (on 14th place) in a list of (20) Assyrian vassals in Egypt. The city of Trenuthis (Akk. *Piḫattiḫurunpiki*, Eg. *Pr-ḥwt-ḥr-nbt-mfkt*) was situated in the eastern Nile delta (RGTC 7/2-2, p. 479).

Ēšâ

The 30th individual of this category is *Ēšâ*. The name of this individual gives a hypocorrected form of the name of the Egyptian goddess Isis. Contextual data reveal this individual as a male individual. *Ēšâ* is mentioned in a text (StAT 2 139) from Assur and the seventh century BCE (probably reign of Ashurbanipal or later) as the buyer of a boy (whose name is not preserved) for twelve shekels of silver from *Bibīa*, the boy's father.[89]

On the basis of the above data, identities, properties, and settings can be identified. *Ēšâ* seems to have been an Egyptian, a male, an adult, and a commoner. He lived in the seventh century BCE (probably reign of Ashurbanipal or later), and he seems to have been a resident of the city of Assur. The circumstances leading to this individual being in Assyria are difficult to pin down, but it is likely that he or older relatives of his came to Assyria forcibly by means of deportation.[90]

Eša-rṭeše

The 31st individual of this category is *Eša-rṭeše*. The name of this individual of feminine gender is fully Egyptian and means "it is Isis who has given her" (Eg. *ꜣst-ir-di-st*). *Eša-rṭeše* appears in a text (SAA 11 169) from Nineveh and the seventh century BCE as one of four weavers (*ušpartu*). The document in question lists Egyptian deportees and their possessions.[91]

On the basis of the above data, the interrogative words who, what, when, and where can be responded to. *Eša-rṭeše* seems to have been an Egyptian, a female, an adult, and a commoner. She lived some time in the seventh century BCE, and she seems to have been a resident of the city of Nineveh. Although the exact circumstances leading to the presence of *Eša-rṭeše* in Assyria are unclear, it is evident that she came to Assyria forcibly via deportation.[92]

---

[89] Drawing from the text publication and the PNA-entry of W. Pempe (PNA 1/II, p. 406).

[90] Regarding etymology, Pempe refers to studies by K. Tallqvist (1914: 255) and R. Zadok (1977a: 27). The name is brought up also in Ranke 1910: 43; 1935: 3:18. "Isis" as a personal name naturally speaks of a close relationship between the goddess and the name bearer. Notably, V. Donbaz and S. Parpola (2001: 102) read *Sasâ* rather than *Ēšâ*. Concerning textual content and context, none of the eleven or twelve witnesses can be tied to African ethnicity. The background of this transaction, outside the Egyptian community, is unclear, although it probably concerned adoption. V. Donbaz and S. Parpola (2001: 102) propose 679 BCE as the date.

[91] Drawing from the text publication and the PNA-entry of R. Mattila (PNA 1/II, p. 407).

[92] Regarding etymology, this name is attested in the Egyptian onomasticon (Ranke 1935: 3:19). The name in question is listed (as *Unš/sard/ṭi*) but unexplained in Ranke 1910: 38 and Tallqvist 1914: 241. The name "it is Isis who has given her" defines the name bearer as a gift of the goddess. Concerning textual content and context, the names of the other three weavers are not preserved. Both named and anonymous Egyptians are enumerated. The total number of Egyptians consists of 17 people, nine men and eight women.

Ḫapi-maniḫi

The 32nd individual of this category is *Ḫapi-maniḫi*. The meaning of the name of this individual of masculine gender is unclear but probably includes the name of the Egyptian divine bull Apis. *Ḫapi-maniḫi* is mentioned in a text (StAT 3 95) from the N31-archive, Assur, and 658 BCE as taking a loan of a mina(?) and five shekels of silver from *Ḫur-waṣi*▪ 6.[93]

On the basis of the above data, identities, properties, and settings can be identified. *Ḫapi-maniḫi* seems to have been an Egyptian, a male, an adult, and a commoner. He lived in the reign of Ashurbanipal, and he seems to have been a resident of the city of Assur. The circumstances leading to this individual being in Assyria are difficult to pin down, but it is likely that he or older relatives of his came to Assyria forcibly through deportation.[94]

Ḫapi-nāu

The 33rd individual of this category is *Ḫapi-nāu*. The name of this individual of masculine gender is fully Egyptian and means "Apis is lenient" (Eg. *Ḥp-nʿi*). *Ḫapi-nāu* is mentioned in a text (*FNLD* 18) from the N31-archive, Assur, and 625 BCE as a witness when *Huṭ-naḫti*▪ and *Puṭi-Mūnu*▪ 2. share the inheritance of their father *Lā-turammanni-Aššur* 3.[95]

On the basis of the above data, the interrogative words who, what, when, and where can be responded to. *Ḫapi-nāu* seems to have been an Egyptian, a male, an adult, and a commoner. He lived in the post-Ashurbanipal period, and he seems to have been a resident of the city of Assur. The question of how this individual ended up in Assyria is difficult to answer, but it is likely that he or older relatives of his came to Assyria forcibly by means of deportation.[96]

---

93 Drawing from the text publication and a PNAo-entry of H.D. Baker (the name and/or individual in question is not listed in PNA).

94 Regarding etymology, *Ḫapi* can refer to the Apis bull (Zadok 1977b: 64; Zeidler 1994: 42). It is likely that the Egyptian name *Ḥp-mnḥ* (Ranke 1935: 237:14), meaning "Apis rejoices", is expressed here (Karlsson 2022a). Concerning textual content and context, the loan is witnessed by five people. None of these have a clearly African name. A clause of this fragmentary text seems to say that the (unnamed) sons of *Ḫapi-maniḫi* will be held as a pledge with the creditor.

95 Drawing from the text publication and the PNA-entry of R. Mattila (PNA 2/I, p. 458).

96 Regarding etymology, Mattila refers to studies by R. Zadok (1977b: 64) and J. Zeidler (1994: 42). The name "Apis is lenient" speaks of the divine Apis bull as merciful towards the name bearer. Concerning textual content and context, *Ḫapi-nāu* appears on third place in the list of (17) witnesses. Numerous individuals mentioned in this text have Egyptian names. *Ḫapi-nāu* was obviously a part of the Egyptian community of Assur.

Ḫaqu-nēši

The 34th individual of this category is *Ḫaqu-nēši*. The name of this individual of masculine gender is fully Egyptian and means “strong ruler” (Eg. *Ḥḳꜣ-nꜥš*). *Ḫaqu-nēši* is brought up in a text (SAA 14 446) from the archive of *Inurta-šarru-uṣur*, Nineveh, and 612 BCE as a witness in a court order concerning a debt of silver owed by *Aṣê*▪.[97]

On the basis of the above data, identities, properties, and settings can be identified. *Ḫaqu-nēši* seems to have been an Egyptian, a male, an adult, and a commoner. He lived in the post-Ashurbanipal period, and he seems to have been a resident of the city of Nineveh. The circumstances leading to this individual being in Assyria are difficult to pin down, but it is likely that he or older relatives of his came to Assyria forcibly through deportation.[98]

Ḫasâ

The 35th individual of this category is *Ḫasâ*. The name of this individual of masculine gender is fully Egyptian and means “praised” (Eg. *Ḥsy*). *Ḫasâ* is mentioned in a text (SAA 14 442) from the archive of *Inurta-šarru-uṣur*, Nineveh, and 634 BCE as a witness when *Puṭi-Atḫiš*▪ buys and adopts the boy *Aḫu-iddina* from his grandfather, the cook *Abdi-Kurra*, for ten shekels of silver.[99]

On the basis of the above data, the interrogative words who, what, when, and where can be responded to. *Ḫasâ* seems to have been an Egyptian, a male, an adult, and a commoner. He lived in the reign of Ashurbanipal, and he seems to have been a resident of the city of Nineveh. The question of how this individual ended up in Assyria is difficult to answer, but it is likely that he or older relatives of his came to Assyria forcibly by means of deportation.[100]

Ḫatpi-Ašte

The 36th individual of this category is *Ḫatpi-Ašte*. The name of this individual of masculine gender is fully Egyptian and means “may Satis be satisfied” (Eg. *Ḥtp-Stt*), referring to the Egyptian goddess Satis. *Ḫatpi-Ašte* is mentioned in a text

---

[97] Drawing from the text publication and the PNA-entry of R. Mattila (PNA 2/I, p. 458).

[98] Regarding etymology, Mattila refers to a study by A. Leahy (1993: 58). The name “strong ruler” arguably conveys a praise of an Egyptian (or the Assyrian) ruler. Concerning textual content and context, *Ḫaqu-nēši* appears as number two of three witnesses. The names of the other witnesses are either non-African or lost.

[99] Drawing from the text publication and the PNA-entry of R. Mattila (PNA 2/I, p. 463).

[100] Regarding etymology, Mattila refers to studies by H. Ranke (1910: 28; 1935: 254:28-29) and A. Leahy (1993: 58). Concerning textual content and context, the names of 17 witnesses (including that of the owner of the archive) have been preserved, and several of these are African. *Ḫasâ* appears as number eight in this list of witnesses.

(StAT 2 181) from the N31-archive, Assur, and 629 BCE as a witness when *Aššur-gārû'a-nēre* buys the slave woman *Issar-tukallanni* from her owner *Daiān-Marduk* for one mina and seven shekels of silver.[101]

On the basis of the above data, identities, properties, and settings can be identified. *Ḫatpi-Ašte* seems to have been an Egyptian, a male, an adult, and a commoner. He lived in the post-Ashurbanipal period, and he seems to have been a resident of Assur. The circumstances leading to this individual being in Assyria are difficult to pin down, but it is likely that he or older relatives of his came to Assyria forcibly through deportation.[102]

Ḫatpi-Mūnu

The 37th individual of this category is *Ḫatpi-Mūnu*. The name of this individual of masculine gender is fully Egyptian and means "may Amun be satisfied" (Eg. *Ḥtp-Imn*), referring to the Egyptian god Amun. *Ḫatpi-Mūnu* is mentioned in texts (SAA 14 119-120) on a tablet and its envelope from Nineveh and 631 BCE as a witness when *Mannu-kī-Arbail* borrows silver from an individual named *Bēlu-lū-balaṭ*.[103]

On the basis of the above data, the interrogative words who, what, when, and where can be responded to. *Ḫatpi-Mūnu* seems to have been an Egyptian, a male, an adult, and a commoner. He lived in the reign of Ashurbanipal, and he appears to have been a resident of the city of Nineveh. The question of how this individual ended up in Assyria is difficult to answer, but it is likely that he or older relatives of his came to Assyria forcibly by means of deportation.[104]

Ḫatpi-Napi

The 38th individual of this category is *Ḫatpi-Napi*. The name of this individual of masculine gender is fully Egyptian and means "may the Beautiful One be satisfied"

---

101 Drawing from the text publication and the PNA-entry of R. Mattila (PNA 2/I, p. 466).

102 Regarding etymology, this name is attested in the Egyptian onomasticon (Ranke 1935: 259:17). A difference between Egyptian and Mesopotamian naming traditions may be expressed here, with this name conveying prospective mood rather than (as in Mesopotamia) imperative mood (with the request of a deity intervening) (Ranke 1952: 254). The name "may Satis be satisfied" implies that the name bearer was a devotee of Satis. Satis was an Egyptian goddess worshipped primarily in the Assuan-region (Shaw and Nicholson 1995: 252-253). As for the Assuan-region and Egyptian deities in Assyria, a statuette of the goddess Anukis has been found in Nineveh (al-Asil 1955: 129). Concerning textual content and context, there are more than 20 witnesses to this purchase, with *Ḫatpi-Ašte* appearing on twelfth place. Several of the witnesses have African names and quite a few are guards, soldiers, and army officers.

103 Drawing from the text publication and the PNA-entry of R. Mattila (PNA 2/I, p. 466).

104 Regarding etymology, Mattila refers to studies by K. Tallqvist (1914: 87) and H. Ranke (1935: 258:1). The name is brought up also in Ranke 1911: 112. The name "may Amun be satisfied" implies that the name bearer was a devotee of Amun. Concerning textual content and context, eight people (two with Egyptian names) witness the loan. *Ḫatpi-Mūnu* appears as the first witness, indicating that he was not an insignificant member of the Egyptian community of Nineveh.

(Eg. *Ḥtp-nfr*), referring to an Egyptian goddess. *Ḫatpi-Napi* is mentioned in a text (StAT 2 207) from the N31-archive, Assur, and 618 BCE as a witness for *Bābilāiu*, who buys a house from *Urdu-Aššur*, son of *Puṭi-ḫutapiša*▪. *Ḫatpi-Napi* is qualified as "the Egyptian" (*Muṣurāiu*).[105]

On the basis of the above data, identities, properties, and settings can be identified. *Ḫatpi-Napi* seems to have been an Egyptian, a male, an adult, and a commoner. He lived in the post-Ashurbanipal period, and he seems to have been a resident of Assur. The circumstances leading to this individual being in Assyria are difficult to pin down, but it is likely that he or older relatives of his came to Assyria forcibly through deportation.[106]

Ḫipirrāu

The 39th individual of this category is *Ḫipirrāu*. The meaning of the name of this individual of masculine gender is unknown, but the name has been identified as safely Egyptian. *Ḫipirrāu* is mentioned in a text (StAT 2 164) from the N31-archive, Assur, and 675 BCE as a witness when *Pabbā'u*▫ gives her daughter *Mullissu-ḫammat*, a votaress of the goddess Ishtar of Arbela, to *Awa* (1.). *Ḫipirrāu* is qualified as a "chief brewer" (*rab sirāšê*) in the text.[107]

On the basis of the above data, the interrogative words who, what, when, and where can be responded to. *Ḫipirrāu* seems to have been an Egyptian, a male, an adult, and a commoner. He lived in the reign of Esarhaddon, and he seems to have been a resident of the city of Assur. The question of how this individual ended up in Assyria is difficult to answer, but it is likely that he or older relatives of his came to Assyria forcibly by means of deportation.[108]

---

105 Drawing from the text publication and the PNA-entry of R. Mattila (PNA 2/I, p. 466).

106 Regarding etymology, the PNA-entry includes an alleged reference to *Ḫatpi-Napi* in text StAT 2 167. However, the name in question is now read *Pamenapi* (Donbaz and Parpola 2001: 121). For the name *Ḥp-nfr* in Egyptian texts, see Ranke 1935: 258:20. The goddess in question may be Hathor, associated with female beauty (Shaw and Nicholson 1995: 119). Concerning textual content and context, also the prominent Egyptian *Kiṣir-Aššur* 45. features as a witness in this transaction. *Ḫatpi-Napi* is one of five men referred to as "Egyptian", being listed on fourth place. All facts combined, this transaction took place firmly in the Egyptian community of Assur.

107 Drawing from the text publication and the PNA-entry of D. Schwemer (PNA 2/I, p. 473).

108 Regarding etymology, Schwemer supposedly focuses on the Egyptian textual context. The name may contain the Egyptian word *ḫpr* and/or the Egyptian prepositional phrase *r.w*, proceeding from the analysis of H. Ranke (1910: 54, 58). Concerning textual content and context, the special status of *Mullissu-hammat*, in her being a votaress of Ishtar of Arbela, is stressed in the document. *Pabbā'u*, in his turn, is presented as a horse keeper of the same goddess. Several of the twelve witnesses are tied to the cultic sphere. A few of the witnesses have Egyptian names. The fact that *Ḫipirrāu* is mentioned as the first witness indicates that he was not an insignificant member of the Egyptian community of Assur. It is unclear to which institution *Ḫipirrāu* belonged as "chief brewer", but the context suggests that it might have been a temple.

Ḫursisu

The 40th individual of this category is *Ḫursisu*. The meaning of the name of this individual of masculine gender is unclear, but the name has been identified as safely Egyptian. This name should be distinguished from the name *Ḫur-ši-Ēšu*▪, treated below. *Ḫursisu* appears in a broken text (SAA 14 309) from Nineveh and the seventh(?) century BCE as a witness in a case whose nature and participants are unclear due to the damaged state of the tablet.[109]

On the basis of the above data, identities, properties, and settings can be identified. *Ḫursisu* seems to have been an Egyptian, a male, an adult, and a commoner. He probably lived some time in the seventh century BCE, and he seems to have been a resident of the city of Nineveh. The circumstances leading to this individual being in Assyria are difficult to pin down, but it is likely that he or older relatives of his came to Assyria forcibly through deportation.[110]

Ḫur-šia

The 41st individual of this category is *Ḫur-šia*. The name of this individual of masculine gender is fully Egyptian and means "Horus (is) son" (Eg. *Ḥr-sꜣ*), referring to the Egyptian god Horus (as son of Isis). *Ḫur-šia* is mentioned in a text (StAT 2 204) from the N31-archive, Assur, and the seventh century BCE as a witness when *[...]-ilu* borrows silver from an individual whose name has not been preserved.[111]

On the basis of the above data, the interrogative words who, what, when, and where can be responded to. *Ḫur-šia* seems to have been an Egyptian, a male, an adult, and a commoner. He lived in the seventh century BCE, and he seems to have been a resident of the city of Assur. The question of how this individual ended up in Assyria is difficult to answer, but it is likely that he or older relatives of his came to Assyria forcibly by means of deportation.[112]

---

109 Drawing from the text publication and the PNA-entry of R. Mattila (PNA 2/I, p. 481).

110 Regarding etymology, Mattila refers to studies by K. Tallqvist (1914: 87) and A. Leahy (1993: 58). Both Tallqvist and Leahy link this name to the name *Ḫur-ši-Ēšu*, with Leahy identifying "a defective writing of the very common Late Period name *Ḥr-sꜣ-ꜣst*". Mattila sees the name as Egyptian but objects to Leahy's interpretation, citing phonology in the Neo-Assyrian dialect. In any case, it seems likely that the Egyptian theonym *Ḥr* forms the first element of this name. Concerning textual content and context, the names of five witnesses are preserved, and the majority of these are non-African. *Ḫursisu* appears first in this list of witnesses.

111 Drawing from the text publication and the PNA-entry of R. Mattila (PNA 2/I, p. 481).

112 Regarding etymology, Mattila adds that the name may be a short form of *Ḫur-ši-Ēšu*. The notion of Horus as son of Isis was important in Egyptian religion, not the least in the Egyptian myth of kingship (Shaw and Nicholson 1995: 133-134, 142-143). Concerning textual content and context, *Ḫur-šia* appears as the third of six witnesses, mentioned right after a man with an Egyptian name. While Mattila dates the text approximately to the seventh century BCE, V. Donbaz and S. Parpola (2001: 140) date the text to 620 BCE.

Ḫur-ši-Ēšu 1.

The 42nd individual of this category is *Ḫur-ši-Ēšu* 1. The name of this individual of masculine gender is fully Egyptian and means "Horus, son of Isis" (Eg. *Ḥr-sꜣ-ꜣst*). *Ḫur-ši-Ēšu* 1. is mentioned in a text (RINAP 5/1 11) from Nineveh and 644-642 BCE as an Assyrian vassal in Egypt, being the ruler of the city of Sebennytos, a ruler installed by Esarhaddon and re-installed by Ashurbanipal after the revolt of Taharqa, king of Kush.[113]

On the basis of the above data, identities, properties, and settings can be identified. *Ḫur-ši-Ēšu* 1. was an Egyptian, a male, an adult, and a member of the elite. He lived in the reigns of Esarhaddon and Ashurbanipal, and he resided in the Egyptian city of Sebennytos. The question of how he became a part of the Neo-Assyrian empire is difficult to answer, but it was voluntary in the sense that he chose not to resist but forced in the sense that he surrendered in light of the threat of Assyrian arms.[114]

Ḫur-ši-Ēšu 2.

The 43rd individual of this category is *Ḫur-ši-Ēšu* 2. This man is mentioned in a text (SAA 7 9) from Nineveh and the reigns of Esarhaddon or Ashurbanipal which gives a list of lodgings for officials. *Ḫur-ši-Ēšu* 2. is presented as "prefect (*šaknu*) of the Hallateans" in this context.[115]

On the basis of the above data, the interrogative words who, what, when, and where can be responded to. *Ḫur-ši-Ēšu* 2. seems to have been an Egyptian, a male, an adult, and a member of the elite. He lived in the reigns of Esarhaddon or Ashurbanipal, and he seems to have been a resident of Nineveh. The question of how this individual ended up in Assyria is difficult to answer, but it is likely that he or older relatives of his came to Assyria forcibly via deportation.[116]

Ḫur-ši-Ēšu 3.

The 44th individual of this category is *Ḫur-ši-Ēšu* 3. This man, likewise highlighting Horus, son of Isis, through his personal name, appears in a text (SAA

---

[113] Drawing from the text publication and the PNA-entry of R. Mattila (PNA 2/I, p. 481).

[114] Regarding etymology, Mattila refers to studies by K. Tallqvist (1914: 86-87), H. Ranke (1910: 28; 1935: 250:13; 1952: 378), and A. Leahy (1993: 58). The name in question is brought up also in Steindorff 1890: 350. Concerning textual content and context, *Ḫur-ši-Ēšu* 1. is referred to (on ninth place) in a list of (20) Assyrian vassals in Egypt. The city of Sebennytos (Akk. *Ṣabnūti*, Eg. *Ṯb-nṯr*) was situated in the delta (RGTC 7/2-2, pp. 549-550).

[115] Drawing from the text publication and the PNA-entry of R. Mattila (PNA 2/I, p. 481).

[116] Mattila adds that this individual may be identical with *Ḫur-ši-Ēšu* 3. Concerning textual content and context, none of the other named people in the list have an African name. The Hallateans were West Semitic tribesmen (presumably Arameans) who served as auxiliaries in the Assyrian army (Zadok 2010: 416). Somehow, Hallateans came under the leadership of the Egyptian *Ḫur-ši-Ēšu* 2.

14 442) from the archive of *Inurta-šarru-uṣur*, Nineveh, and 634 BCE as a witness when *Puṭi-Atḫiš▪* buys and adopts the boy *Aḫu-iddina* from the latter's grandfather, the cook *Abdi-Kurra*.[117]

On the basis of the above data, identities, properties, and settings can be identified. *Ḫur-ši-Ēšu* 3. seems to have been an Egyptian, a male, an adult, and a commoner. He lived in the reign of Ashurbanipal, and he seems to have been a resident of the city of Nineveh. The circumstances leading to this individual being in Assyria are difficult to pin down, but it is likely that he or older relatives of his came to Assyria forcibly through deportation.[118]

Ḫur-tibû 1.

The 45th individual of this category is *Ḫur-tibû* 1. The name of this individual of masculine gender is fully Egyptian and means "Horus of the Tree" (Eg. *Ḥr-tꜣ-bꜣt*). *Ḫur-tibû* 1. appears in a text (SAA 11 169) from Nineveh and the seventh century BCE as an Egyptian deportee listed among other deportees with Egyptian names.[119]

On the basis of the above data, the interrogative words who, what, when, and where can be responded to. *Ḫur-tibû* 1. seems to have been an Egyptian, a male, an adult, and a commoner. He lived some time in the seventh century BCE, and he seems to have been a resident of the city of Nineveh. Although the exact circumstances leading to the presence of *Ḫur-tibû* 1. in Assyria are unclear, it is evident that he came to Assyria forcibly via deportation.[120]

Ḫur-tibû 2.

The 46th individual of this category is *Ḫur-tibû* 2. This man is mentioned in a text (CTN 3 41) from Kalhu and 616 BCE as the father of *Urdu-Mullissu* 10., who borrows (along with *Kalbāia* 2., son of *Pi-san-Eši▪* 2.) silver from *Nabû-aḫu-uṣur*. The people involved in this transaction seem to be tied to the city of Napisina.[121]

On the basis of the above data, identities, properties, and settings can be identified. *Ḫur-tibû* 2. seems to have been an Egyptian, a male, an adult, and a commoner. He lived in the post-Ashurbanipal period, and he seems to have been a

117 Drawing from the text publication and the PNA-entry of R. Mattila (PNA 2/I, p. 481).
118 Mattila adds that this individual may be identical with *Ḫur-ši-Ēšu* 2. Concerning textual content and context, the man in question appears as number seven of the around 20 witnesses, of whom several have African names. The archive owner *Inurta-šarru-uṣur* 2. is listed on second place.
119 Drawing from the text publication and the PNA-entry of R. Mattila (PNA 2/I, p. 481).
120 Regarding etymology, Mattila refers to studies by H. Ranke (1910: 28) and K. Tallqvist (1914: 87) and adds that the name should not be confused with the Egyptian title *ḥry-tp* (rendered as *ḫar-ṭi-bi* in the cuneiform script). As for the name "Horus of the Tree", trees were viewed as sacred in ancient Egypt, in the sense that certain kinds of trees (such as sycamore and persea) were associated with specific deities and with the afterlife (Shaw and Nicholson 1995: 295). Concerning textual content and context, *Ḫur-tibû* 1. appears as the third of the eleven preserved personal names.
121 Drawing from the text publication and the PNA-entry of R. Mattila (PNA 2/I, p. 481).

resident of the city of Napisina. The circumstances leading to this individual being in Assyria are difficult to pin down, but it is likely that he or older relatives of his came to Assyria forcibly through deportation.[122]

Ḫūru 1.

The 47th individual of this category is *Ḫūru* 1. The name of this individual of masculine gender is Egyptian, referring to the Egyptian god Horus. It is a short form of names containing this theophoric element (Eg. *Ḥr*). *Ḫūru* 1. is mentioned (along with *Niḫarā'u*▪ and *Ḫur-waṣi*▪ 3.) in a text (SAA 7 1) from Nineveh and the reign of Esarhaddon as an "Egyptian scribe" (*ṭupšar Muṣurāiu*). The text lists scholars at the Assyrian court.[123]

On the basis of the above data, the interrogative words who, what, when, and where can be responded to. *Ḫūru* 1. seems to have been an Egyptian, a male, an adult, and a member of the elite. He lived in the reign of Esarhaddon, and he seems to have been a resident of Nineveh. The question of how this individual ended up in Assyria is difficult to answer, but it is likely that he or older relatives of his came to Assyria forcibly by means of deportation. It can not be excluded, however, that *Ḫūru* 1., with his special skills, arrived in Assyria as a result of peaceful negotiations between the Assyrian king and an African ruler.[124]

Ḫūru 2.

The 48th individual of this category is *Ḫūru* 2. This man appears in several texts from the N31-archive, Assur, and the time range of 645-613 BCE. He appears as a party in transactions when he lends 15 shekels of silver to *Mannu-kī-Arbail* (StAT 2 168), and when he (and five other men) owe three horses, *iškaru*-tax of the king, to *Urdu-Aššur* 5. (StAT 2 213). He also appears as the father of *Aḫu-dūr-enši* 2., who borrows silver from *Urdu-Aššur* 5. (StAT 2 191). He also features as a witness, namely in a court case involving unnamed Egyptian merchants who had been attacked by six men in the house of *Ḫakkubāia* (StAT 2 173-174), in a text (StAT 2 178) about *Kiṣir-Aššur* 45. buying the slave woman *Bānât-Esaggil* from *Nabû-mētu-balliṭ*, in a text (*FNLD* 18) where *Huṭ-naḫti*▪ and *Puṭi-Mūnu*▪ 2. share the

---

[122] Only the names of three witnesses have been preserved. One of these has a possibly Egyptian name. The city of Napisina may have been situated somewhere near Kalhu (RGTC 7/2-2, p. 447).
[123] Drawing from the text publication and the PNA-entry of R. Mattila (PNA 2/I, p. 481).
[124] Regarding etymology, Mattila refers to studies by H. Ranke (1910: 29), K. Tallqvist (1914: 90), R. Zadok (1977b: 64), and J. Zeidler (1994: 47-48). The name in question is brought up also in Ranke 1935: 245:18 and Zeidler 1994: 43-47. The bearer of the (divine) name was probably imagined to be under the protection of the deity in question (in this case Horus). Concerning textual content and context, *Ḫūru* 1. is mentioned first of the three Egyptian scribes. This group of three concludes the list of experts. The directly preceding group of experts consists of three (Egyptian) dream interpreters. For Egyptian scholars as spoils of war, see the royal inscriptions of Esarhaddon, specifically RINAP 4 9.

inheritance of their father *Lā-turammanni-Aššur* 3., and in a text (StAT 2 184) about *Ata'*□ giving his sister *Silim-Puṭi-lumur* in marriage to *Riḫpi-Mūnu*□. Finally, *Ḫūru* 2. is a witness when *Lā-turammanni-Aššur* 3., *Awa* (2.), and *Pi'u*▪ 2. pay the servants of the king for a horse given to *Paši*□ 3. (StAT 3 87), when *K[isir]i* borrows silver from *Kiṣir-Aššur* 45. (StAT 3 92), and when *Nāṣirī*(?) settles a lawsuit with *Zamunu*(?) (StAT 3 79). *Ḫūru* 2. is presented as active in the military sphere, namely as a "cohort commander" (*rab kiṣri*).[125]

On the basis of the above data, identities, properties, and settings can be identified. *Ḫūru* 2. seems to have been an Egyptian, a male, an adult, and a member of the elite. He lived in the reign of Ashurbanipal and later, and he seems to have been a resident of the city of Assur. The circumstances leading to this individual being in Assyria are difficult to pin down, but it is likely that he or older relatives of his came to Assyria forcibly through deportation.[126]

Ḫūru 3.

The 49th individual of this category is *Ḫūru* 3. This man, whose name likewise points to the Egyptian god Horus, is mentioned in a text (StAT 1 36) from Assur and 614 BCE as a witness to the pledge of the woman *Aḫā[tī]* and her unnamed son in relation to a creditor whose name has not been preserved in full (*Ḫa[...]*).[127]

On the basis of the above data, the interrogative words who, what, when, and where can be responded to. *Ḫūru* 3. seems to have been an Egyptian, a male, an adult, and a commoner. He lived in the post-Ashurbanipal period, and he seems to have been a resident of the city of Assur. The question of how this individual ended up in Assyria is difficult to answer, but it is likely that he or older relatives of his came to Assyria forcibly by means of deportation.[128]

Ḫūru-[...] (1.)

The 50th individual of this category is *Ḫūru-[...]* (1.) The incomplete name of this individual of masculine gender is Egyptian and probably contains the theophoric element Horus. *Ḫūru-[...]* (1.) is mentioned in a text (SAA 11 169) from Nineveh and the seventh century BCE as an Egyptian deportee listed among other deportees with Egyptian names.[129]

---

125 Drawing from the text publications, the PNA-entry of R. Mattila (PNA 2/I, p. 481), and three PNAo-entries of H.D. Baker.

126 *Ḫūru* 2. frequently features with the prominent Egyptians *Lā-turammanni-Aššur* 3., *Kiṣir-Aššur* 45., and *Urdu-Aššur* 5. (StAT 2 168; 178; 184; 191; StAT 3 92). He heads three of the relevant lists (StAT 2 213, StAT 3 92; 79). Thus, *Ḫūru* 2. must have been an important member of the Egyptian community in Assur. Notably, *Ḫūru* 2. appears both as patronym and witness in StAT 2 191.

127 Drawing from the text publication and the PNA-entry of R. Mattila (PNA 2/I, p. 481).

128 *Ḫūru* 3. counts as number four of six witnesses and is the only witness with an African name.

129 Drawing from the text publication and the PNA-entry of R. Mattila (PNA 2/I, p. 481).

On the basis of the above data, identities, properties, and settings can be identified. *Ḫūru-[...]* (1.) seems to have been an Egyptian, a male, an adult, and a commoner. He lived some time in the seventh century BCE, and he appears to have been a resident of the city of Nineveh. Although the exact circumstances leading to the presence of *Ḫūru-[...]* (1.) in Assyria are unclear, it is evident that he came to Assyria forcibly via deportation.[130]

Ḫūru-[...] (2.)

The 51st individual of this category is *Ḫūru-[...]* (2.) This man is mentioned in a text (WVDOG 152 II.7) from the Assur 52b-archive, Assur, and the reign of Ashurbanipal as borrowing four and a half and a fifth shekels of silver from a man named *Tap[...]*ᵒ.[131]

On the basis of the above data, the interrogative words who, what, when, and where can be responded to. *Ḫūru-[...]* (2.) seems to have been an Egyptian, a male, an adult, and a commoner. He lived in the reign of Ashurbanipal, and he seems to have been a resident of the city of Assur. The question of how this individual ended up in Assyria is difficult to answer, but it is likely that he or older relatives of his came to Assyria forcibly by means of deportation.[132]

Ḫur-waṣi 1.

The 52nd individual of this category is *Ḫur-waṣi* 1. The name of this individual of masculine gender is fully Egyptian and means "Horus is sound" (Eg. *Ḥr-wḏꜣ*), referring to the Egyptian god Horus. *Ḫur-waṣi* 1. is mentioned in a text (SAA 6 142) from Nineveh and 692 BCE as a witness for the Egyptian scribe *Ṣil-Aššur* 2., who buys a house in Nineveh from *Šarru-lū-dāri*, *Atar-suru*, and the woman *Amat-Su'la*, wife of *Bēl-dūrī*. *Ḫur-waṣi* 1. is qualified as a "third man" (*tašlīšu*) of a chariot team, thus being tied to the military sphere.[133]

On the basis of the above data, identities, properties, and settings can be identified. *Ḫur-waṣi* 1. seems to have been an Egyptian, a male, an adult, and a commoner. He lived in the reign of Sennacherib, and he appears to have been a resident of the city of Nineveh. The circumstances leading to this individual being in Assyria are difficult to pin down, but it is likely that he or older relatives of his came to Assyria forcibly through deportation.[134]

---

[130] This man is mentioned as number five of the eleven people whose names are preserved.

[131] Drawing from the text publication. *Ḫūru-[...]* (2.) is not listed in PNA or PNAo.

[132] The contract lists at least four witnesses, of whom one is an Egyptian and two have possibly Egyptian names. In other words, this loan took place in the Egyptian community of Assur.

[133] Drawing from the text publication and the PNA-entry of R. Mattila (PNA 2/I, pp. 481-482).

[134] Regarding etymology, Mattila refers to studies by A. Leahy (1993: 59), R. Zadok (1977b: 64), E. Edel (1980: 25-28), and J. Zeidler (1994: 43-47). For this name in Egyptian texts, see Ranke 1935: 246:23. By contrast, H. Ranke (1910: 34) and K. Tallqvist (1914: 206) list the name in question as

***Ḫur-waṣi* 2.**

The 53rd individual of this category is *Ḫur-waṣi* 2. This man is mentioned in a text (SAA 6 142) from Nineveh and 692 BCE as a witness when the Egyptian scribe *Ṣil-Aššur* 2. buys a house in Nineveh from *Šarru-lū-dāri*, *Atar-suru*, and the woman *Amat-Su'la*, wife of *Bēl-dūrī*. *Ḫur-waṣi* 2. is presented as a "chief boatman" (*rab mallāḫi*) in the document in question.[135]

On the basis of the above data, the interrogative words who, what, when, and where can be responded to. *Ḫur-waṣi* 2. seems to have been an Egyptian, a male, an adult, and a commoner. He lived in the reign of Sennacherib, and he seems to have been a resident of the city of Nineveh. The question of how this individual ended up in Assyria is difficult to answer, but it is likely that he or older relatives of his came to Assyria forcibly by means of deportation.[136]

***Ḫur-waṣi* 3.**

The 54th individual of this category is *Ḫur-waṣi* 3. This man is mentioned (along with *Ḫūru*▪ 1. and *Niḫarā'u*▪) in a text (SAA 7 1) from Nineveh and the reign of Esarhaddon as an "Egyptian scribe" (*ṭupšar Muṣurāiu*). The text lists various scholars at the Assyrian court.[137]

On the basis of the above data, identities, properties, and settings can be identified. *Ḫur-waṣi* 3. seems to have been an Egyptian, a male, an adult, and a member of the elite. He lived in the reign of Esarhaddon, and he seems to have been a resident of Nineveh. The circumstances leading to this individual being in Assyria are difficult to pin down, but it is likely that he or older relatives of his came to Assyria forcibly by means of deportation. It can not be excluded, however, that *Ḫur-waṣi* 3., with his special skills, came to Assyria as a result of peaceful negotiations between rulers.[138]

***Ḫur-waṣi* 4.**

The 55th individual of this category is *Ḫur-waṣi* 4. This man is mentioned in a fragmentary text (PEF 36 229) from Gezer (a town situated in a vassal state) and

---

Ṣuwaṣu. The former links it to Egyptian *Ḏ(d)-Wꜣḏy(t)*. The name "Horus is sound" probably refers to the healing power of Horus in relation to his violent clashes with his uncle Seth over the throne of Osiris (Shaw and Nicholson 1995: 133-134). Concerning textual content and context, the man in question appears as number two (after the prominent Libyan *Susinqu* 1.) of ten witnesses, of whom several bear African names.

135 Drawing from the text publication and the PNA-entry of R. Mattila (PNA 2/I, p. 482).

136 This man appears as number five of ten witnesses, of whom several bear African names.

137 Drawing from the text publication and the PNA-entry of R. Mattila (PNA 2/I, p. 482).

138 *Ḫur-waṣi* 3. appears last of the three Egyptian scribes. This group of three concludes the list of experts. The directly preceding group of experts consists of three (Egyptian) dream interpreters. For Egyptian scholars as spoils of war, see the royal inscriptions of Esarhaddon, specifically RINAP 4 9.

652 BCE as a witness when *Marduk-erība* and *Abī-erība* sell houses, land, and people to someone whose name has not been preserved. He is qualified as a "mayor" (*ḫazannu*) in the document in question.[139]

On the basis of the above data, the interrogative words who, what, when, and where can be responded to. *Ḫur-waṣi* 4. seems to have been an Egyptian, a male, an adult, and a member of the elite. He lived in the reign of Ashurbanipal, and he resided in the city of Gezer. The circumstances leading to the presence of *Ḫur-waṣi* 4. outside Egypt are difficult to pin down, but it is likely that he or older relatives of his came to Gezer forcibly via deportation.[140]

Ḫur-waṣi 5.

The 56th individual of this category is *Ḫur-waṣi* 5. This man is mentioned in a fragmentary text (TIM 11 29) said to come from the archive of *Inurta-šarru-uṣur*, Nineveh, and the reign of Ashurbanipal or later where he is referred to as potentially joining (or simply assisting) a lawsuit. The writer of the letter-text in question informs his superior that he ought to speak to *Atmanni*(?), show him *Ḫur-waṣi* 5., and plead a lawsuit with him.[141]

On the basis of the above data, identities, properties, and settings can be identified. *Ḫur-waṣi* 5. seems to have been an Egyptian, a male, an adult, and a commoner. He lived in the reign of Ashurbanipal or later, and he appears to have been a resident of the city of Nineveh. The circumstances leading to this individual being in Assyria are difficult to pin down, but it is likely that he or older relatives of his came to Assyria forcibly through deportation.[142]

Ḫur-waṣi 6.

The 57th individual of this category is *Ḫur-waṣi* 6. This man is mentioned in several texts from the N31-archive, Assur, and the time range of 658-613 BCE. He features as a neighbour of *Lā-turammanni-Aššur* 3. and as a witness when *Huṭ-naḫti*▪ and *Puṭi-Mūnu*▪ 2. share the inheritance of their father *Lā-turammanni-Aššur* 3. (*FNLD* 18). He is also a witness when *Mannu-kī-Arbail* borrows silver from *Ḫūru*▪ 2. (StAT 2 168), when two unknown people and *Puṭi-Bina[...]*▪ borrow silver from *Indî* (StAT 2 77), when six men borrow four horses from *Urdu-Aššur* 8. (StAT 2 210-211), when *Urdu-Bēlti* borrows silver from *Urdu-Aššur* 5. (StAT 2 192), and

---

[139] Drawing from the text publication and the PNA-entry of R. Mattila (PNA 2/I, p. 482).

[140] Supposedly, *Ḫur-waṣi* 4. was the mayor of Gezer, situated in modern-day Israel (RGTC 7/1, pp. 74-75). It is unclear how *Ḫur-waṣi* 4. reached this position. Probably, he was installed by the Assyrians. For more on this individual, see Giveon 1972. There are no further African names in the document. The mayor appears on fifth place in the list of (twelve) witnesses. The other person with a profession title is qualified as a merchant.

[141] Drawing from the text publication and the PNA-entry of R. Mattila (PNA 2/I, p. 482).

[142] It is unclear what the lawsuit concerned and who the sender and receiver of the letter were.

when *Kiṣir-Aššur* 45. buys the female slave *Bānât-Esaggil* from *Nabû-mētu-ballit* (StAT 2 178). He also functions as a witness when *Qurdi-Issar* and *Abu-lē'i* borrow barley from *Urdu-Aššur* 5. and *Kiṣir-Aššur* 45. (StAT 2 187), when *Balāssu* borrows silver from *Qurdi-Issar* (StAT 1 11), when *Apâ*▪ borrows silver from *Urdu-Aššur* 5. (StAT 2 216-217), when *Ata'*▫ gives his sister *Silim-Puṭi-lumur* in marriage to *Riḫpi-Mūnu*▫ (StAT 2 184), and when a redemption of a pledge involving *Šamaš-ibni* and *Urdu-Aššur* 5. takes place (StAT 2 229). He also borrows (together with at least two unknown people) silver from an unknown person (StAT 3 97), and he lends silver to *Ḫapi-maniḫi*▪ (StAT 3 95). *Ḫur-waṣi* 6. is qualified as the son of *Ki[r...]*.[143]

On the basis of the above data, the interrogative words who, what, when, and where can be responded to. *Ḫur-waṣi* 6. seems to have been an Egyptian, a male, an adult, and a member of the elite. He lived in the reign of Ashurbanipal and the following period, and he seems to have been a resident of Assur. The question of how he ended up in Assyria is difficult to answer, but it is likely that he or older relatives of his came to Assyria forcibly via deportation.[144]

Ḫur-waṣi 7.

The 58th individual of this category is *Ḫur-waṣi* 7. This man is mentioned in a text (StAT 2 207) from the N31-archive, Assur, and 618 BCE as a witness when *Bābilāiu* purchases a house in Assur from *Urdu-Aššur*, son of *Puṭi-ḫutapiša*▪.[145]

On the basis of the above data, identities, properties, and settings can be identified. *Ḫur-waṣi* 7. seems to have been an Egyptian, a male, an adult, and a commoner. He lived in the post-Ashurbanipal period, and he seems to have been a resident of the city of Assur. The circumstances leading to this individual being in Assyria are difficult to pin down, but it is likely that he or older relatives of his came to Assyria forcibly through deportation.[146]

---

143 Drawing from the text publications, the PNA-entry of R. Mattila (PNA 2/I, p. 482), and two PNAo-entries of H.D. Baker.

144 Mattila adds that this individual may be identical with *Ḫur-waṣi* 7., 10., or 11. Baker notes that the following texts contain references to anyone of *Ḫur-waṣi* 6.-11., namely StAT 2 198, r. 4 (witness), StAT 3 78 (witness), StAT 3 87 (witness), and StAT 3 114 (witness). Concerning textual content and context, and as noted in the PNA-entry, *Ḫur-waṣi* 6. was active in the circle of the prominent Egyptians *Lā-turammanni-Aššur* 3., *Urdu-Aššur* 5., and *Kiṣir-Aššur* 45., as he witnessed many of their documents from the N31-archive. However, there are few clues regarding his own position or activities. Still, considering his frequent mention in texts and his prominent positions in lists, he can be regarded as an individual of high social rank. It is noteworthy that StAT 2 77 is the only text outside the N31-archive, that there are *two* witnesses named *Ḫur-waṣi* in StAT 2 184 (the other being *Ḫur-waṣi* 9.), and that the time range 658-613 BCE can be established by the two documents StAT 3 95 (658) and StAT 2 216-217 (613).

145 Drawing from the text publication and the PNA-entry of R. Mattila (PNA 2/I, p. 482).

146 Mattila adds that this individual may be identical with *Ḫur-waṣi* 6. or 9. Concerning textual content and context, numerous people have Egyptian names. *Ḫur-waṣi* 7. counts as number three of

Ḫur-waṣi 8.

The 59th individual of this category is *Ḫur-waṣi* 8. This man appears in a text (StAT 2 207) from the N31-archive, Assur, and 618 BCE as a witness when *Bābilāiu* buys a house from *Urdu-Aššur*, son of *Puṭi-ḫutapiša*▪. *Ḫur-waṣi* 8. is presented as a son of *Tarḫursi*.[147]

On the basis of the above data, the interrogative words who, what, when, and where can be responded to. *Ḫur-waṣi* 8. seems to have been an Egyptian, a male, an adult, and a commoner. He lived in the post-Ashurbanipal period, and he seems to have been a resident of the city of Assur. The question of how this individual ended up in Assyria is difficult to answer, but it is likely that he or older relatives of his came to Assyria forcibly by means of deportation.[148]

Ḫur-waṣi 9.

The 60th individual of this category is *Ḫur-waṣi* 9. This man is mentioned in a text (StAT 2 184) from the N31-archive, Assur, and the reign of Ashurbanipal or the following period as a witness when *Ata'*▫ gives his sister *Silim-Puṭi-lumur* as a wife to *Riḫpi-Mūnu*▫.[149]

On the basis of the above data, identities, properties, and settings can be identified. *Ḫur-waṣi* 9. seems to have been an Egyptian, a male, an adult, and a commoner. He lived in the reign of Ashurbanipal or later, and he seems to have been a resident of the city of Assur. The circumstances leading to this individual being in Assyria are difficult to pin down, but it is likely that he or older relatives of his came to Assyria forcibly through deportation.[150]

Ḫur-waṣi 10.

The 61st individual of this category is *Ḫur-waṣi* 10. This man is mentioned in a broken text (KAV 189) from the N31-archive, Assur, and the post-Ashurbanipal period as a witness, together with *Amu-rṭēše*▪ 3. and *Ra'[...]*, in an unclear context.

---

15 witnesses. The piece of the tablet which defined what occupation he had is destroyed. The people listed right before and after him are qualified as "cohort commander" or gate guard.

[147] Drawing from the text publication and the PNA-entry of R. Mattila (PNA 2/I, p. 482).

[148] Mattila adds that this individual may be identical with *Ḫur-waṣi* 9., 10., or 11. Concerning textual content and context, numerous people have Egyptian names. *Ḫur-waṣi* 8. counts as number twelve of 15 witnesses. He appears after *Kiṣir-Aššur* 45. but before a "superintendent of the crown prince". Notably, there are *two* witnesses named *Ḫur-waṣi* in this text (the other being *Ḫur-waṣi* 7.).

[149] Drawing from the text publication and the PNA-entry of R. Mattila (PNA 2/I, p. 482).

[150] Mattila adds that this individual may be identical with *Ḫur-waṣi* 7., 8., 10., or 11. Concerning textual content and context, *Ḫur-waṣi* 9. appears on 16th place in the list of (more than 20) witnesses. The list includes the prominent Egyptians *Lā-turammanni-Aššur* 3.-4. and *Urdu-Aššur* 5, as well as several people with Egyptian names. It is noteworthy that there are *two* witnesses named *Ḫur-waṣi* in this text (the other being *Ḫur-waṣi* 6.).

He may also be a witness in a text (StAT 2 179) from the N31-archive, Assur, and 625 BCE in which an individual whose name has not been preserved buys the slave *[...]aya* from *Sinqi-[...]*. *Ḫur-waṣi* 10. is referred to as a "commander-of-fifty" (*rab ḫanšê*) in the former document.[151]

On the basis of the above data, the interrogative words who, what, when, and where can be responded to. *Ḫur-waṣi* 10. seems to have been an Egyptian, a male, an adult, and a member of the elite. He lived in the post-Ashurbanipal period, and he seems to have been a resident of the city of Assur. The question of how this individual ended up in Assyria is difficult to answer, but it is likely that he or older relatives of his came to Assyria forcibly by means of deportation.[152]

Ḫur-waṣi 11.

The 62nd individual of this category is *Ḫur-waṣi* 11. This man is mentioned in a text (StAT 2 201) from the N31-archive, Assur, and 622 BCE as a witness in a case about an inheritance that involves people whose names have not been preserved. *Ḫur-waṣi* 11. is presented as a cook (*nuḫatimmu*) in the document in question.[153]

On the basis of the above data, identities, properties, and settings can be identified. *Ḫur-waṣi* 11. seems to have been an Egyptian, a male, an adult, and a commoner. He lived in the post-Ashurbanipal period, and he appears to have been a resident of the city of Assur. The circumstances leading to this individual being in Assyria are difficult to pin down, but it is likely that he or older relatives of his came to Assyria forcibly through deportation.[154]

Ḫur-waṣi (12.)

The 63rd individual of this category is *Ḫur-waṣi* (12.), originally classified as *Ḫur-asu* 1. This man is mentioned in a text (StAT 2 181) from the N31-archive, Assur, and 629 BCE as one of the witnesses when *Aššur-gārû'a-nēre* purchases the female slave *Issar-tukallanni* from her owner *Daiān-Marduk*. *Ḫur-waṣi* (12.) is qualified as the father of *[...]-Aššur*.[155]

On the basis of the above data, the interrogative words who, what, when, and where can be responded to. *Ḫur-waṣi* (12.) seems to have been an Egyptian, a male,

---

151 Drawing from the text publications and the PNA-entry of R. Mattila (PNA 2/I, p. 482).

152 Mattila adds that this individual may be identical with *Ḫur-waṣi* 6., 8., or 9. Concerning textual content and context and with regard to document StAT 2 179, *Ḫur-waṣi* 10. is the only witness (of at least twelve) whose name is preserved. He appears to be the first witness, and he is qualified as the son of someone whose name has not been preserved.

153 Drawing from the text publication and the PNA-entry of R. Mattila (PNA 2/I, p. 482).

154 Mattila adds that this individual may be identical with *Ḫur-waṣi* 6., 8., or 9. Concerning textual content and context, *Ḫur-waṣi* 11. appears as number four of nine witnesses. One other witness has a possibly Egyptian name. It is not clear to what institution *Ḫur-waṣi* 11. belonged (the textual content does not give a clear indication).

155 Drawing from the text publication and the PNA-entry of R. Mattila (PNA 2/I, p. 480).

an adult, and a commoner. He lived in the post-Ashurbanipal period, and he seems to have been a resident of the city of Assur. The question of how this individual ended up in Assyria is difficult to answer, but it is likely that he or older relatives of his came to Assyria forcibly by means of deportation.[156]

Ḫur-waṣi (13.)

The 64th individual of this category is *Ḫur-waṣi* (13.), originally classified as *Ḫur-asu* 2. This man is mentioned in a text (StAT 2 198) from the N31-archive, Assur, and 623 BCE as a witness to an imposition of a fine concerning a crime which a *Bēl-lēšir* committed in the house of *Urdu-Aššur* 19. *Ḫur-waṣi* (13.) is presented as an "eunuch" (*ša rēši*).[157]

On the basis of the above data, identities, properties, and settings can be identified. *Ḫur-waṣi* (13.) seems to have been an Egyptian, a male, an adult, and a member of the elite. He lived in the post-Ashurbanipal period, and he appears to have been a resident of the city of Assur. The circumstances leading to this individual being in Assyria are difficult to pin down, but it is likely that he or older relatives of his came to Assyria forcibly through deportation.[158]

Ḫur-waṣi (14.)

The 65th individual of this category is *Ḫur-waṣi* (14.). This man is mentioned in a text (*ZA* 105) from Qalat-i Dinka (east of the Assyrian heartland) and 725 BCE as a witness when *Ḫazā* sells his female slave *Kablā*. *Ḫur-waṣi* (14.) is qualified as a servant (*ardu*) of the "palace herald" (*nāgir ekalli*).[159]

On the basis of the above data, the interrogative words who, what, when, and where can be responded to. *Ḫur-waṣi* (14.) seems to have been an Egyptian, a male, an adult, and a member of the elite. He lived in the reign of Shalmaneser V, and he seems to have lived east of the Assyrian heartland. The question of how this

---

[156] Regarding etymology, the change of reading in question comes from a PNAo-entry of H.D. Baker. Baker also proposes that this individual may be identical with anyone of *Ḫur-waṣi* 6.-11., with *Ḫur-waṣi* 6. as the most likely one. Concerning textual content and context, *Ḫur-waṣi* (12.) and his son appear as number eight and 13 of the more than 20 witnesses. The individuals whose professions are stated are either officers, soldiers, or guards. Several personal names are Egyptian. The name of his son tells of assimilation, in its including the name of the Assyrian god Ashur.

[157] Drawing from the text publication and the PNA-entry of R. Mattila (PNA 2/I, p. 480).

[158] Regarding etymology, the change of reading in question comes from a PNAo-entry of H.D. Baker. Concerning textual content and context, *Ḫur-waṣi* (13.) appears as the first of six witnesses. His namesake (anyone of *Ḫur-waṣi* 6.-11.) is listed on fourth place. Several witnesses bear likely or certain Egyptian names. His prominent position in the list, together with his status as a royal(?) eunuch, indicate that he was an individual of high social rank.

[159] Drawing from the text publication and the description of this text by R. Zadok (2018).

individual ended up in this corner of Assyria is difficult to answer, but it is likely that he or older relatives of his came to Assyria forcibly through deportation.[160]

Ḫuṭ-naḫti

The 66th individual of this category is *Ḫuṭ-naḫti*. The name of this individual of masculine gender is fully Egyptian and means "the attack is strong" (Eg. *Hd-nḫt(w))*. *Ḫuṭ-naḫti* appears in a text (*FNLD* 18) from the N31-archive, Assur, and 625 BCE as sharing (together with *Puṭi-Mūnu*▪ 2.) the inheritance of their father *Lā-turammanni-Aššur* 3. In addition to his share of his father's house, *Ḫuṭ-naḫti* inherits the slave woman *Ṣil-urkittu* and the sum of 16 shekels of silver.[161]

On the basis of the above data, identities, properties, and settings can be identified. *Ḫuṭ-naḫti* seems to have been an Egyptian, a male, an adult, and a member of the elite. He lived in the post-Ashurbanipal period, and he seems to have been a resident of the city of Assur. The circumstances leading to this individual being in Assyria are difficult to pin down, but it is likely that he or older relatives of his came to Assyria forcibly by means of deportation.[162]

Išpimāṭu

The 67th individual of this category is *Išpimāṭu*. The name of this individual of masculine gender is Egyptian and means "he belongs to the holy staff" (Eg. *Ns-pꜣ-mdw*). *Išpimāṭu* is mentioned in a text (RINAP 5/1 11) from Nineveh and 644-642 BCE as the ruler of the Egyptian city of Thinis, a ruler appointed as vassal by Esarhaddon and re-appointed by Ashurbanipal.[163]

On the basis of the above data, the interrogative words who, what, when, and where can be responded to. *Išpimāṭu* was an Egyptian, a male, an adult, and a member of the elite. He lived in the reigns of Esarhaddon and Ashurbanipal, and he resided in the Egyptian city of Thinis. The question of how he became a part of the Neo-Assyrian empire is difficult to answer, but it was voluntary in the sense

---

160 *Ḫur-waṣi* (14.) is the second and last witness, with the other witness bearing an Akkadian name. His position as a/the servant of the palace herald indicates that he was a man of influence. Zadok suggests that *Ḫur-waṣi* (14.) was brought to this part of Assyria following Tiglath-pileser III's campaign against Gaza (supported by Egypt) in 734 BCE.

161 Drawing from the text publication and the PNA-entry of R. Mattila (PNA 2/I, p. 483).

162 Regarding etymology, Mattila refers to studies by J. Osing (1978: 37), R. Zadok (1977b: 64), and J. Zeidler (1994: 48). For this name in Egyptian texts, see Ranke 1935: 231:20. The interpretation of Zadok, which is rejected by Osing, offers the reading *Ḥꜣt-nḫt*. The meaning of the name "the attack is strong" is unclear, but it may refer to a personal quality of the name bearer or of a deity. Concerning textual content and context, there are several Egyptian names also in the list of witnesses. *Ḫuṭ-naḫti* can be regarded as a member of the elite in his being a son of the prominent Egyptian *Lā-turammanni-Aššur* 3.

163 Drawing from the text publication and the PNA-entry of E. Frahm (PNA 2/I, p. 586).

that he chose not to resist but forced in the sense that he surrendered in light of the threat of Assyrian arms.[164]

Kurarâ

The 68th individual of this category is *Kurarâ*. The meaning of the name of this individual of masculine gender is unclear, but it has been identified as safely Egyptian. *Kurarâ* is mentioned in a text (SAA 11 169) from Nineveh and the seventh century BCE as an Egyptian deportee listed among other deportees with Egyptian names.[165]

On the basis of the above data, identities, properties, and settings can be identified. *Kurarâ* seems to have been an Egyptian, a male, an adult, and a commoner. He lived some time in the seventh century BCE, and he seems to have been a resident of the city of Nineveh. Although the exact circumstances leading to the presence of *Kurarâ* in Assyria are unclear, it is evident that he came to Assyria forcibly via deportation.[166]

Lamintu

The 69th individual of this category is *Lamintu*. The meaning of the name of this individual of masculine gender is unclear, but the name has been identified as safely Libyan. *Lamintu* corresponds to Nimlot (*Nmrt*). *Lamintu* / Nimlot II is mentioned in a text (RINAP 5/1 11) from Nineveh and 644-642 BCE as the ruler of the Egyptian city of Hermopolis, a ruler who was appointed as vassal by Esarhaddon and re-appointed by Ashurbanipal.[167]

On the basis of the above data, the interrogative words who, what, when, and where can be responded to. *Lamintu* was a Libyan, a male, an adult, and a member of the elite. He lived in the reigns of Esarhaddon and Ashurbanipal, and he resided in the Egyptian city of Hermopolis. The question of how he became a part of the

---

[164] Regarding etymology, Frahm refers to studies by H. Ranke (1935: 175:1; 1952: 365), K. Tallqvist (1914: 105), and H.-U. Onasch (1994: 56-57). The name is brought up also in Steindorff 1890: 354, Ranke 1910: 29, Fecht 1958: 114-116, and Leahy 1979. The meaning of the name "he belongs to the holy staff" is unclear, but it may refer to an attachment to divine or royal insignia or to his position of authority. As noted by Frahm, *Išpimāṭu* was also an Egyptian "vizier" (*ṯꜣty*). Concerning textual content and context, *Išpimāṭu* appears (on 19th place) in a list of (20) Assyrian vassals in Egypt. Thinis (Akk. *Tayani*, Eg. *Tny*) was a city in southern Egypt, near Abydos (RGTC 7/2-2, pp. 582-583). Fecht suggests that the city which *Išpimāṭu* resided in was Assuan. This idea is rejected by Onasch, citing phonological evidence.

[165] Drawing from the text publication and the PNA-entry of R. Mattila (PNA 2/I, p. 639).

[166] Regarding etymology, the name in question is brought up also in Tallqvist 1914: 118. Mattila supposedly focuses on the Egyptian textual context in her etymological classification. The Egyptian words *kꜣ* (*ku*) and/or *ir* (*ar*) may be part of this name, proceeding from the analysis of H. Ranke (1910: 45, 60). Concerning textual content and context, *Kurarâ* is mentioned towards the end of the list. The likely reconstructed "ditto-sign" describes this individual as a "fugitive" (*ḫalqu*) deportee.

[167] Drawing from the text publication and the PNA-entry of E. Frahm (PNA 2/II, p. 652).

Neo-Assyrian empire is difficult to answer, but it was voluntary in the sense that he chose not to resist but forced in the sense that he surrendered in light of the threat of Assyrian arms.[168]

Manti-me-ḫē

The 70th individual of this category is *Manti-me-ḫē* (Fig. 7). The name of this individual of masculine gender is fully Egyptian and means "Month is in the lead" (Eg. *Mnṯw-m-ḥꜣt*), referring to the Egyptian god Month. *Manti-me-ḫē* is mentioned in a text (RINAP 5/1 11) from Nineveh and 644-642 BCE as the ruler of the Egyptian city of Thebes, a ruler who was appointed as vassal by Esarhaddon and re-appointed by Ashurbanipal. In Egyptian sources, this figure is described as in possession of the prestigious offices of "mayor (*ḥꜣty-ꜥ*) of Thebes", "governor (*imy-r*) of Upper Egypt", and "fourth prophet (*ḥm-nṯr*) of Amun".[169]

On the basis of the above data, identities, properties, and settings can be identified. *Manti-me-ḫē* was an Egyptian, a male, an adult, and a member of the elite. He lived in the reigns of Esarhaddon and Ashurbanipal, and he resided in the Egyptian city of Thebes. The question of how he became a part of the Neo-Assyrian empire is hard to answer, but it was voluntary in the sense that he chose not to resist but forced in the sense that he surrendered in light of the threat of Assyrian arms.[170]

Matanaḫte

The 71st individual of this category is *Matanaḫte*. The meaning of the name of this individual of masculine gender is unclear, but the name has been identified as safely Egyptian. *Matanaḫte* appears in a text (StAT 2 208) from the N31-archive, Assur,

---

[168] Regarding etymology, Frahm refers to studies by H. Ranke (1910: 30; 1935: 204:11), K. Tallqvist (1914: 120), and J. Yoyotte (1960: 23-24). The name is brought up also in Steindorff 1890: 353-354. The meaning of this name is unclear, in its being non-Egyptian. Concerning textual content and context, and as remarked by Frahm, *Lamintu* was a successor and (possibly) grandson to Nimlot D, who opposed Piye, king of Kush, in the latter's campaign for control over the whole of Egypt. *Lamintu* appears (on 18th place) in a list of (20) Assyrian vassals in Egypt. Hermopolis (Akk. *Ḫimuni*, Eg. *Ḫmnw*) was a city in middle Egypt (RGTC 7/2-1, p. 227).

[169] Drawing from the text publication and the PNA-entry of E. Frahm (PNA 2/II, p. 701).

[170] Regarding etymology, Frahm refers to studies by H. Ranke (1910: 30; 1935: 154:7; 1952: 361) and K. Tallqvist (1914: 127). The name is brought up also in Steindorff 1890: 354-356. Evidently, the name of this ruler conveys a praise of the god Month. Month was a god linked to warfare and Thebes (Shaw and Nicholson 1995: 189-190). Concerning textual content and context, *Manti-me-ḫē* appears last in a list of (20) Assyrian vassals in Egypt. This final position reflects the geographic order of the list rather than any social rank. As noted by Frahm, *Manti-me-ḫē* recognized the Egyptian ruler Psammetichus I as king of Egypt some years later, in 656 BCE. Thebes (Akk. *Nī'*, Eg. *Niwt*) was a city in southern Egypt (RGTC 7/2-2, p. 454).

and 616 BCE as borrowing (along with *Lā-turammanni-Aššur* 3. and *Ṭab[...]*) two minas and ten shekels of silver from *Urdu-Aššur* 5.[171]

On the basis of the above data, the interrogative words who, what, when, and where can be responded to. *Matanaḫte* seems to have been an Egyptian, a male, an adult, and a commoner. He lived in the post-Ashurbanipal period, and he seems to have been a resident of the city of Assur. The circumstances leading to this individual being in Assyria are difficult to pin down, but it is likely that he or older relatives of his came to Assyria forcibly through deportation.[172]

Meia

The 72nd individual of this category is *Meia*. The name of this individual of feminine gender is Egyptian and means "beloved" (Eg. *Mry*). *Meia* is mentioned in a text (CT 53 974) from Assur and the seventh century BCE which consists of a letter from a *Gula-ēṭir* 3. The writer of the letter expresses the wish that *Meia* should not go out, and gives the information that he will join *Meia* in ten days. This man and a man named *Rībāia* 11. appear to be brothers of *Meia*.[173]

On the basis of the above data, identities, properties, and settings can be identified. *Meia* seems to have been an Egyptian, a female, an adult, and a commoner. She lived some time in the seventh century BCE, and she seems to have been a resident of the city of Assur. The question of how this individual ended up in Assyria is difficult to answer, but it is likely that she or older relatives of her came to Assyria forcibly by means of deportation.[174]

Nabareu

The 73rd individual of this category is *Nabareu*. The meaning of the name of this individual of masculine gender is unclear, but the name has been identified as safely Egyptian. *Nabareu* is mentioned in a text (StAT 2 228) from the N31-archive,

---

[171] Drawing from the text publication and the PNA-entry made by G. Van Buylaere (PNA 2/II, pp. 744-745).

[172] Van Buylaere adds that this name/person may be identical with *Amman-tanaḫti* (1.). Regarding etymology, Van Buylaere obviously identifies the Egyptian word *nḫtw* in this name. Concerning textual content and context, *Matanaḫte* is mentioned last of the three debtors, implying a lower social status. Two people with possibly or likely Egyptian names and the prominent Egyptian *Lā-turammanni-Aššur* 3. are among the witnesses.

[173] Drawing from the PNA-entry of E. Lipiński (PNA 2/II, p. 747).

[174] Regarding etymology, this name appears in the Egyptian onomasticon (Ranke 1935: 160:1). Concerning textual content and context, the background of the instruction in question is unclear, although an inferior position (with restriction of free movement) of this woman in relation to her brothers may be implied. As remarked by Lipiński, the letter carries two texts (on the same tablet), one addressed to *Rībāia* 11., one addressed to *Meia*.

Assur, and the reign of Ashurbanipal or the following period as a witness when *Šulmu-lušeri* borrows silver from *Urdu-Aššur* 5.[175]

On the basis of the above data, the interrogative words who, what, when, and where can be responded to. *Nabareu* seems to have been an Egyptian, a male, an adult, and a commoner. He lived in the later half of the seventh century BCE, and he seems to have been a resident of the city of Assur. The circumstances leading to this individual being in Assyria are difficult to pin down, but it is likely that he or older relatives of his came to Assyria forcibly through deportation.[176]

Naḫkê

The 74th individual of this category is *Naḫkê*. The name of this individual of masculine gender is Egyptian and means "the desired" (Eg. *Pꜣ-nhḳ*). *Naḫkê* appears in a text (RINAP 5/1 11) from Nineveh and 644-642 BCE as the ruler of the Egyptian city of Herakleopolis parva, a ruler appointed as vassal by Esarhaddon and re-appointed by Ashurbanipal. He also appears in two texts (RINAP 5/1 6; 7) from Nineveh and Kalhu and 647-642 BCE as one of the Egyptian vassals who fled from Taharqa and were re-installed by Ashurbanipal.[177]

On the basis of the above data, identities, properties, and settings can be identified. *Naḫkê* was an Egyptian, a male, an adult, and a member of the elite. He lived in the reigns of Esarhaddon and Ashurbanipal, and he resided in the Egyptian city of Herakleopolis parva. The question of how he became a part of the Neo-Assyrian empire is difficult to answer, but it was voluntary in the sense that he chose not to resist but forced in the sense that he surrendered in light of the threat of Assyrian arms.[178]

Naḫti-ḫuru-ansini

The 75th individual of this category is *Naḫti-ḫuru-ansini*. The name of this individual of masculine gender is fully Egyptian and means "the Horus of the trees is strong" (Eg. *Nḫt-Ḥr-nꜣ-šnw*), referring to the Egyptian god Horus. *Naḫti-ḫuru-*

---

175 Drawing from the text publication and the PNA-entry of P. Charlier (PNA 2/II, p. 788).

176 Regarding etymology, Charlier supposedly focuses on the Egyptian textual context. Proceeding from the analysis of H. Ranke (1910: 54), it is possible that the Egyptian prepositional phrase *r.w* is expressed in this name, then appearing as *areu* instead of *arau*. Concerning textual content and context, this man is mentioned last of five witnesses, supposedly indicating a lower social status. None of the other preserved names in the list of witnesses are African.

177 Drawing from the text publication and the PNA-entry of E. Frahm (PNA 2/II, p. 922).

178 Regarding etymology, Frahm refers to studies by K. Tallqvist (1914: 166) and E. Lüddeckens *et al.* (1980-2000: 193). The name is brought up also in Steindorff 1890: 349 and Ranke 1910: 30. Steindorff proposes that the Egyptian word *ꜥnḫ* forms the initial part of the name. Concerning textual content and context, *Naḫkê* is mentioned (on sixth place) in a list of (20) Assyrian vassals in Egypt in text RINAP 5/1 11. Herakleopolis parva (Akk. *Ḫininši*, Eg. *Pr-ḥry-š.f-nb-nn-nsw*) was a city situated in the Nile delta (RGTC 7/2-1, p. 231).

ansini is mentioned in a text (RINAP 5/1 11) from Nineveh and 644-642 BCE as the ruler of the Egyptian city of Pishapdia, a ruler who was appointed as vassal by Esarhaddon and re-appointed by Ashurbanipal.[179]

On the basis of the above data, the interrogative words who, what, when, and where can be responded to. *Naḫti-ḫuru-ansini* was an Egyptian, a male, an adult, and a member of the elite. He lived in the reigns of Esarhaddon and Ashurbanipal, and he resided in the Egyptian city of Pishapdia. The question of how he became a part of the Neo-Assyrian empire is difficult to answer, but it was voluntary in the sense that he chose not to resist but forced in the sense that he surrendered in light of the threat of Assyrian arms.[180]

Nibiḫis (1.)

The 76th individual of this category is *Nibiḫis* (1.). The meaning of the name of this individual of masculine gender is unclear, but it has been identified as safely Egyptian. *Nibiḫis* (1.) is mentioned in a text (StAT 2 198) from the N31-archive, Assur, and 623 BCE as a witness in a legal case dealing with a fine for a crime committed by *Bēl-lēšir* against *Urdu-Aššur* 19.[181]

On the basis of the above data, identities, properties, and settings can be identified. *Nibiḫis* (1.) seems to have been an Egyptian, a male, an adult, and a commoner. He lived in the post-Ashurbanipal period, and he seems to have been a resident of the city of Assur. The question of how this individual ended up in Assyria is difficult to answer, but it is likely that he or older relatives of his came to Assyria forcibly by means of deportation.[182]

---

[179] Drawing from the text publication and the PNA-entry of E. Frahm (PNA 2/II, p. 922).

[180] Regarding etymology, Frahm refers to studies by H. Ranke (1910: 30; 1935: 211:5) and K. Tallqvist (1914: 166). The name is brought up also in Steindorff 1890: 353. As for the name of this ruler, "the Horus of the trees is strong", certain kinds of trees were regarded as sacred in ancient Egypt (Shaw and Nicholson 1995: 295). Also, a quality (strength) of Horus is alluded to. Concerning textual content and context, *Naḫti-ḫuru-ansini* is referred to (on 15th place) in a list of (20) Assyrian vassals in Egypt. As concluded by Frahm, this ruler probably was "little more than a local mayor and a chief of second rank". Pishapdia (Eg. *Pr-Spdw-m-iꜣ.ti*) was a city possibly situated near Fayoum (RGTC 7/2-2, p. 481).

[181] Drawing from the text publication and the PNA-entry of F.S. Reynolds (PNA 2/II, p. 960).

[182] Regarding etymology, Reynolds supposedly centres on the Egyptian textual context. The Egyptian word *nb* (transcribed as *nib* in cuneiform) may be a part of this name, proceeding from the analysis of H. Ranke (1910: 52). Concerning textual content and context, this man appears as number five of six witnesses, of whom four have Egyptian names. Thus, this document is embedded in the Egyptian community of Assur.

Nibiḫis (2.)

The 77th individual of this category is *Nibiḫis* (2.). This man, whose name formerly was read *Nipiḫītu*, is mentioned in a text (StAT 3 46) from Assur and 623 BCE as a witness when *Ubru-Egissi* lends barley to *Šēp-Aššur*.[183]

On the basis of the above data, the interrogative words who, what, when, and where can be responded to. *Nibiḫis* (2.) seems to have been an Egyptian, a male, an adult, and a commoner. He lived in the post-Ashurbanipal period, and he seems to have been a resident of the city of Assur. The circumstances leading to this individual being in Assyria are difficult to pin down, but it is likely that he or older relatives of his came to Assyria forcibly through deportation.[184]

Niḫarā'u

The 78th individual of this category is *Niḫarā'u*. The meaning (and reading) of the name of this individual of masculine gender is unclear, but it has been identified as safely Egyptian. *Niḫarā'u* appears in a text (SAA 7 1) from Nineveh and the reign of Esarhaddon as an "Egyptian scribe" (*ṭupšar Muṣurāiu*) (along with *Ḫūru*▪ 1. and *Ḫur-waṣi*▪ 3.) listed among other (groups of) experts at the Assyrian court.[185]

On the basis of the above data, identities, properties, and settings can be identified. *Niḫarā'u* seems to have been an Egyptian, a male, an adult, and a member of the elite. He lived in the reign of Esarhaddon, and he seems to have been a resident of the city of Nineveh. The question of how this individual ended up in Assyria is difficult to answer, but it is likely that he or older relatives of his came to Assyria forcibly by means of deportation. It can not be excluded, however, that *Niḫarā'u*, with his special skills, arrived in Assyria as a result of peaceful negotiations between rulers.[186]

Niḫti-Eša-rau

The 79th individual of this category is *Niḫti-Eša-rau*. The name of this individual of feminine gender is fully Egyptian and means "Isis is strong against them" (Eg. *Nḫt-ꜣst-r.w*), referring to the Egyptian goddess Isis. *Niḫti-Eša-rau* is mentioned in

---

183 Drawing from the text publication and the PNA-entry of H.D. Baker (PNA 2/II, p. 965).

184 Regarding the etymology, the revised reading of the name of this individual comes from a PNAo-entry of H.D. Baker. Concerning textual content and context, this individual features as the fifth of nine witnesses. No other witness bears an African name.

185 Drawing from the text publication and the PNA-entry of R. Mattila (PNA 2/II, p. 960).

186 Regarding etymology, Mattila refers to a study by H. Ranke (1910: 31). The name is brought up also in Tallqvist 1914: 173. Ranke (1910: 31, 54) sees a connection with the Coptic name Niharau and identifies the Egyptian prepositional phrase *r.w*. F.M. Fales and J.N. Postgate, the publishers of the text, give the reading *Nimmurau*. Concerning textual content and context, this man appears second in this group of Egyptian experts at the Assyrian court in Nineveh. The group in question concludes the list and is directly preceded by a group of (three) Egyptian dream interpreters.

a text (SAA 14 161) from Nineveh and 623 BCE as buying *Mullissu-ḫāṣinat*, daughter of *Nabû-rēḫtu-uṣur* 17. (son of an Egyptian), as a wife for her son *Ṣi-hû*▪ 4. at the cost of 18 shekels of silver.[187]

On the basis of the above data, the interrogative words who, what, when, and where can be responded to. *Niḫti-Eša-rau* seems to have been an Egyptian, a female, an adult, and a commoner. She lived in the post-Ashurbanipal period, and she seems to have been a resident of the city of Nineveh. The circumstances leading to this individual being in Assyria are difficult to pin down, but it is likely that she or older relatives of her came to Assyria forcibly through deportation.[188]

Nikkû

The 80th individual of this category is *Nikkû*. The name of this individual of masculine gender is Egyptian and means "the one to whom belongs a Ka" (Eg. *Nkꜣw*), referring to the Egyptian concept of a soul. *Nikkû* (Necho I), ruler of the Egyptian cities of Memphis and Sais, features both in state letters and documents and in royal inscriptions from Assyria. As for the former source, the actions of *Nikkû* and *Šarru-lū-dāri* 13. (ruler of the Egyptian city of Pelusium) are highlighted in a query to the sun-god (SAA 4 88). A question whether these two men will attack (kill and loot) an envoy of Esarhaddon (*Ša-Nabû-šû*) to Egypt is posed. As for the latter source, the annals of Ashurbanipal (primarily RINAP 5/1 6; 7; 11, from Nineveh and Kalhu and the time range of 647-642 BCE) also mention *Nikkû*. He appears first in a list of 20 Assyrian vassals in Egypt, installed by Esarhaddon and re-installed by Ashurbanipal. *Nikkû*, *Šarru-lū-dāri* 13., and *Pa-qruru*▪ (ruler of the Egyptian city/nome of Per-Sopdu) later rebel against the agreement with Ashurbanipal and make overtures to Taharqa, king of Kush. Ashurbanipal's men in Egypt hear of this and have *Nikkû* and *Šarru-lū-dāri* 13. arrested and brought in front of Ashurbanipal in Nineveh. The Assyrian king takes pity on *Nikkû* and restores him to office, making him a primary Assyrian ally in Egypt. The fate of *Nikkû* at the re-conquest of Egypt by the Kushite king Tanutamon in 664 BCE is unknown, but he may have died in battle.[189]

On the basis of the above data, identities, properties, and settings can be identified. *Nikkû* was an Egyptian, a male, an adult, and a member of the elite. He

---

[187] Drawing from the text publication and the PNA-entry of R. Mattila (PNA 2/II, p. 960).

[188] Regarding etymology, Mattila refers to a study by H. Ranke (1910: 31). The name is brought up also in Tallqvist 1914: 173. The name of this individual, "Isis is strong against them", probably tells of the goddess Isis fighting the god Seth and his supporters, who threatened her son and legitimate heir Horus (Shaw and Nicholson 1995: 142-143). Concerning textual content and context, there are several people with Egyptian names among the listed guarantors and witnesses. This document illustrates the relative economic freedom enjoyed by some Egyptian women in Assyria.

[189] Drawing from the text publications and the PNA-entry of M.P. Streck (PNA 2/II, p. 963). *Nikkû* is also brought up in RINAP 5/1 2 and 8, and in Ashurbanipal 118 and 207 (available at http://oracc.org/rinap/Q003817/ and http://oracc.org/rinap/Q007615/ respectively; accessed 2021-07-26).

lived in the reigns of Esarhaddon and Ashurbanipal, and he resided in the Egyptian cities of Memphis and Sais. The question of how he became a part of the Neo-Assyrian empire is difficult to answer, but it was voluntary in the sense that he initially and subsequently chose not to resist but forced in the sense that he repeatedly surrendered in light of the threat of Assyrian arms.[190]

Nummurīja

The 81st individual of this category is *Nummurīja*. The name of this individual of masculine gender is Egyptian and probably means "Ra is lord of truth" (Eg. *Nb-mꜣʿt-Rʿ*), referring to the Egyptian god Ra and the Egyptian concept of Order (*mꜣʿt*). *Nummurīja* appears in a text (SAA 3 29) from Nineveh and the reign of Ashurbanipal as an alleged ally of the traitor *Ṣallâ*. In this literary text, which contains invectives against *Bēl-ēṭir* of Bit-Iba, a certain *Ṣallâ* is spoken of in unflattering terms and called a "raped comrade" (*tappê nīku*) of *Nummurīja*.[191]

On the basis of the above data, the interrogative words who, what, when, and where can be responded to. *Nummurīja* seems to have been an Egyptian, a male, an adult, and a member of the elite. He lived in the reign of Ashurbanipal, but his place of residence is unclear. He may have had his base in Egypt, but it is also possible that he acted from another vassal state or from Assyria proper. The question of how he (in some form) became a part of Assyria is difficult to answer, considering the great uncertainties surrounding the identity of this individual. Apparently, he worked against Assyrian interests in some way.[192]

---

190 Regarding etymology, the name is brought up also in Steindorff 1890: 346-347, Ranke 1910: 31; 1935: 213:16, and Tallqvist 1914: 173. Steindorff regards the name as Libyan. As for the meaning of the name "the one to whom belongs a Ka", the *kꜣ* was a fundamental aspect in the Egyptian belief in an afterlife (Shaw and Nicholson 1995: 146). Concerning textual content and context, the prominent position *Nikkû* had for Assyria in Egypt is not the least manifested in his being mentioned first in the said list. Memphis (Akk. *Mempi*, Eg. *Mn-nfr*) was a city situated at the apex of the delta, and Sais (Akk. *Sai*, Eg. *Sꜣw*) was a city in the north-western part of the delta. The latter city was given the Akkadian name *Kār-bēl-mātāti* by the Assyrians (RGTC 7/2-2, pp. 424-425, 517-518).

191 Drawing from the text publication and the PNA-entry made by H.D. Baker and S. Parpola (PNA 2/II, p. 967).

192 Regarding etymology, Baker and Parpola refer to a study by H. Ranke (1910: 14). The name in question is brought up also in Tallqvist 1914: 173. The name conveys a statement about the supreme power of the god Ra. Ra was the main sun-god, closely tied to the upholding of Order, in Egyptian religion (Shaw and Nicholson 1995: 166, 239). As observed by Parpola, the name is otherwise not attested as a personal name (but see the throne name of Amenhotep III, as expressed in the Amarna letters: *ni-im-mu-ri-ia*, etc.). Concerning textual content and context, the background to the mention of *Nummurīja* is not clarified in the text, which is referred to as "warning to *Bel-eṭir*" by A. Livingstone in his text publication. *Nummurīja* apparently belonged to the elite, in his being linked to state policy and to an important enemy of Assyria. For the toponym of Bit-Iba (not found in RGTC 7/1-2), see Parpola 1970: 83.

Pa-qruru

The 82nd individual of this category is *Pa-qruru*. The name of this individual of masculine gender is Egyptian and means "the frog" (Eg. *Pꜣ-ḳrr*). *Pa-qruru*, ruler of the Egyptian city/nome of Per-Sopdu, features in Assyrian royal inscriptions. The annals of Ashurbanipal (primarily RINAP 5/1 6; 7; 11, from Nineveh and Kalhu and the time range of 647-642 BCE) mention *Pa-qruru*. He appears on fourth place in a list of 20 Assyrian vassals in Egypt, installed by Esarhaddon and re-installed by Ashurbanipal. *Nikkû*▪ (ruler of the Egyptian cities of Memphis and Sais), *Šarru-lū-dāri* 13. (ruler of the Egyptian city of Pelusium), and *Pa-qruru* subsequently rebel against the agreement with Ashurbanipal and make diplomatic overtures to Taharqa, king of Kush. A punishment imposed upon *Pa-qruru* is not attested.[193]

On the basis of the above data, identities, properties, and settings can be identified. *Pa-qruru* was an Egyptian, a male, an adult, and a member of the elite. He lived in the reigns of Esarhaddon and Ashurbanipal, and he resided in the Egyptian city/nome of Per-Sopdu. The question of how he became a part of the Neo-Assyrian empire is difficult to answer, but it appears that the integration in question was both voluntary and forced, considering his initial submission (being a vassal) and his subsequent resistance (being a rebel).[194]

Pīlušu

The 83rd individual of this category is *Pīlušu*. The meaning of the name of this individual of masculine gender is unclear, but it has been identified as safely Egyptian (Eg. *Pꜣy-rws* or *Pꜣy-iws*). *Pīlušu* is mentioned in a number of texts from the N31-archive, Assur, and the time range of 629-615 BCE. He appears as a witness when *Aššur-gārû'a-nēre* buys the female slave *Issar-tukallanni* from *Daiān-Marduk* (StAT 2 181), when *Urdu-Bēlti* borrows silver from *Urdu-Aššur* 5. (StAT 2 192), when *Ḫatta[ya]* borrows silver from *Urdu-Aššur* 5. (StAT 2 195), and when the estate of *Lā-turammanni-Aššur* 3. is divided between *Ḫuṭ-naḫti*▪ and *Puṭi-Mūnu*▪ 2. (*FNLD* 18). He also features as a witness in a broken text where the case and parties are missing (StAT 2 211), when *Ata'*▫ gives his sister *Silim-Puṭi-lumur* to *Riḫpi-Mūnu*▫ as a wife (StAT 2 184), when two people whose names are

---

[193] Drawing from the text publication and the PNA-entry of A.M. Bagg (PNA 3/I, p. 988). *Pa-qruru* is also brought up in RINAP 5/1 2 and 8, and in Ashurbanipal 118 and 207 (available at http://oracc.org/rinap/Q003817/ and http://oracc.org/rinap/Q007615/ respectively; accessed 2021-07-27).
[194] Regarding etymology, Bagg refers to studies by G. Steindorff (1890: 348), K. Tallqvist (1914: 180), H. Ranke (1910: 31; 1935: 120:1), and H.-U. Onasch (1994: 42). As for the meaning of the name, frogs were linked to fertility, creation, and regeneration in ancient Egypt. For example, frogs were central in the creation myth of Hermopolis (Shaw and Nicholson 1995: 103-104). Concerning textual content and context, the omitted mention of a punishment imposed on *Pa-qruru* indicates that he managed to escape from the Assyrian punitive forces. Per-Sopdu (Akk. *Pišaptu*; Eg. *Pr-Spdw*) was situated in the eastern delta (RGTC 7/2-2, pp. 481-482).

missing borrow silver from *Urdu-Aššur* 5. (StAT 2 225), and when *Lā-turammanni-Aššur* 3. and two other individuals (whose names are lost) borrow silver from *Urdu-Aššur* 5. (StAT 2 209).[195]

On the basis of the above data, the interrogative words who, what, when, and where can be responded to. *Pīlušu* seems to have been an Egyptian, a male, an adult, and a commoner. He lived in the post-Ashurbanipal period, and he seems to have been a resident of the city of Assur. The circumstances leading to this individual being in Assyria are difficult to pin down, but it is likely that he or older relatives of his came to Assyria forcibly through deportation.[196]

Pīnapi

The 84th individual of this category is *Pīnapi*. The name of this individual of masculine gender is Egyptian and means "the beautiful" (Eg. *Pꜣ-nfr*). *Pīnapi* appears in a broken text (StAT 2 77) from Assur and 643 BCE as a witness when two people whose names are lost and *Puṭi-bina[...]*▪, son of an Egyptian, borrow silver from a man named *Indî*.[197]

On the basis of the above data, identities, properties, and settings can be identified. *Pīnapi* seems to have been an Egyptian, a male, an adult, and a commoner. He lived in the reign of Ashurbanipal, and he seems to have been a resident of the city of Assur. The question of how this individual ended up in Assyria is difficult to answer, but it is likely that he or older relatives of his came to Assyria forcibly by means of deportation.[198]

Pir'û

The 85th individual of this category is *Pir'û*. The name of this individual of masculine gender is Egyptian and means "the great house / pharaoh" (Eg. *Pr-ꜥꜣ*). *Pir'û*, king of Egypt (*šar māt Muṣuri*), features in royal inscriptions of Sargon II. In the annals (RINAP 2 1) and a summary inscription (RINAP 2 7) from Dur-

---

195 Drawing from the text publications and the PNA-entry of R. Pruzsinszky (PNA 3/1, p. 994).

196 Regarding etymology, Pruzsinszky refers to a study by J. Zeidler (1994: 49-50). Zeidler suggests that this (demotic) name can be tied to hieroglyphic *Pꜣ-nsy* (Ranke 1935: 114:1). Ranke does not provide a translation of the name in question. Concerning textual content and context, there are several Egyptian names in the lists of witnesses. In text StAT 2 184, the three prominent Egyptians *Lā-turammanni-Aššur* 3.-4., *Urdu-Aššur* 5., and *Kiṣir-Aššur* 45. all appear as witnesses. It is evident then that *Pīlušu* was an integral part of the Egyptian community in Assur. He generally holds a low position in the lists of witnesses in which he appears, thus indicating a relatively low social rank.

197 Drawing from the text publication and the PNA-entry made by R. Mattila and R. Pruzsinszky (PNA 3/I, p. 995).

198 Regarding etymology, this name is attested in the Egyptian onomasticon (Ranke 1935: 113:1). Concerning textual content and context, *Pīnapi* is the second of four witnesses. Another man with an Egyptian name and the prominent Egyptian *Lā-turammanni-Aššur* 3. are also witnesses. Thus, this transaction took place in the Egyptian community of Assur.

Sharrukin and 708-706 BCE, *Pir'û* gives (along with *Samsi*, queen of the Arabs, and *It'amar*, the Sabaean) "tribute" (*maddattu*) to Sargon II consisting of gold, precious stones, ivory, ebony, aromatics, horses, and camels. These three rulers may be the ones described as "kings from the seacoast and desert" (*šarrāni ša aḫi tâmtim u madbari*). In the annals (RINAP 2 82) from Nineveh and 711 BCE, *Pir'û* is approached by rulers in the Levant (represented by Philistia, Judah, Edom, and Moab), who had turned against Assyria. These give "presents" (*šulmānu*) to *Pir'û* and repeatedly ask him for military aid. Sargon II describes *Pir'û* in condescending terms as "a ruler who could not save them" (*malku lā mušēzibšunu*).[199]

On the basis of the above data, the interrogative words who, what, when, and where can be responded to. *Pir'û* was an Egyptian, a male, an adult, and a member of the elite. He lived in the reign of Sargon II, and he probably resided in a city in the Egyptian delta. The question of how he became a part of the Neo-Assyrian empire is difficult to answer, but it was voluntary in the sense that he chose not to resist but forced in the sense that he surrendered (by giving tribute) faced with Assyrian might.[200]

Pi-san-Eši 1.

The 86th individual of this category is *Pi-san-Eši* 1. The name of this individual of masculine gender is fully Egyptian and means "son of Isis" (Eg. *Pꜣ-šry-n-ꜣst*), referring to the Egyptian goddess Isis. *Pi-san-Eši* 1. appears in a text (SAA 14 91) from Nineveh and 648 BCE as a witness when *Gīr-Hâ* purchases a Tabalian servant named *Kamabānu* from *Adad-rapa*. *Pi-san-Eši* 1. is qualified further as a "commander-of-fifty" (*rab ḫanšê*).[201]

On the basis of the above data, identities, properties, and settings can be identified. *Pi-san-Eši* 1. seems to have been an Egyptian, a male, an adult, and a member of the elite. He lived in the reign of Ashurbanipal, and he seems to have been a resident of the city of Nineveh. The question of how this individual ended up in Assyria is difficult to answer, but it is likely that he or older relatives of his came to Assyria forcibly by means of deportation.[202]

---

[199] Drawing from the text publication and the PNA-entry made by R. Mattila and M. Weszeli (PNA 3/I, p. 996).

[200] Regarding etymology, Mattila and Weszeli refer to a study by H. Ranke (1910: 32). The name is brought up also in Steindorff 1890: 342-343 and Tallqvist 1914: 181. Concerning textual content and context, the identity of this ruler is disputed, but he is often equated with Osorkon IV of Tanis (see e.g. Kitchen 1973: 143-144). The bribes (offered by the Levantine rulers in question) do not seem to have had the desired effect. For the ideological significance of tribute in the ancient Near East, see Liverani 2001: 141-195.

[201] Drawing from the text publication and the PNA-entry of R. Mattila (PNA 3/I, p. 996).

[202] Regarding etymology, Mattila refers to a study by E. Edel (1980: 31-33). The name is brought up also in Tallqvist 1914: 181 and Ranke 1935: 118:7. Edel suggests the form *Pꜣ-sn-(ny)-ꜣst*. This interpretation is rejected by Mattila, citing phonological evidence. The name "son of Isis" refers to the god Horus (Shaw and Nicholson 1995: 133-134, 142-143). Concerning textual content and

Pi-san-Eši 2.

The 87th individual of this category is *Pi-san-Eši* 2. This man is mentioned in a text (CTN 3 41) from Kalhu and 616 BCE as the father of *Kalbāia* 2., who (together with *Urdu-Mullissu* 10., son of an Egyptian) owes *Nabû-aḫu-uṣur* a sum of silver. The debtors are tied to the town of Napisina.[203]

On the basis of the above data, the interrogative words who, what, when, and where can be responded to. *Pi-san-Eši* 2. seems to have been an Egyptian, a male, an adult, and a commoner. He lived in the post-Ashurbanipal period, and he seems to have been a resident of the town of Napisina. The circumstances leading to this individual being in Assyria are difficult to pin down, but it is likely that he or older relatives of his came to Assyria forcibly through deportation.[204]

Pi-san-Eši 3.

The 88th individual of this category is *Pi-san-Eši* 3. This man is mentioned in a text (SAA 14 171) from Nineveh and 613 BCE as a witness for *Mannu-kī-māt-Aššur*, who had seized his debtor *Nabû-šallim-aḫḫē* on account of a surety not provided by this man.[205]

On the basis of the above data, identities, properties, and settings can be identified. *Pi-san-Eši* 3. seems to have been an Egyptian, a male, an adult, and a commoner. He lived in the post-Ashurbanipal period, and he seems to have been a resident of the city of Nineveh. The question of how this individual ended up in Assyria is difficult to answer, but it is likely that he or older relatives of his came to Assyria forcibly by means of deportation.[206]

Pišamelki

The 89th individual of this category is *Pišamelki*. The name of this individual of masculine gender is Egyptian and means "the negus vendor" (Eg. *Psmṯk*). *Pišamelki* (i.e. Psammetichus I) is mentioned in a text (RINAP 5/1 11) from Nineveh and 644-642 BCE as a former vassal of Assyria (known under the name *Nabû-šēzibanni*) who had renounced his position and, with military support from Gyges, king of Lydia, had become *the* "king of Egypt" (*šar māt Muṣur*). *Pišamelki*,

---

context, the names of four witnesses are preserved. The other three names are not African. As noted by Mattila, *Pi-san-Eši* 1. and *Gīr-Hâ* (also a "commander-of-fifty") were colleagues.

203 Drawing from the text publication and the PNA-entry of R. Mattila (PNA 3/I, p. 996).

204 *Kalbāia* 2., son of *Pi-san-Eši* 2., is mentioned first, possibly indicative of higher social rank. Of the three names of witnesses that are preserved, one of them is (likely) Egyptian.

205 Drawing from the text publication and the PNA-entry of R. Mattila (PNA 3/I, p. 966).

206 The man in question appears last of four witnesses. One other witness has an Egyptian name. The act of seizing by the creditor was apparently due to the debtor's lack of re-payment.

son of *Nikkû*▪ (i.e. Necho I), is here described as someone "who had cast off the yoke of my (i.e. Ashurbanipal's) lordly majesty" (*ša iṣlû nīr bēlūtīya*).[207]

On the basis of the above data, the interrogative words who, what, when, and where can be responded to. *Pišamelki* was an Egyptian, a male, an adult, and a member of the elite. He lived in the reigns of Esarhaddon and Ashurbanipal, and he resided in the Egyptian cities of Memphis and Sais. The question of how he became a part of the Neo-Assyrian empire is difficult to answer, but as *Nabû-šēzibanni* it was voluntary in the sense that he chose not to resist but forced in the sense that he surrendered in light of the threat of Assyrian arms. As *Pišamelki*, he was not truly a part of the Neo-Assyrian empire, as he offered resistance successfully.[208]

Pi-šan-Ḫuru

The 90th individual of this category is *Pi-šan-Ḫuru*. The name of this individual of masculine gender is fully Egyptian and means "the brother of Horus" (Eg. *Pꜣ-sn-n-Ḥr*), referring to the Egyptian god Horus. *Pi-šan-Ḫuru* is mentioned in a text (RINAP 5/1 11) from Nineveh and 644-642 BCE as the ruler of the Egyptian city of Natho, a ruler who served as a vassal of Esarhaddon and Ashurbanipal. He also appears in two texts (RINAP 5/1 6; 7) from Nineveh and Kalhu and 647-642 BCE as one of the Egyptian vassals who fled from Taharqa and were re-installed by Ashurbanipal.[209]

On the basis of the above data, identities, properties, and settings can be identified. *Pi-šan-Ḫuru* was an Egyptian, a male, an adult, and a member of the elite. He lived in the reigns of Esarhaddon and Ashurbanipal, and he resided in the Egyptian city of Natho. The question of how he became a part of the Neo-Assyrian empire is hard to answer, but it was voluntary in the sense that he chose not to resist but forced in the sense that he surrendered in light of the threat of Assyrian arms.[210]

---

[207] Drawing from the text publication and the PNA-entry of R. Mattila (PNA 3/I, p. 997).

[208] Regarding etymology, Mattila refers to studies by G. Steindorff (1890: 360-361), H. Ranke (1910: 32), K. Tallqvist (1914: 181-182), and A. Gardiner (1961: 352-353). The name is brought up also in Edel 1980: 36-37 and Ranke 1935: 136:8. By contrast, Edel concludes that this name is without certain Egyptian etymology and that it may be of foreign origin. The meaning of the name of *Pišamelki*, "the negus vendor", is unclear. Concerning textual content and context, in the aftermath of the revolt of 667 BCE, Psammetichus I was brought with his father Necho I to Nineveh. Back in Egypt, he became the ruler of the city of Athribis, only to ascend his father's throne in 664 BCE. In 656 BCE, Psammetichus I was recognized as king over a united and independent Egypt (Shaw and Nicholson 1995: 229).

[209] Drawing from the text publication and the PNA-entry of R. Mattila (PNA 3/I, p. 997). *Pi-šan-Ḫuru* also appears in text Ashurbanipal 118 (available at http://oracc.org/rinap/Q003817/; accessed 2021-07-28).

[210] Regarding etymology, Mattila refers to studies by E. Edel (1980: 31-33) and A. Leahy (1983: 37-39). For the name *Pꜣ-sn-n-Ḥr* in Egyptian texts, see Ranke 1935: 110:28. The name is brought up also in Steindorff 1890: 347-348, Ranke 1910: 32, and Tallqvist 1914: 182. That said, all these three scholars suggest the form *Pꜣ-šry-n-Ḥr*. As for his name "the brother of Horus", a religious link to the

***Pi'u* 1.**

The 91st individual of this category is *Pi'u* 1. The meaning of the name of this individual of masculine gender is unclear, but it has been identified as safely Egyptian, pointing to a hypocorrected form of the definite article *pꜣ*. *Pi'u* 1. appears in a text (ND 2321) from Kalhu and 624 BCE as a scribe (*ṭupšarru*) and as a witness when *Issar-šumu-iddina* lends a quantity of barley to *Lamkiat*(?) and *Nīnuāiu*.[211]

On the basis of the above data, the interrogative words who, what, when, and where can be responded to. *Pi'u* 1. seems to have been an Egyptian, a male, an adult, and a member of the elite. He lived in the post-Ashurbanipal period, and he seems to have been a resident of the city of Kalhu. The circumstances leading to this individual being in Assyria are difficult to pin down, but it is likely that he or older relatives of his came to Assyria forcibly through deportation.[212]

***Pi'u* 2.**

The 92nd individual of this category is *Pi'u* 2. This man is mentioned in a text (*FNLD* 18) from the N31-archive, Assur, and 625 BCE as the son of *Taḫ-artišu*▪ 1. and as a witness when *Ḫuṭ-naḫti*▪ *and Puṭi-Mūnu*▪ 2. divide the inheritance of their father *Lā-turammanni-Aššur* 3. He also appears in a text (StAT 3 87) from the same archive and city (but from 617 BCE) which consists of a receipt stating that *Pi'u* 2. (along with *Lā-turammanni-Aššur* 3. and *Awa* (2.)) have paid the servants of the king for a horse which was at the disposal of *Pašî*▫ 3.[213]

On the basis of the above data, identities, properties, and settings can be identified. *Pi'u* 2. seems to have been an Egyptian, a male, an adult, and a commoner. He lived in the post-Ashurbanipal period, and he seems to have been a resident of the city of Assur. The question of how this individual ended up in Assyria is difficult to answer, but it is likely that he or older relatives of his came to Assyria forcibly by means of deportation.[214]

---

god Horus is probably alluded to (Shaw and Nicholson 1995: 133-134). Concerning textual content and context, *Pi-šan-Ḫuru* appears (on third place) in a list of (20) Assyrian vassals in Egypt. Natho (Eg. *Nꜣy-n-tꜣ-ḥwt*) was a city in the Nile delta (RGTC 7/2-2, p. 451).

211 Drawing from the description of this text by B. Parker (1954: 41) and the PNA-entry of R. Mattila (PNA 3/I, p. 998).

212 Regarding etymology, Mattila refers to studies by R. Zadok (1977b: 64) and J. Zeidler (1994: 49). For the definite article *pꜣ* as a personal name in Egypt, see Ranke 1935: 99:22. Concerning textual content and context, Parker (1954: 41) states that *Pi'u* 1. is one of five witnesses, with only four of the names of witnesses legible. Parker dates the document to 671 or 666 BCE.

213 Drawing from the text publications, the PNA-entry of R. Mattila (PNA 3/I, p. 998), and a PNAo-entry of H.D. Baker.

214 As for the latter text, it is noticeable that *Pi'u* 2. is mentioned after *Lā-turammanni-Aššur* 3. and *Awa* (2.), supposedly indicating relative social rank. The three witnesses of this text all bear Egyptian names. In the former text, *Pi'u* 2. appears on ninth place in the list of 17 witnesses, which includes numerous Egyptian names.

Pūiama

The 93rd individual of this category is *Pūiama*. The name of this individual of masculine gender is Egyptian and means "the sea" (Eg. *Pꜣ-ym*). *Pūiama* is mentioned in a text (RINAP 5/1 11) from Nineveh and 644-642 BCE as the ruler of the Egyptian city of Mendes, a ruler who was installed as a vassal by Esarhaddon and then was re-installed by Ashurbanipal.[215]

On the basis of the above data, the interrogative words who, what, when, and where can be responded to. *Pūiama* was an Egyptian, a male, an adult, and a member of the elite. He lived in the reigns of Esarhaddon and Ashurbanipal, and he resided in the Egyptian city of Mendes. The question of how he became a part of the Neo-Assyrian empire is difficult to answer, but it was voluntary in the sense that he chose not to resist but forced in the sense that he surrendered in light of the threat of Assyrian arms.[216]

Pūlušu

The 94th individual of this category is *Pūlušu*. The meaning of the name of this individual of masculine gender is unclear, but it has been identified as safely Egyptian. *Pūlušu* is mentioned in a text (StAT 3 82) from the N31-archive, Assur, and 617 BCE as one of the witnesses when *Kiṣir-Aššur* 45. lends silver to *Unabi*, *Mušallim-Adad*, and *Kapī[ru?]*.[217]

On the basis of the above data, identities, properties, and settings can be identified. *Pūlušu* seems to have been an Egyptian, a male, an adult, and a commoner. He lived in the post-Ashurbanipal period, and he seems to have been a resident of the city of Assur. The question of how this individual ended up in Assyria is difficult to answer, but it is likely that he or older relatives of his came to Assyria forcibly by means of deportation.[218]

---

215 Drawing from the text publication and the PNA-entry made by R. Mattila and G. Van Buylaere (PNA 3/I, p. 999).

216 Regarding etymology, Mattila and Van Buylaere refer to a study by H.-U. Onasch (1994: 53). The name is brought up also in Steindorff 1890: 351, Ranke 1910: 27, Tallqvist 1914: 182, and Fecht 1958: 114-115. Among these, only Fecht identifies *Pꜣ-ym*. Tallqvist offers the reading *P-wꜣ-r-m*. For the name *Pꜣ-ym* in Egyptian texts, see Ranke 1935: 100:15. Regarding his name "the sea", it is possible that the cosmogonic and sacred qualities of water are alluded to (Shaw and Nicholson 1995: 304). Concerning textual content and context, *Pūiama* is referred to (on tenth place) in a list of (20) Assyrian vassals in Egypt. Mendes (Akk. *Pinṭiṭi*, Eg. *Pꜣ-bꜣ-nb-ḏdt*) was a city situated in the delta (RGTC 7/2-2, p. 480).

217 Drawing from the text publication and a PNAo-entry of H.D. Baker (the name and/or individual in question is not listed in PNA).

218 Baker suggests that this *Pūlušu* may represent the same person and name as the Egyptian *Pīlušu* (which conveys the Egyptian forms *pꜣ-rws* or *pꜣ-iws*). Alternatively, the name is the same but the person is different. Concerning textual content and context, this man is mentioned last of four witnesses, with the prominent Egyptian *Lā-turammanni-Aššur* 3. heading the list and with a man bearing an Egyptian name following directly after.

Pūnašti

The 95th individual of this category is *Pūnašti*. The meaning of the name of this individual of masculine gender is unclear, but it has been identified as safely Egyptian. *Pūnašti* is mentioned in a document (StAT 2 177) from the N31-archive, Assur, and 617 BCE as borrowing 15 shekels of silver from *Kiṣir-Aššur* 45. and *Urdu-Aššur* 5.[219]

On the basis of the above data, the interrogative words who, what, when, and where can be responded to. *Pūnašti* seems to have been an Egyptian, a male, an adult, and a commoner. He lived in the post-Ashurbanipal period, and he seems to have been a resident of the city of Assur. The circumstances leading to this individual being in Assyria are difficult to pin down, but it is likely that he or older relatives of his came to Assyria forcibly through deportation.[220]

Puṭi[...] (1.)

The 96th individual of this category is *Puṭi[...]* (1.). The name of this individual of masculine gender is Egyptian and means "one given (by NN/DN)" (Eg. *Pꜣ-di*). *Puṭi[...]* (1.) is mentioned in a fragmentary text (WVDOG 152 II.2) from the Assur 52b-archive, Assur, and 647 BCE as a witness when the woman *Tamurtašu*▫ borrows silver from *Puqulāya*. He also appears as a witness in a text (WWDOG 152 II.7) from the same archive and city which centres on *Ḫūru-[...]*▪ (2.) borrowing a quantity of silver from *Tap[...]*▫.[221]

On the basis of the above data, identities, properties, and settings can be identified. *Puṭi[...]* (1.) seems to have been an Egyptian, a male, an adult, and a commoner. He lived in the reign of Ashurbanipal, and he seems to have been a resident of the city of Assur. The question of how this individual ended up in Assyria is difficult to answer, but it is likely that he or older relatives of his came to Assyria forcibly by means of deportation.[222]

---

219 Drawing from the text publication and the PNA-entry of M. Capraro (PNA 3/I, p. 1000).
220 Regarding etymology, Capraro supposedly focuses on the Egyptian textual context. Proceeding from the analysis of H. Ranke (1910: 47), the definite article *pꜣ*, which can be written *pu* in cuneiform, may form the initial part of this name. Concerning textual content and context, there are four witnesses to this debt note. The prominent Egyptian *Lā-turammanni-Aššur* 3. heads the list, followed by two men with Libyan or Egyptian names, stressing the African context of *Pūnašti*.
221 Drawing from the text publication. *Puṭi[...]* (1.) is not listed in PNA or PNAo.
222 Regarding etymology, the form *Puṭi[...]* is brought up also in Tallqvist 1914: 182 and Leahy 1993: 59. For Egyptian names beginning with *pꜣ-di*, see Ranke 1935: 121:17-126:15. Concerning textual content and context, the list of witnesses in text II.7 contains three names that are or may be of African origins.

Puṭi[...] (2.)

The 97th individual of this category is *Puṭi[...]* (2.). This man is mentioned in a text (RINAP 4 9) from Nineveh and the reign of Esarhaddon as an official placed by Esarhaddon over the Egyptian (re-named) city of *Aššur-nāsiḫ-gallî* after this king's victory over Taharqa.[223]

On the basis of the above data, the interrogative words who, what, when, and where can be responded to. *Puṭi[...]* (2.) seems to have been an Egyptian, a male, an adult, and a member of the elite. He lived in the reign of Esarhaddon, and he had the Egyptian city of *Aššur-nāsiḫ-gallî* as his place of residence. The question of how this individual was integrated into the Neo-Assyrian empire is complex, but it is clear that he at some stage, more or less voluntarily, agreed to co-operate with the Assyrian state and administration.[224]

Puṭi-Atḫiš

The 98th individual of this category is *Puṭi-Atḫiš*. The name of this individual of masculine gender is fully Egyptian and probably contains the element *pꜣ-di* and an unidentified theophoric name. *Puṭi-Atḫiš* appears in a text (SAA 14 442) from the archive of *Inurta-šarru-uṣur*, Nineveh, and 634 BCE as the buyer and adoptive father of the boy *Aḫu-iddina*, son of an unnamed temple votaress. He buys him from the boy's grandfather *Abdi-Kurra* for ten shekels of silver.[225]

On the basis of the above data, identities, properties, and settings can be identified. *Puṭi-Atḫiš* seems to have been an Egyptian, a male, an adult, and a commoner. He lived (late) in the reign of Ashurbanipal, and he seems to have been a resident of the city of Nineveh. The question of how this individual ended up in Assyria is difficult to answer, but it is likely that he or older relatives of his came to Assyria forcibly by means of deportation.[226]

---

223 Drawing from the text publication. *Puṭi[...]* (2.) is not listed in PNA or PNAo.

224 Regarding etymology, the textual context and the preserved bits of his name (^{m}*pu-ṭi-*^{d}) make it virtually certain that an Egyptian is referred to. Concerning textual content and context, the fragmentary royal inscription in question seems to focus on deportees and booty from Egypt, and on the re-organization of Egypt. The phenomenon of an Egyptian truly being a part of the Assyrian state naturally tells of integration. The identity of the said city is unclear, although a location of it to the Nile delta seems likely. The relevant RGTC-entry (7/2-1, p. 82) merely states that this city was situated in Egypt.

225 Drawing from the text publication and the PNA-entry of R. Mattila (PNA 3/I, p. 1001).

226 Regarding etymology, Mattila refers to a study by A. Leahy (1993: 59). Concerning textual content and context, several of the around 20 witnesses bear African names. This transaction clearly took place in the Egyptian community of Nineveh. Also the archive owner and prominent Egyptian *Inurta-šarru-uṣur* 2. appears as a witness. The boy *Aḫu-iddina* is stated as the eldest son and heir of *Puṭi-Atḫiš*, regardless of any subsequent progeny, and as of three spans height.

Puṭi-Bina[...]

The 99th individual of this category is *Puṭi-Bina[...]*. The meaning of the name of this individual of masculine gender is unclear, but it has been identified as safely Egyptian, containing the Egyptian element *pꜣ-di*. *Puṭi-Bina[...]* is mentioned in a text (StAT 2 77) from Assur and 643 BCE as (along with two men whose names are lost) owing *Indî* three and a half minas of silver. *Puṭi-Bina[...]* is referred to as a son of *Tap-naḫte*▪ 4. and as "the Egyptian" (*Muṣurāiu*).[227]

On the basis of the above data, the interrogative words who, what, when, and where can be responded to. *Puṭi-Bina[...]* seems to have been an Egyptian, a male, an adult, and a commoner. He lived in the reign of Ashurbanipal, and he seems to have been a resident of the city of Assur. The circumstances leading to this individual being in Assyria are difficult to pin down, but it is likely that he or older relatives of his came to Assyria forcibly through deportation.[228]

Puṭi-Eše

The 100th individual of this category is *Puṭi-Eše*. The name of this individual of masculine gender is fully Egyptian and means "the one whom Isis has given" (Eg. *Pꜣ-di-ꜣst*), referring to the Egyptian goddess Isis. *Puṭi-Eše* is mentioned in several texts from the archive of *Inurta-šarru-uṣur*, Nineveh, and the post-Ashurbanipal period (only one text carries a date, 612 BCE). He buys *Al-ḫapi-mepi*▪ from her father *Puṭu-Mehēši*▪ 2. as a wife for half a mina of silver (SAA 14 443). He also acts as a witness, namely when *Inurta-šarru-uṣur* 2. purchases the slave woman *Puṭu-šisi[...]*▪ from *Hallabēše*▫ 2. (SAA 14 435), when *Ēdu-šal[lim]* borrows barley from *Inurta-šarru-uṣur* 2. (SAA 14 436), in the case of a court order involving *Bal[...]* and *Kanūn[āiu]* (SAA 14 449), and in a court decision about an adoption which involves (at least) the claimant(?) *Nūr-šarru-[uṣur]*, the adoptive father *Nabû-mār-šarri-uṣur*, and the adopted boy *Aptir[a...]* (SAA 14 450).[229]

On the basis of the above data, identities, properties, and settings can be identified. *Puṭi-Eše* seems to have been an Egyptian, a male, an adult, and a commoner. He lived in the post-Ashurbanipal period, and he seems to have been a resident of the city of Nineveh. The question of how this individual ended up in Assyria is difficult to answer, but it is likely that he or older relatives of his came to Assyria forcibly by means of deportation.[230]

---

227 Drawing from the text publication and the PNA-entry of R. Mattila (PNA 3/I, p. 1001).

228 Of the four witnesses, two of them bear Egyptian names and another one (*Lā-turammanni-Aššur* 3.) is indirectly identifiable as an Egyptian.

229 Drawing from the text publication and the PNA-entry of R. Mattila (PNA 3/I, p. 1001).

230 Regarding etymology, Mattila refers to a study by A. Leahy (1993: 60). For this name in Egyptian texts, see Ranke 1935: 121:18-19. The name "the one whom Isis has given" points to the idea of *Puṭi-Eše* as god-given. Concerning textual content and context, and as noted in the PNA-entry, he belonged to the circle of the prominent Egyptian *Inurta-šarru-uṣur* 2. *Puṭi-Eše* was

Puṭi-Ḫūru

The 101st individual of this category is *Puṭi-Ḫūru*. The name of this individual of masculine gender is fully Egyptian and means "the one whom Horus has given" (Eg. *Pꜣ-di-Ḥr*), referring to the Egyptian god Horus. *Puṭi-Ḫūru* is mentioned in a text (SAA 11 169) from Nineveh and the reign of Esarhaddon or Ashurbanipal as an Egyptian deportee listed among other deportees with Egyptian names.[231]

On the basis of the above data, the interrogative words who, what, when, and where can be responded to. *Puṭi-Ḫūru* seems to have been an Egyptian, a male, an adult, and a commoner. He lived in the reign of Esarhaddon or Ashurbanipal, and he seems to have been a resident of the city of Nineveh. Although the exact circumstances leading to the presence of *Puṭi-Ḫūru* in Assyria are unclear, it is evident that he came to Assyria forcibly via deportation.[232]

Puṭi-ḫutapiša

The 102nd individual of this category is *Puṭi-ḫutapiša*. The meaning of the name of this individual of masculine gender is unclear, but it has been identified as safely Egyptian, probably containing the Egyptian element *pꜣ-di*. *Puṭi-ḫutapiša* is mentioned in a text (StAT 2 207) from the N31-archive, Assur, and 618 BCE as the father of *Urdu-Aššur* 7. and as the owner (together with his son) of a house being sold to *Bābilāiu* for two and a half minas of silver.[233]

On the basis of the above data, identities, properties, and settings can be identified. *Puṭi-ḫutapiša* seems to have been an Egyptian, a male, an adult, and a commoner. He lived in the post-Ashurbanipal period, and he seems to have been a resident of the city of Assur. The question of how this individual ended up in Assyria is difficult to answer, but it is likely that he or older relatives of his came to Assyria forcibly by means of deportation.[234]

---

apparently an integral part of the Egyptian community of Nineveh. With regard to text SAA 14 443, a divorce clause states that *Al-ḫapi-mepi* and her sons will belong to the temple of Ishtar of Arbela as long as *Puṭi-Eše* lives. Concerning text SAA 14 436, it is unclear what to make of the ^{d}NIN following the name *Puṭi-Eše*.

[231] Drawing from the text publication and the PNA-entry of R. Mattila (PNA 3/I, p. 1001).

[232] Regarding etymology, Mattila refers to a study by H. Ranke (1910: 33). The name in question is also brought up in Tallqvist 1914: 182 and Ranke 1935: 124:19. "The one whom Horus has given" points to the idea of *Puṭi-Ḫūru* as god-given. Concerning textual content and context, the man in question is enumerated on fourth place in the list of eleven preserved names.

[233] Drawing from the text publication and the PNA-entry of R. Mattila (PNA 3/I, p. 1001).

[234] Several of the 15 witnesses have Egyptian names and/or are referred to as "Egyptian" (*Muṣurāiu*). Almost all of those whose professions are stated are linked to the military sphere.

Puṭi-Māni

The 103rd individual of this category is *Puṭi-Māni*. The name of this individual of masculine gender is fully Egyptian and means "the one whom Min has given" (Eg. *Pꜣ-di-Mn*), including the Egyptian element *pꜣ-di* and referring to the Egyptian god Min. *Puṭi-Māni* is mentioned in a text (SAA 11 169) from Nineveh and the reign of Esarhaddon or Ashurbanipal as an Egyptian deportee listed among other deportees with Egyptian names.[235]

On the basis of the above data, the interrogative words who, what, when, and where can be responded to. *Puṭi-Māni* seems to have been an Egyptian, a male, an adult, and a commoner. He lived in the reign of Esarhaddon or Ashurbanipal, and he seems to have been a resident of the city of Nineveh. Although the exact circumstances leading to the presence of *Puṭi-Māni* in Assyria are unclear, it is evident that he came to Assyria forcibly via deportation.[236]

Puṭi-Mūnu 1.

The 104th individual of this category is *Puṭi-Mūnu* 1. The name of this individual of masculine gender is fully Egyptian and means "the one whom Amun has given" (Eg. *Pꜣ-di-Imn*), referring to the Egyptian god Amun. *Puṭi-Mūnu* 1. is mentioned in a text (*ZA* 73 11) from the N31-archive, Assur, and 640 BCE as a witness when *Nabû-mētu-ballit* buys the female slave *Bānât-Esaggil* from *Iadī'-Iāu*.[237]

On the basis of the above data, identities, properties, and settings can be identified. *Puṭi-Mūnu* 1. seems to have been an Egyptian, a male, an adult, and a commoner. He lived in the reign of Ashurbanipal, and he seems to have been a resident of the city of Assur. The question of how this individual ended up in Assyria is difficult to answer, but it is likely that he or older relatives of his came to Assyria forcibly by means of deportation.[238]

---

235 Drawing from the text publication and the PNA-entry of R. Mattila (PNA 3/I, p. 1001).

236 Regarding etymology, the name is also brought up in Ranke 1910: 37; 1935: 123:18, and Tallqvist 1914: 182. The name "the one whom Min has given" presents its bearer as god-given. The god Min was associated with fertility and (male) potency as well as with the city of Coptos and the mining areas in the Eastern Desert (Shaw and Nicholson 1995: 187-188). Concerning textual content and context, this man appears on seventh place in the list of eleven preserved names. As noted in the PNA-entry, the "ditto" in the text probably qualifies him as a "fugitive" (*ḫalqu*).

237 Drawing from the text publication and the PNA-entry of R. Mattila (PNA 3/I, p. 1001).

238 Regarding etymology, Mattila refers to studies by R. Zadok (1977b: 64) and J. Zeidler (1994: 50). For this name in Egyptian texts, see Ranke 1935: 121:23. The name bearer is presented, through his name, as a gift from Amun. Concerning textual content and context, *Puṭi-Mūnu* 1. appears on second place in the fragmentary list of (around ten) witnesses. This position indicates that he was not an insignificant member of the Egyptian community of Assur.

Puṭi-Mūnu 2.

The 105th individual of this category is *Puṭi-Mūnu* 2. This man is mentioned in a text (*FNLD* 18) from the N31-archive, Assur, and 625 BCE as the brother of *Ḫuṭ-naḫti*▪ and as inheriting his father *Lā-turammanni-Aššur* 3. Apart from a share of his father's house, three people (*Bēlet-issē'a* 2., *Amman-tanaḫti*▪ 2., and *Apî*▪ 1.) are assigned to *Puṭi-Mūnu* 2. as his portion. He also appears in a text (StAT 3 79) from the same archive and city (but from 626 BCE) as a witness when *Nāṣirī*(?) and *Zamunu*(?) settle a lawsuit between themselves.[239]

On the basis of the above data, the interrogative words who, what, when, and where can be responded to. *Puṭi-Mūnu* 2. seems to have been an Egyptian, a male, an adult, and a member of the elite. He lived in the post-Ashurbanipal period, and he seems to have been a resident of the city of Assur. The circumstances leading to this individual being in Assyria are difficult to pin down, but it is likely that he or older relatives of his came to Assyria forcibly through deportation.[240]

Puṭi-Nūnu

The 106th individual of this category is *Puṭi-Nūnu*. The name of this individual of masculine gender is fully Egyptian and means "the one whom Nun has given" (Eg. *Pꜣ-di-Nnw*), referring to the Egyptian god Nun. *Puṭi-Nūnu* appears in a text (StAT 2 194) from the N31-archive, Assur, and 626 BCE as borrowing half a mina of silver from *Urdu-Aššur* 5.[241]

On the basis of the above data, identities, properties, and settings can be identified. *Puṭi-Nūnu* seems to have been an Egyptian, a male, an adult, and a commoner. He lived in the post-Ashurbanipal period, and he seems to have been a resident of the city of Assur. The question of how this individual ended up in Assyria is difficult to answer, but it is likely that he or older relatives of his came to Assyria forcibly by means of deportation.[242]

---

[239] Drawing from the text publications, the PNA-entry of R. Mattila (PNA 3/I, p. 1001), and a PNAo-entry of H.D. Baker.

[240] This man can be described as a member of the elite in his being a son of the prominent Egyptian *Lā-turammanni-Aššur* 3. With regard to text StAT 3 79, three out of six witnesses have Egyptian names. *Puṭi-Mūnu* 2. appears on fourth place in this list of witnesses.

[241] Drawing from the text publication and the PNA-entry of R. Mattila (PNA 3/I, p. 1002).

[242] Regarding etymology, the name bearer is presented, through his name, as a gift from Nun. In Egyptian cosmogony, the god Nun personified the original formless waters of chaos from which the primeval mound arose (Shaw and Nicholson 1995: 206-207). Concerning textual content and context, none of the three witnesses have African names.

Puṭiše 1.

The 107th individual of this category is *Puṭiše* 1. The name of this individual of masculine gender is abbreviated, fully Egyptian, and means "the one whom DN has given" (Eg. *Pꜣ-di-sw*). *Puṭiše* 1. features as a witness in several documents from the archive of *Inurta-šarru-uṣur*, Nineveh, and the time range of 634-612 BCE. He acts as a witness when *Puṭi-Athiš*▪ buys the boy *Aḫu-iddina* from the latter's grandfather *Abdi-Kurra* (SAA 14 442), in a court order on behalf of *Inurta-šarru-uṣur* 2. against *Nabû-šallim-aḫḫē* concerning some donkeys (SAA 14 430), in a silver loan where the names of the parties of the transaction are lost (SAA 14 445), when *Inurta-šarru-uṣur* 2. rents land in the Village of Smiths and from its manager *Ilâ-erība* (SAA 14 434), and when *Inurta-šarru-uṣur* 2. lends barley to *Ēdu-šal[lim]* (SAA 14 436). *Puṭiše* 1. is referred to as a "commander-of-fifty" (*rab ḫanšê*).[243]

On the basis of the above data, the interrogative words who, what, when, and where can be responded to. *Puṭiše* 1. seems to have been an Egyptian, a male, an adult, and a member of the elite. He lived in the reign of Ashurbanipal and later, and he seems to have been a resident of the city of Nineveh. The circumstances leading to this individual being in Assyria are difficult to pin down, but it is likely that he or older relatives of his came to Assyria forcibly through deportation.[244]

Puṭiše 2.

The 108th individual of this category is *Puṭiše* 2. This man is mentioned in a text (StAT 2 176) from the N31-archive, Assur, and 633 BCE as a witness when the king's eunuch *Idrāia* pays wages (in silver) to *Mannu-kī-Ešarra*.[245]

On the basis of the above data, identities, properties, and settings can be identified. *Puṭiše* 2. seems to have been an Egyptian, a male, an adult, and a commoner. He lived in (the later part of) the reign of Ashurbanipal, and he seems to have been a resident of the city of Assur. The question of how this individual ended up in Assyria is difficult to answer, but it is likely that he or older relatives of his came to Assyria forcibly via deportation.[246]

---

243 Drawing from the text publication and the PNA-entry of R. Mattila (PNA 3/I, p. 1002).

244 Regarding etymology, Mattila states that the name form *Puṭiše* should be distinguished from *Puṭi-Eše*, and refers to the works by R. Zadok (1977b: 65), J. Zeidler (1994: 51-52), and A. Leahy (1993: 60). Zeidler also gives two alternative readings: *Pꜣ-di-ꜣst* and *Pꜣ-di-Zpꜣ*. For the name *Pꜣ-di-sw* in Egyptian texts, see Ranke 1935: 126:6. Concerning textual content and context, this man obviously belonged to the circle of *Inurta-šarru-uṣur* 2. and the Egyptian community of Nineveh. Indicative of his elevated social status, he heads the list of (c. 20) witnesses in text SAA 14 442. His name (with title) is directly followed by that of the archive owner *Inurta-šarru-uṣur* 2.

245 Drawing from the text publication and the PNA-entry of R. Mattila (PNA 3/I, p. 1002).

246 Mattila adds that this individual may be identical with *Puṭiše* 3. Concerning textual content and context, *Puṭiše* 2. appears on second place in the list of (four) witnesses. He is the only witness with an African name.

Puṭiše 3.

The 109th individual of this category is *Puṭiše* 3. This man is mentioned in a text (*FNLD* 18) from the N31-archive, Assur, and 625 BCE as the father of *Puṭi-Šīri*▪ 5., who acts as a witness for *Ḫuṭ-naḫti*▪ and *Puṭi-Mūnu*▪ 2. in their dividing the inheritance of their father *Lā-turammanni-Aššur* 3.[247]

On the basis of the above data, the interrogative words who, what, when, and where can be responded to. *Puṭiše* 3. seems to have been an Egyptian, a male, an adult, and a commoner. He lived in the post-Ashurbanipal period, and he seems to have been a resident of the city of Assur. The circumstances leading to this individual being in Assyria are difficult to pin down, but it is likely that he or older relatives of his came to Assyria forcibly through deportation.[248]

Puṭi-Šīri 1.

The 110th individual of this category is *Puṭi-Šīri* 1. The name of this individual of masculine gender is fully Egyptian and means "the one whom Osiris has given" (Eg. *P3-di-Wsir*), referring to the Egyptian god Osiris. *Puṭi-Šīri* 1. is mentioned in a text (SAA 7 5) from Nineveh and the (later part of the) reign of Esarhaddon which gives a list of military and other officials, many of them belonging to the troops of the crown prince, the queen mother, and the chief eunuch. *Puṭi-Šīri* 1. is referred to as "the Egyptian" (*Muṣurāiu*) in the document.[249]

On the basis of the above data, identities, properties, and settings can be identified. *Puṭi-Šīri* 1. seems to have been an Egyptian, a male, an adult, and (possibly) a member of the elite. He lived in the reign of Esarhaddon, and he seems to have been a resident of the city of Nineveh. The question of how he ended up in Assyria is difficult to answer, but it is likely that he or older relatives of his came to Assyria forcibly via deportation.[250]

---

[247] Drawing from the text publication and the PNA-entry of R. Mattila (PNA 3/I, p. 1002).

[248] Mattila adds that this individual may be identical with *Puṭiše* 2. Concerning textual content and context, the son of this man appears on eleventh place in the list of 17 witnesses. A significant share of the witnesses bears Egyptian names. All in all, it is evident that *Puṭiše* 3. formed a part of the Egyptian community of Assur.

[249] Drawing from the text publication and the PNA-entry of R. Mattila (PNA 3/I, p. 1002).

[250] Mattila adds that this individual may be identical with *Puṭi-Širi* 6. Regarding etymology, Mattila refers to studies by R. Zadok (1977b: 65) and J. Zeidler (1994: 51). H. Ranke (1910: 37) and K. Tallqvist (1914: 182) both list the name in question. Tallqvist suggests (without explaining) the form *Budi-Šēri*. For the name *P3-di-Wsir* in Egyptian texts, see Ranke 1935: 123:1. As for the name *Puṭi-Šīri*, which presents the name bearer as god-given, the god Osiris was mainly associated with death, resurrection, and fertility (Shaw and Nicholson 1995: 213-215). Concerning textual content and context, *Puṭi-Šīri* 1., who appears in the later part of the list, is surrounded by men with Akkadian names and the professions of chariot driver and royal bodyguard. The professions given to the listed individuals are many and varied.

Puṭi-Šīri 2.

The 111th individual of this category is *Puṭi-Šīri* 2. This man is mentioned in a text (SAA 11 169) from Nineveh and the reign of Esarhaddon or Ashurbanipal as an Egyptian deportee listed among other deportees with Egyptian names. By means of the "ditto-sign", *Puṭi-Šīri* 2. is qualified as a "fugitive" (*ḫalqu*) deportee.[251]

On the basis of the above data, the interrogative words who, what, when, and where can be responded to. *Puṭi-Šīri* 2. seems to have been an Egyptian, a male, an adult, and a commoner. He lived in the reign of Esarhaddon or Ashurbanipal, and he seems to have been a resident of the city of Nineveh. Although the exact circumstances leading to the presence of *Puṭi-Šīri* 2. in Assyria are unclear, it is evident that he came to Assyria forcibly via deportation.[252]

Puṭi-Šīri 3.

The 112th individual of this category is *Puṭi-Šīri* 3. This man is mentioned in a text (CTN 6 112) from Kalhu and the reign of Ashurbanipal or later which contains a list of debts and debtors. In this context, *Puṭi-Šīri* 3. is described as owing one shekel of silver.[253]

On the basis of the above data, identities, properties, and settings can be identified. *Puṭi-Šīri* 3. seems to have been an Egyptian, a male, an adult, and a commoner. He lived in the reign of Ashurbanipal or later, and he seems to have been a resident of the city of Kalhu. The question of how this individual ended up in Assyria is difficult to answer, but it is likely that he or older relatives of his came to Assyria forcibly by means of deportation.[254]

Puṭi-Šīri 4.

The 113th individual of this category is *Puṭi-Šīri* 4. This man is mentioned in a text (StAT 1 11) from Assur and 627 BCE as a witness when *Balāssu* borrows silver from *Qurdi-Issar*, with the female slave of *Balāssu*, *Bānītu-dūrī*, functioning as a pledge in this transaction.[255]

On the basis of the above data, the interrogative words who, what, when, and where can be responded to. *Puṭi-Šīri* 4. seems to have been an Egyptian, a male, an adult, and a commoner. He lived in the post-Ashurbanipal period, and he seems to have been a resident of the city of Assur. The circumstances leading to this

---

[251] Drawing from the text publication and the PNA-entry of R. Mattila (PNA 3/I, p. 1002).

[252] This individual appears as number eight of the eleven deportees whose names are preserved.

[253] Drawing from the text publication and the PNA-entry of R. Mattila (PNA 3/I, p. 1002).

[254] Nine debtors are listed. *Puṭi-Šīri* 3. is listed on last place and is the only one with an Egyptian name. The nine debtors taken together owe eleven shekels of silver.

[255] Drawing from the text publication and the PNA-entry of R. Mattila (PNA 3/I, p. 1002).

individual being in Assyria are difficult to pin down, but it is likely that he or older relatives of his came to Assyria forcibly through deportation.[256]

***Puṭi-Šīri* 5.**

The 114th individual of this category is *Puṭi-Šīri* 5. This man is mentioned in a text (*FNLD* 18) from the N31-archive, Assur, and 625 BCE as a witness when *Ḫuṭ-naḫti*▪ and *Puṭi-Mūnu*▪ 2. share the inheritance of their father *Lā-turammanni-Aššur* 3. *Puṭi-Šīri* 5. is referred to as the son of *Puṭiše*▪ 3. in this context. He also appears in a text (StAT 3 79) from the same archive and city (but from 626 BCE) as a witness when *Nāṣirī*(?) and *Zamunu*(?) settle a lawsuit between themselves.[257]

On the basis of the above data, identities, properties, and settings can be identified. *Puṭi-Šīri* 5. seems to have been an Egyptian, a male, an adult, and a commoner. He lived in the post-Ashurbanipal period, and he seems to have been a resident of the city of Assur. The question of how this individual ended up in Assyria is difficult to answer, but it is likely that he or older relatives of his came to Assyria forcibly by means of deportation.[258]

***Puṭi-Šīri* 6.**

The 115th individual of this category is *Puṭi-Šīri* 6. This man is mentioned in a text (SAA 16 57) from Nineveh and the seventh century BCE as the recipient of a letter (of which only the greeting formula has been preserved) from *Nabû-ilā'i*.[259]

On the basis of the above data, the interrogative words who, what, when, and where can be responded to. *Puṭi-Šīri* 6. seems to have been an Egyptian, a male, an adult, and a commoner. He lived some time in the seventh century BCE, and he seems to have been a resident of the city of Nineveh. The circumstances leading to this individual being in Assyria are difficult to pin down, but it is likely that he or older relatives of his came to Assyria forcibly through deportation.[260]

---

[256] There are eight witnesses to this transaction. *Puṭi-Šīri* 4. appears on the penultimate place, supposedly telling of a lower social rank. Two of the names in the list of witnesses are African.
[257] Drawing from the text publications, the PNA-entry of R. Mattila (PNA 3/I, p. 1002), and a PNAo-entry of H.D. Baker.
[258] *Puṭi-Širi* 5. can be found in the middle (position eleven out of 17 and three out of six respectively) of the two lists of witnesses. Both documents are rich in Egyptian names.
[259] Drawing from the text publication and the PNA-entry of R. Mattila (PNA 3/I, p. 1002).
[260] Mattila adds that this individual may be identical with *Puṭi-Šīri* 1. Concerning textual content and context, the preserved part of the letter reads, "[A tablet of Na]bû-ila'i [to Pu]ṭi-Širi. [Good he]alth to my brother! [May Nabû a]nd Marduk [bles]s my brother!". The letter also mentions "40 wooden…". The brotherhood in question should probably not be understood literally.

Puṭu-Bāšti 1.

The 116th individual of this category is *Puṭu-Bāšti* 1. The name of this individual of masculine gender is fully Egyptian and means "the one whom Bastet has given" (Eg. *Pꜣ-di-Bꜣstt*), referring to the Egyptian goddess Bastet. *Puṭu-Bāšti* 1. is mentioned in a text (RINAP 5/1 11) from Nineveh and 644-642 BCE as the ruler of the Egyptian city of Tanis, a ruler who was installed as a vassal by Esarhaddon and then was re-installed by Ashurbanipal.[261]

On the basis of the above data, identities, properties, and settings can be identified. *Puṭu-Bāšti* 1. was an Egyptian, a male, an adult, and a member of the elite. He lived in the reigns of Esarhaddon and Ashurbanipal, and he resided in the Egyptian city of Tanis. The question of how he became a part of the Neo-Assyrian empire is hard to answer, but it was voluntary in the sense that he chose not to resist but forced in the sense that he surrendered faced with Assyrian might.[262]

Puṭu-Bāšti 2.

The 117th individual of this category is *Puṭu-Bāšti* 2. This man is mentioned in a text (*ZA* 73 11) from the N31-archive, Assur, and 640 BCE as a witness when *Nabû-mētu-balliṭ* buys the female slave *Bānât-Esaggil* from *Iadī'-Iāu*.[263]

On the basis of the above data, the interrogative words who, what, when, and where can be responded to. *Puṭu-Bāšti* 2. seems to have been an Egyptian, a male, an adult, and a commoner. He lived in the reign of Ashurbanipal, and he seems to have been a resident of the city of Assur. The circumstances leading to this individual being in Assyria are difficult to pin down, but it is likely that he or older relatives of his came to Assyria forcibly through deportation.[264]

Puṭu-Bāšti 3.

The 118th individual of this category is *Puṭu-Bāšti* 3. This man appears in texts (StAT 2 173-174) on a tablet and its envelope from the N31-archive, Assur, and

---

261 Drawing from the text publication and the PNA-entry of R. Mattila (PNA 3/I, p. 1002).

262 Regarding etymology, Mattila refers to studies by G. Steindorff (1890: 349-350) and H. Ranke (1910: 33). The name in question is also brought up in Tallqvist 1914: 182 and Ranke 1935: 123:5. The name "the one whom Bastet has given" presents *Puṭu-Bāšti* 1. as god-given. Bastet was a cat-goddess, worshipped in Bubastis and regarded as the daughter of the sun-god (Shaw and Nicholson 1995: 50). Concerning textual content and context, *Puṭu-Bāšti* 1. appears (on seventh place) in a list of (20) Assyrian vassals in Egypt. Tanis (Akk. *Ṣa'nu*, Eg. *Ḏʿnt*) was a city in the eastern part of the Nile delta (RGTC 7/2-2, pp. 550-551).

263 Drawing from the text publication and the PNA-entry of R. Mattila (PNA 3/I, p. 1002).

264 *Puṭu-Bāšti* 2. appears on third place in the fragmentary list of (around ten) witnesses, which does not contain (as preserved) any other personal name of African origin.

636 or 625 BCE as a witness in a court case concerning six people having attacked "Egyptian merchants" (*tankarāni Muṣurāiu*) in the house of *Ḫakkubāia*.[265]

On the basis of the above data, identities, properties, and settings can be identified. *Puṭu-Bāšti* 3. seems to have been an Egyptian, a male, an adult, and a commoner. He lived in the reign of Ashurbanipal or later, and he seems to have been a resident of the city of Assur. The question of how this individual ended up in Assyria is difficult to answer, but it is likely that he or older relatives of his came to Assyria forcibly by means of deportation.[266]

Puṭubikišu

The 119th individual of this category is *Puṭubikišu*. The meaning of the name of this individual of masculine gender is unclear, but it is certainly Egyptian, in its containing the Egyptian linguistic element *pꜣ-di*. *Puṭubikišu* is mentioned in a fragmentary text (WVDOG 152 II.1) from the Assur 52b-archive, Assur, and 658 BCE as a witness when *[...]-mu[...]* borrows silver from an individual whose name is not preserved.[267]

On the basis of the above data, the interrogative words who, what, when, and where can be responded to. *Puṭubikišu* seems to have been an Egyptian, a male, an adult, and a commoner. He lived in the reign of Ashurbanipal, and he seems to have been a resident of the city of Assur. The circumstances leading to this individual being in Assyria are difficult to pin down, but it is likely that he or older relatives of his came to Assyria forcibly through deportation.[268]

Puṭubišu

The 120th individual of this category is *Puṭubišu*. The meaning of the name of this individual of masculine gender is unclear, but it is certainly Egyptian, in its containing the Egyptian linguistic element *pꜣ-di*. *Puṭubišu* is mentioned in a text (WVDOG 152 II.6) from the Assur 52b-archive, Assur, and the reign of Ashurbanipal or the following period as buying the woman *Kurilītu* for ten shekels of silver from her father *Bēl-rēmanni*.[269]

On the basis of the above data, identities, properties, and settings can be identified. *Puṭubišu* seems to have been an Egyptian, a male, an adult, and a commoner. He lived in the reign of Ashurbanipal or later, and he seems to have

[265] Drawing from the text publication and the PNA-entry of R. Mattila (PNA 3/I, p. 1002).
[266] There are twelve witnesses, several with Egyptian names. *Puṭu-Bāšti* 3. appears as number three in the lists, preceding the prominent Egyptian *Kiṣir-Aššur* 45. None of the attackers have Egyptian names. It is a matter of debate whether the attack signified ethnic conflict or property dispute, or both (Karlsson 2021a).
[267] Drawing from the text publication. *Puṭubikišu* is not listed in PNA or PNAo.
[268] This individual is the second of three witnesses. The name of the first witness is likely Egyptian.
[269] Drawing from the text publication. *Puṭubišu* is not listed in PNA or PNAo.

been a resident of the city of Assur. The question of how this individual ended up in Assyria is difficult to answer, but it is likely that he or older relatives of his came to Assyria forcibly by means of deportation.[270]

Puṭu-ḫabišu

The 121st individual of this category is *Puṭu-ḫabišu*. The meaning of the name of this individual of masculine gender is unclear, but it is certainly Egyptian, containing the element *pꜣ-di*. *Puṭu-ḫabišu* appears in a text (WVDOG 152 II.3) from the Assur 52b-archive, Assur, and 631 BCE as the father of *Puṭu-Paiti*▪ 1., who borrows silver from *Zaḫâ*▫.[271]

On the basis of the above data, the interrogative words who, what, when, and where can be responded to. *Puṭu-ḫabišu* seems to have been an Egyptian, a male, an adult, and a commoner. He lived in the reign of Ashurbanipal, and he seems to have been a resident of the city of Assur. The circumstances leading to this individual being in Assyria are difficult to pin down, but it is likely that he or older relatives of his came to Assyria forcibly through deportation.[272]

Puṭukiše

The 122nd individual of this category is *Puṭukiše*. The meaning of the name of this individual of masculine gender is unclear, but it is certainly Egyptian, containing the element *pꜣ-di*. *Puṭukiše* appears in a fragmentary text (WVDOG 152 II.10) from the Assur 52b-archive, Assur, and the reign of Ashurbanipal or later as a litigator against the woman *Lābê*▫ (2.) and *Puṭupašte*▪ because of his son *Sabutî*.[273]

On the basis of the above data, identities, properties, and settings can be identified. *Puṭukiše* seems to have been an Egyptian, a male, an adult, and a commoner. He lived in the reign of Ashurbanipal or later, and he seems to have been a resident of the city of Assur. The question of how this individual ended up in Assyria is difficult to answer, but it is likely that he or older relatives of his came to Assyria forcibly by means of deportation.[274]

---

270 There is only one witness to this purchase, probably the scribe (who has an Akkadian name) of the document.

271 Drawing from the text publication and the PNA-entry of R. Mattila (PNA 3/I, p. 1002).

272 In total, nine witnesses are listed. Several of the names in question are certain or probably Egyptian. By contrast, K. Radner (2016: 122) gives 640 BCE as the date of the document.

273 Drawing from the text publication. *Puṭukiše* is not listed in PNA or PNAo.

274 The names of the witnesses have not been preserved. It is unclear what the case in question concerns. Supposedly, it deals with a conflict on the basis of an adoption.

Puṭu-Meḫēši 1.

The 123rd individual of this category is *Puṭu-Meḫēši* 1. The name of this individual of masculine gender is fully Egyptian and means "the one whom Mahes has given" (Eg. *Pꜣ-di-mꜣy-ḥsꜣ*), referring to the Egyptian god Mahes. *Puṭu-Meḫēši* 1. is mentioned in a text (SAA 14 161) from Nineveh and 623 BCE as a witness when the woman *Nihti-Eša-rau*▪ buys *Mullissu-ḫāṣinat* from her father *Nabû-rēḫtu-uṣur* 17. as a wife for her son *Ṣi-ḫû*▪ 4.[275]

On the basis of the above data, the interrogative words who, what, when, and where can be responded to. *Puṭu-Meḫēši* 1. seems to have been an Egyptian, a male, an adult, and a commoner. He lived in the post-Ashurbanipal period, and he seems to have been a resident of the city of Nineveh. The circumstances leading to this individual being in Assyria are difficult to pin down, but it is likely that he or older relatives of his came to Assyria forcibly through deportation.[276]

Puṭu-Meḫēši 2.

The 124th individual of this category is *Puṭu-Meḫēši* 2. This man is mentioned in a text (SAA 14 443) from the archive of *Inurta-šarru-uṣur*, Nineveh, and the post-Ashurbanipal period as the father of *Al-ḫapi-mepi*▪, whom he sells for half a mina of silver to *Puṭi-Eše*▪ as a wife.[277]

On the basis of the above data, identities, properties, and settings can be identified. *Puṭu-Meḫēši* 2. seems to have been an Egyptian, a male, an adult, and a commoner. He lived in the post-Ashurbanipal period, and he seems to have been a resident of the city of Nineveh. The question of how this individual ended up in Assyria is difficult to answer, but it is likely that he or older relatives of his came to Assyria forcibly via deportation.[278]

Puṭupašte

The 125th individual of this category is *Puṭupašte*. The meaning of the name of this individual of masculine gender is unclear, but it is certainly Egyptian, containing

---

[275] Drawing from the text publication and the PNA-entry of R. Mattila (PNA 3/I, pp. 1002-1003).
[276] Regarding etymology, Mattila refers to studies by H. Ranke (1910: 34) and A. Leahy (1993: 60). The name is also brought up in Tallqvist 1914: 182 and Ranke 1935: 123:15. *Puṭu-Meḫēši* 1. is presented as a gift of god through his name. Mahes, "the wild lion", was the son of Bastet or Sakhmet and was worshipped in the delta cities of Bubastis and Taremu (Quirke 1992: 73). Leahy (1993: 62) also concludes that this name identifies the name bearer as coming from Lower Egypt. Concerning textual content and context, *Puṭu-Meḫēši* 1. appears on fourth place in the list of (15) witnesses. There are several Egyptian names in the document.
[277] Drawing from the text publication and the PNA-entry of R. Mattila (PNA 3/I, p. 1003).
[278] Notably, a divorce clause links his daughter and her sons to the Assyrian goddess Ishtar of Arbela. Regarding the list of witnesses, only one name is preserved, and the man in question bears an Egyptian name.

the element *pꜣ-di*. *Puṭupašte* is mentioned in a text (WVDOG 152 II.10) from the Assur 52b-archive, Assur, and the reign of Ashurbanipal or the following period as the son of *Aššur-dūrī* (6.) and as (together with the woman *Lābê*▫ (2.)) targeted legally by *Puṭukiše*▪ because of the boy *Sabutî*.[279]

On the basis of the above data, the interrogative words who, what, when, and where can be responded to. *Puṭupašte* seems to have been an Egyptian, a male, an adult, and a commoner. He lived in the reign of Ashurbanipal or later, and he seems to have been a resident of the city of Assur. The circumstances leading to this individual being in Assyria are difficult to pin down, but it is likely that he or older relatives of his came to Assyria forcibly through deportation.[280]

Puṭu-Paiti 1.

The 126th individual of this category is *Puṭu-Paiti* 1. The name of this individual of masculine gender is fully Egyptian and means "the one whom the Ruler has given" (Eg. *Pꜣ-di-pꜣ-ity*). *Puṭu-Paiti* 1. appears in a text (WVDOG 152 II.3) from the Assur 52b-archive, Assur, and 640 BCE as the son of *Puṭu-ḫabišu*▪ and as borrowing five shekels of silver from *Zahâ*▫.[281]

On the basis of the above data, identities, properties, and settings can be identified. *Puṭu-Paiti* 1. seems to have been an Egyptian, a male, an adult, and a commoner. He lived in the reign of Ashurbanipal, and he seems to have been a resident of the city of Assur. The question of how this individual ended up in Assyria is difficult to answer, but it is likely that he or older relatives of his came to Assyria forcibly by means of deportation.[282]

Puṭu-Paiti 2.

The 127th individual of this category is *Puṭu-Paiti* 2. This man is mentioned in a text (SAA 14 161) from Nineveh and 623 BCE as a witness when the woman *Nihti-Eša-rau*▪ buys *Mullissu-ḫāṣinat* from her father *Nabû-rēḫtu-uṣur* 17. as a wife for her son *Ṣi-ḫû*▪ 4.[283]

On the basis of the above data, the interrogative words who, what, when, and where can be responded to. *Puṭu-Paiti* 2. seems to have been an Egyptian, a male,

---

279 Drawing from the text publication. *Puṭupašte* is not listed in PNA or PNAo.

280 The names of the witnesses have not been preserved. It is unclear what the case in question concerns. Supposedly, it deals with a conflict on the basis of an adoption.

281 Drawing from the text publication and the PNA-entry of R. Mattila (PNA 3/I, p. 1003).

282 Regarding etymology, the name of this individual is read *Puṭupate* in the text publication by K. Radner (2016: 122-123). The name in question is also brought up in Ranke 1910: 34 and Tallqvist 1914: 183. As for "the one whom the Ruler has given", "the Ruler" (*ity*) is probably a generic reference. If specific, it probably refers to an Egyptian ruler rather than to the Assyrian king. The name bearer is portrayed as a gift of the (divine) ruler. Concerning textual content and context, nine (in total) witnesses are listed, of whom at least one has an Egyptian name.

283 Drawing from the text publication and the PNA-entry of R. Mattila (PNA 3/I, p. 1003).

an adult, and a commoner. He lived in the post-Ashurbanipal period, and he seems to have been a resident of the city of Nineveh. The circumstances leading to this individual being in Assyria are difficult to pin down, but it is likely that he or older relatives of his came to Assyria forcibly through deportation.[284]

Puṭu-šisi[…]

The 128th individual of this category is *Puṭu-šisi[...]*. The meaning of the name of this individual of feminine gender is unclear, but it is certainly Egyptian, containing the element *pꜣ-di*. *Puṭu-šisi[...]* appears in a text (SAA 14 435) from the archive of *Inurta-šarru-uṣur*, Nineveh, and 612 BCE as a female slave being bought by *Inurta-šarru-uṣur* 2. from *Hallabēše*▫ 2. for the sum of 50 shekels of silver.[285]

On the basis of the above data, identities, properties, and settings can be identified. *Puṭu-šisi[...]* seems to have been an Egyptian, a female, an adult, and a slave. She lived in the post-Ashurbanipal period, and she seems to have been a resident of the city of Nineveh. The question of how this individual ended up in Assyria is difficult to answer, but it is likely that she or older relatives of her came to Assyria forcibly by means of deportation.[286]

Puṭušu

The 129th individual of this category is *Puṭušu*. The meaning of the name of this individual of masculine gender is unclear, but it is certainly Egyptian, containing the element *pꜣ-di*. *Puṭušu* appears in a broken text (WVDOG 152 II.8) from the Assur 52b-archive, Assur, and the reign of Ashurbanipal or later as borrowing two and a half shekels of silver from *Šumma-Nabû*.[287]

On the basis of the above data, the interrogative words who, what, when, and where can be responded to. *Puṭušu* seems to have been an Egyptian, a male, an adult, and a commoner. He lived in the reign of Ashurbanipal or later, and he seems to have been a resident of the city of Assur. The circumstances leading to this individual being in Assyria are difficult to pin down, but it is likely that he or older relatives of his came to Assyria forcibly through deportation.[288]

---

284 There are 15 witnesses in this document. Several of these have Egyptian names. *Puṭu-Paiti* 2. appears on 13th place, arguably telling of the relative social rank of this individual.

285 Drawing from the text publication and the PNA-entry of R. Mattila (PNA 3/I, p. 1003).

286 Regarding etymology, Mattila refers to a study by A. Leahy (1993: 61). Leahy notes that the use of masculine *pꜣ* for a woman's name is unexpected but not without parallels. Concerning textual content and context, a clause states that the buyer is insured against the slave getting epilepsy for 100 days (and against fraud forever). There are 13 witnesses, of which one has an Egyptian name.

287 Drawing from the text publication. *Puṭušu* is not listed in PNA or PNAo.

288 Regarding etymology, the name in question may be linked to the Egyptian name *Pꜣ-di-sw* (Ranke 1935: 126:6). Concerning textual content and context, the names of two witnesses are preserved, of whom one is possibly Egyptian.

Putu-zutaḫa

The 130th individual of this category is *Putu-zutaḫa*. The meaning of the name of this individual of masculine gender is unclear, but it has been identified as safely Egyptian, incorporating the Egyptian participle element *pꜣ-di*, which means "one given (by NN/DN)". *Putu-zutaḫa* is mentioned in a text (WVDOG 152 II.3) from the Assur 52b-archive, Assur, and 640 BCE as a witness when *Puṭu-Paiti*▪ 1. borrows silver from *Zahâ*▫.[289]

On the basis of the above data, identities, properties, and settings can be identified. *Putu-zutaḫa* seems to have been an Egyptian, a male, an adult, and a commoner. He lived in the reign of Ashurbanipal, and he seems to have been a resident of the city of Assur. The question of how this individual ended up in Assyria is difficult to answer, but it is likely that he or older relatives of his came to Assyria forcibly by means of deportation.[290]

Puṭu-[...]

The 131st individual of this category is *Puṭu-[...]*. The meaning of the name of this individual of masculine gender is unclear, but it is certainly Egyptian, containing the element *pꜣ-di*. *Puṭu-[...]* appears in a text (SAA 14 442) from the archive of *Inurta-šarru-uṣur*, Nineveh, and 634 BCE as a witness when *Puṭi-Athiš*▪ purchases the boy *Aḫu-iddina* from the latter's grandfather, the cook *Abdi-Kurra*.[291]

On the basis of the above data, the interrogative words who, what, when, and where can be responded to. *Puṭu-[...]* seems to have been an Egyptian, a male, an adult, and a commoner. He lived in the later part of the reign of Ashurbanipal, and he seems to have been a resident of the city of Nineveh. The circumstances leading to this individual being in Assyria are difficult to pin down, but it is likely that he or older relatives of his came to Assyria forcibly through deportation.[292]

Qašḫamete

The 132nd individual of this category is *Qašḫamete*. The name of this individual of masculine gender is Egyptian and may mean "woman's young", then based on Demotic *ḳi* "young" and *sḫmt* "woman". *Qašḫamete* appears in a text (StAT 2 169)

---

289 Drawing from the text publication and the PNA-entry of R. Mattila (PNA 3/I, p. 1003).

290 Regarding etymology, the name of this individual is read *Puṭetaḫa* in the publication by K. Radner (2016: 122-123). Concerning textual content and context, the names of nine (in total) witnesses are preserved. *Putu-zutaḫa* is the only clearly African name.

291 Drawing from the text publication and the PNA-entry of R. Mattila (PNA 3/I, p. 1003).

292 Regarding etymology, this broken name is noted by A. Leahy (1993: 61), who states that it contains the form *pꜣ-di*. Concerning textual content and context, there are around 20 witnesses to this purchase, of whom several have Egyptian or Libyan names. The man in question appears on 17th place, indicative of his social rank.

from the N31-archive, Assur, and 641 BCE as a witness for *Kiṣir-Aššur* 45., who buys the female slave *Rēmtu-dūrī* from *Adda-pisia* and *Adda-lûkidi*, and in a text (StAT 2 197) from the N31-archive, Assur, and 625 BCE as a witness in a lawsuit from Kalhu which centres on *Urdu-Aššur* 5. and *Nabû-aḫu-uṣur*.[293]

On the basis of the above data, identities, properties, and settings can be identified. *Qašḫamete* seems to have been an Egyptian, a male, an adult, and a commoner. He lived in the reign of Ashurbanipal and later, and he seems to have been a resident of the city of Assur. The question of how this individual ended up in Assyria is difficult to answer, but it is likely that he or older relatives of his came to Assyria forcibly by means of deportation.[294]

Quni-Ḫūru

The 133rd individual of this category is *Quni-Ḫūru*. The name of this individual of masculine gender is fully Egyptian and means "Horus is strong" (Eg. *Ḳn-Ḥr*), referring to the Egyptian god Horus. *Quni-Ḫūru* is mentioned in a text (SAA 14 171) from Nineveh and 613 BCE as a witness when *Mannu-kī-māt-Aššur* seizes his debtor *Nabû-šallim-aḫḫē*.[295]

On the basis of the above data, the interrogative words who, what, when, and where can be responded to. *Quni-Ḫūru* seems to have been an Egyptian, a male, an adult, and a commoner. He lived in the post-Ashurbanipal period, and he seems to have been a resident of the city of Nineveh. The circumstances leading to this individual being in Assyria are difficult to pin down, but it is likely that he or older relatives of his came to Assyria forcibly through deportation.[296]

Raḫpau 1.

The 134th individual of this category is *Raḫpau* 1. The name of this individual of masculine gender is fully Egyptian and means "may Apis reach old age" (Eg. *Iry-Ḥpy-iȝwt*), referring to the divine bull from the Egyptian city of Memphis. *Raḫpau* 1. is mentioned in a text (StAT 2 164) from the N31-archive, Assur, and 675 BCE

---

[293] Drawing from the text publication and the PNA-entry of E. Lipiński (PNA 3/I, p. 1009).
[294] There are nine witnesses in the first document and three in the latter one. *Qašḫamete* is the only African name, and he appears at (or towards) the end of the two lists of witnesses. The latter text (StAT 2 197) is actually dated to 638 BCE by V. Donbaz and S. Parpola (2001: 137).
[295] Drawing from the text publication and the PNA-entry of R. Mattila (PNA 3/I, p. 1018).
[296] Regarding etymology, Mattila refers to a study by H. Ranke (1911: 112). The name in question is also brought up in Tallqvist 1914: 184 and Ranke 1935: 334:21. As for "Horus is strong", the strength which the god Horus displayed in his struggle against his rival and uncle Seth may be alluded to (Shaw and Nicholson 1995: 133-134). Concerning textual content and context, there are four witnesses in this document. Two of them have Egyptian names, and *Quni-Ḫūru* appears on third place, telling of his relative social rank.

as a witness when *Pabbā'u*▫ gives his daughter *Mullissu-ḫammat* to *Awa* (1.), son of *Tap-naḫte*▪ 1., in marriage.[297]

On the basis of the above data, identities, properties, and settings can be identified. *Raḫpau* 1. seems to have been an Egyptian, a male, an adult, and a commoner. He lived in the reign of Esarhaddon, and he seems to have been a resident of the city of Assur. The question of how this individual ended up in Assyria is difficult to answer, but it is likely that he or older relatives of his came to Assyria forcibly by means of deportation.[298]

Raḫpau 2.

The 135th individual of this category is *Raḫpau* 2. This man is mentioned in a text (*FNLD* 18) from the N31-archive, Assur, and 625 BCE as a witness when *Ḫuṭ-naḫti*▪ and *Puṭi-Mūnu*▪ 2. divide the estate of their father *Lā-turammanni-Aššur* 3., and in a text (StAT 2 207) from the same archive and city (but from 618 BCE) as a witness when *Bābilāiu* buys a house in Assur from *Urdu-Aššur*, son of *Puṭi-ḫutapiša*▪. The title "cohort commander" (*rab kiṣri*) in the latter document may refer to *Raḫpau* 2.[299]

On the basis of the above data, the interrogative words who, what, when, and where can be responded to. *Raḫpau* 2. seems to have been an Egyptian, a male, an adult, and a member of the elite. He lived in the post-Ashurbanipal period, and he seems to have been a resident of the city of Assur. The circumstances leading to this individual being in Assyria are difficult to pin down, but it is likely that he or older relatives of his came to Assyria forcibly through deportation.[300]

Ra'sî

The 136th individual of this category is *Ra'sî*. The meaning of the name of this individual of masculine gender is uncertain, but it has been identified as safely Egyptian. *Ra'sî* appears in a text (SAA 7 1) from Nineveh and the reign of Esarhaddon or Ashurbanipal as an Egyptian scholar (*ḫarṭibu*) at the royal court of Nineveh. The text gives a list of experts at court. Two other such scholars (*[...]gurši*▪ and *Ṣi-ḫû*▪ 2.) are mentioned alongside *Ra'sî*.[301]

---

297 Drawing from the text publication and the PNA-entry of R. Mattila (PNA 3/I, p. 1030).

298 Regarding etymology, Mattila refers to a study by J. Zeidler (1994: 52-54). For this name in Egyptian texts, see Ranke 1935: 40:4. Concerning textual content and context, twelve people witness this purchase, with several of these having clearly or likely Egyptian names. *Raḫpau* 1. appears on seventh place. Several of the witnesses are referred to as priests.

299 Drawing from the text publications and the PNA-entry of R. Mattila (PNA 3/I, p. 1030).

300 There are 15 witnesses to the house purchase, including the prominent Egyptian *Kiṣir-Aššur* 45. Several people have Egyptian names and five people are referred to as "Egyptians". Quite a few are presented as militaries and guards. *Raḫpau* 2. appears on second place in this list. In text *FNLD* 18, he appears on eighth place in the list of (17) witnesses, which contains numerous Egyptian names.

301 Drawing from the text publication and the PNA-entry of R. Mattila (PNA 3/I, p. 1033).

On the basis of the above data, identities, properties, and settings can be identified. *Ra'sî* seems to have been an Egyptian, a male, an adult, and a member of the elite. He lived in the reign of Esarhaddon or Ashurbanipal, and he seems to have been a resident of Nineveh. The question of how this individual ended up in Assyria is difficult to answer, but it is likely that he or older relatives of his came to Assyria forcibly by means of deportation. It can not be excluded, however, that *Ra'sî*, with his special skills, arrived in Assyria as a result of peaceful negotiations between rulers.[302]

Rasū'

The 137th individual of this category is *Rasū'*. The meaning of the name of this individual of masculine gender is uncertain, but it has been identified as safely Egyptian, expressing the Egyptian form *rsw*. *Rasū'* is mentioned in a text (SAA 6 142) from Nineveh and 692 BCE as a witness for the Egyptian scribe *Ṣil-Aššur* 2., who buys a house in Nineveh from *Šarru-lū-dāri*, *Atar-suru*, and *Amat-Su'la*. *Rasū'* is qualified as a "chief boatman" (*rab mallāḫi*).[303]

On the basis of the above data, the interrogative words who, what, when, and where can be responded to. *Rasū'* seems to have been an Egyptian, a male, an adult, and a commoner. He lived in the reign of Sennacherib, and he seems to have been a resident of the city of Nineveh. The circumstances leading to this individual being in Assyria are difficult to pin down, but it is likely that he or older relatives of his came to Assyria forcibly through deportation.[304]

Ra'û 1.

The 138th individual of this category is *Ra'û* 1. The meaning of the name of this individual of masculine gender is uncertain, but it has been identified as safely Egyptian, giving the Egyptian form *r-ȝw*. *Ra'û* 1. appears in an unpublished text

[302] Regarding etymology, the name in question is brought up also in Ranke 1910: 37 and Tallqvist 1914: 186. Mattila supposedly focuses on the Egyptian textual context in her etymological classification. It is not impossible that the name of the sun-god *Rʿ* is a part of this name, although the vowel *i* rather than the vowel *a* would be expected initially in the name written *ra-a'-si-i* (Ranke 1910: 54). Concerning textual content and context, the Egyptian scholars referred to as *ḫarṭibu* were specialized on interpreting dreams (Radner 2009; Baker 2016: 35). The group (of three) to which this individual belonged is enumerated as the penultimate group in the list, and it is followed only by a group of (three) Egyptian scribes. *Ra'sî* appears on second place.

[303] Drawing from the text publication and the PNA-entry of R. Mattila (PNA 3/I, p. 1033).

[304] Regarding etymology, Mattila refers to a study by R. Zadok (1977b: 66). The name is brought up also in Tallqvist 1914: 186. The name *Rsw*, which is attested in Egyptian texts (Ranke 1935: 227:1), means "aufwachen" or "wachen, wach sein" (Wb II, pp. 449-450). Concerning textual content and context, there are ten witnesses to this purchase, of whom several have Egyptian or Libyan names. *Rasū'* is listed on third place. *Ḫur-waṣi* 2. on fifth place is also qualified as a "chief boatman".

(VAT 20337) from Assur and 693 or 688 BCE as a witness for *Aḫ-abû*, who is owed copper. *Ra'û* 1. is qualified by the term *kasubu*.[305]

On the basis of the above data, identities, properties, and settings can be identified. *Ra'û* 1. seems to have been an Egyptian, a male, an adult, and a commoner. He lived in the reign of Sennacherib, and he seems to have been a resident of the city of Assur. The question of how this individual ended up in Assyria is difficult to answer, but it is likely that he or older relatives of his came to Assyria forcibly by means of deportation.[306]

Ra'û 2.

The 139th individual of this category is *Ra'û* 2. This man is mentioned in a text (StAT 2 296) from Assur and the reign of Ashurbanipal as the father of *Barīku* 8., who borrows 58 shekels of silver from the royal *iškaru* income of the mausoleum of *Sangû-Issar*.[307]

On the basis of the above data, the interrogative words who, what, when, and where can be responded to. *Ra'û* 2. seems to have been an Egyptian, a male, an adult, and a commoner. He lived in the reign of Ashurbanipal, and he seems to have been a resident of the city of Assur. The circumstances leading to this individual being in Assyria are difficult to pin down, but it is likely that he or older relatives of his came to Assyria forcibly through deportation.[308]

Ra'û 3.

The 140th individual of this category is *Ra'û* 3. This man appears in texts (SAA 14 119-120) on a tablet with envelope from Nineveh and 631 BCE as a witness when *Mannu-kī-Arbail* borrows a quantity of silver from *Bēlu-lū-balaṭ*.[309]

On the basis of the above data, identities, properties, and settings can be identified. *Ra'û* 3. seems to have been an Egyptian, a male, an adult, and a commoner. He lived in the later part of the reign of Ashurbanipal, and he seems to have been a resident of the city of Nineveh. The question of how this individual ended up in Assyria is difficult to answer, but it is likely that he or older relatives of his came to Assyria forcibly through deportation.[310]

---

305 Drawing from the PNA-entry of R. Mattila (PNA 3/I, p. 1036).

306 Regarding etymology, Mattila refers to a study by R. Zadok (1977b: 65). The name in question is brought up also in Tallqvist 1914: 186. The form *r-ȝw*, which means "ganz, ingesamt" (Wb I, p. 4), is attested in the Egyptian onomasticon (Ranke 1935: 216:10). Concerning textual content and context, the meaning of the term *kasubu* (supposedly indicating profession) is unclear.

307 Drawing from the text publication and the PNA-entry of H.D. Baker (PNA 3/I, p. 1036).

308 The exact nature of the funds in question is unclear. There are five witnesses to this loan. None of the names of these witnesses are of African origin.

309 Drawing from the text publication and the PNA-entry of R. Mattila (PNA 3/I, p. 1036).

310 *Ra'û* 3. appears as the second witness, preceded by another man with an Egyptian name. The lists of witnesses on the envelope and on the inner tablet differ somewhat. However, the afore-

Ra'û 4.

The 141st individual of this category is *Ra'û* 4. This man is mentioned in a fragmentary text (KAV 189) from the N31-archive, Assur, and the reign of Ashurbanipal or the following period as a witness in some legal affair.[311]

On the basis of the above data, the interrogative words who, what, when, and where can be responded to. *Ra'û* 4. seems to have been an Egyptian, a male, an adult, and a commoner. He lived in the reign of Ashurbanipal or later, and he seems to have been a resident of the city of Assur. The circumstances leading to this individual being in Assyria are difficult to pin down, but it is likely that he or older relatives of his came to Assyria forcibly through deportation.[312]

Ra'û 5.

The 142nd individual of this category is *Ra'û* 5. This man is mentioned in a highly fragmentary text (SAA 14 244) from Nineveh and the seventh century BCE as a witness to the purchase of a slave, with the names of all parties missing.[313]

On the basis of the above data, identities, properties, and settings can be identified. *Ra'û* 5. seems to have been an Egyptian, a male, an adult, and a commoner. He lived some time in the seventh century BCE, and he seems to have been a resident of the city of Nineveh. The question of how this individual ended up in Assyria is difficult to answer, but it is likely that he or older relatives of his came to Assyria forcibly by means of deportation.[314]

Rē'e

The 143rd individual of this category is *Rē'e* (also read *Ra'ê*). The meaning of the name of this individual of masculine gender is unclear, but it has been identified as safely Egyptian. *Rē'e* appears in the annals (RINAP 2 1) and a summary inscription (RINAP 2 7) of Sargon II from Dur-Sharrukin and 708-706 BCE as an Egyptian "field marshal" (*turtānu*) who was dispatched in 720 BCE by an unknown Egyptian ruler to aid Hanunu of Gaza against Assyria. The coalition was defeated, Hanunu was captured, and *Rē'e* escaped (presumably to Egypt).[315]

---

mentioned people are the only ones with African names, and they are listed in the same order in both text versions.

311 Drawing from the text publication and the PNA-entry of R. Mattila (PNA 3/I, p. 1036).

312 *Ra'û* 4. is mentioned after two individuals with clearly Egyptian names in the list of witnesses. All in all, it is obvious that *Ra'û* 4. was a member of the Egyptian community of Assur.

313 Drawing from the text publication and the PNA-entry of R. Mattila (PNA 3/I, p. 1036).

314 The names of six witnesses are preserved, with *Ra'û* 5. appearing on fourth place. The other names in the list have a non-African etymology.

315 Drawing from the text publication and the PNA-entry of A. Fuchs (PNA 3/I, p. 1037).

On the basis of the above data, the interrogative words who, what, when, and where can be responded to. *Rēʾe* seems to have been an Egyptian, a male, an adult, and a member of the elite. He lived in the reign of Sargon II, and he supposedly had his base somewhere in Egypt. *Rēʾe* was integrated into the Neo-Assyrian empire only in the sense that he belonged to the sphere of Assyria. Effectively, *Rēʾe* resisted and escaped the Neo-Assyrian empire.[316]

Ri-m-pi-aue

The 144th individual of this category is *Ri-m-pi-aue*. The name of this individual of masculine gender is fully Egyptian and means "Ra is in the bark" (Eg. *Rʿ-m-pꜣ-wiꜣ*), referring to the Egyptian god Ra. *Ri-m-pi-aue* appears in a text (StAT 2 184) from the N31-archive, Assur, and the reign of Ashurbanipal or later as a witness when *Ataʾ*▫ gives away his sister *Silim-Puṭi-lumur* in marriage to *Riḫpi-Mūnu*▫.[317]

On the basis of the above data, identities, properties, and settings can be identified. *Ri-m-pi-aue* seems to have been an Egyptian, a male, an adult, and a commoner. He lived in the reign of Ashurbanipal or later, and he seems to have been a resident of the city of Assur. The question of how this individual ended up in Assyria is difficult to answer, but it is likely that he or older relatives of his came to Assyria forcibly by means of deportation.[318]

Sa-ḫpi-māu

The 145th individual of this category is *Sa-ḫpi-māu*. The name of this individual of masculine gender is fully Egyptian and means "May Apis seize him!" (Eg. *Ṯꜣ-Ḥp-*

---

316 Regarding etymology, Fuchs refers to a study by R. Borger (1960) and adds that the name in question is written with the logogram SIPA, which means "shepherd". He notes that a pun is expressed here, which conveys the irony that "the shepherd" abandons (rather than saves) his flock. An Egyptian field marshal hardly had an Akkadian name. The Egyptian onomasticon offers a wide range of options with regard to the Egyptian form of the name *Rēʾe*, such as *Rꜣiꜣ* and *Rꜣy* (Ranke 1935: 216-217, specifically 216:23-24). The name is discussed and/or listed (as *Sibʾe*) in studies by G. Steindorff (1890: 339-342), H. Ranke (1910: 38), and K. Tallqvist (1914: 195). Concerning textual content and context, RINAP 2 1 claims that Hanunu and *Rēʾe* were defeated at Raphia by the command of the god Ashur, and that the latter "then fled off by himself, like a shepherd whose flock had been stolen, and got away". RINAP 2 7 refers to *Rēʾe* as "the field marshal of Egypt", states that Sargon II defeated the coalition, and then argues that, "*Rēʾe* took fright at the clangor of my weapons and fled; his whereabouts have never been discovered". In either case, *Rēʾe* is portrayed as weak and cowardly. Concerning the identity of the king who dispatched *Rēʾe*, K. Kitchen (1973: 155) suggests Osorkon IV of Tanis or another delta ruler.

317 Drawing from the text publication and the PNA-entry of R. Mattila (PNA 3/I, p. 1053).

318 Regarding etymology, this name is attested in Egyptian texts (Ranke 1935: 217:15). As for "Ra is in the bark", the sun-god Ra was believed to traverse the heavens in a bark (Shaw and Nicholson 1995: 48, 239). Concerning textual content and context, there are around 20 witnesses to this marriage transaction, of whom several bear Egyptian names. *Ri-m-pi-aue* is number four in the list, preceded by (e.g.) *Lā-turammanni-Aššur* 4. and *Urdu-Aššur* 5.

im.w). *Sa-ḫpi-māu* is mentioned in a text (SAA 14 161) from Nineveh and 623 BCE as one of three men (along with *Bēl-šumu-iddina* and *Ubru-Mullissi*) who are named as guarantors (*bēl qātāti*) for *Mullissu-ḫāṣinat*, whom the woman *Niḫti-Eša-rau*▪ buys from *Nabû-rēḫtu-uṣur* 17. as a wife for her son *Ṣi-ḫû*▪ 4. *Sa-ḫpi-māu* is qualified as a "perfume-maker" (*muraqqiu*) in the text.[319]

On the basis of the above data, the interrogative words who, what, when, and where can be responded to. *Sa-ḫpi-māu* seems to have been an Egyptian, a male, an adult, and a commoner. He lived in the post-Ashurbanipal period, and he seems to have been a resident of the city of Nineveh. The circumstances leading to this individual being in Assyria are difficult to pin down, but it is likely that he or older relatives of his came to Assyria forcibly through deportation.[320]

***Susinqu* 1.**

The 146th individual of this category is *Susinqu* 1. The meaning of the name of this individual of masculine gender is unknown, but it has been identified as safely Libyan, expressing the Libyan linguistic element *ššnḳ*. *Susinqu* 1. is mentioned in a text (SAA 6 142) from Nineveh and 692 BCE as a witness when the Egyptian scribe *Ṣil-Aššur* 2. buys a house in Nineveh from *Šarru-lū-dāri*, *Atar-suru*, and the woman *Amat-Su'la*. *Susinqu* 1. is qualified as "the king's (probably the *Assyrian* king's) brother/son-in-law" (*ḫatan šarri*).[321]

On the basis of the above data, identities, properties, and settings can be identified. *Susinqu* 1. seems to have been a Libyan, a male, an adult, and a member of the elite. He lived in the reign of Sennacherib, and he seems to have been a resident of the city of Nineveh. The question of how this individual ended up in Assyria is difficult to answer, but it is likely that he or older relatives of his came to Assyria forcibly by means of deportation.[322]

---

[319] Drawing from the text publication and the PNA-entry of R. Mattila (PNA 3/I, p. 1062).

[320] Regarding etymology, Mattila refers to a study by H. Ranke (1910: 35). The name in question is brought up also in Tallqvist 1914: 190 and Ranke 1935: 388:2. As for "May Apis seize him!", an aggressive (against this man's enemies) or protective (towards the name bearer) aspect of the Apis bull may be deduced (Shaw and Nicholson 1995: 35-36). Concerning textual content and context, *Sa-ḫpi-māu* is listed first of the three guarantors, telling of his rank. He is a guarantor against "a fine, stolen property, and debts". There are 15 witnesses to the affair, several with Egyptian names. The profession of fuller appears repeatedly.

[321] Drawing from the text publication and the PNA-entry made by H.D. Baker and R. Mattila (PNA 3/I, p. 1161).

[322] Regarding etymology, Baker and Mattila refer to studies by G. Steindorff (1890: 351) and H. Ranke (1910: 34). The name is brought up also in Tallqvist 1914: 226, Ranke 1935: 330:6, and Yoyotte 1960: 23-24. Sheshonq was a common royal name in Egypt of the third intermediate period (Shaw and Nicholson 1995: 268). Concerning textual content and context, there are ten witnesses, and the list is headed by *Susinqu* 1. Several of the other witnesses have Egyptian names. As concluded by Baker and Mattila, the in-law was probably the Assyrian king, although the possibility that it was an Egyptian ruler can not be excluded entirely. W. Struve (1927) and K. Radner (2012a)

Susinqu 2.

The 147th individual of this category is *Susinqu* 2. This man is mentioned in a text (RINAP 5/1 11) from Nineveh and 644-642 BCE as the ruler of the Egyptian city of Busiris, a ruler who was installed as a vassal by Esarhaddon and then was re-installed by Ashurbanipal.[323]

On the basis of the above data, the interrogative words who, what, when, and where can be responded to. *Susinqu* 2. was a Libyan, a male, an adult, and a member of the elite. He lived in the reigns of Esarhaddon and Ashurbanipal, and he resided in the Egyptian city of Busiris. The question of how he became a part of the Neo-Assyrian empire is difficult to answer, but it was voluntary in the sense that he chose not to resist but forced in the sense that he surrendered in light of the threat of Assyrian arms.[324]

Ṣi-ḫû 1.

The 148th individual of this category is *Ṣi-ḫû* 1. The name of this individual of masculine gender is fully Egyptian and means "the face (of DN) has said" (Eg. *Ḏd-ḥr*). *Ṣi-ḫû* 1. is mentioned in a text (RINAP 5/1 11) from Nineveh and 644-642 BCE as the ruler of the Egyptian city of Siut, a ruler who was installed as a vassal by Esarhaddon and re-installed by Ashurbanipal.[325]

On the basis of the above data, identities, properties, and settings can be identified. *Ṣi-ḫû* 1. was an Egyptian, a male, an adult, and a member of the elite. He lived in the reigns of Esarhaddon and Ashurbanipal, and he resided in the Egyptian city of Siut. The question of how he became a part of the Neo-Assyrian empire is hard to answer, but it was voluntary in the sense that he chose not to resist but forced in the sense that he surrendered in light of the threat of Assyrian arms.[326]

---

both argue that the king was Sennacherib. For the idea that *Susinqu* 1. was married to Sennacherib's daughter *Šaddītu*, see the PNA-entry *Sîn-aḫḫē-erība* by E. Frahm (PNA 3/I, p. 1115).

323 Drawing from the text publication and the PNA-entry made by A. Fuchs and R. Mattila (PNA 3/I, p. 1161).

324 *Susinqu* 2. is referred to (on eleventh place) in a list of (20) Assyrian vassals in Egypt. Busiris (Akk. *Puširu*, Eg. *Pr-Wsir*) was a city situated in the Nile delta (RGTC 7/2-2, p. 483).

325 Drawing from the text publication and the PNA-entry of R. Mattila (PNA 3/I, p. 1170).

326 Regarding etymology, Mattila refers to studies by G. Steindorff (1890: 353), H. Ranke (1910: 34, 38), K. Tallqvist (1914: 205), and E. Edel (1980: 30-31). For this name in Egyptian texts, see Ranke 1935: 411:12. The name of this individual seems to express the idea of the name bearer as attentive to the wishes of an unnamed deity. Concerning textual content and context, *Ṣi-ḫû* 1. is referred to (on 17th place) in a list of (20) Assyrian vassals in Egypt. Siut (Akk. *Šiyāutu*, Eg. *Sȝwt*) was a city situated in middle Egypt (RGTC 7/2-2, p. 569).

Ṣi-ḫû 2.

The 149th individual of this category is *Ṣi-ḫû* 2. This man is mentioned in a text (SAA 7 1) from Nineveh and the reign of Esarhaddon or Ashurbanipal which lists experts at the royal court in Nineveh. *Ṣi-ḫû* 2. is here referred to as an Egyptian scholar (*ḫarṭibu*), along with *[...]gurši*▪ and *Ra'sî*▪.[327]

On the basis of the above data, the interrogative words who, what, when, and where can be responded to. *Ṣi-ḫû* 2. seems to have been an Egyptian, a male, an adult, and a member of the elite. He lived in the reign of Esarhaddon or Ashurbanipal, and he seems to have been a resident of Nineveh. The circumstances leading to this individual being in Assyria are difficult to pin down, but it is likely that he or older relatives of his came to Assyria forcibly through deportation. It can not be excluded, however, that *Ṣi-ḫû* 2., with his special skills, arrived in Assyria as a result of peaceful negotiations between rulers.[328]

Ṣi-ḫû 3.

The 150th individual of this category is *Ṣi-ḫû* 3. This man is mentioned in a text (SAA 11 169) from Nineveh and the reign of Esarhaddon or Ashurbanipal as an Egyptian deportee listed among other deportees with Egyptian names.[329]

On the basis of the above data, identities, properties, and settings can be identified. *Ṣi-ḫû* 3. seems to have been an Egyptian, a male, an adult, and a commoner. He lived in the reign of Esarhaddon or Ashurbanipal, and he seems to have been a resident of the city of Nineveh. Although the exact circumstances leading to the presence of *Ṣi-ḫû* 3. in Assyria are unclear, it is evident that he came to Assyria forcibly via deportation.[330]

Ṣi-ḫû 4.

The 151st individual of this category is *Ṣi-ḫû* 4. This man appears in a text (SAA 14 161) from Nineveh and 623 BCE as a son of the woman *Niḫti-Eša-rau*▪, who buys him *Mullissu-ḫāṣinat*, daughter of *Nabû-rēḫtu-uṣur* 17. and granddaughter of *Amu-rṭēše*▪ 2., as his wife.[331]

On the basis of the above data, the interrogative words who, what, when, and where can be responded to. *Ṣi-ḫû* 4. seems to have been an Egyptian, a male, an adult, and a commoner. He lived in the post-Ashurbanipal period, and he seems to

---

[327] Drawing from the text publication and the PNA-entry of R. Mattila (PNA 3/I, p. 1170).
[328] These scholars were experts with regard to dream interpretation (Radner 2009). A group of three Egyptian scribes follows the group to which *Ṣi-ḫû* 2. belongs as the third and final member.
[329] Drawing from the text publication and the PNA-entry of R. Mattila (PNA 3/I, p. 1170).
[330] This individual is listed as number ten of the eleven named deportees. The (reconstructed) "ditto-sign" that preceded his name suggests that he was a "fugitive" (*ḫalqu*) deportee.
[331] Drawing from the text publication and the PNA-entry of R. Mattila (PNA 3/I, p. 1170).

have been a resident of the city of Nineveh. The circumstances leading to this individual being in Assyria are difficult to pin down, but it is likely that he or older relatives of his came to Assyria forcibly through deportation.[332]

Ṣi-Ḫuru 1.

The 152nd individual of this category is *Ṣi-Ḫuru* 1. The name of this individual of masculine gender is fully Egyptian and means "Horus has said" (Eg. *Ḏd-Ḥr*), referring to the Egyptian god Horus. *Ṣi-Ḫuru* 1. appears in two texts (SAA 7 1; 2) from Nineveh and the reign of Esarhaddon or Ashurbanipal which provide lists of experts at the royal court in Nineveh. *Ṣi-Ḫuru* 1. is here brought up as a member of two group of physicians (*asû*), one comprising nine people and the other four (the others being *Inurta-ballissu*, *Sîn-šarru-uṣur*, and *Puglu*).[333]

On the basis of the above data, identities, properties, and settings can be identified. *Ṣi-Ḫuru* 1. seems to have been an Egyptian, a male, an adult, and a member of the elite. He lived in the reign of Esarhaddon or Ashurbanipal, and he seems to have been a resident of the city of Nineveh. The question of how this individual ended up in Assyria is difficult to answer, but it is likely that he or older relatives of his came to Assyria forcibly by means of deportation. It can not be excluded, however, that *Ṣi-Ḫuru* 1., with his special skills, arrived in Assyria as a result of peaceful negotiations between rulers.[334]

Ṣi-Ḫuru 2.

The 153rd individual of this category is *Ṣi-Ḫuru* 2. This man is mentioned in a text (RINAP 4 9) from Nineveh and the reign of Esarhaddon as an official placed by Esarhaddon over the Egyptian (re-named) city of *Aššur-māssu-urappiš* after this king's victory over Taharqa.[335]

On the basis of the above data, the interrogative words who, what, when, and where can be responded to. *Ṣi-Ḫuru* 2. seems to have been an Egyptian, a male, an adult, and a member of the elite. He lived in the reign of Esarhaddon, and he apparently resided in the Egyptian city of *Aššur-māssu-urappiš*. The question of how this individual was integrated into the Neo-Assyrian empire is complex, but it

---

332 There are 15 witnesses to this deal, of whom several have Egyptian names. One of the three guarantors has an Egyptian name. The profession of fuller is mentioned repeatedly in the document.
333 Drawing from the text publication and the PNA-entry of R. Mattila (PNA 3/I, p. 1170).
334 Regarding etymology, Mattila refers to a study by E. Edel (1980: 30-31). The name is brought up also in Tallqvist 1914: 205 and Ranke 1935: 411:12. It seems to express the idea of the name bearer as attentive to the wishes of Horus. Concerning textual content and context, *Ṣi-Ḫuru* 1. appears last of nine physicians, of whom he is the only one with an Egyptian name in text SAA 7 1. A group of Egyptian scholars and a group of Egyptian scribes conclude the list. In text SAA 7 2, he appears as the second of four physicians, of whom he is the only one with an Egyptian name.
335 Drawing from the text publication and the PNA-entry made by H.D. Baker and R. Mattila (PNA 3/I, p. 1170).

is clear that he at some stage, more or less voluntarily, agreed to co-operate with the Assyrian state and administration.[336]

Ṣumaššeri

The 154th individual of this category is *Ṣumaššeri*. The meaning of the name of this individual of masculine gender is unclear, but it has been identified as safely Egyptian. *Ṣumaššeri* is mentioned in a text (SAA 11 169) from Nineveh and the reign of Esarhaddon or Ashurbanipal as an Egyptian deportee listed among other deportees with Egyptian names. *Ṣumaššeri* is qualified as a "fugitive" (*ḫalqu*) deportee in the document.[337]

On the basis of the above data, identities, properties, and settings can be identified. *Ṣumaššeri* seems to have been an Egyptian, a male, an adult, and a commoner. He lived in the reign of Esarhaddon or Ashurbanipal, and he seems to have been a resident of the city of Nineveh. Although the exact circumstances leading to the presence of *Ṣumaššeri* in Assyria are unclear, it is evident that he came to Assyria forcibly via deportation.[338]

Šabakû

The 155th individual of this category is *Šabakû*. The meaning of the name of this individual of masculine gender is unclear, but it can be regarded as safely Kushite. *Šabakû* appears in a text (RINAP 5/1 11) from Nineveh and 644-642 BCE through a patronym of Tanutamon, king of Kush. Tanutamon is here introduced as a "son of Shabaka" (*mār Šabakû*).[339]

On the basis of the above data, the interrogative words who, what, when, and where can be responded to. *Šabakû* was a Kushite, a male, an adult, and a member of the elite. He lived in the reign of Sargon II, and he resided in the Kushite city of Napata or in the Egyptian city of Memphis. *Šabakû* was integrated into the Neo-

---

[336] This fragmentary royal inscription seems to focus on deportees and booty from Egypt and on the re-organization of Egypt. The phenomenon of an Egyptian truly being a part of the Assyrian state naturally tells of integration. The identity of the said city is unclear, although a location of it to the Nile delta seems likely. The relevant RGTC-entry (7/2-1, p. 82) merely states that this city was situated in Egypt.

[337] Drawing from the text publication and the PNA-entry of R. Mattila (PNA 3/I, p. 1178).

[338] Regarding etymology, the name in question is brought up also in Ranke 1910: 38 and Tallqvist 1914: 206. Both of these scholars interpret the name as possibly Egyptian and read *Ṣumašše*. Mattila presumably focuses on these analyses and the Egyptian textual context. Proceeding from the analysis of H. Ranke (1910: 51), the name may contain the Egyptian word *ms*. Concerning textual content and context, this individual is listed as number six of the eleven named deportees.

[339] Drawing from the text publication and the PNA-entry made by H.D. Baker and R. Mattila (PNA 3/II, p. 1180).

Assyrian empire in the sense that he was in direct contact with Assyria. After his conquest of Lower Egypt, Kush and Assyria shared borders.[340]

Šapataku'

The 156th individual of this category is *Šapataku'*. The meaning of the name of this individual of masculine gender is unclear, but it can be assumed to be Kushite. *Šapataku'* appears in a text (RINAP 2 116) from Tang-i Var (in the Zagros mountains) and the reign of Sargon II as the king of Kush who extradited Yamani of Ashdod, an enemy of Assyria, to Sargon II around 706 BCE, after this Yamani had fled to African territory in 712 BCE.[341]

On the basis of the above data, identities, properties, and settings can be identified. *Šapataku'* was a Kushite, a male, an adult, and a member of the elite. He lived in the reigns of Sargon II and Sennacherib, and he resided in the Kushite city of Napata or in the Egyptian city of Memphis. *Šapataku'* was integrated into the Neo-Assyrian empire in the sense that he was in direct contact with Assyria, in his extradition of the said Assyrian enemy.[342]

Šē'i-Ēši

The 157th individual of this category is *Šē'i-Ēši*. The name of this individual of masculine gender is partly Akkadian and partly Egyptian (through the theonym Isis) and means "(the one who is) seeking Isis". *Šē'i-Ēši* appears in a text (SAA 14 446) from the archive of *Inurta-šarru-uṣur*, Nineveh, and 612 BCE as a witness in a fragmentary contract concerning a debt of *Aṣê*▪, son of *Taḫ-arṭiše*▪ 2.[343]

On the basis of the above data, the interrogative words who, what, when, and where can be responded to. *Šē'i-Ēši* seems to have been an Egyptian, a male, an adult, and a commoner. He lived in the post-Ashurbanipal period, and he seems to have been a resident of the city of Nineveh. The circumstances leading to this

340 Regarding etymology, Baker and Mattila refer to a study by K. Tallqvist (1914: 207). The name in question is brought up also in Steindorff 1890: 360 and Ranke 1910: 35. Concerning textual content and context, it is unclear what relations this ruler had with Assyria, whether friendly or hostile. For the chronology of this reign and the supposed co-regency of Shabaka and Shebitku, see Kahn 2001. Napata was an important city of the Kushite state and was situated near the fourth Nile cataract (Shaw and Nicholson 1995: 195).

341 Drawing from the text publication and the PNA-entry of K. Kessler (PNA 3/II, p. 1228).

342 His name can be reconstructed in a broken text (RINAP 2 113) from Melidu (south-eastern Anatolia) which claims that Shebitku "was overwhelmed by fear of the brilliance of the gods Ashur, Nabu, and Marduk" in the same context. Sargon II narrates that Yamani fled from Ashdod in Philistia to the region of Meluhha (another name for Kush), that Shebitku "heard of the might of the gods Ashur, Nabu, and Marduk" from afar, that he placed Yamani in handcuffs and manacles, and that he brought him in bondage in front of Sargon II. Later, Shebitku played a role in the battle at Eltekeh (between Assyrian and Levantine-African forces) in 701 BCE. For the chronology of this reign and the supposed co-regency of Shabaka and Shebitku, see Kahn 2001.

343 Drawing from the text publication and the PNA-entry of M. Weszeli (PNA 3/II, p. 1255).

individual being in Assyria are difficult to pin down, but it is likely that he or older relatives of his came to Assyria forcibly through deportation.[344]

Šumma-Ēši

The 158th individual of this category is *Šumma-Ēši* (or *Šumma-Eššu*). The name of this individual of masculine gender is partly Akkadian and partly Egyptian (through the theonym Isis) and means "truly Isis". *Šumma-Ēši* appears in a text (StAT 2 37) from Assur and 666 BCE regarding the charioteer *Nabû'a* receiving the debt payment of the officer *Epšanni-Issar*. *Nabû'a* is under the command of *Šēp-Issar*, who is "in the service of" (*ša ina maḫri*) *Šumma-Ēši*.[345]

On the basis of the above data, identities, properties, and settings can be identified. *Šumma-Ēši* seems to have been an Egyptian, a male, an adult, and a member of the elite. He lived in the reign of Ashurbanipal, and he seems to have been a resident of the city of Assur. The question of how this individual ended up in Assyria is difficult to answer, but it is likely that he or older relatives of his came to Assyria forcibly by means of deportation.[346]

Taḫ-arṭiše 1.

The 159th individual of this category is *Taḫ-arṭiše* 1. The name of this individual of masculine gender is fully Egyptian and means "it is Ptah who has given him" (Eg. *Ptḥ-ir-di-sw*), referring to the Egyptian god Ptah. *Taḫ-arṭiše* 1. is mentioned in some texts from the N31-archive and Assur, namely in a text (StAT 2 192) from 629 BCE where he acts as a witness when *Urdu-Aššur* 5. lends silver to *Urdu-Bēlti*, in a text (*FNLD* 18) from 625 BCE in which he is referred to as the father of *Pi'u*▪ 2., who (together with his father) witness the division of the estate of *Lā-turammanni-Aššur* 3. between *Ḫut-naḫti*▪ and *Puṭi-Mūnu*▪ 2., and in a text (StAT 3 87) from 617 BCE where he acts as a witness when *Lā-turammanni-Aššur* 3., *Awa* (2.), and *Pi'u*▪ 2. give horses to the servants of the king.[347]

On the basis of the above data, the interrogative words who, what, when, and where can be responded to. *Taḫ-arṭiše* 1. seems to have been an Egyptian, a male, an adult, and a commoner. He lived in the post-Ashurbanipal period, and he seems

---

344 Regarding etymology, Weszeli refers to studies by K. Tallqvist (1914: 255) and R. Zadok (1977a: 27). By contrast, A. Leahy (1993: 61) identifies (without further comment) the fully Egyptian name *Sꜣ ꜣst*, meaning "son of Isis". The name "(the one who is) seeking Isis" implies that the name bearer was someone who piously turned to Isis. Concerning textual content and context, there are three witnesses in this document. The names of two of these are preserved, and the other name is not African. *Šē'i-Ēši* appears as the final witness, telling of his relative social rank.

345 Drawing from the text publication and the PNA-entry of M. Luukko (PNA 3/II, p. 1286).

346 Regarding etymology, Luukko refers to a study by J.J. Stamm (1939: 135). The name in question seems to convey a praise of Isis. Concerning textual content and context, there are nine witnesses, all of them with non-African names. The transaction obviously took place in military circles.

347 Drawing from the text publications and the PNA-entry of R. Mattila (PNA 3/II, pp. 1302-1303).

to have been a resident of the city of Assur. The circumstances leading to this individual being in Assyria are difficult to pin down, but it is likely that he or older relatives of his came to Assyria forcibly through deportation.[348]

Taḫ-arṭiše 2.

The 160th individual of this category is *Taḫ-arṭiše* 2. This man is mentioned in a text (SAA 14 446) from the archive of *Inurta-šarru-uṣur*, Nineveh, and 612 BCE as the father of *Aṣê*•, who features in a badly preserved document concerning a court order as owing silver.[349]

On the basis of the above data, identities, properties, and settings can be identified. *Taḫ-arṭiše* 2. seems to have been an Egyptian, a male, an adult, and a commoner. He lived in the post-Ashurbanipal period, and he seems to have been a resident of the city of Nineveh. The question of how this individual ended up in Assyria is difficult to answer, but it is likely that he or older relatives of his came to Assyria forcibly by means of deportation.[350]

Takilāti

The 161st individual of this category is *Takilāti*. The meaning of the name of this individual of masculine gender is unclear, but it has been identified as safely Libyan (Lib. *Ṯklṯ*). *Takilāti* is mentioned in a text (SAA 14 26) from Nineveh and 645 BCE as a witness when *Luqu* lends silver to *Sukki-Aya* and *Rēmut-ilāni*, and in a text (SAA 14 154) from Nineveh and 627 BCE as a witness when *Abdūnu* buys the slave girl *Aḫāt-abīša* from *Nabû-bēlu-uṣur*.[351]

On the basis of the above data, the interrogative words who, what, when, and where can be responded to. *Takilāti* seems to have been a Libyan, a male, an adult, and a commoner. He lived in the reign of Ashurbanipal and later, and he seems to have been a resident of the city of Nineveh. The circumstances leading to this

---

348 Regarding etymology, Mattila refers to studies by A. Leahy (1993: 61) and J. Zeidler (1994: 54-56). The name in question is brought up also in Steindorff 1890: 352, Ranke 1910: 29; 1935: 138:16, Tallqvist 1914: 101, and Fecht 1958: 113-114. The name bearer is presented as a gift of the god Ptah. Ptah was a god associated with creation and with the city of Memphis (Shaw and Nicholson 1995: 230-231). Leahy (1993: 62) also concludes that this name identifies the name bearer as coming from Lower Egypt. Concerning textual content and context, there are five witnesses in the document StAT 2 192. Most of these have Egyptian names. *Taḫ-arṭiše* 1. appears as number two in the list, preceded only by *Lā-turammanni-Aššur* 3. He appears as the first of three witnesses in text StAT 3 87. The other two names are also Egyptian. The same position is found in text *FNLD* 18, which contains the names of 17 witnesses. In other words, *Taḫ-arṭiše* 1. was not an insignificant member of the Egyptian community of Assur.

349 Drawing from the text publication and the PNA-entry of R. Mattila (PNA 3/II, p. 1303).

350 Three people witness this court order. The names of two of these are preserved, and one of them is Egyptian.

351 Drawing from the text publication and the PNA-entry made by M. Capraro and R. Zadok (PNA 3/II, p. 1303).

individual being in Assyria are difficult to pin down, but it is likely that he or older relatives of his came to Assyria forcibly through deportation.[352]

Tanut-Amani

The 162nd individual of this category is *Tanut-Amani* (Fig. 6). The meaning of the name of this individual of masculine gender is unclear, but it can be assumed to be Kushite. It may include the element Amun, pointing to the Egyptian god so named (*Tnt-Imn*). *Tanut-Amani*, ruler of Kush, features in Assyrian royal inscriptions (RINAP 5/1 3; 4; 6; 9; 11). In 664 BCE, he and his army march to Lower Egypt and attack Memphis and the Assyrian garrison stationed there. Ashurbanipal hears of this, sends his army to Egypt, with the effect that *Tanut-Amani* flees to Thebes. Memphis is conquered and Egyptian rulers surrender. The army of Ashurbanipal follows him southwards, with the effects that the Kushite king flees to Kipkipi, and Thebes is conquered and sacked. *Tanut-Amani* is not heard of again.[353]

On the basis of the above data, identities, properties, and settings can be identified. *Tanut-Amani* was a Kushite, a male, an adult, and a member of the elite. He lived in the reign of Ashurbanipal, and he resided in the Kushite city of Napata or in the Egyptian city of Thebes. *Tanut-Amani* was integrated into the Neo-Assyrian empire in the sense that he was in direct contact with Assyria, clashing with the army of Ashurbanipal and having territories (Upper and Lower Egypt) which he claimed as his conquered by Assyria.[354]

Tap-naḫte 1.

The 163rd individual of this category is *Tap-naḫte* 1. The name of this individual of masculine gender is fully Egyptian and means "his strength" (Eg. *Tꜣy.f-nḫtt*). *Tap-naḫte* 1. is mentioned in a text (StAT 2 164) from the N31-archive, Assur, and

---

352 Regarding etymology, Capraro and Zadok refer to studies by K. Tallqvist (1914: 228) and G. Vittmann (1984: 65:1). The name is brought up also in Yoyotte 1960: 23-24. Takelot is a royal name in Egypt of later times (Shaw and Nicholson 1995: 311). Concerning textual content and context, *Takilāti* appears on fourth (of seven) and second (of 22) place in the lists of witnesses. The name in question is the only African name.

353 Drawing from the text publications and the PNA-entry of R. Mattila and R. Pruszynszki (PNA 3/II, pp. 1310-1311). *Tanut-Amani* is also mentioned in Ashurbanipal 121, 122, 197, and 207 (available at http://oracc.org/rinap/Q003820/, http://oracc.org/rinap/Q003821/, http://oracc.org/rinap/Q007605/, http://oracc.org/rinap/Q007615/ respectively; accessed 2021-08-05).

354 Regarding etymology, Mattila and Pruszynszki refer to studies by G. Steindorff (1890: 356-359), H. Ranke (1910: 36), W. Struve (1927), and A.C. Piepkorn (1933: 37, n. 7). The name is brought up also in Tallqvist 1914: 243. Tallqvist classifies the name as Egyptian. Concerning textual content and context, the historical aspect of this reign is treated e.g. by H.-U. Onasch (1994). For the ideological aspect, see Karlsson 2020b. Kipkipi may be a derogative Assyrian term for Napata (Karlsson 2019). As for the location of Kipkipi, see also RGTC 7/2-1, p. 343.

675 BCE as the father of *Awa* (1.), who marries *Mullissu-ḫammat*, daughter of *Pabbā'u*▫ and a votaress of Ishtar of Arbela.[355]

On the basis of the above data, the interrogative words who, what, when, and where can be responded to. *Tap-naḫte* 1. seems to have been an Egyptian, a male, an adult, and a commoner. He lived in the reign of Esarhaddon, and he seems to have been a resident of the city of Assur. The circumstances leading to this individual being in Assyria are difficult to pin down, but it is likely that he or older relatives of his came to Assyria forcibly through deportation.[356]

Tap-naḫte 2.

The 164th individual of this category is *Tap-naḫte* 2. This man is mentioned in a text (RINAP 5/1 11) from Nineveh and 644-642 BCE as the ruler of the Egyptian city of Punubu, a ruler who was appointed as vassal by Esarhaddon and re-appointed by Ashurbanipal.[357]

On the basis of the above data, identities, properties, and settings can be identified. *Tap-naḫte* 2. was an Egyptian, a male, an adult, and a member of the elite. He lived in the reigns of Esarhaddon and Ashurbanipal, and he resided in the Egyptian city of Punubu. The question of how he became a part of the Neo-Assyrian empire is hard to answer, but it was voluntary in the sense that he chose not to resist but forced in the sense that he surrendered in light of the threat of Assyrian arms.[358]

Tap-naḫte 3.

The 165th individual of this category is *Tap-naḫte* 3. This man is mentioned in some texts from the N31-archive and Assur, namely in a text (StAT 2 167) from 646 BCE where he, instead of his share of the inheritance, receives "a house of six seahs in front of the *ekiri* house" from nine or ten individuals (most of these bearing Egyptian names), in a text (StAT 3 99) from 635 BCE in which he is a witness when *[...]āiu* borrows silver from *Nabû-d[ūrī]*, and in a text (StAT 3 78) from 631 BCE where he lends nine shekels of silver to *Baṭṭūṭu*.[359]

On the basis of the above data, the interrogative words who, what, when, and where can be responded to. *Tap-naḫte* 3. seems to have been an Egyptian, a male,

---

355 Drawing from the text publication and the PNA-entry of R. Mattila (PNA 3/II, p. 1311).

356 Regarding etymology, Mattila refers to studies by G. Steindorff (1890: 352) and H. Ranke (1910: 35). The name is brought up also in Tallqvist 1914: 230 and Ranke 1935: 375:21. It is unclear what it refers to, whether a quality that belongs to a deity, the king, or the name bearer. Concerning textual content and context, twelve people witness this deal, several with Egyptian names.

357 Drawing from the text publication and the PNA-entry of R. Mattila (PNA 3/II, p. 1311).

358 *Tap-naḫte* 2. is referred to (on twelfth place) in a list of (20) Assyrian vassals in Egypt. Punubu (Eg. *Pr-inbw*) was a city situated in Lower Egypt, probably at the western fringes of the delta (RGTC 7/2-2, p. 483).

359 Drawing from the text publications and the PNA-entry of R. Mattila (PNA 3/II, p. 1311).

an adult, and a commoner. He lived in the reign of Ashurbanipal, and he seems to have been a resident of the city of Assur. The circumstances leading to this individual being in Assyria are difficult to pin down, but it is likely that he or older relatives of his came to Assyria forcibly through deportation.[360]

Tap-naḫte 4.

The 166th individual of this category is *Tap-naḫte* 4. This man appears in a text (StAT 2 77) from Assur and 643 BCE as the father of *Puṭi-Bina[...]*▪, "the Egyptian" (*Muṣurāiu*), who together with two other men (whose names are lost) owe an amount of silver to *Indî*.[361]

On the basis of the above data, identities, properties, and settings can be identified. *Tap-naḫte* 4. seems to have been an Egyptian, a male, an adult, and a commoner. He lived in the reign of Ashurbanipal, and he seems to have been a resident of the city of Assur. The question of how this individual ended up in Assyria is difficult to answer, but it is likely that he or older relatives of his came to Assyria forcibly by means of deportation.[362]

Tarqû

The 167th individual of this category is *Tarqû* (Fig. 5). The meaning of the name of this individual of masculine gender is unclear, but it can be assumed to be Kushite. *Tarqû*, ruler of Kush, features both in state letters and documents and in royal inscriptions from Assyria. As for the former source, two queries to the sun-god ask whether Esarhaddon should go to Egypt and wage war against *Tarqû* (SAA 4 84; 130). As for the latter source and the inscriptions of Esarhaddon, *Tarqû* is described as fomenting rebellion in the Levant (befriending *Ba'alu* of Tyre), and Esarhaddon decides to go to Egypt with his army. The Assyrian forces march victoriously through the delta and conquer Memphis. *Tarqû* is said to have been wounded five times with arrows. *Tarqû* flees to Thebes, while his family and court are taken as prisoners of war by the Assyrians. An Assyrian administration is established in Egypt (RINAP 4 8; 15; 34; 38; 39; 60; 98; 103). The inscriptions of Ashurbanipal narrate that *Tarqû* had re-conquered Memphis and that he had turned

---

360 Mattila adds that this individual may be identical with *Tap-naḫte* 4. Concerning textual content and context, a clause states that anyone who will oppose the house transfer shall pay five minas to *Tap-naḫte* 3. Egyptian names appear in all three lists of witnesses. *Tap-naḫte* 3. was clearly a part of the Egyptian community of Assur.

361 Drawing from the text publication and the PNA-entry of R. Mattila (PNA 3/II, p. 1311).

362 Mattila adds that this individual may be identical with *Tap-naḫte* 3. Regarding etymology, V. Donbaz and S. Parpola (2001: 57) refer to "Tar-nah[te]" rather than to *Tap-naḫte*. For the emendation of the form Tar-nah[te] in StAT 2, see Faist 2007: 130. Concerning textual content and context, there are four witnesses in this document, including two with Egyptian names and *Lā-turammanni-Aššur* 3., a prominent individual in the N31-archive.

against Assyrian loyalists in Egypt. Ashurbanipal hears of this and sends his army to Egypt, with 22 kings of the sea-coast joining the Assyrian army on its way. The Assyrian forces defeat the African troops on the battlefield, *Tarqû* flees (yet again) to Thebes, the Assyrian army re-conquers Memphis, and the Assyrian administration in Egypt is re-established. A conspiracy among the Egyptian vassals, seeking support from *Tarqû*, is detected and quelled. *Tarqû* is then said to die, following being overwhelmed by "the awesome terror of the weapon of the god Ashur (*rašubbat kakki Aššur*)" (RINAP 5/1 2; 3; 4; 6; 7; 8; 11; 15).[363]

On the basis of the above data, the interrogative words who, what, when, and where can be responded to. *Tarqû* was a Kushite, a male, an adult, and a member of the elite. He lived in the reigns of Esarhaddon and Ashurbanipal, and he resided in the Kushite city of Napata or in the Egyptian cities of Memphis and Thebes. *Tarqû* was integrated into the Neo-Assyrian empire in the sense that he was in direct contact with Assyria, clashing with Esarhaddon and Ashurbanipal and having a territory (Lower Egypt) which he claimed as his conquered by Assyria.[364]

Tattapḫa(?)

The 168th individual of this category is *Tattapḫa(?)*. The name of this individual of feminine gender is unclear, but it has been classified as safely Egyptian. *Tattapḫa(?)* appears in a text (SAA 11 169) from Nineveh and the reign of Esarhaddon or Ashurbanipal as an Egyptian deportee listed among other deportees with Egyptian names.[365]

On the basis of the above data, identities, properties, and settings can be identified. *Tattapḫa(?)* seems to have been an Egyptian, a female, an adult, and a commoner. She lived in the reign of Esarhaddon or Ashurbanipal, and she seems to have been a resident of the city of Nineveh. Although the exact circumstances leading to the presence of *Tattapḫa(?)* in Assyria are unclear, it is evident that she came to Assyria forcibly via deportation.[366]

---

363 Drawing from the text publications and the PNA-entry of H.D. Baker (PNA 3/II, pp. 1317-1318). *Tarqû* is also mentioned in the texts Ashurbanipal 72, 73, 117, 118, 119, 121, 122, 196, 197, and 207 (available at http://oracc.org/rinap/Q003771/, http://oracc.org/rinap/Q003772/, http://oracc.org/rinap/Q003816/, http://oracc.org/rinap/Q003817/, http://oracc.org/rinap/Q003818/, http://oracc.org/rinap/Q003820/, http://oracc.org/rinap/Q003821/, and http://oracc.org/rinap/Q007604/, http://oracc.org/rinap/Q007605/, http://oracc.org/rinap/Q007615/ respectively; accessed 2021-08-05).

364 Regarding etymology, the name is brought up also in Steindorff 1890: 345-346, Ranke 1910: 35, and Tallqvist 1914: 231. Concerning textual content and context, the historical aspect of this reign is treated e.g. by H.-U. Onasch (1994). For the ideological aspect, see Karlsson 2020b. Esarhaddon claims to have conquered Kush beside Lower and Upper Egypt (see e.g. RINAP 4 60), but that claim is clearly exaggerated. Although they reached southern Egypt (under Ashurbanipal), Assyrian troops never entered the territory of Kush proper (Kahn 2006).

365 Drawing from the text publication and the PNA-entry of R. Mattila (PNA 3/II, p. 1321).

366 Regarding etymology, the name is also brought up in Ranke 1910: 38 and Tallqvist 1914: 241. Ranke and Tallqvist classify the name as possibly Egyptian and offer the transcription *Ummatḫa*. Mattila presumably focuses on these analyses and the Egyptian textual context in her etymological

Unamunu

The 169th individual of this category is *Unamunu*. The name of this individual of masculine gender is fully Egyptian and means "Amun is there" (Eg. *Wn-Imn*), referring to the Egyptian god Amun. *Unamunu* is mentioned in a text (RINAP 5/1 11) from Nineveh and 644-642 BCE as the ruler of the Egyptian city of Nathu, a ruler who was appointed as vassal by Esarhaddon and re-appointed by Ashurbanipal.[367]

On the basis of the above data, the interrogative words who, what, when, and where can be responded to. *Unamunu* was an Egyptian, a male, an adult, and a member of the elite. He lived in the reigns of Esarhaddon and Ashurbanipal, and he resided in the Egyptian city of Nathu. The question of how he became a part of the Neo-Assyrian empire is difficult to answer, but it was voluntary in the sense that he chose not to resist but forced in the sense that he surrendered in light of the threat of Assyrian arms.[368]

Usilkanu 1.

The 170th individual of this category is *Usilkanu* 1. The meaning of the name of this individual of masculine gender is unclear, but it has been identified as safely Libyan (Lib. *Wsrkn*). *Usilkanu* 1. is mentioned in two texts (RINAP 2 63; 82) from Assyria and the reign of Sargon II as "the king of Egypt" (*šar māt Muṣri*) who delivers an "audience gift" (*tāmartu*) of twelve large horses to Sargon II when Assyrian forces approach Egyptian territory in 716 BCE. *Usilkanu* 1. is probably to be identified with Osorkon IV of Tanis.[369]

On the basis of the above data, identities, properties, and settings can be identified. *Usilkanu* 1. seems to have been a Libyan, a male, an adult, and a member of the elite. He lived in the reign of Sargon II, and he seems to have resided in the Egyptian delta city of Tanis. *Usilkanu* 1. was integrated into the Neo-Assyrian

---

classification. Proceeding from the analysis of H. Ranke (1910: 60), the name may contain the Egyptian definite article *tꜣ*. Concerning textual content and context, this individual is listed first of the eleven named deportees, possibly indicating a higher rank.

367 Drawing from the text publication and the PNA-entry of E. Lipiński (PNA 3/II, p. 1386).

368 Regarding etymology, the name in question is brought up also in Steindorff 1890: 350, Ranke 1910: 36, Tallqvist 1914: 241, and Ranke 1935: 78:21. Steindorff stands out by not being able to explain the name. The personal name in question may imply the presence of the god Amun, for the benefit of the bearer of the name. Concerning textual content and context, *Unamunu* is referred to (on eighth place) in a list of (20) Assyrian vassals in Egypt. Nathu (Eg. *Nꜣy-n-tꜣ-Ḥw.t*) was a city situated in Lower Egypt (RGTC 7/2-2, p. 451).

369 Drawing from the text publication and the PNA-entry made by D. Schwemer (PNA 3/II, pp. 1421-1422).

empire in the sense that he was in direct contact with Assyria, delivering exclusive gifts to the Assyrian king.[370]

Usilkanu 2.

The 171st individual of this category is *Usilkanu* 2. This man appears in a broken text (StAT 2 268) from Assur and 644 or 629 BCE as the sealer of a document whose details are unclear, although it seems to bring up an obligation for *Usilkanu* 2. to pay one mina of silver. *Usilkanu* 2. is defined as a "servant of the paternal household" (*ardu ša bīt abīšu*) of *Šumma-Nabû*.[371]

On the basis of the above data, the interrogative words who, what, when, and where can be responded to. *Usilkanu* 2. seems to have been a Libyan, a male, an adult, and a commoner. He lived in the reign of Ashurbanipal or later, and he seems to have been a resident of the city of Assur. The circumstances leading to this individual being in Assyria are difficult to pin down, but it is likely that he or older relatives of his came to Assyria forcibly through deportation.[372]

Usilkanu 3.

The 172nd individual of this category is *Usilkanu* 3. This man is mentioned in a poorly preserved text (StAT 3 97) from the N31-archive, Assur, and the later part of the seventh century BCE as a witness in a debt note concerning silver. *Ḫur-waṣi* 6. and (at least) two other individuals (with names partly lost) borrow silver from an individual whose name is not preserved.[373]

On the basis of the above data, identities, properties, and settings can be identified. *Usilkanu* 3. seems to have been a Libyan, a male, an adult, and a commoner. He lived in the later part of the seventh century BCE, and he seems to have been a resident of the city of Assur. The question of how this individual ended

---

370 Regarding etymology, Schwemer refers to studies by W.F. Albright (1956: 24) and H.-U. Onasch (1994: 6-7). The name is brought up also in Yoyotte 1960: 23-24. As noted by Schwemer, the form *Šilkanni* is a product of *aphaeresis* (loss of initial vowel). Osorkon/*Usilkanu* was a common royal name in third intermediate period Egypt (Shaw and Nicholson 1995: 215). Concerning textual content and context, Egypt is described as remote, and *Usilkanu* 1. is spoken of as "overwhelmed by fear of the brilliance of the god Ashur", leading to his sending of the "audience gifts", portrayed as exclusive. According to D. Kahn (2001: 9), *Usilkanu* 1. was a vassal to the Kushite king Shabaka. As already noted, Tanis was a city in the north-eastern part of the delta.

371 Drawing from the text publication and the PNA-entry of D. Schwemer (PNA 3/II, p. 1422).

372 There are six witnesses listed. None of these have an African name. The text is classified by V. Donbaz and S. Parpola (2001: 189) as a document about the "purchase(?) of a slave".

373 Drawing from the text publication and the PNA-entry made by H.D. Baker and D. Schwemer (PNA 3/II, p. 1422).

up in Assyria is difficult to answer, but it is likely that he or older relatives of his came to Assyria forcibly by means of deportation.[374]

Usta-Ḫuru

The 173rd individual of this category is *Usta-Ḫuru*. The name of this individual of masculine gender is fully Egyptian and means "May Horus be sound!" (Eg. *Wḏ3-Ḥr*), referring to the Egyptian god Horus. *Usta-Ḫuru* is mentioned in a text (CTN 3 44) from Kalhu and 621 BCE as one of seven men who owe *Dūr-mākî-Ninurta*, *Dauskunu*, and *Urdu-Nabû* 15 homers of barley.[375]

On the basis of the above data, the interrogative words who, what, when, and where can be responded to. *Usta-Ḫuru* seems to have been an Egyptian, a male, an adult, and a commoner. He lived in the post-Ashurbanipal period, and he seems to have been a resident of the city of Kalhu. The circumstances leading to this individual being in Assyria are difficult to pin down, but it is likely that he or older relatives of his came to Assyria forcibly through deportation.[376]

Uṣi-Ḫanša

The 174th individual of this category is *Uṣi-Ḫanša*. The name of this individual of masculine gender is fully Egyptian and means "Khonsu is prosperous" (Eg. *Wḏ3-Ḫnsw*), referring to the Egyptian god Khonsu. *Uṣi-Ḫanša* is mentioned in a text (SAA 11 169) from Nineveh and the reign of Esarhaddon or Ashurbanipal as an Egyptian deportee listed among other deportees with Egyptian names.[377]

On the basis of the above data, identities, properties, and settings can be identified. *Uṣi-Ḫanša* seems to have been an Egyptian, a male, an adult, and a commoner. He lived in the reign of Esarhaddon or Ashurbanipal, and he seems to have been a resident of the city of Nineveh. Although the exact circumstances leading to the presence of *Uṣi-Ḫanša* in Assyria are unclear, it is evident that he came to Assyria forcibly via deportation.[378]

---

374 The names of four witnesses have been preserved. *Usilkanu* 3. is listed as number two, and the name of one other witness may be Egyptian.

375 Drawing from the text publication and the PNA-entry of R. Mattila (PNA 3/II, p. 1422).

376 Regarding etymology, Mattila refers to a study by A. Leahy (1993: 60-61), but adds that this scholar's explanation (as above) of the name should be considered tentative. For this name in Egyptian texts, see Ranke 1935: 88:26. The personal name in question probably alludes to the healing power of the god Horus (Shaw and Nicholson 1995: 133-134). Concerning textual content and context, none of the other debtors have an African name. There are five witnesses, none with an African name. The text comes from the office of the palace manageress of Fort Shalmaneser.

377 Drawing from the text publication and the PNA-entry of R. Mattila (PNA 3/II, p. 1422).

378 Regarding etymology, Mattila refers to a study by H. Ranke (1910: 36). The name is brought up also in Tallqvist 1914: 244 and Ranke 1935: 89:2. His personal name conveys a praise to the Egyptian god Khonsu. Khonsu was a god associated with the moon and tied to the cult of Amun in

Uš-Anaḫuru

The 175th individual of this category is *Uš-Anaḫuru*. The name of this individual of masculine gender is fully Egyptian (even though the man himself was a Kushite) and means "he belongs to Onuris" (Eg. *Ns-Inḥrt*), referring to the Egyptian god Onuris. *Uš-Anaḫuru* appears in two texts (RINAP 4 98; 103) from Assyria and the reign of Esarhaddon as the crown prince (*mār ridûti*) of Taharqa who was taken captive by Assyrian forces in the aftermath of the fall of Memphis in 671 BCE.[379]

On the basis of the above data, the interrogative words who, what, when, and where can be responded to. *Uš-Anaḫuru* was a Kushite, a male, an adult, and a member of the elite. He lived in the reign of Esarhaddon, and he seems to have resided in the Egyptian city of Memphis. The circumstances leading to the presence of *Uš-Anaḫuru* in Assyria (an exile which may be assumed) and Nineveh(?) point to a situation in which *Uš-Anaḫuru* functioned as a prisoner of war.[380]

Uširiḫiuḫurti

The 176th individual of this category is *Uširiḫiuḫurti*. The name of this individual of masculine gender is unclear, but it has been identified as safely Egyptian, probably containing the name of the Egyptian god Osiris (Eg. *Wsir*). *Uširiḫiuḫurti* is mentioned in a text (StAT 2 53) from Assur and 700 BCE as a witness when *Qišerāia* buys a building of unclear function in Guzana from *Sama'*, who is qualified as a "Damascene".[381]

On the basis of the above data, identities, properties, and settings can be identified. *Uširiḫiuḫurti* seems to have been an Egyptian, a male, an adult, and a commoner. He lived in the reign of Sennacherib, and he seems to have been a resident of the city of Guzana. The question of how he ended up in this corner of Assyria is difficult to answer, but it is likely that he or older relatives of his came to Assyria forcibly by means of deportation.[382]

Thebes, as the son of Amun and his consort Mut (Shaw and Nicholson 1995: 151-152). Concerning textual content and context, *Uṣi-Ḫanša* is listed second of the eleven named deportees.

379 Drawing from the text publication and the PNA-entry of R. Mattila (PNA 3/II, p. 1422).

380 Regarding etymology, Mattila refers to studies by H. Ranke (1935: 174:2) and H.-U. Onasch (1994: 19). The name is brought up also in Ranke 1910: 36 and Tallqvist 1914: 244. His personal name speaks of an attachment to the Egyptian god Onuris. Onuris was a god associated with warfare and hunting, as well as (suitably enough) with the Nubian region (Shaw and Nicholson 1995: 211). Concerning textual content and context, *Uš-Anaḫuru* was carried off along with the wife, court ladies, the rest of the sons and daughters, and courtiers and attendants of his father Taharqa. In connection with this narration, Esarhaddon exclaims that, "he (I) tore out (*nasāḫu*) the roots (*šuršu*) of Kush from Egypt". The crown prince may be the one depicted (together with a Phoenician ruler) as a prisoner of war on royal stelae of Esarhaddon from Syria (Fig. 4).

381 Drawing from the text publication and the PNA-entry made by H.D. Baker and R. Mattila (PNA 3/II, p. 1422).

382 Regarding etymology, this name has also been interpreted as Libyan (Draper 2015: 2-3). Still, *Uširiḫiuḫurti* is referred to as "the Egyptian" (*Miṣirāiu*) in the document. Concerning textual

Uta-Ḫūru

The 177th individual of this category is *Uta-Ḫūru*. The name of this individual of masculine gender is Egyptian and probably means "May Horus be sound!" (Eg. *Wḏ3-Ḥr*), referring to the Egyptian god Horus. *Uta-Ḫūru* is mentioned in a text (SAA 14 442) from the archive of *Inurta-šarru-uṣur*, Nineveh, and 634 BCE as a witness when *Puṭi-Athiš*▪ buys the boy *Aḫu-iddina* from the latter's grandfather, the cook *Abdi-Kurra*, for the purpose of adoption.[383]

On the basis of the above data, the interrogative words who, what, when, and where can be responded to. *Uta-Ḫūru* seems to have been an Egyptian, a male, an adult, and a commoner. He lived in the reign of Ashurbanipal, and he seems to have been a resident of the city of Nineveh. The circumstances leading to this individual being in Assyria are difficult to pin down, but it is likely that he or older relatives of his came to Assyria forcibly through deportation.[384]

2.1.2 People identified as Africans via ethnonyms

The second subsection highlights Africans identifiable on the identification ground ethnonyms, meaning that someone is revealed as African through ethnonyms (as name or qualifier). 43 individuals will be presented and discussed in this subsection.[385]

Ašāia

The first individual of this category is *Ašāia*. This individual of feminine gender is presented as "the Egyptian" (*Muṣurītu*). She appears in texts from Assur and the reign of Ashurbanipal or later. She is referred to as "the Egyptian" when she contributes six shekels of silver to a trade trip of *Muqallil-kabti* (WVDOG 152 I.38), and in a financial statement tied to three shekels (I.57). Referred to as "from the household of a priest" (*ina bīt šangû*), she contributes six shekels to a trade trip of *Ḫabil-kēnu* (I.33). Called "from the household of *Nādin(u)*", she appears in a

---

content and context, the individual in question appears on fourth place in the list of around 20 witnesses. No other name in this list has been identified as African. Guzana was a city in the Habur region, situated (north-)west of the Assyrian heartland (RGTC 7/2-1, pp. 187-189).

[383] Drawing from the text publication and the PNA-entry of R. Mattila (PNA 3/II, p. 1424).

[384] Regarding etymology, Mattila refers to a study by A. Leahy (1993: 61-62), but adds that this scholar's explanation (as above) of the name should be considered tentative. The personal name in question probably alludes to the healing power of the god Horus (Shaw and Nicholson 1995: 133-134). Concerning textual content and context, *Uta-Ḫūru* appears on fifth place in the list of witnesses, which contains around 20 names. The archive owner appears on second place, and several of the names of witnesses can be identified as African.

[385] A note on exclusion: the woman *Kusitu* (MÍ.GÚ.ZI-*i-tú*) in text StAT 2 235 is not included, due to the writing of her name (cf. *Kūsītu*, "the Kushite (woman)") and the non-African context in which she appears.

financial statement tied to an unknown amount (I.59), she contributes six and three quarters of a shekel to a trade trip of *Kiṣir-Nabû* (I.36), and she contributes half a mina and seven shekels to a trade trip of *Muqallil-kabti* (I.39). Qualified as "from the household of the son of *Nādin(u)*", she appears in a financial statement tied to twelve shekels (I.56).[386]

On the basis of the above data, the interrogative words who, what, when, and where can be responded to. *Ašāia* seems to have been an Egyptian, a female, an adult, and a commoner. She lived in the reign of Ashurbanipal or the following period, and she seems to have been a resident of the city of Assur. The question of how she ended up in Assyria is difficult to answer, but it is likely that she or older relatives of her came to Assyria forcibly via deportation.[387]

Bur-Kūbi

The second individual of this category is *Bur-Kūbi*. This individual of masculine gender is presented as "the Egyptian" (*Muṣurāiu*). *Bur-Kūbi* appears in texts from the N31-archive and Assur, such as in a text (StAT 2 207) from 618 BCE where he witnesses when *Bābilāiu* buys a house in Assur from *Urdu-Aššur*, son of *Puṭi-ḫutapiša*▪, a house neigbouring his own. It is in this text (only) that *Bur-Kūbi* is presented as "the Egyptian". He is also a witness when *Kiṣir-Aššur* 45. buys the slave woman *Bānât-Esaggil* from *Nabû-mētu-balliṭ* (StAT 2 178, dated to 629 BCE), when *Aššur-gārû'a-nēre* buys the slave woman *Issar-tukallanni* from *Daiān-Marduk* (StAT 2 181, dated to 629 BCE), and when *Ḫur-waṣi*▪ 6. and (at least) two others (with their names lost) borrow silver from someone whose name is lacking (StAT 3 97).[388]

On the basis of the above data, identities, properties, and settings can be identified. *Bur-Kūbi* seems to have been an Egyptian, a male, an adult, and a commoner. He lived in the post-Ashurbanipal period, and he seems to have been a resident of the city of Assur. The circumstances leading to this individual being in Assyria are difficult to pin down, but it is likely that he or older relatives of his came to Assyria forcibly through deportation.[389]

---

386 Drawing from the text publication and the PNA-entry of P.D. Gesche (PNA 1/I, p. 139).
387 Gesche states that the language and meaning of the name are unclear. Supposedly, the priest in question can be equated with *Nādin(u)*. The texts come from the archive of *Dūrī-Aššur* (known as Assur 52a), which mentions numerous Egyptians. The term "financial statement" is a direct translation of Radner's "Finanzaufstellung" and refers to a list of investors and investments.
388 Drawing from the text publications, the PNA-entry of H.D. Baker (PNA 1/II, p. 354), and a PNAo-entry of H.D. Baker.
389 Baker suggests that the name is West Semitic, meaning "son of Kubu". The identity of Kubu is unclear. The name element in question is not preceded by a personal or divine determinative in any of the four texts. *Bur-Kūbi* appears as the first of twelve witnesses in text StAT 2 178, even before the prominent Egyptian *Lā-turammanni-Aššur* 3. All four lists are rich with African names.

Dāri-šarru 2.

The third individual of this category is *Dāri-šarru* 2. This individual of masculine gender is presented as a "Kushite eunuch" (*ša rēši Kūsāiu*). He appears in a text (SAA 7 47) from Nineveh and the reign of Esarhaddon or early reign of Ashurbanipal, which conveys a memorandum concerning debts owed in the western part of Assyria. *Dāri-šarru* 2. collects silver (in one case by force) from some individuals. He may also be mentioned (but then without the ethnonym preserved) in a broken text (SAA 7 48) from Nineveh and the reign of Esarhaddon or early reign of Ashurbanipal, which is a document concerning silver payments in relation to the queen mother.[390]

On the basis of the above data, the interrogative words who, what, when, and where can be responded to. *Dāri-šarru* 2. seems to have been a Kushite, a male, an adult, and a member of the elite. He lived in the reign of Esarhaddon or Ashurbanipal, and he may have been a resident of western Assyria. The question of how he ended up in this part of Assyria is difficult to answer, but it is likely that he or older relatives of his came to Assyria forcibly by means of deportation.[391]

Ezibtu 2.

The fourth individual of this category is *Ezibtu* 2. This individual of feminine gender is presented as "the Egyptian" (*Muṣurītu*). She is mentioned in texts from Assur and the reign of Ashurbanipal or later, namely in a text (WVDOG 152 I.38) where *Ezibtu* 2. contributes six shekels to a trade trip of *Muqallil-kabti*, in a text (I.36) in which she contributes an unknown amount to a trade trip of *Kiṣir-Nabû*, in a text (1.41) where she contributes one shekel to a trade trip of *Mušēzib-Aššur*, and in a text (I.68) which gives a financial statement in which she is tied to 30 shekels. *Ezibtu* 2. is referred to as "the Egyptian" in texts I.38 and I.41.[392]

On the basis of the above data, identities, properties, and settings can be identified. *Ezibtu* 2. seems to have been an Egyptian, a female, an adult, and a commoner. She lived in the reign of Ashurbanipal or later, and she seems to have been a resident of the city of Assur. The circumstances leading to this individual

---

[390] Drawing from the text publication and the PNA-entry of H.D. Baker (PNA 1/II, p. 380).

[391] Baker identifies the name as Akkadian, meaning "the king is everlasting". Notably, the name conveys a loyalist tone. Text SAA 7 47 reports that *Dāri-šarru* 2. "came up for an emergency concerning the case of *Aḫu-sapa* of Kummuh and received 1 talent of silver", that he "took 2 minas of silver *by force* (and) wrote 5 minas in the debt-note", and that he made something of "4 minas, capital of his silver". The facts that the text is fragmentary and much is implicit make it difficult to fully understand the activities of this Kushite eunuch. The toponyms (Rasappa, Lahiru, Kummuh) in the same text suggest a western setting.

[392] Drawing from the text publication and the PNA-entry of W. Pempe (PNA 1/II, p. 410).

being in Assyria are difficult to pin down, but it is likely that she or older relatives of her came to Assyria forcibly through deportation.[393]

Ispiniša

The fifth individual of this category is *Ispiniša*. This individual of feminine gender is presented as "the Egyptian" (*Muṣurītu*). She is mentioned in a text (WVDOG 152 I.38) from Assur and the reign of Ashurbanipal or later as involved in the financing (making a contribution of six shekels of silver) of a trade trip conducted by *Muqallil-kabti*.[394]

On the basis of the above data, the interrogative words who, what, when, and where can be responded to. *Ispiniša* seems to have been an Egyptian, a female, an adult, and a commoner. She lived in the reign of Ashurbanipal or later, and she seems to have been a resident of the city of Assur. The question of how this individual ended up in Assyria is difficult to answer, but it is likely that she or older relatives of her came to Assyria forcibly via deportation.[395]

Karānūtu

The sixth individual of this category is *Karānūtu*. This individual of feminine gender is presented as "the Egyptian" (*Muṣurītu*). She is mentioned in texts from Assur and the reign of Ashurbanipal or later. *Karānūtu* is referred to as "the Egyptian" when she contributes three shekels of silver to a trade trip of *Mušēzib-Aššur* (WVDOG 152 I.41), and when she gives an unknown amount to a trade trip of someone whose name is missing (I.43). She appears without the ethnonym, but together with a woman named *Muṣurītu* (2.), in two financial statements in which she is (in both cases) tied to three shekels (I.56; I.58). *Karānūtu* also contributes (without the ethnonym preserved) an unknown amount to a trade trip conducted by *Muqallil-kabti* (I.37).[396]

On the basis of the above data, identities, properties, and settings can be identified. *Karānūtu* seems to have been an Egyptian, a female, an adult, and a commoner. She lived in the reign of Ashurbanipal or later, and she seems to have been a resident of the city of Assur. The circumstances leading to this individual

---

393 Pempe identifies the name as Akkadian, meaning "the abandoned one". The ethnonym in question may have been expressed in the destroyed parts of the other tablets. The texts come from the archive of *Dūrī-Aššur* (known as Assur 52a), which mentions numerous Egyptians.

394 Drawing from the text publication. This name and individual are not listed in PNA or PNAo, other than in PNA 4/I, p. 249.

395 The document comes from the archive of *Dūrī-Aššur* (known as Assur 52a), which mentions numerous Egyptians.

396 Drawing from the text publication and the PNA-entry of A. Berlejung (PNA 2/I, p. 606).

being in Assyria are difficult to pin down, but it is likely that she or older relatives of her came to Assyria forcibly through deportation.[397]

Kiṣir-Aššur (66.)

The seventh individual of this category is *Kiṣir-Aššur* (66.). This individual of masculine gender is presented as "the Egyptian" (*Muṣurāiu*). *Kiṣir-Aššur* (66.) appears in a text (WVDOG 152 II.9) from the Assur 52b-archive, Assur, and the reign of Ashurbanipal or later as owing four shekels of silver to *Abu-dūrī*, *Urdu-Nanāia*, and *Aḫū'a-erība*. He is also qualified as a son of *Urdu-Nabû* 13. and as having "fled" (*ḫalāqu*) from Assur, presumably on account of his debt.[398]

On the basis of the above data, the interrogative words who, what, when, and where can be responded to. *Kiṣir-Aššur* (66.) seems to have been an Egyptian, a male, an adult, and a commoner. He lived in the reign of Ashurbanipal or later, and he seems to have been a resident of the city of Assur. The question of how this individual ended up in Assyria is difficult to answer, but it is likely that he or older relatives of his came to Assyria forcibly via deportation.[399]

Kūsāiâ 1.

The eighth individual of this category is *Kūsāiâ* 1. This individual of masculine gender is presented through his name as "the Kushite". *Kūsāiâ* 1. is mentioned in a document (VS 1 86) from Assur and 620 BCE as a witness when *Nabû-mušēṣi*, *Nabû-šallimšunu*, and *Ḫannî* buy a slave woman from *Nabû-aḫḫē-erība*, a native of Kannu'.[400]

On the basis of the above data, identities, properties, and settings can be identified. *Kūsāiâ* 1. seems to have been a Kushite, a male, an adult, and a commoner. He lived in the post-Ashurbanipal period, and he seems to have been a resident of the city of Kannu'. The circumstances leading to this individual being in Assyria are difficult to pin down, but it is likely that he or older relatives of his came to Assyria forcibly through deportation.[401]

---

397 Berlejung identifies the name in question as Akkadian, meaning "grape cluster". Along with *Muṣurītu* (2.), this woman heads the financial statement of text WVDOG 152 I.56, thus indicating her rank. Judging by the phrase *ina qāt*, it seems like *Karānūtu* invested with silver borrowed from *Muṣurītu* (2.). The texts come from the archive of *Dūrī-Aššur* (known as Assur 52a), which mentions numerous Egyptians.

398 Drawing from the text publication. This individual does not seem to be listed in PNA or PNAo, other than in PNA 4/I, p. 249.

399 It is, of course, possible that this man can be equated with one of the other individuals with this name. His Akkadian name (incorporating the name of the main Assyrian god) naturally tells of assimilation.

400 Drawing from the text publication and the PNA-entry of E. Lipiński (PNA 2/I, pp. 642-643).

401 Lipiński identifies the name in question as Aramaic, meaning "man from Cush". Kannu' was a city situated somewhere in the Assyrian heartland (RGTC 7/2-1, pp. 287-288).

***Kūsāiâ* 2.**

The ninth individual of this category is *Kūsāiâ* 2. This individual of masculine gender is presented via his name as "the Kushite". *Kūsāiâ* 2. is mentioned in a text (VS 1 86) from Assur and 620 BCE as a witness for *Nabû-mušēṣi*, *Nabû-šallimšunu*, and *Ḫannî*, who buy a slave woman from *Nabû-aḫḫē-erība*, a native of Kannu'. He or *Kūsāiâ* 1. also appears as a witness with regard to purchases of slaves in two other texts (*OLZ* 8 131; VS 1 89) from Assur.[402]

On the basis of the above data, the interrogative words who, what, when, and where can be responded to. *Kūsāiâ* 2. seems to have been a Kushite, a male, an adult, and a commoner. He lived in the post-Ashurbanipal period, and he seems to have been a resident of the city of Kannu'. The question of how this individual ended up in Assyria is difficult to answer, but it is likely that he or older relatives of his came to Assyria forcibly by means of deportation.[403]

***Kūsāiu* 1.**

The tenth individual of this category is *Kūsāiu* 1. This individual of masculine gender is presented through his name as "the Kushite". *Kūsāiu* 1. is mentioned in a text (SAA 11 201) of a census character from Nineveh and the reign of Sargon II as the son of *Sē'-aqāba* and as the younger brother of *Šēr-manāni*. *Kūsāiu* 1. is described as of four spans' height. His father *Sē'-aqāba* is qualified as "guardian of the grove" (*maṣṣar qabli*) in the town of Yanibir-Suhuri.[404]

On the basis of the above data, identities, properties, and settings can be identified. *Kūsāiu* 1. seems to have been a Kushite, a male, a child, and a commoner. He lived in the reign of Sargon II, and he seems to have been a resident of western Assyria. The circumstances leading to this individual being in this corner of Assyria are difficult to pin down, but it is likely that he or older relatives of his came to Assyria forcibly via deportation.[405]

---

402 Drawing from the text publications and the PNA-entry of E. Lipiński (PNA 2/I, p. 643).

403 In other words, there are two people with the name *Kūsāiâ* in text VS 1 86. It is possible that the naming tradition, attested in ancient Egypt by contrast to Mesopotamia, of family members sharing the same name is expressed here (Ranke 1952: 253). *Kūsāiâ* 1. or 2. appears on second place in the list of (seven) witnesses in text *OLZ* 8 131. The two individuals in question are the only ones who speak of African ethnicity in these three documents from Kannu'.

404 Drawing from the text publication and the PNA-entry of H. Hunger (PNA 2/I, p. 643).

405 The description of this individual as of four spans' height is made simply by the sign for "four" (after the phrase, *māršu*). There are no other people with explicit African background listed in the census. Generally, the other people in this text are (also) described as dealing with cultivation. Yanibir-Suhuri was situated near Harran. Harran was a city in the western part of Assyria, near the Balih river (RGTC 7/2-1, pp. 212-215).

***Kūsāiu* 2.**

The eleventh individual of this category is *Kūsāiu* 2. This individual of masculine gender is presented via his name as "the Kushite". *Kūsāiu* 2. is mentioned in a text (SAA 14 29) from Nineveh and 636 BCE as a witness when *Kiṣir-Aššur* 24. buys the slave girl *Arbail-šarrat* from *Bēl-aḫḫēšu*. He is probably a witness also in another text (SAA 14 110) from the same city and date where *Urdu-Aia* lends silver to *Qītī-Bēl*. Through the "ditto-sign" in the former document, he is qualified as a "horse trainer" (*šušānu*).[406]

On the basis of the above data, the interrogative words who, what, when, and where can be responded to. *Kūsāiu* 2. seems to have been a Kushite, a male, an adult, and a commoner. He lived in the reign of Ashurbanipal, and he seems to have been a resident of the city of Nineveh. The question of how this individual ended up in Assyria is difficult to answer, but it is likely that he or older relatives of his came to Assyria forcibly by means of deportation.[407]

***Kūsāiu* 3.**

The twelfth individual of this category is *Kūsāiu* 3. This individual of masculine gender is presented through his name as "the Kushite". *Kūsāiu* 3. is mentioned in a text (StAT 1 37) from Assur and the post-Ashurbanipal period as the future receiver of 50 shekels of silver from *Šēp-Aššur* when the latter makes a settlement with his business partner *Nabû-balassu-iqbi*. In another text (StAT 1 55), conveying a fragmentary letter, *Mutakkil-Aššur* 23., son of *Kūsāiu* 3., is instructed to give good-quality silver to someone whose name has not been preserved.[408]

On the basis of the above data, identities, properties, and settings can be identified. *Kūsāiu* 3. seems to have been a Kushite, a male, an adult, and a commoner. He lived in the post-Ashurbanipal period, and he seems to have been a resident of the city of Assur. The circumstances leading to this individual being in Assyria are difficult to pin down, but it is likely that he or older relatives of his came to Assyria forcibly through deportation.[409]

---

[406] Drawing from the text publication and the PNA-entry of H. Hunger (PNA 2/I, p. 643).

[407] *Kūsāiu* 2. appears as number nine of 18 witnesses in SAA 14 29 and as number five of five witnesses in SAA 14 110. None of the names of the other witnesses of these two documents indicate African etymology. The former document is rich with individuals having authority and being in the military sphere (13 people are horse trainers). For the identification of Kush as specialized in horse breeding, see Heidorn 1997.

[408] Drawing from the text publication and the PNA-entry of H. Hunger (PNA 2/I, p. 643).

[409] Hunger identifies the name as Akkadian, meaning "man from Cush". Notably, K. Radner (1999: 183), the translator of the text, speaks of "the *Kūsāyu*". The document does not preserve any names of witnesses. Both the document and the letter come from the goldsmiths' archive, labelled N33.

***Kūsāiu* 4.**

The 13th individual of this category is *Kūsāiu* 4. This individual of masculine gender is presented via his name as "the Kushite". *Kūsāiu* 4. is mentioned in a text (TH 108) from Guzana and 625 BCE as borrowing (together with *Abu-lēšir*) straw and barley from *Adad-milki-ilā'ī*. He also appears in a fragmentary text (TH 110) from 613 BCE as a witness in a legal settlement whose precise nature is unclear, although an individual named *Nīnuāiu* seems to be centred on. *Kūsāiu* 4. is referred to as a son of *Zabad* 4. in the former document.[410]

On the basis of the above data, the interrogative words who, what, when, and where can be responded to. *Kūsāiu* 4. seems to have been a Kushite, a male, an adult, and a commoner. He lived in the post-Ashurbanipal period, and he seems to have been a resident of the city of Guzana. The question of how he ended up in this corner of Assyria is difficult to answer, but it is likely that he or older relatives of his came to Assyria forcibly by means of deportation.[411]

***Kūsāiu* 5.**

The 14th individual of this category is *Kūsāiu* 5. This individual of masculine gender is presented through his name as "the Kushite". *Kūsāiu* 5. is mentioned in a text (BATSH 6 3) from Dur-Katlimmu and the period after the fall of Nineveh as a witness for *Zēru-ukīn*, who buys the slave woman *Šulme-ra'īm*(?) from *Apil-Addu-na'id*(?). *Kūsāiu* 5. seems to be qualified as a brick mason (*urāsu*).[412]

On the basis of the above data, identities, properties, and settings can be identified. *Kūsāiu* 5. seems to have been a Kushite, a male, an adult, and a commoner. He lived in the post-imperial period, and he seems to have been a resident of the city of Dur-Katlimmu. The circumstances leading to this individual being in this corner of Assyria are difficult to pin down, but it is likely that he or older relatives of his came to Assyria forcibly through deportation.[413]

---

410 Drawing from the text publication and the PNA-entry of H. Hunger (PNA 2/I, p. 643).

411 None of the two documents contain further African names. *Kūsāiu* 4. appears as number three of the four preserved names of witnesses. His profession is not stated (due to a lacuna?), but the other witnesses seem to be tied to a palace. Both documents derive from the archive of the Assyrian governor in Guzana, *Mannu-kī-Aššur*.

412 Drawing from the text publication and the PNA-entry of H. Hunger (PNA 2/I, p. 643).

413 In her PNAo-entry, H.D. Baker modifies the reading of the profession title from ^{lú}*ra-si* to ^{lú}(*ú*)-*ra-si*. This Kushite individual appears as number four of the seven preserved names of witnesses. No other name of this document indicates an African ethnicity. Dur-Katlimmu (Aramaic Magdalu) was a city situated in the Laqe region, along the lower Habur (RGTC 7/2-1, pp. 152-153).

***Kūsāiu* 6.**

The 15th individual of this category is *Kūsāiu* 6. This individual of masculine gender is presented through his name as "the Kushite". *Kūsāiu* 6. is mentioned in a text (SAA 7 30) from Nineveh and the seventh century BCE as "the chariot driver of the prefect of the land" (*mukīl appāti šakin māti*), being in charge of 15(?) "corral-men" (*ma'āssu*).[414]

On the basis of the above data, the interrogative words who, what, when, and where can be responded to. *Kūsāiu* 6. seems to have been a Kushite, a male, an adult, and a member of the elite. He lived some time in the seventh century BCE, and he may have been a resident of the city of Nineveh. The question of how he ended up in Assyria is difficult to answer, but it is likely that he or older relatives of his came to Assyria forcibly by means of deportation.[415]

***Kūsāiu* (7.)**

The 16th individual of this category is *Kūsāiu* (7.). This individual of masculine gender is presented through his name as "the Kushite". *Kūsāiu* (7.) appears in a text (StAT 3 35) from Assur and the reign of Ashurbanipal or later tied to one homer and five seahs of grain in a list entry.[416]

On the basis of the above data, identities, properties, and settings can be identified. *Kūsāiu* (7.) seems to have been a Kushite, a male, an adult, and a commoner. He lived in the reign of Ashurbanipal or later, and he seems to have been a resident of the city of Assur. The circumstances leading to this individual being in Assyria are difficult to pin down, but it is likely that he or older relatives of his came to Assyria forcibly through deportation.[417]

***Kūsāiu* (8.)**

The 17th individual of this category is *Kūsāiu* (8.). This individual of masculine gender is presented through his name as "the Kushite". *Kūsāiu* (8.) is mentioned in a text (StAT 3 4) from Assur and 630 BCE as a witness when *Lā-turammanni-Aššur* and *Balāssu* buy 18 slaves (men, women, children) for ten minas of silver

---

[414] Drawing from the text publication and the PNA-entry of H. Hunger (PNA 2/I, p. 643).

[415] The document in question is described as a "list of various debts" in SAA 7 (Fales and Postgate 1992). Also the expression "at the disposal of" (*ina qāt*) indicates that *Kūsāiu* 6. was in debt. No other name of this document points to an African ethnicity.

[416] Drawing from the text publication and a PNAo-entry of H.D. Baker (this individual does not seem to be listed in PNA).

[417] As suggested by Baker, it is possible that this individual can be equated with *Kūsāiu* 3. Right after the grain quantifications, the phrases "out of the house" and "a fourth" appear (followed by the name). *Kūsāiu* (7.) is listed towards the end. The other names in the document seem to be Akkadian.

from (at least) *Šarru-iddi[n]a*, *[Mannu-kī]-Arbail*, and *Ḫattiānu*. *Kūsāiu* (8.) is qualified as a son of *[...]āyu* and as from *Libbi-āli* (Assur).[418]

On the basis of the above data, the interrogative words who, what, when, and where can be responded to. *Kūsāiu* (8.) seems to have been a Kushite, a male, an adult, and a commoner. He lived in the post-Ashurbanipal period, and he seems to have been a resident of the city of Assur. The question of how he ended up in Assyria is difficult to answer, but it is likely that he or older relatives of his came to Assyria forcibly by means of deportation.[419]

Kūsāiu (9.)

The 18th individual of this category is *Kūsāiu* (9.). This individual of masculine gender is presented via his name as "the Kushite". *Kūsāiu* (9.) appears in a broken text (WVDOG 152 I.24) from Assur and the reign of Ashurbanipal or later as borrowing something (probably silver) from someone whose name is lost. *Kūsāiu* (9.) is qualified as a son of *Mutakkil-Aššur* 23.[420]

On the basis of the above data, identities, properties, and settings can be identified. *Kūsāiu* (9.) seems to have been a Kushite, a male, an adult, and a commoner. He lived in the reign of Ashurbanipal or later, and he seems to have been a resident of the city of Assur. The circumstances leading to this individual being in Assyria are difficult to pin down, but it is likely that he or older relatives of his came to Assyria forcibly through deportation.[421]

Kūsāiu (10.)

The 19th individual of this category is *Kūsāiu* (10.). This individual of masculine gender is presented via his name as "the Kushite". *Kūsāiu* (10.) is mentioned in two texts from Assur. In the one text (WVDOG 152 I.17) from 635 BCE, he is a witness when *Dūrī-Aššur* buys or rents farmland from *Bakuri*. In the other text (I.47), he is listed as one of the share holders (receiving ten and a half shekels of silver) in a trade enterprise.[422]

---

418 Drawing from the text publication and a PNAo-entry of H.D. Baker (this individual does not seem to be listed in PNA).

419 As suggested by Baker, it is possible that this individual can be equated with *Kūsāiu* 3. There are 14 witnesses to this transaction, with *Kūsāiu* (8.) appearing on ninth place. No other witness bears an African name. Several of the witnesses have positions of authority and some of them are scribes. According to a PNAo-entry of H.D. Baker, the *Lā-turammanni-Aššur* who appears in this document has not been attested before.

420 Drawing from the text publication. *Kūsāiu* (9.) is not listed in PNA or PNAo.

421 Since *Mutakkil-Aššur* 23. is linked to another man named *Kūsāiu* in another text (StAT 1 55), it is likely that he is the one who appears in this text also. The tablet is destroyed where the list of witnesses would have been. The text comes from the archive of *Dūrī-Aššur* (known as Assur 52a), which mentions numerous Egyptians.

422 Drawing from the text publication. *Kūsāiu* (10.) is not listed in PNA or PNAo.

On the basis of the above data, the interrogative words who, what, when, and where can be responded to. *Kūsāiu* (10.) seems to have been a Kushite, a male, an adult, and a commoner. He lived in the reign of Ashurbanipal, and he seems to have been a resident of the city of Assur. The question of how he ended up in Assyria is difficult to answer, but it is likely that he or older relatives of his came to Assyria forcibly by means of deportation.[423]

Kusî

The 20th individual of this category is *Kusî*. This individual of masculine gender is presented through his name as "the Nubian-like". *Kusî* appears in texts (NWL 6; 19) from Kalhu and the eighth century BCE as a receiver of rations of wine in his being a member of the court of Kalhu. He may also appear in a third administrative text dealing with wine rations (CTN 3 120).[424]

On the basis of the above data, identities, properties, and settings can be identified. *Kusî* seems to have been a Kushite, a male, an adult, and (probably) a member of the elite. He lived some time in the eighth century BCE, and he seems to have been a resident of the city of Kalhu. The circumstances leading to this individual being in Assyria are difficult to pin down, but it is likely that he or older relatives of his came to Assyria forcibly through deportation.[425]

Kūsītu

The 21st individual of this category is *Kūsītu*. This individual of feminine gender is presented via her name as "the Kushite". *Kūsītu* is mentioned in a text (*Iraq* 41 56) from Nineveh and the seventh century BCE, which consists of a list of women or feminine names.[426]

On the basis of the above data, the interrogative words who, what, when, and where can be responded to. *Kūsītu* seems to have been a Kushite, a female, an adult, and a commoner. She lived some time in the seventh century BCE, and she seems to have been a resident of the city of Nineveh. The question of how she ended up

---

423 *Kūsāiu* (10.) appears as number five of eight witnesses, with one more possibly African name in the document. He appears as number two of seven share holders, with no other African name in the document. The texts come from the archive of *Dūrī-Aššur* (known as Assur 52a), which mentions numerous Egyptians.

424 Drawing from the text publications and the PNA-entry of E. Lipiński (PNA 2/I, p. 643).

425 Lipiński identifies the name as West Semitic, meaning "Nubian-like". In texts NWL 6 and 19, this individual is listed as the receiver of unknown (due to lacunae) quantities of wine. The name in question is surrounded (in both documents) by titles of prestigious offices. This circumstance, together with the fact that he was a part of the court, indicate that *Kusî* was of high social rank. No other name in the texts is African. In text CTN 3 120, he is the receiver of two liters of wine.

426 Drawing from the text publication and the PNA-entry of H. Hunger (PNA 2/I, p. 644).

in Assyria is difficult to answer, but it is likely that she or older relatives of her came to Assyria forcibly by means of deportation.[427]

Mannu-kī-Nīnua 13.

The 22nd individual of this category is *Mannu-kī-Nīnua* 13. This individual of masculine gender is presented as "the Egyptian" (*Muṣurāiu*). *Mannu-kī-Nīnua* 13. is mentioned in a text (CTN 3 34) from Kalhu and 638 BCE as selling his unnamed daughter to the "harem manageress" (*šakintu*) of the queen's household of the Review Palace of Kalhu for an unknown (due to a lacuna) amount of silver. He may also be mentioned in a text (CTN 3 54) from Kalhu and 642 BCE as a witness when *Šēpē-Ninurta*, *Mannu-kī-Adad*, and *Nurtî* sell an orchard and a well(?) to someone whose name has not been preserved.[428]

On the basis of the above data, identities, properties, and settings can be identified. *Mannu-kī-Nīnua* 13. seems to have been an Egyptian, a male, an adult, and a commoner. He lived in the reign of Ashurbanipal, and he seems to have been a resident of the city of Kalhu. The circumstances leading to this individual being in Assyria are difficult to pin down, but it is likely that he or older relatives of his came to Assyria forcibly through deportation.[429]

Menas(s)ê 3.

The 23rd individual of this category is *Menas(s)ê* 3. This individual of masculine gender is presented as "the Egyptian" (*Muṣurāiu*). *Menas(s)ê* 3. appears in a text (StAT 3 105) from Assur and (probably) the post-Ashurbanipal period as selling (along with *Zab[i?...]*) their (unnamed) slave to *Aššur-šēzibanni* for one mina and three shekels of silver.[430]

On the basis of the above data, the interrogative words who, what, when, and where can be responded to. *Menas(s)ê* 3. seems to have been an Egyptian, a male, an adult, and a commoner. He probably lived in the post-Ashurbanipal period, and he seems to have been a resident of the city of Assur. The question of how he ended up in Assyria is difficult to answer, but it is likely that he or older relatives of his came to Assyria forcibly by means of deportation.[431]

---

427 Hunger identifies the name in question as Akkadian, meaning "woman from Cush". There are no descriptive elements in this text. *Kūsītu* appears in the mid section of this name list, which does not convey any other genuinely African name.

428 Drawing from the text publication and the PNA-entry of H.D. Baker (PNA 2/II, p. 696).

429 Baker identifies the name in question as Akkadian, meaning "Who is like Nineveh?". None of the seven witnesses in CTN 3 34 have an African name. There are 14 witnesses listed in CTN 3 54, and *Mannu-kī-Nīnua* 13.(?) is heading the list (which does not give any African name). His Akkadian name (incorporating the name of the Assyrian capital) naturally tells of assimilation.

430 Drawing from the text publication and the PNA-entry of E. Frahm (PNA 2/II, p. 749).

431 Frahm identifies the name in question as West Semitic, possibly meaning "the one who makes forget". By contrast, B. Faist (2007: 156-159) gives the date 634 BCE and reads *Ṣurrāiu* ("man from

Muṣurāiu 1.

The 24th individual of this category is *Muṣurāiu* 1. This individual of masculine gender is presented through his name as "the Egyptian". *Muṣurāiu* 1. is mentioned in a text (SAA 16 50) from Nineveh and the reign of Esarhaddon as one of 14 people (both men and women) who are to be admitted to the palace, by the order of the chief scribe *Nabû-zēru-lēšir* to the unnamed palace manager. *Muṣurāiu* 1. here appears as a member of the palace personnel, in his being admitted and referred to as a "son of the palace" (*mār ekalli*).[432]

On the basis of the above data, identities, properties, and settings can be identified. *Muṣurāiu* 1. seems to have been an Egyptian, a male, an adult, and a member of the elite. He lived in the reign of Esarhaddon, and he seems to have been a resident of the city of Nineveh. The circumstances leading to this individual being in Assyria are difficult to pin down, but it is likely that he or older relatives of his came to Assyria forcibly through deportation.[433]

Muṣurāiu 2.

The 25th individual of this category is *Muṣurāiu* 2. This individual of masculine gender is presented via his name as "the Egyptian". *Muṣurāiu* 2. is mentioned in a text (SAA 14 16) from Nineveh and 639 BCE as the father of *Ḫuddāia* 4., who sells the slave *[Il-ḫ]azi* and his mother *Aḫātī-ṭābat* to the royal eunuch *Nīnuāiu* for an unknown (due to a lacuna) amount of silver.[434]

On the basis of the above data, the interrogative words who, what, when, and where can be responded to. *Muṣurāiu* 2. seems to have been an Egyptian, a male, an adult, and a commoner. He lived in the reign of Ashurbanipal, and he seems to have been a resident of the city of Nineveh. The question of how he ended up in Assyria is difficult to answer, but it is likely that he or older relatives of his came to Assyria forcibly by means of deportation.[435]

Tyre") as the ethnonym. However, this reading of the ethnonym is far from certain (as she herself admits on p. 158), and the ethnonym *Ṣurrāiu* is comparatively rare and almost restricted to royal inscriptions in the Neo-Assyrian text corpus (cf. Baker 2016: 252). There are no African names in the list of (twelve) witnesses.

[432] Drawing from the text publication and the PNA-entry of M. Jursa (PNA 2/II, pp. 772).

[433] Jursa identifies the name in question as Akkadian, meaning "the Egyptian". *Muṣurāiu* 1. appears as number four in this list, which only contains Akkadian names. Among the admitted enterers are the children of the chief scribe *Nabû-zēru-lēšir*. One other person is referred to as a *mār ekalli*.

[434] Drawing from the text publication and the PNA-entry of M. Jursa (PNA 2/II, pp. 772).

[435] The names of two witnesses are preserved, and both of these are Akkadian.

Muṣurāiu 3.

The 26th individual of this category is *Muṣurāiu* 3. This individual of masculine gender is presented through his name as "the Egyptian". *Muṣurāiu* 3. is mentioned in a text (CTN 3 7) from Kalhu and 620 BCE as a witness in a legal case which conveys the order that *Nabû-nādin-aḫḫē* should give an individual named *Sūsu* to the unnamed palace manager (of Fort Shalmaneser).[436]

On the basis of the above data, identities, properties, and settings can be identified. *Muṣurāiu* 3. seems to have been an Egyptian, a male, an adult, and a commoner. He lived in the post-Ashurbanipal period, and he seems to have been a resident of the city of Kalhu. The circumstances leading to this individual being in Assyria are difficult to pin down, but it is likely that he or older relatives of his came to Assyria forcibly through deportation.[437]

Muṣurāiu 4.

The 27th individual of this category is *Muṣurāiu* 4. This individual of masculine gender is presented via his name as "the Egyptian". *Muṣurāiu* 4. is mentioned in a text (WVDOG 152 I.37) from Assur and the post-Ashurbanipal period as the father of *Sukkāia* 43., who contributes seven shekels of silver to a trade trip conducted by *Muqallil-kabti*.[438]

On the basis of the above data, the interrogative words who, what, when, and where can be responded to. *Muṣurāiu* 4. seems to have been an Egyptian, a male, an adult, and a commoner. He lived in the post-Ashurbanipal period, and he seems to have been a resident of the city of Assur. The question of how he ended up in Assyria is difficult to answer, but it is likely that he or older relatives of his came to Assyria forcibly by means of deportation.[439]

Muṣurāiu 5.

The 28th individual of this category is *Muṣurāiu* 5. This individual of masculine gender is presented through his name as "the Egyptian". *Muṣurāiu* 5. is mentioned in a text (AssU6) from Assur and the seventh century BCE as one of the witnesses

---

436 Drawing from the text publication and the PNA-entry of M. Jursa (PNA 2/II, pp. 772).

437 *Muṣurāiu* 3., who is not given any title, appears as the second of six witnesses. The only witness with a profession title is qualified as a merchant. There are no African names in this document. By contrast, S. Dalley and J.N. Postgate (1984: 5) date this text to 618 BCE.

438 Drawing from the text publication and the PNA-entry of M. Jursa (PNA 2/II, pp. 772).

439 This man appears in the middle of this financial statement, which includes both men and women and brings up a great variety of profession titles. K. Radner (2016: 105) seems to regard the ethnonym as attributive, in her translating "Sieben Scheqel des Sukkāja Sohn eines Ägypters". The text in question comes from the archive of *Dūrī-Aššur* (known as Assur 52a), which mentions numerous Egyptians.

for *[...]ysy*. The text is an Aramaic loan contract, and *Muṣurāiu* 5. is qualified further as a son of *Šarru-lū-dāri* 33.[440]

On the basis of the above data, identities, properties, and settings can be identified. *Muṣurāiu* 5. seems to have been an Egyptian, a male, an adult, and a commoner. He lived some time in the seventh century BCE, and he seems to have been a resident of the city of Assur. The circumstances leading to this individual being in Assyria are difficult to pin down, but it is likely that he or older relatives of his came to Assyria forcibly through deportation.[441]

Muṣurāiu 6.

The 29th individual of this category is *Muṣurāiu* 6. This individual of masculine gender is presented via his name as "the Egyptian". *Muṣurāiu* 6. is mentioned in a text (BATSH 6 40) from Dur-Katlimmu and 600 BCE as the father of *Sīn-na'di* 27., who acts as one of the witnesses when *Arrî* purchases land from four men (with non-African names).[442]

On the basis of the above data, the interrogative words who, what, when, and where can be responded to. *Muṣurāiu* 6. seems to have been an Egyptian, a male, an adult, and a commoner. He lived in the post-imperial period (reign of Nebuchadnezzar II), and he seems to have been a resident of Dur-Katlimmu. The question of how he ended up in this corner of Assyria is difficult to answer, but it is likely that he or older relatives of his came to Assyria forcibly by means of deportation.[443]

Muṣurī

The 30th individual of this category is *Muṣurī*. This individual of masculine gender is presented through his name as "the Egyptian". *Muṣurī* features in Assyrian royal inscriptions as a king of the Levantine state of Moab. In texts (RINAP 4 1; 5) from Nineveh and 673-670 BCE, this ruler is mentioned as one of the vassal kings who participated in Esarhaddon's reconstruction of the Review Palace in Nineveh. In another text (RINAP 5/1 6), this time from Nineveh and the reign of Ashurbanipal (probably 647 BCE), *Muṣurī* is listed among the vassal kings who took part in Ashurbanipal's first Egyptian campaign in 667 BCE.[444]

On the basis of the above data, identities, properties, and settings can be identified. *Muṣurī* seems to have been an Egyptian, a male, an adult, and a member of the elite. He lived in the reigns of Esarhaddon and Ashurbanipal, and he resided

---

[440] Drawing from the PNA-entry of M. Jursa (PNA 2/II, pp. 772).
[441] The archival context (among other things) of this document is unclear.
[442] Drawing from the text publication and the PNA-entry of M. Jursa (PNA 2/II, pp. 772).
[443] *Sīn-na'di* 27., son of *Muṣurāiu* 6., appears as the second of eight witnesses, telling of his rank. No other name in the list of witnesses indicates an African ethnicity.
[444] Drawing from the text publications and the PNA-entry of M. Jursa (PNA 2/II, pp. 772).

in the land of Moab. The question of how he became a part of the Neo-Assyrian empire is hard to answer, but it was voluntary in the sense that he chose not to resist but forced in the sense that he surrendered in light of the threat of Assyrian arms.[445]

Muṣur(ītu) (1.)

The 31st individual of this category is *Muṣur(ītu)* (1.). This individual of feminine gender is presented via her name as "the Egyptian". *Muṣur(ītu)* (1.) is mentioned in a text (WVDOG 152 I.35) from Assur and the reign of Ashurbanipal or later as the contributor of an unknown (due to a lacuna) amount of silver to a trade trip of *Kiṣir-Nabû*.[446]

On the basis of the above data, the interrogative words who, what, when, and where can be responded to. *Muṣur(ītu)* (1.) seems to have been an Egyptian, a female, an adult, and a commoner. She lived in the reign of Ashurbanipal or later, and she seems to have been a resident of the city of Assur. The question of how she ended up in Assyria is difficult to answer, but it is likely that she or older relatives of her came to Assyria forcibly via deportation.[447]

Muṣurītu (2.)

The 32nd individual of this category is *Muṣurītu* (2.). This individual of feminine gender is presented via her name as "the Egyptian". *Muṣurītu* (2.) appears in texts (WVDOG 152 I.56; I.58) from Assur and the reign of Ashurbanipal or later as (together with *Karānūtu*) tied to three and three shekels of silver in two financial statements.[448]

On the basis of the above data, identities, properties, and settings can be identified. *Muṣurītu* (2.) seems to have been an Egyptian, a female, an adult, and a commoner. She lived in the reign of Ashurbanipal or later, and she seems to have

---

445 Jursa identifies the name in question as West Semitic. Esarhaddon orders "twelve kings from the shore of the sea (i.e. the Levant)" and ten Cypriot rulers (from "the midst of the sea") to send timber and stone for his building project. *Muṣurī* is listed on fourth place. This constellation and relative position are virtually intact in the text of Ashurbanipal, who claims that the 22 rulers gave "audience gifts" (*tāmartu*), kissed his feet, and went with his troops to Egypt along with their forces and boats. Telling of their status, the 22 rulers are called "[serva]nts who belonged to me" (*[ard]āni dāgil pānīya*). It should be noted that the reading "the Egyptian" is disputed. No doubt, such a name for a Moabite ruler surprises (but note *Ḫur-waṣi* 4., mayor of Gezer). For a discussion of the identity and etymology of *Muṣurī*, see Karlsson 2022b.

446 Drawing from the text publication. *Muṣur(ītu)* (1.) is not listed in PNA or PNAo, other than in PNA 4/I, p. 250.

447 It is also possible that *Muṣur(ītu)* is an attribute to a name that has not been preserved, and/or that it conveys masculine gender (but see Radner 2016: 104). This woman is enumerated in the middle of the financial statement in question. Both men and women appear as investors, and one of the investors has architect as his profession. The text in question comes from the archive of *Dūrī-Aššur* (known as Assur 52a), which mentions numerous Egyptians.

448 Drawing from the text publication. *Muṣurītu* (2.) is not listed in PNA or PNAo.

been a resident of the city of Assur. The circumstances leading to this individual being in Assyria are difficult to pin down, but it is likely that she or older relatives of her came to Assyria forcibly through deportation.[449]

Muṣurītu (3.)

The 33rd individual of this category is *Muṣurītu* (3.). This individual of feminine gender is presented via her name as "the Egyptian". *Muṣurītu* (3.) appears in a text (WVDOG 152 I.58) from Assur and the reign of Ashurbanipal or later as tied to six shekels of silver in a financial statement. She is qualified further as "from the household of *Ubrūtu*" (*ina bīt Ubrūte*).[450]

On the basis of the above data, the interrogative words who, what, when, and where can be responded to. *Muṣurītu* (3.) seems to have been an Egyptian, a female, an adult, and a commoner. She lived in the reign of Ashurbanipal or later, and she seems to have been a resident of the city of Assur. The question of how she ended up in Assyria is difficult to answer, but it is likely that she or older relatives of her came to Assyria forcibly via deportation.[451]

Qīšāia 2.

The 34th individual of this category is *Qīšāia* 2. This individual of masculine gender is presented as "the Egyptian" (*Muṣurāiu*). *Qīšāia* 2. is mentioned in a text (StAT 2 207) from the N31-archive, Assur, and 618 BCE as a witness when *Bābilāiu* buys a house in Assur from *Urdu-Aššur*, son of *Puṭi-ḫutapiša*▪.[452]

On the basis of the above data, identities, properties, and settings can be identified. *Qīšāia* 2. seems to have been an Egyptian, a male, an adult, and a commoner. He lived in the post-Ashurbanipal period, and he seems to have been a resident of the city of Assur. The circumstances leading to this individual being in Assyria are difficult to pin down, but it is likely that he or older relatives of his came to Assyria forcibly through deportation.[453]

---

[449] This woman is enumerated first and last in the financial statements in question. Both men and women appear as investors, and the investors have professions like gardener and smith. Judging by the phrase *ina qāt*, it seems like *Karānūtu* invested with silver borrowed from *Muṣurītu* (2.). The text in question comes from the archive of *Dūrī-Aššur* (known as Assur 52a), which mentions numerous Egyptians.

[450] Drawing from the text publication. *Muṣurītu* (3.) is not listed in PNA or PNAo.

[451] This woman is enumerated first in the financial statement. Both men and women appear as investors, and one of the investors comes from the household of the mayor. The text in question derives from the archive of *Dūrī-Aššur* (known as Assur 52a), which mentions numerous Egyptians.

[452] Drawing from the text publication and the PNA-entry of J. Llop (PNA 3/I, p. 1015).

[453] Llop identifies the name as Akkadian, meaning "granted by Aia". *Qīšāia* 2. is listed as the eighth of 15 witnesses. He is one of five individuals who are presented with the ethnonym in question. Several of the names in this list of witnesses are African. His Akkadian name (incorporating the name of a Mesopotamian deity) naturally tells of assimilation.

***Ṣil-Aššur* 2.**

The 35th individual of this category is *Ṣil-Aššur* 2. This individual of masculine gender is presented as "an Egyptian" (*Muṣurāiu*). *Ṣil-Aššur* 2. is mentioned in a text (SAA 6 142) from Nineveh and 692 BCE as the buyer of a house in Nineveh for one mina of silver from *Šarru-lū-dāri*, *Attar-suri*, and the woman *Amat-Sula*. *Ṣil-Aššur* 2. is qualified as an "Egyptian scribe" (*ṭupšar Muṣurāiu*) in the document.[454]

On the basis of the above data, the interrogative words who, what, when, and where can be responded to. *Ṣil-Aššur* 2. seems to have been an Egyptian, a male, an adult, and a member of the elite. He lived in the reign of Sennacherib, and he seems to have been a resident of the city of Nineveh. The question of how he ended up in Assyria is difficult to answer, but it is likely that he or older relatives of his came to Assyria forcibly by means of deportation.[455]

***Šarru-lū-dāri* 12.**

The 36th individual of this category is *Šarru-lū-dāri* 12. This individual of masculine gender is presented as "the Egyptian" (*Miṣirāiu*). *Šarru-lū-dāri* 12. is mentioned in a text (SAA 10 112) from Nineveh and the reign of Esarhaddon. In this letter, the Babylonian astrologer *Bēl-ušēzib* informs the Assyrian king that *Šarru-lū-dāri* 12., "the Egyptian", a friend (*bēl ṭābti*) of *Bēl-ēṭir* (governor of ḪAR) and *Sasî*, may have been induced (*dabābu* Š) to join the conspiracy (*sīḫu*) of *Šumu-iddina*, governor of Nippur. In a letter (YBC 11382, dated to 671 BCE) from Nineveh and a *Nabû-ušallim* to the king, the former claims that *Šarru-lū-dāri* 12. turned to *Sasî* instead of to the Assyrian king regarding a suspected plot involving *Sasî* and *Abdâ*, governor of Assur.[456]

On the basis of the above data, identities, properties, and settings can be identified. *Šarru-lū-dāri* 12. seems to have been an Egyptian, a male, an adult, and a member of the elite. He lived in the reign of Esarhaddon, and he may have resided (as a high official?) in a city somewhere in Babylonia. The circumstances leading to this individual being in Babylonia are difficult to pin down, but it is likely that he or older relatives of his came to southern Mesopotamia forcibly by means of deportation.[457]

---

454 Drawing from the text publication and the PNA-entry of F.S. Reynolds (PNA 3/I, p. 1171).

455 Reynolds identifies the name as Akkadian, meaning "shade (i.e. protection) of (the god) Ashur". There are ten witnesses to this purchase, several with African names. The list starts with *Susinqu* 1., the king's brother/son-in-law. Clearly, *Ṣil-Aššur* 2. was an integral part of the Egyptian community in Nineveh. His Akkadian name (incorporating the name of the main Assyrian god) naturally tells of assimilation.

456 Drawing from the text publication and the PNA-entry of H.D. Baker (PNA 3/II, p. 1248).

457 For text YBC 11382, see Frahm 2010: 91-95. Baker identifies the name as Akkadian, meaning "May the king be eternal!". Ironically enough, his (Akkadian) name conveys a loyalist tone. *Bēl-ušēzib* adds that, "the king should be wary of all of them". The identity of the Egyptian in question is unclear (cf. Frahm 2010: 126-127), although it looks as if he was an important figure and tied in

Šašmâ 1.

The 37th individual of this category is *Šašmâ* 1. This individual of masculine gender is presented as "the Egyptian" (*Muṣurāiu*). *Šašmâ* 1. is mentioned in a text (T. Hadid 2) from Tel Hadid (in the Levant) and 664 BCE as a witness when *Ki-[...]* lends silver to *Ši?[...]*.[458]

On the basis of the above data, the interrogative words who, what, when, and where can be responded to. *Šašmâ* 1. seems to have been an Egyptian, a male, an adult, and a commoner. He lived in the reign of Ashurbanipal, and he seems to have been a resident of the Levantine town of Tel Hadid. The question of how he ended up in this Assyrian vassal state is difficult to answer, but it is likely that he or older relatives of his came there forcibly via deportation.[459]

Šulmu-šarri 12.

The 38th individual of this category is *Šulmu-šarri* 12. This individual of masculine gender is presented as a "Kushite eunuch" (*ša rēši Kūsāiu*). *Šulmu-šarri* 12. appears in a text (SAA 7 47) from Nineveh and the reign of Esarhaddon or Ashurbanipal, which gives a memorandum on the activities of the Kushite eunuchs *Dāri-šarru* 2. and *Šulmu-šarri* 12. in western Assyria. The text says that *Kiṣir-Issar*, a provider of limestone, entered the service of *Šulmu-šarri* 12., and that the latter sent a royal bodyguard to some man in order to extract 20 minas of silver from him, and gave three minas of silver to an unnamed supervisor of military(?) equipment.[460]

On the basis of the above data, identities, properties, and settings can be identified. *Šulmu-šarri* 12. seems to have been a Kushite, a male, an adult, and a member of the elite. He lived in the reign of Esarhaddon or Ashurbanipal, and he seems to have been a resident of western Assyria. The circumstances leading to this individual being in this corner of Assyria are difficult to pin down, but it is likely that he or older relatives of his came to Assyria forcibly by means of deportation.[461]

---

some way to the Assyrian administration. He seems to equal a governor in rank, and he is described as having the obligation to warn the Assyrian king of any insurrection plans. *Šarru-lū-dāri* 12. may, of course, have been an Assyrian official in Egypt, but the textual context (sender, toponyms, etc.) indicates that he was an Assyrian official in Babylonia. For the toponym of ḪAR (not found in RGTC 7/1-2), see Parpola 1970: 149.

458 Drawing from the text publication and the PNA-entry made by M. Weszeli and R. Zadok (PNA 3/II, p. 1253).

459 Weszeli and Zadok identify the name as "Semitic" and as based on the theophoric element *Ssm*. Explaining the presence of an Egyptian in Tel Hadid, this town is after all situated near Egypt. *Šašmâ* 1. appears third of four witnesses, with the names of the other witnesses being non-African.

460 Drawing from the text publication and the PNA-entry of K. Radner (PNA 3/II, p. 1278).

461 Radner identifies the name as Akkadian, meaning "well-being of the king". The facts that the text is fragmentary and much is implicit make it difficult to fully understand the activities of this Kushite eunuch. *Šulmu-šarri* 12. is said to have extracted the 20 minas of silver in question "by force" (*dannatti*). Notably, his name conveys a loyalist tone, telling of his assimilation. The toponyms (Rasappa, Lahiru, Kummuh) in the same text suggest a western setting.

***Ta'lâ* 5.**

The 39th individual of this category is *Ta'lâ* 5. This individual of masculine gender is presented as "the Egyptian" (*Muṣurāiu*). *Ta'lâ* 5. is mentioned in a text (*SAAB* 9 77) from Assur and the reign of Ashurbanipal or later as a witness for *Kusasu*, who purchases the slave *Atar-nūrī* from an individual named *Rāši-ili*.[462]

On the basis of the above data, the interrogative words who, what, when, and where can be responded to. *Ta'lâ* 5. seems to have been an Egyptian, a male, an adult, and a commoner. He lived in the reign of Ashurbanipal or later, and he seems to have been a resident of the city of Assur. The question of how this individual ended up in Assyria is difficult to answer, but it is likely that he or older relatives of his came to Assyria forcibly by means of deportation.[463]

***Tamūzītu* 1.**

The 40th individual of this category is *Tamūzītu* 1. (or *Du'ūzītu*). This individual of feminine gender is presented as "the Egyptian" (*Muṣur(ītu)*). She is mentioned in a text (WVDOG 152 I.35) from Assur and the reign of Ashurbanipal or later as contributing two shekels of silver to a trade trip of *Kiṣir-Nabû*. She is qualified further as a daughter of *Urdu-Nanāia* 20.[464]

On the basis of the above data, identities, properties, and settings can be identified. *Tamūzītu* 1. seems to have been an Egyptian, a female, an adult, and a commoner. She lived in the reign of Ashurbanipal or later, and she seems to have been a resident of the city of Assur. The circumstances leading to this individual being in Assyria are difficult to pin down, but it is likely that she or older relatives of her came to Assyria forcibly through deportation.[465]

***Ṭāb-Bēl* 8.**

The 41st individual of this category is *Ṭāb-Bēl* 8. This individual of masculine gender is presented as "the Egyptian" (*Muṣurāiu*). *Ṭāb-Bēl* 8. appears in a text (StAT 2 273) from Assur and 636 BCE as the seller of his female slave *Adimasia*ᵒ to *Adda-dimrī* for 46 shekels of silver.[466]

---

462 Drawing from the text publication and the PNA-entry of P. Talon (PNA 3/II, p. 1305).

463 Talon identifies the name as Aramaic, meaning "fox". The names of seven witnesses have been preserved, and *Ta'lâ* 5. appears on fifth place in the list. The others have Akkadian names and a variety of professions (scribe, eunuch, merchant, baker).

464 Drawing from the text publication and the PNA-entry of C. Jean (PNA 3/II, p. 1309).

465 Jean identifies the name in question as Akkadian, meaning "the one (fem.) born in the month *Tamūz*". This Egyptian woman appears in the first half of the financial statement, which brings up both men and women as well as a variety of professions (architect, temple official, physician). The text in question comes from the archive of *Dūrī-Aššur* (known as Assur 52a), which mentions numerous Egyptians.

466 Drawing from the text publication and the PNA-entry of J. Llop (PNA 3/II, p. 1339).

On the basis of the above data, the interrogative words who, what, when, and where can be responded to. *Ṭāb-Bēl* 8. seems to have been an Egyptian, a male, an adult, and a commoner. He lived in the later part of the reign of Ashurbanipal, and he seems to have been a resident of the city of Assur. The question of how this individual ended up in Assyria is difficult to answer, but it is likely that he or older relatives of his came to Assyria forcibly via deportation.[467]

Urkittu-kallat

The 42nd individual of this category is *Urkittu-kallat*. This individual of feminine gender is presented as "the Egyptian" (*Muṣurītu*). *Urkittu-kallat* is mentioned in a text (WVDOG 152 I.38) from Assur and the reign of Ashurbanipal or later as contributing twelve shekels of silver to a trade trip of *Muqallil-kabti*.[468]

On the basis of the above data, identities, properties, and settings can be identified. *Urkittu-kallat* seems to have been an Egyptian, a female, an adult, and a commoner. She lived in the reign of Ashurbanipal or later, and she seems to have been a resident of the city of Assur. The circumstances leading to this individual being in Assyria are difficult to pin down, but it is likely that she or older relatives of her came to Assyria forcibly through deportation.[469]

Zateubatte

The 43rd individual of this category is *Zateubatte*. This individual of masculine gender is presented as "the Egyptian" (*Muṣurāiu*). *Zateubatte* appears in a text (StAT 2 207) from the N31-archive, Assur, and 618 BCE as a witness when *Bābilāiu* buys a house in Assur from *Urdu-Aššur*, son of *Puṭi-ḫutapiša*▪.[470]

On the basis of the above data, the interrogative words who, what, when, and where can be responded to. *Zateubatte* seems to have been an Egyptian, a male, an adult, and a commoner. He lived in the post-Ashurbanipal period, and he seems to have been a resident of the city of Assur. The question of how this individual ended

---

467 Llop identifies the name as Akkadian, meaning "the/my lord is good". The identity of "the lord" (*bēlu*) referred to in his name is unclear. It may point to a deity or to a king. It is noticeable that the tablet on which the text is written contains scarab seal impressions, thus pointing to Egypt. V. Donbaz and S. Parpola (2001: 192) date the text to 625 BCE.

468 Drawing from the text publication and the PNA-entry of H.D. Baker (PNA 3/II, p. 1416).

469 Baker identifies the name as Akkadian, meaning "the Urukite (i.e. Ishtar) is the god". *Urkittu-kallat* appears in the beginning (on third place) of the financial statement in question. Her name, which brings up the Mesopotamian goddess Ishtar in her form at Uruk (a city in southern Mesopotamia), naturally tells of assimilation. The text in question comes from the archive of *Dūrī-Aššur* (known as Assur 52a), which mentions numerous Egyptians.

470 Drawing from the text publication and the PNA-entry of H.D. Baker (PNA 3/II, p. 1439).

up in Assyria is difficult to answer, but it is likely that he or older relatives of his came to Assyria forcibly by means of deportation.[471]

2.1.3 People identified as Africans via family relations

The third subsection focuses on Africans identifiable on the identification ground family relations, meaning that someone is revealed as African through family ties to an identified African. 33 individuals will be presented and discussed in this subsection.

***Aḫu-dūr-enši* 2.**

The first individual of this category is *Aḫu-dūr-enši* 2. This individual of masculine gender is presented as a son of *Ḫūru*▪ 2., whose name is Egyptian. *Aḫu-dūr-enši* 2. is mentioned in a text (StAT 2 191) from the N31-archive, Assur, and 629 BCE as the borrower of half a mina and five shekels of silver from *Urdu-Aššur* 5.[472]

On the basis of the above data, the interrogative words who, what, when, and where can be responded to. *Aḫu-dūr-enši* 2. seems to have been an Egyptian, a male, an adult, and a commoner. He lived in the post-Ashurbanipal period, and he seems to have been a resident of Assur. The question of how this individual ended up in Assyria is difficult to answer, but it is likely that he or older relatives of his came to Assyria forcibly by means of deportation.[473]

Apâ

The second individual of this category is *Apâ*. This individual of masculine gender is presented as a son of *Apiḫuniṣi[...]* (now read *Apiḫuniawa*▪), whose name is Egyptian. Also, the name of this individual has been classified as Egyptian, although its exact meaning is unknown. *Apâ* appears in texts (StAT 2 216-217) on a tablet and its envelope from the N31-archive, Assur, and the seventh century BCE as a son of *Apiḫuniawa* and as borrowing 15 shekels of silver from *Urdu-Aššur* 5.[474]

On the basis of the above data, identities, properties, and settings can be identified. *Apâ* seems to have been an Egyptian, a male, an adult, and a commoner.

---

471 Baker states that the meaning and origin of the name in question are unknown. *Zateubatte* is listed as the tenth of 15 witnesses. He is one of five individuals who are presented with the ethnonym in question. Several of the names in this list of witnesses are African.

472 Drawing from the text publication and the PNA-entry of K. Radner (PNA 1/I, p. 72).

473 Radner identifies the name as Akkadian, meaning "the brother is a protective wall for the weak". This loan of silver is witnessed by three people, one with an Egyptian name (on second place), and the others being the prominent Egyptians *Lā-turammanni-Aššur* 3. and *Kiṣir-Aššur* 45. Radner suggests the dates 644, 629, or 610 BCE. The date 629 BCE appears in the publication by V. Donbaz and S. Parpola (2001: 135).

474 Drawing from the text publication and the PNA-entry of R. Mattila (PNA 1/I, p. 112).

He lived some time in the seventh century BCE, and he seems to have been a resident of the city of Assur. The circumstances leading to this individual being in Assyria are difficult to pin down, but it is likely that he or older relatives of his came to Assyria forcibly through deportation.[475]

***Aššur-dūri* (6.)**

The third individual of this category is *Aššur-dūri* (6.). This individual of masculine gender is presented as the father of *Puṭupašte*▪, that is, of a man with an Egyptian name. *Aššur-dūri* (6.) is mentioned in a text (WVDOG 152 II.10) from the Assur 52b-archive, Assur, and the reign of Ashurbanipal or later as the father of *Puṭupašte*, who is sued (along with the woman *Lābê*▫ (2.)) by *Puṭukiše*▪ on account of the latter's son *Sabutī*.[476]

On the basis of the above data, the interrogative words who, what, when, and where can be responded to. *Aššur-dūri* (6.) seems to have been an Egyptian, a male, an adult, and a commoner. He lived in the reign of Ashurbanipal or later, and he seems to have been a resident of the city of Assur. The question of how this individual ended up in Assyria is difficult to answer, but it is likely that he or older relatives of his came to Assyria forcibly via deportation.[477]

***Awa* (1.)**

The fourth individual of this category is *Awa* (1.). This individual of masculine gender is presented as a son of *Tap-naḫte*▪ 1., that is, of a man with an Egyptian name. *Awa* (1.) is mentioned in a text (StAT 2 164) from the N31-archive, Assur, and 675 BCE as marrying *Mullissu-ḫammat*, daughter of *Pabbā'u*▫ and a votaress of the Assyrian goddess Ishtar of Arbela, with wedding money and dowry exchanged.[478]

On the basis of the above data, identities, properties, and settings can be identified. *Awa* (1.) seems to have been an Egyptian, a male, an adult, and a commoner. He lived in the reign of Esarhaddon, and he seems to have been a resident of the city of Assur. The circumstances leading to this individual being in

[475] Mattila states that the meaning of the name is unknown but that it is "probably Egyptian". Four individuals, several of these with Egyptian names and with *Kiṣir-Aššur* 45. on first place, witness this loan. V. Donbaz and S. Parpola (2001: 146) suggest the date 613 BCE.

[476] Drawing from the text publication. It is unclear if this individual can be tied to someone listed with this name in PNA.

[477] The name means "Aššur is my protective wall" (K. Åkerman, PNA 1/I, p. 180). *Aššur-dūri* (6.) is clearly linked to the Egyptian community in Assur. That said, his personal name, which incorporates the name of the main Assyrian god, naturally tells of some degree of assimilation.

[478] Drawing from the text publication and the PNA-entry of H.D. Baker (PNA 1/II, p. 433).

Assyria are difficult to pin down, but it is likely that he or older relatives of his came to Assyria forcibly through deportation.[479]

***Barīku* 8.**

The fifth individual of this category is *Barīku* 8. This individual of masculine gender is presented as a son of *Ra'û*▪ 2., whose name is Egyptian. *Barīku* 8. appears in a text (StAT 2 296) from Assur and the early reign of Ashurbanipal as the borrower of 58 shekels of silver from *Sangû-Issar*, derived from the "royal *iškaru* income of the mausoleum of *Sangû-Issar*".[480]

On the basis of the above data, the interrogative words who, what, when, and where can be responded to. *Barīku* 8. seems to have been an Egyptian, a male, an adult, and a commoner. He lived in the early reign of Ashurbanipal, and he seems to have been a resident of Assur. The question of how this individual ended up in Assyria is difficult to answer, but it is likely that he or older relatives of his came to Assyria forcibly by means of deportation.[481]

***Bēlet-issē'a* 2.**

The sixth individual of this category is *Bēlet-issē'a* 2. This individual of feminine gender is presented as the mother of *Apî*▪ 1., whose name is Egyptian. *Bēlet-issē'a* 2. is mentioned in a text (*FNLD* 18) from the N31-archive, Assur, and 625 BCE as being inherited (along with her female child *Apî* and her husband *Amman-tanaḫti*▪ 2.) by *Puṭi-Mūnu*▪ 2. when the inheritance of the latter's father *Lā-turammanni-Aššur* 3. is divided.[482]

On the basis of the above data, identities, properties, and settings can be identified. *Bēlet-issē'a* 2. seems to have been an Egyptian, a female, an adult, and a slave. She lived in the post-Ashurbanipal period, and she seems to have been a resident of Assur. The circumstances leading to this individual being in Assyria are

---

479 Also text StAT 2 184 is referred to in the PNA-entry. However, as noticed by Baker herself in a PNAo-entry, the signs *a-ú-e* are actually part of the (Egyptian) name *Ri-m-pi-aue* (m*ri-im-pi-a-ú-e*) in the text publication by V. Donbaz and S. Parpola (2001: 131). Baker proposes that *Awa* is West Semitic, based on a verb meaning "to desire". Still, the Egyptian setting of *Awa* (1.) appears through the list of witnesses, which contains several Egyptian names. The multicultural character of the Neo-Assyrian empire is reflected in the West Semitic name for an Egyptian and in the fact that a woman married to an Egyptian is tied to an Assyrian goddess. The professions stated in the document suggest a cultic environment.

480 Drawing from the text publication and the PNA-entry of D.R. Brown (PNA 1/II, p. 271).

481 Brown identifies the name as West Semitic, meaning "blessed". The names of five witnesses have been fully or partly preserved. There is no African name among these.

482 Drawing from the text publication and the PNA-entry of G.J. Selz (PNA 1/II, p. 297).

difficult to pin down, but it is likely that she or older relatives of her came to Assyria forcibly through deportation.[483]

Gula-ēṭir 3.

The seventh individual of this category is *Gula-ēṭir* 3. This individual of masculine gender is presented as a brother of *Meia*▪, whose name is Egyptian. *Gula-ēṭir* 3. is mentioned in a text (CT 53 974) from Assur and the seventh century BCE as the writer of letters (written on the same tablet) to his brother *Rībāia* 11. and to his sister *Meia*, in which he urges his brother to be vigilant and not allow *Meia* to go out of the house.[484]

On the basis of the above data, the interrogative words who, what, when, and where can be responded to. *Gula-ēṭir* 3. seems to have been an Egyptian, a male, an adult, and a commoner. He lived some time in the seventh century BCE, and he seems to have been a resident of Assur. The question of how this individual ended up in Assyria is difficult to answer, but it is likely that he or older relatives of his came to Assyria forcibly by means of deportation.[485]

Ḫuddāia 4.

The eighth individual of this category is *Ḫuddāia* 4. This individual of masculine gender is presented as a son of *Muṣurāiu*▪ 2., whose name means "the Egyptian". *Ḫuddāia* 4. is mentioned in a text (SAA 14 19) from Nineveh as the seller of *Asalluḫi-ḫutnī* and his brother *Addî* to the royal eunuch *Nīnuāiu* for one mina (by the mina of Carchemish) and 30 shekels of silver, and in a text (SAA 14 16) from Nineveh and 639 BCE as the seller of *Il-ḫazi* and his mother *Aḫātī-ṭābat* to the same *Nīnuāiu* for an unknown (due to a lacuna) quantity of silver (but with the measure of mina mentioned).[486]

On the basis of the above data, identities, properties, and settings can be identified. *Ḫuddāia* 4. seems to have been an Egyptian, a male, an adult, and a commoner. He lived in the reign of Ashurbanipal, and he seems to have been a resident of Nineveh. The circumstances leading to this individual being in Assyria

---

[483] Selz identifies the name as Akkadian, meaning "*Belet* (= the Lady) is with me". The identity of the goddess(?) *Bēlet* is unclear. The name of *Bēlet-issē'a* 2. appears before those of her relations, and she is qualified by GÉME, meaning "slave". Several of the 17 witnesses have Egyptian names.
[484] Drawing from the text publication and the PNA-entry of M. Weszeli (PNA 1/II, p. 429).
[485] Weszeli identifies the name as Akkadian, meaning "Gula has saved". It is not clear why it was so important to not let his sister go out of the house. The name of *Gula-ēṭir* 3., incorporating the name of a Mesopotamian goddess, naturally tells of assimilation.
[486] Drawing from the text publication and the PNA-entry of K. Fabritius (PNA 2/I, p. 476).

are difficult to pin down, but it is likely that he or older relatives of his came to Assyria forcibly through deportation.[487]

Issar-dūrī 26.

The ninth individual of this category is *Issar-dūrī* 26. This individual of masculine gender is presented as a son of *Abši-Ešu*▪, "the Egyptian". *Issar-dūrī* 26. is mentioned in a text (SAA 6 311) from Nineveh and 666 BCE as the seller (together with his brother *Lū-šakin* 14.) of a house in the city of Bet-Eriba-ilu to the "chief chariot driver of Ashurbanipal", *Rēmanni-Adad*, for four minas of silver, by the mina of Carchemish.[488]

On the basis of the above data, the interrogative words who, what, when, and where can be responded to. *Issar-dūrī* 26. seems to have been an Egyptian, a male, an adult, and a commoner. He lived in the reign of Ashurbanipal, and he seems to have been a resident of the western city of Bet-Eriba-ilu. The question of how he ended up in this part of Assyria is difficult to answer, but it is likely that he or older relatives of his came there forcibly by means of deportation.[489]

Kalbāia 2.

The tenth individual of this category is *Kalbāia* (or *Kalbi-Aia*) 2. This individual of masculine gender is presented as a son of *Pi-san-Eši*▪ 2., whose name is Egyptian. *Kalbāia* 2. appears in a text (CTN 3 41) from Kalhu and 616 BCE as borrowing (together with *Urdu-Mullissu* 10., from the town Napisina) half a mina and two shekels of silver from *Nabû-aḫu-uṣur*.[490]

On the basis of the above data, identities, properties, and settings can be identified. *Kalbāia* 2. seems to have been an Egyptian, a male, an adult, and a commoner. He lived in the post-Ashurbanipal period, and he seems to have been a resident of the town of Napisina. The circumstances leading to this individual being in Assyria are difficult to pin down, but it is likely that he or older relatives of his came to Assyria forcibly through deportation.[491]

---

487 Fabritius states that the meaning and origin of this name are unknown. All in all, the names of seven witnesses have been preserved. None of these are of African origin.

488 Drawing from the text publication and the PNA-entry of H.D. Baker (PNA 2/I, p. 570).

489 Baker identifies the name as Akkadian, meaning "*Ištar* is my (protective) wall". There are six witnesses to this house transaction. None of these have an African name. The name of *Issar-dūrī* 26., incorporating the name of a Mesopotamian goddess, naturally tells of assimilation.

490 Drawing from the text publication and the PNA-entry of A. Berlejung (PNA 2/I, p. 598).

491 By contrast, S. Dalley and J.N. Postgate (1984: 95-96) propose *Ribaya*(?) instead of *Kalbāia*. Berlejung identifies the name as Akkadian, meaning "dog" or "dog/servant of Ea". His loan partner, *Urdu-Mullissu* 10., is qualified by an Egyptian patronym, re-inforcing the African context. The names of three witnesses are preserved, with one of these being possibly Egyptian. The name of *Kalbāia* 2., which may incorporate the name of an important Mesopotamian deity, naturally speaks of assimilation.

Lā-turammanni-Aššur 3.-4.

The eleventh individual of this category is *Lā-turammanni-Aššur* 3.-4. This individual of masculine gender is presented as the father of *Ḫut-naḫti*▪ and *Puṭi-Mūnu*▪ 2., both bearing Egyptian names. *Lā-turammanni-Aššur* 3. is mentioned in numerous texts from the N31-archive, Assur, and the time range of 655-613 BCE. He appears partly as the father of *Ḫut-naḫti* and *Puṭi-Mūnu* 2., namely when his estate is divided between these two (*FNLD* 18), partly as a party of transactions, such as when he and two others (whose names are lost) borrow silver from *Urdu-Aššur* 5. for a commercial enterprise (StAT 2 209), and partly as a witness, such as when he acts as a witness for *Kiṣir-Aššur* 45. and *Urdu-Aššur* 5., who lend silver to *Pūnašti*▪ (StAT 2 177), and when he functions as a witness when *Tap-naḫte*▪ 3. receives a house from nine or ten men (most of them with Egyptian names) in a case of inheritance (StAT 2 167). He is qualified further as a "commander-of-fifty" (*rab ḫanšê*) (e.g. *FNLD* 18), and as a son of *Mannu-kī-Aššur* (e.g. StAT 3 80). *Lā-turammanni-Aššur* 4. is probably to be equated with *Lā-turammanni-Aššur* 3. *Lā-turammanni-Aššur* 4. is referred to as "servant (*ardu*) (and) commander-of-fifty", and he is a witness when *Ata'*▫ gives his sister *Silim-Puṭi-lumur* to *Riḫpi-Mūnu*▫ as a wife in a text (StAT 2 184) from the N31-archive and Assur.[492]

On the basis of the above data, the interrogative words who, what, when, and where can be responded to. *Lā-turammanni-Aššur* 3.-4. seems to have been an Egyptian, a male, an adult, and a member of the elite. He lived in the reign of Ashurbanipal and later, and he seems to have been a resident of the city of Assur. The question of how he ended up in Assyria is difficult to answer, but it is likely that he or older relatives of his came there forcibly via deportation.[493]

---

[492] Drawing from the text publications, the PNA-entries of R. Pruzsinszky (PNA 2/II, pp. 658-659), and (five) PNAo-entries by H.D. Baker. For more texts regarding him as a transaction party, see StAT 2 208; StAT 3 80; 81; 87; WVDOG 152 II.5. For more texts concerning him as a witness, see A 1809; *BagM* 16 31; StAT 2 77; 178; 183; 191; 192; 208; 211; 231; StAT 3 82; 92.

[493] Pruzsinszky identifies the name as Akkadian, meaning "Do not forsake me, O Aššur!". *Lā-turammanni-Aššur* 3.-4. frequently features together with Egyptians (see e.g. *FNLD* 18; StAT 2 167; 208), and he appears to have been of high social rank, as indicated by his profession title and the circumstance that he is often mentioned first or early in the lists of witnesses (see e.g. StAT 2 167; 178; 191). He belonged to the circles of *Urdu-Aššur* 5. and *Kiṣir-Aššur* 45., the principal protagonists of the N31-archive. As for the ethnicity and status of this man, Pruzsinszky concludes that, "he himself may have been of Egyptian extraction", and O. Pedersén (1986: 127) argues that, "it seems reasonable to assume that most of the people attested in this archive [N31] belong to a group of partly assimilated Egyptians, probably under the leadership of La-turammanni-Aššur". His name, which calls upon the main Assyrian deity, naturally tells of assimilation. The above-mentioned time range of 655-613 BCE is defined by StAT 3 81 (655) and StAT 3 92 (613).

Lū-šakin 14.

The twelfth individual of this category is *Lū-šakin* 14. This individual of masculine gender is presented as a son of *Abši-Ešu*▪, whose name is Egyptian and accompanied by an Egyptian ethnonym. *Lū-šakin* 14. appears in a text (SAA 6 311) from Nineveh and 666 BCE as the seller (with his brother *Issar-dūrī* 26.) of a house in Bet-Eriba-ilu to *Rēmanni-Adad*, "chief chariot driver of Ashurbanipal", for four minas of silver, by the mina of Carchemish.[494]

On the basis of the above data, identities, properties, and settings can be identified. *Lū-šakin* 14. seems to have been an Egyptian, a male, an adult, and a commoner. He lived in the reign of Ashurbanipal, and he seems to have been a resident of the western city of Bet-Eriba-ilu. The circumstances leading to this individual being in this part of Assyria are difficult to pin down, but it is likely that he or older relatives of his came to Assyria forcibly via deportation.[495]

Mullissu-ḫāṣinat

The 13th individual of this category is *Mullissu-ḫāṣinat*. This individual of feminine gender is presented as the granddaughter of *Amu-rṭēše*▪ 2., whose name is Egyptian. *Mullissu-ḫāṣinat* appears in a text (SAA 14 161) from Nineveh and 623 BCE as sold by her father *Nabû-rēḫtu-uṣur* 17. for 18 shekels of silver to the woman *Niḫti-Eša-rau*▪ as a wife for her son *Ṣi-ḫû*▪ 4.[496]

On the basis of the above data, the interrogative words who, what, when, and where can be responded to. *Mullissu-ḫāṣinat* seems to have been an Egyptian, a female, an adult, and a commoner. She lived in the post-Ashurbanipal period, and he seems to have been a resident of Nineveh. The question of how this individual ended up in Assyria is difficult to answer, but it is likely that she or older relatives of her came there forcibly by means of deportation.[497]

Mutakkil-Aššur 23.

The 14th individual of this category is *Mutakkil-Aššur* 23. This individual of masculine gender is presented as the son of *Kūsāiu* 3., whose name means "the Kushite". In a text (StAT 1 55) from Assur and the seventh century BCE, *Mutakkil-Aššur* 23., son of *Kūsāiu* 3., is instructed to give good-quality silver to someone

---

494 Drawing from the text publication and the PNA-entry of A. Berlejung (PNA 2/II, p. 671).

495 Berlejung identifies the name in question as Akkadian, meaning "May he be placed!". There is no African name among the six names of witnesses to the transaction in question. Also, the Akkadian name of this Egyptian naturally tells of some degree of assimilation.

496 Drawing from the text publication and the PNA-entry of M. Weszeli (PNA 2/II, p. 766).

497 Weszeli identifies the name as Akkadian, meaning "Mullissu is the one who protects". There are Egyptian names, both among the three guarantors and among the 15 witnesses. The name of this individual, incorporating the name of an Assyrian goddess, naturally tells of assimilation.

whose name has not been preserved. Probably the same man is mentioned in a fragmentary text (WVDOG 152 I.24) from Assur and the reign of Ashurbanipal or later as the father of *Kusāiu* (9.), who owes someone unknown silver.[498]

On the basis of the above data, identities, properties, and settings can be identified. *Mutakkil-Aššur* 23. seems to have been a Kushite, a male, an adult, and a commoner. He lived in the reign of Ashurbanipal or the following period, and he seems to have been a resident of Assur. The circumstances leading to this individual being in Assyria are difficult to pin down, but it is likely that he or older relatives of his came to Assyria forcibly through deportation.[499]

Nabû-rēḫtu-uṣur 17.

The 15th individual of this category is *Nabû-rēḫtu-uṣur* 17. This individual of masculine gender is presented as a son of *Amu-rṭēše*▪ 2., whose name is Egyptian. *Nabû-rēḫtu-uṣur* 17. is mentioned in a text (SAA 14 161) from Nineveh and 623 BCE as selling his daughter *Mullissu-ḫāṣinat* to the woman *Niḫti-Eša-rau*▪ as a wife for her son *Ṣi-ḫû*▪ 4. for 18 shekels of silver. He is also qualified as "the Hasaean, employee of *Ur[du-Issar]*, from Fuller Town" (*Ḫasāiu ša qāt Ur[du-Issar] ša libbi āl ašlākī*).[500]

On the basis of the above data, the interrogative words who, what, when, and where can be responded to. *Nabû-rēḫtu-uṣur* 17. seems to have been an Egyptian, a male, an adult, and a commoner. He lived in the post-Ashurbanipal period, and he seems to have been a resident of Nineveh. The question of how this individual ended up in Assyria is difficult to answer, but it is likely that he or older relatives of his came to Assyria forcibly by means of deportation.[501]

Nādinu (26.)

The 16th individual of this category is *Nādinu* (26.). This individual of masculine gender is presented as a close relative to *Ašāia*, "the Egyptian (woman)". *Nādinu* (26.) is mentioned in several texts from Assur and the reign of Ashurbanipal or later, such as in the texts where *Ašāia* "of the household of *Nādinu*" (*(ina) bīt*

---

498 Drawing from the text publications and the PNA-entry of H.D. Baker (PNA 2/I, pp. 782-784).

499 Baker identifies the name as Akkadian, meaning "the one who inspires trust is *Aššur*". Both the father and a son of this man then had the name *Kūsāiu*. His personal name, which incorporates the name of the main Assyrian god, naturally tells of assimilation. The text in question comes from the archive of *Dūrī-Aššur* (known as Assur 52a), which mentions numerous Egyptians.

500 Drawing from the text publication and the PNA-entry of H.D. Baker (PNA 2/II, p. 862).

501 Baker identifies the name as Akkadian, meaning "O *Nabû*, protect the remaining one!". There are Egyptian names, both among the three guarantors and among the 15 witnesses. Apparently, he was a fuller (*ašlāku*) and had some connection to the toponym of Hasa. For the toponym of Hasa (not found in RGTC 7/1-2), see PNA 4/I, p. 243. *Nabû-rēḫtu-uṣur* 17. is also presented as having two sons, named *Kanūnāiu* and *Silim-Adad*, in the document. His personal name, which incorporates the name of an important Mesopotamian god, naturally tells of assimilation.

Nādin) contributes silver to trade trips conducted by *Kiṣir-Nabû* (WVDOG 152 I.36), by *Muqallil-kabti* (I.39), and by someone whose name has not been preserved (I.43). *Ašāia*, as a part "of the household of the son of *Nādinu*" (*ina bīt apal Nādin*), features in a financial statement tied to an amount of silver (I.56).[502]

On the basis of the above data, identities, properties, and settings can be identified. *Nādinu* (26.). appears to have been an Egyptian, a male, an adult, and a commoner. He lived in the reign of Ashurbanipal or later, and he seems to have been a resident of Assur. The circumstances leading to this individual being in Assyria are difficult to pin down, but it is likely that he or older relatives of his came to Assyria forcibly through deportation.[503]

Pašî 9.

The 17th individual of this category is *Pašî* 9. This individual of masculine gender is presented as the (young) son of *Apî*▪ 2., whose name is Egyptian. Also, the name of this individual has been identified as possibly Egyptian, although its exact meaning is unclear. *Pašî* 9. is mentioned in a text (KAN 4 7) from Assur and 624 BCE where *Ṭāb-Bēl* 7. pays 30 shekels of silver to *Bīšâ* and thereby redeems his sister *Apî* 2. and her son *Pašî* 9.[504]

On the basis of the above data, the interrogative words who, what, when, and where can be responded to. *Pašî* 9. seems to have been an Egyptian, a male, a child, and a commoner. He lived in the post-Ashurbanipal period, and he appears to have been a resident of the city of Assur. The question of how this individual ended up in Assyria is difficult to answer, but it is likely that he or older relatives of his came to Assyria forcibly by means of deportation.[505]

Rībāia 11.

The 18th individual of this category is *Rībāia* (or *Rība-Aya*) 11. This individual of masculine gender is presented as a brother of *Meia*▪, whose name is Egyptian. *Rībāia* 11. appears in a text (CT 53 974) from Assur and the seventh century BCE as the receiver of a letter from his brother *Gula-ēṭir* 3., in which he is urged to be vigilant and not let *Meia* go out of the house.[506]

---

502 Drawing from the text publication. This individual does not seem to be included in PNA(o).

503 It is possible but doubtful that he can be equated with *Nādin(u)* 16.-18. (with 18. the most likely one). H.D. Baker (PNA 2/II, pp. 919-921) identifies the name as abbreviated and as Akkadian, meaning "the one who gives". It is likely that the woman in question was a close relative to *Nādinu* (26.), and not a servant or a slave. Otherwise, *Ašāia* could hardly have acted as independently as she did. The texts in question come from the archive of *Dūrī-Aššur* (known as Assur 52a), which mentions numerous Egyptians.

504 Drawing from the text publication and the PNA-entry of A.M. Bagg (PNA 3/I, p. 992).

505 Bagg suggests that the name is either Egyptian or Akkadian. It is not clear who this *Bīšâ* was and how *Apî* 2. became subservient to him.

506 Drawing from the text publication and the PNA-entry of M.C. Perroudon (PNA 3/I, p. 1051).

On the basis of the above data, identities, properties, and settings can be identified. *Rībāia* 11. seems to have been an Egyptian, a male, an adult, and a commoner. He lived some time in the seventh century BCE, and he seems to have been a resident of Assur. The circumstances leading to this individual being in Assyria are difficult to pin down, but it is likely that he or older relatives of his came to Assyria forcibly through deportation.[507]

Sabutî

The 19th individual of this category is *Sabutî*. This individual of masculine gender is presented as a son of *Puṭikiše*▪, whose name is Egyptian. *Sabutî* is mentioned in a fragmentary text (WVDOG 152 II.10) from the Assur 52b-archive, Assur, and the reign of Ashurbanipal or later as the object of litigation, with his father *Puṭikiše* on one side and *Puṭupašte*▪ and the woman *Lābê*▫ (2.) on the other side.[508]

On the basis of the above data, the interrogative words who, what, when, and where can be responded to. *Sabutî* seems to have been an Egyptian, a male, a child, and a commoner. He lived in the reign of Ashurbanipal or later, and he seems to have been a resident of the city of Assur. The question of how this individual ended up in Assyria is difficult to answer, but it is likely that he or older relatives of his came to Assyria forcibly by means of deportation.[509]

Sē'-aqāba 1.

The 20th individual of this category is *Sē'-aqāba* 1. This individual of masculine gender is presented as the father of the boy *Kūsāiu*▪ 1., whose name means "the Kushite". *Sē'-aqāba* 1. appears in a text (SAA 11 201) from Nineveh and the reign of Sargon II as listed (together with his sons *Šēr-manāni* and *Kūsāiu* 1.) in a census over people in the Harran region. He is the head of a family of dependent workers responsible for a grove of *šaššūgu*-trees in the town of Yanibir-suhuri. In this context, *Sē'-aqāba* 1. is defined as "guardian of the grove" (*maṣṣar qabli*).[510]

On the basis of the above data, identities, properties, and settings can be identified. *Sē'-aqāba* 1. seems to have been a Kushite, a male, an adult, and a commoner. He lived in the reign of Sargon II, and he seems to have been a resident of the western part of Assyria. The circumstances leading to this individual being

---

[507] Perroudon identifies the name as Akkadian, meaning "Replace, O *Ea*!". It is not clear why it was so important to not let his sister go out of the house. His personal name, which incorporates the name of an important Mesopotamian deity, naturally tells of assimilation.

[508] Drawing from the text publication. This name/individual is not listed in PNA or PNAo.

[509] The language behind the name *Sabutî* has not been identified. The litigation supposedly concerned an adoption. The text does not state how old *Sabutî* was at the time. The child in question apparently lived in the Egyptian community of Assur.

[510] Drawing from the text publication and the PNA-entry of F.M. Fales (PNA 3/I, p. 1098).

in this corner of Assyria are difficult to pin down, but it is likely that he or older relatives of his came to Assyria forcibly via deportation.[511]

***Sīn-na'di* 27.**

The 21st individual of this category is *Sīn-na'di* 27. This individual of masculine gender is presented as a son of *Muṣurāiu*▪ 6., whose name means "the Egyptian". *Sīn-na'di* 27. is mentioned in a text (BATSH 6 40) from Dur-Katlimmu and 600 BCE as a witness when four individuals (with non-African names) sell a field in Dur-Katlimmu to *Arrî*.[512]

On the basis of the above data, the interrogative words who, what, when, and where can be responded to. *Sīn-na'di* 27. seems to have been an Egyptian, a male, an adult, and a commoner. He lived in the post-imperial period (reign of Nebuchadnezzar II), and he seems to have been a resident of Dur-Katlimmu. The question of how he ended up in this corner of Assyria is difficult to answer, but it is likely that he or older relatives of his came to Assyria forcibly by means of deportation.[513]

***Sukkāia* 43.**

The 22nd individual of this category is *Sukkāia* (or *Sukki-Aia*) 43. This individual of masculine gender is presented as a son of *Muṣurāiu*▪ 4., whose name means "the Egyptian". *Sukkāia* 43. appears in a number of texts from Assur and the reign of Ashurbanipal or later, such as in two texts (WVDOG 152 I.37; I.42) where he, as a son of *Muṣurāiu* 4., contributes seven shekels of silver to a trade trip of *Muqallil-kabti* and at least nine shekels to a trade trip of *Mušēzib-Aššur*. As a "door-keeper of the Nabu temple" (*etû Nabû*), he contributes one quarter of a shekel to another trade trip of *Mušēzib-Aššur* (I.41). Without any attribute attached to his name, he appears tied to half a mina of silver in a financial statement (I.68).[514]

On the basis of the above data, identities, properties, and settings can be identified. *Sukkāia* 43. seems to have been an Egyptian, a male, an adult, and a commoner. He lived in the reign of Ashurbanipal or later, and he seems to have been a resident of the city of Assur. The circumstances leading to this individual

---

511 Fales identifies the name as West Semitic, meaning "Se' has protected". No female individual of this family is listed, with the entry in question ending with the words "a total of 3 people". Judging by his West Semitic name, *Sē'-aqāba* 1. appears to have been integrated. There are no African names listed in the census, which clearly focuses on people involved in cultivation activities.

512 Drawing from the text publication and the PNA-entry of K. Radner (PNA 3/I, p. 1138).

513 Radner identifies the name in question as Akkadian, meaning "Sin is praised". *Sīn-na'di* 27. appears on second place among the eight witnesses, thus telling of his relative social rank. There are no African names in the document. Moreover, his personal name, which incorporates the name of a prominent Mesopotamian god, speaks of some degree of assimilation.

514 Drawing from the text publications and the PNA-entry of K. Radner (PNA 3/I, pp. 1155-1156).

being in Assyria are difficult to pin down, but it is likely that he or older relatives of his came to Assyria forcibly through deportation.[515]

***Šarru-lū-dāri* 33.**

The 23rd individual of this category is *Šarru-lū-dāri* 33. This individual of masculine gender is presented as the father of *Muṣurāiu*▪ 5., whose name means "the Egyptian". *Šarru-lū-dāri* 33. is mentioned in an Aramaic loan contract (AssU6) from Assur and the seventh century BCE as the father of *Muṣurāiu* 5., who acts as a witness for *[...]ysy*.[516]

On the basis of the above data, the interrogative words who, what, when, and where can be responded to. *Šarru-lū-dāri* 33. seems to have been an Egyptian, a male, an adult, and a commoner. He lived some time in the seventh century BCE, and he seems to have been a resident of the city of Assur. The question of how he ended up in Assyria is difficult to answer, but it is likely that he or older relatives of his came to Assyria forcibly via deportation.[517]

Šēr-manāni

The 24th individual of this category is *Šēr-manāni*. This individual of masculine gender is presented as the older brother of *Kūsāiu*▪ 1., whose name means "the Kushite". *Šēr-manāni* appears in a text (SAA 11 201) from Nineveh and the reign of Sargon II as "adolescent" (*ṣa(ḫurtu)*), as living in the Harran region, and as having *Sē'-aqāba* 1., "guardian of the grove" (*maṣṣar qabli*), as his father and *Kūsāiu* 1. as his little brother.[518]

On the basis of the above data, identities, properties, and settings can be identified. *Šēr-manāni* seems to have been a Kushite, a male, a child, and a commoner. He lived in the reign of Sargon II, and he seems to have been a resident of the Harran region. The circumstances leading to this individual being in this

---

[515] The index of K. Radner (2016: 131) also lists WVDOG 152 I.38, I.48, I.52, and II.11 under the entry "Sukkāia". In a PNAo-entry, H.D. Baker suggests that the reference to a *Sukkāia* in StAT 3 67 points to a new individual or to *Sukkāia* 43.-47. The sign A, expressing "son (of)", is actually missing in text I.42. The same supposedly applies in text WVDOG 152 I.33, in which a *Sukkāia* contributes at least two shekels of silver to a trade trip of *Ḫabil-kēnu*. Radner identifies the name as Akkadian, meaning "shrine" or "shrine of Ea". Regarding assimilation, *Sukkāia* 43. has an Akkadian name, and this name (probably) incorporates the name of the Mesopotamian god Ea. Moreover, he was in the service of the Mesopotamian god Nabu, functioning as a door-keeper in the temple dedicated to this deity in Assur. The texts come from the archive of *Dūrī-Aššur* (known as Assur 52a), which mentions numerous Egyptians.

[516] Drawing from the PNA-entry of H.D. Baker (PNA 3/II, p. 1250).

[517] Baker identifies the name as Akkadian, meaning "May the king be eternal!". His Akkadian name, which conveys a loyalist tone (in relation to the Assyrian king and empire), naturally speaks of some degree of assimilation.

[518] Drawing from the text publication and the PNA-entry of H.D. Baker (PNA 3/II, p. 1264).

corner of Assyria are difficult to pin down, but it is likely that he or older relatives of his came to Assyria forcibly through deportation.[519]

Tarḫursi 2.

The 25th individual of this category is *Tarḫursi* 2. This individual of masculine gender is presented as the father of *Ḫur-waṣi*■ 8., whose name is Egyptian. *Tarḫursi* 2. is mentioned in a text (StAT 2 207) from the N31-archive, Assur, and 618 BCE as the father of *Ḫur-waṣi* 8., who acts as a witness when *Bābilāiu* buys a house in Assur from *Urdu-Aššur*, son of *Puṭi-ḫutapiša*■.[520]

On the basis of the above data, the interrogative words who, what, when, and where can be responded to. *Tarḫursi* 2. seems to have been an Egyptian, a male, an adult, and a commoner. He lived in the post-Ashurbanipal period, and he seems to have been a resident of Assur. The question of how he ended up in Assyria is difficult to answer, but it is likely that he or older relatives of his came there forcibly by means of deportation.[521]

Ṭāb-Bēl 7.

The 26th individual of this category is *Ṭāb-Bēl* 7. This individual of masculine gender is presented as the brother of *Apî*■ 2., whose name is Egyptian. *Ṭāb-Bēl* 7. is mentioned in a text (KAN 4 7) from Assur and 624 BCE as redeeming his sister *Apî* 2. and her son *Pašî*□ 9. from an individual named *Bīšâ*, thus setting his relatives free. He takes the money from his share of an inheritance, and the redemption takes place in the presence of several high officials.[522]

On the basis of the above data, identities, properties, and settings can be identified. *Ṭāb-Bēl* 7. seems to have been an Egyptian, a male, an adult, and a commoner. He lived in the post-Ashurbanipal period, and he seems to have been a resident of Assur. The circumstances leading to this individual being in Assyria are difficult to pin down, but it is likely that he or older relatives of his came to Assyria forcibly through deportation.[523]

---

519 Baker identifies the name as Aramaic, meaning "*Šēr* has assigned me". No female individual of this family is listed, with the entry in question ending with the words "a total of 3 people". Judging by his Aramaic name, *Šēr-manāni* 1. appears to have been integrated. There are no African names listed in the census, which clearly focuses on people involved in cultivation activities.

520 Drawing from the text publication and the PNA-entry of R. Pruzsinszky (PNA 3/II, p. 1316).

521 Pruzsinszky proposes that the name is Anatolian. There are 15 witnesses to this property transaction, with the son of *Tarḫursi* appearing on twelfth place. Several of the names of the witnesses bear Egyptian names. The multicultural nature of the Neo-Assyrian empire is evident in this case, with an Egyptian having an Anatolian name and living in the Assyrian heartland.

522 Drawing from the text publication and the PNA-entry of J. Llop (PNA 3/II, p. 1339).

523 Llop identifies the name as Akkadian, meaning "the lord is good / my lord is good". It is not clear why his sister was in this predicament. Possibly, an unpaid debt lead to her slavery.

Ubru-Mullissu

The 27th individual of this category is *Ubru-Mullissu*. This individual of masculine gender is presented as a son of *Ati'*▪, whose name is Egyptian. *Ubru-Mullissu* is mentioned in a text (SAA 14 161) from Nineveh and 623 BCE as a guarantor (along with *Sa-ḫpi-māu*▪ and *Bēl-šumu-iddina*) when *Nabû-rēḫtu-uṣur* 17. sells his daughter *Mullissu-ḫāṣinat* to the woman *Niḫti-Eša-rau*▪ as a wife for her son *Ṣi-ḫû*▪ 4. He (and/or *Ati'*) is qualified as a fuller (*ašlāku*).[524]

On the basis of the above data, the interrogative words who, what, when, and where can be responded to. *Ubru-Mullissu* seems to have been an Egyptian, a male, an adult, and a commoner. He lived in the post-Ashurbanipal period, and he seems to have been a resident of Nineveh. The question of how he ended up in Assyria is difficult to answer, but it is likely that he or older relatives of his came there forcibly by means of deportation.[525]

Ubrūtu 4.

The 28th individual of this category is *Ubrūtu* 4. This individual of masculine gender is presented as the head of a household in which a woman named *Muṣurītu*▪ (3.) (whose name means "the Egyptian") lived. *Ubrūtu* 4. is mentioned in a text (WVDOG 152 I.58) from Assur and the reign of Ashurbanipal or later, which conveys a financial statement, in which six shekels of silver are tied to *Muṣurītu* (3.) "of the household of *Ubrūtu*" (*ina bīt Ubrūte*).[526]

On the basis of the above data, identities, properties, and settings can be identified. *Ubrūtu* 4. seems to have been an Egyptian, a male, an adult, and a commoner. He lived in the reign of Ashurbanipal or later, and he seems to have been a resident of the city of Assur. The circumstances leading to this individual being in Assyria are difficult to pin down, but it is likely that he or older relatives of his came to Assyria forcibly through deportation.[527]

---

[524] Drawing from the text publication and the PNA-entry of H.D. Baker (PNA 3/II, p. 1365).

[525] Baker identifies the name as Akkadian, meaning "client of Mullissu". There are Egyptian names, both among the three guarantors and among the 15 witnesses. His personal name, which incorporates the name of an Assyrian goddess, naturally tells of assimilation.

[526] Drawing from the text publication and the PNA-entry of H.D. Baker (PNA 3/II, p. 1371).

[527] Baker identifies the name as Akkadian, meaning "clientship". Since this woman seems to have acted independently, she must have belonged to the household as a family member rather than as a servant or slave. *Muṣurītu* (3.) of the household of *Ubrūtu* 4. represents the first entry of the list of investors. The Akkadian name of *Ubrūtu* 4. suggests some degree of assimilation. The text comes from the archive of *Dūrī-Aššur* (known as Assur 52a), which mentions numerous Egyptians.

Urdu-Aššur 7.

The 29th individual of this category is *Urdu-Aššur* 7. This individual of masculine gender is presented as a son of *Puṭi-ḫutapiša*▪, whose name is Egyptian. *Urdu-Aššur* 7. appears in a text (StAT 2 207) from the N31-archive, Assur, and 618 BCE as the seller of a house in Assur to *Bābilāiu* for two and a half minas of silver.[528]

On the basis of the above data, the interrogative words who, what, when, and where can be responded to. *Urdu-Aššur* 7. seems to have been an Egyptian, a male, an adult, and a commoner. He lived in the post-Ashurbanipal period, and he seems to have been a resident of Assur. The question of how he ended up in Assyria is difficult to answer, but it is likely that he or older relatives of his came there forcibly by means of deportation.[529]

Urdu-Mullissu 10.

The 30th individual of this category is *Urdu-Mullissu* 10. This individual of masculine gender is presented as a son of *Ḫur-tibû*▪ 2., whose name is Egyptian. *Urdu-Mullissu* 10. appears in a text (CTN 3 41) from Kalhu and 616 BCE as the borrower (together with *Kalbāia* 2., son of *Pi-san-Eši*▪ 2., from Napisina) of half a mina and two shekels of silver from *Nabû-aḫu-uṣur*.[530]

On the basis of the above data, identities, properties, and settings can be identified. *Urdu-Mullissu* 10. seems to have been an Egyptian, a male, an adult, and a commoner. He lived in the post-Ashurbanipal period, and he seems to have been a resident of the town of Napisina. The circumstances leading to this individual being in Assyria are difficult to pin down, but it is likely that he or older relatives of his came to Assyria forcibly through deportation.[531]

Urdu-Nabû 13.

The 31st individual of this category is *Urdu-Nabû* 13. This individual of masculine gender is presented as the father of *Kiṣir-Aššur* (66.), who is referred to as "the Egyptian". *Urdu-Nabû* 13. appears in a text (WVDOG 152 II.9) from the Assur 52b-archive, Assur, and the reign of Ashurbanipal or later as the father of *Kiṣir-*

---

528 Drawing from the text publication and the PNA-entry of R. Jas (PNA 3/II, p. 1400).

529 Jas adds that this individual may be identical with *Urdu-Aššur* 5., and identifies the name as Akkadian, meaning "servant of *Aššur*". There are 15 witnesses to this property transaction. Several of the names of the witnesses bear Egyptian names. His name, which incorporates the name of the main Assyrian god, naturally tells of assimilation.

530 Drawing from the text publication and the PNA-entry of K. Radner (PNA 3/II, p. 1408).

531 Radner identifies the name as Akkadian, meaning "servant of Mullissu". His loan partner, *Kalbaiu* 2., is qualified by an Egyptian patronym, re-inforcing the African context. The names of three witnesses are preserved, with one of these being possibly Egyptian. His personal name, which incorporates the name of an Assyrian goddess, naturally tells of assimilation.

Aššur (66.), an Egyptian who fled Assur and Assyria while owing *Abu-dūrī*, *Urdu-Nanāia*, and *Ahū'a-erība* four shekels of silver.[532]

On the basis of the above data, the interrogative words who, what, when, and where can be responded to. *Urdu-Nabû* 13. seems to have been an Egyptian, a male, an adult, and a commoner. He lived in the reign of Ashurbanipal or later, and he seems to have been a resident of the city of Assur. The question of how he ended up in Assyria is difficult to answer, but it is likely that he or older relatives of his came to Assyria forcibly by means of deportation.[533]

***Urdu-Nanāia* 20.**

The 32nd individual of this category is *Urdu-Nanāia* 20. This individual of masculine gender is presented as the father of the woman *Tamūzītu* 1., who is referred to as "the Egyptian". *Urdu-Nanāia* 20. is mentioned in a text (WVDOG 152 I.35) from Assur and the reign of Ashurbanipal or later as the father of *Tamūzītu* 1., who contributes two shekels of silver to a trade trip of *Kiṣir-Nabû*.[534]

On the basis of the above data, identities, properties, and settings can be identified. *Urdu-Nanāia* 20. seems to have been an Egyptian, a male, an adult, and a commoner. He lived in the reign of Ashurbanipal or later, and he seems to have been a resident of the city of Assur. The circumstances leading to this individual being in Assyria are difficult to pin down, but it is likely that he or older relatives of his came to Assyria forcibly through deportation.[535]

***Zabad* 4.**

The 33rd individual of this category is *Zabad* 4. This individual of masculine gender is presented as the father of *Kūsāiu*▪ 4., whose name means "the Kushite". *Zabad* 4. appears in a text (TH 108) from Guzana and 625 BCE as the father of *Kūsāiu* 4., who (together with *Abu-lēšir*) owe *Adad-milki-ilā'ī* straw and barley.[536]

On the basis of the above data, the interrogative words who, what, when, and where can be responded to. *Zabad* 4. seems to have been a Kushite, a male, an adult, and a commoner. He lived in the post-Ashurbanipal period, and he seems to have been a resident of the city of Guzana. The question of how he ended up in this part

---

[532] Drawing from the text publication and the PNA-entry of K. Radner (PNA 3/II, p. 1410).

[533] Radner identifies the name in question as Akkadian, meaning "servant of *Nabû*". Although the Egyptian context of this individual can be seen clearly, his personal name, which incorporates the name of an important Mesopotamian god, speaks of assimilation.

[534] Drawing from the text publication and the PNA-entry of K. Radner (PNA 3/II, p. 1412).

[535] Radner adds that it is possible that this individual may be identical with *Urdu-Nanāia* 21., and identifies the name as Akkadian, meaning "servant of *Nanāia*". His name, which incorporates the name of a Mesopotamian goddess, speaks of assimilation. The text in question comes from the archive of *Dūrī-Aššur* (known as Assur 52a), which mentions numerous Egyptians.

[536] Drawing from the text publication and the PNA-entry of H.D. Baker (PNA 3/II, p. 1426).

of Assyria is difficult to answer, but it is likely that he or older relatives of his came to Assyria forcibly via deportation.[537]

2.1.4 People identified as Africans via institutional affiliations

The fourth subsection brings up Africans identifiable on the identification ground institutional affiliations, meaning that someone is revealed as African through links to an African institution. Four individuals will be presented and discussed in this subsection.

[...]gurši

The first individual of this category is *[...]gurši*. This individual of masculine gender can be identified as an African on account of institutional affiliation, in his being an Egyptian scholar. *[...]gurši* is mentioned in a text (SAA 7 1) from Nineveh and the reign of Esarhaddon or Ashurbanipal which gives a list of experts at court. *[...]gurši*, *Ra'sî*▪, and *Ṣi-ḫû*▪ 2. are here described as *ḫarṭibu*, namely "(Egyptian) dream interpreters".[538]

On the basis of the above data, the interrogative words who, what, when, and where can be responded to. *[...]gurši* seems to have been an Egyptian, a male, an adult, and a member of the elite. He lived in the reign of Esarhaddon or Ashurbanipal, and he seems to have been a resident of Nineveh. The question of how he ended up in Assyria is difficult to answer, but it is likely that he or older relatives of his came there forcibly by means of deportation. It can not be excluded, however, that *[...]gurši*, with his special skills, arrived in Assyria as a result of peaceful negotiations between rulers.[539]

***Nabû-šēzibanni* 12.**

The second individual of this category is *Nabû-šēzibanni* 12. This individual of masculine gender can be identified as an African on account of institutional affiliation, in his being an Egyptian ruler. *Nabû-šēzibanni* 12. (future Psammetichus I) features in Assyrian royal inscriptions as a main Assyrian vassal in Egypt. He is defined as the son of Necho I (*Nikkû*▪) and as the ruler of the Egyptian city of Athribis. His Assyrian connections are stressed via his Akkadian name and via the Akkadian name (*Limmer-iššak-Aššur*) given to his residential city. Ultimately,

---

537 Baker identifies the name as Aramaic, meaning "he has given". The document does not contain any African names proper. The document derives from the archive of the Assyrian governor in Guzana, *Mannu-kī-Aššur*.

538 Drawing from the text publication. This individual/name is not listed in PNA or PNAo.

539 The language with which this name is written is unclear but likely Egyptian. This group of Egyptian scholars is the penultimate group in this list of experts at court, followed only by a group of three Egyptian scribes. *[...]gurši* appears on first place in the group, possibly indicating rank.

Nabû-šēzibanni 12. became the king of an independent Egypt (as *Pišamilki*▪). Ashurbanipal narrates (after words on pardoning Necho I) that he "appointed (*paqādu*) *Nabû-šēzibanni*, his son, in the city Athribis", and that he "performed (*epēšu*) more kind (and) good deed(s) (*ṭābtu damiqtu*) for him than the father who had engendered me (Esarhaddon)" (RINAP 5/1 6; 11).[540]

On the basis of the above data, identities, properties, and settings can be identified. *Nabû-šēzibanni* 12. was an Egyptian, a male, an adult, and a member of the elite. He lived in the reign of Esarhaddon and Ashurbanipal, and he resided in the Egyptian city of Athribis. The question of how he became integrated into the Neo-Assyrian empire is complex, but it was voluntary in the sense that he (initially) did not offer any resistance.[541]

Qibīt-Aššur 30.

The third individual of this category is *Qibīt-Aššur* 30. This individual of masculine gender can be identified as an African on account of institutional affiliation, in his being an Egyptian priest. *Qibīt-Aššur* 30. is mentioned in a text (*SAAB* 9 127) from Assur and 639 or 636 BCE as a priest in a sanctuary dedicated to the Egyptian god Horus. In this document, he acts as a witness when *Qurdi-Gula* buys the slave *Aššur-balliṭ* from his owner *Zērî*.[542]

On the basis of the above data, the interrogative words who, what, when, and where can be responded to. *Qibīt-Aššur* 30. seems to have been an Egyptian, a male, an adult, and a member of the elite. He lived in the reign of Ashurbanipal, and he seems to have been a resident of the city of Assur. The circumstances leading to this individual being in Assyria are difficult to pin down, but it is likely that he or older relatives of his came there forcibly by means of deportation.[543]

---

[540] Drawing from the text publications and the PNA-entry of E. Frahm (PNA 2/II, p. 881). *Nabû-šēzibanni* 12. is also brought up in Ashurbanipal 207 (available at http://oracc.org/rinap/Q007615/; accessed 2021-08-13).

[541] Frahm identifies this name as Akkadian, meaning "O, *Nabû*, save me!". The text passage in question goes on with narrations of Taharqa's death and the re-conquest activities of Tanutamon. As already noted, the integration of *Nabû-šēzibanni* 12. into the Assyrian sphere is obvious in his being a close Assyrian ally and in the Akkadian names of him and his city. Tellingly, crown princes during Egypt's 22nd and 23rd dynasties were often installed in Athribis (Onasch 1994: 154).

[542] Drawing from the text publication and the PNA-entry of H.D. Baker (PNA 3/I, p. 1013).

[543] Baker brings up the suggestion (see Radner 1999: 74) that he may be equated with *Qibīt-Aššur* 17., a priest of the Babylonian god Nabu. Baker also identifies the name in question as Akkadian, meaning "command of *Aššur*". There are 15 witnesses to this transaction, none with an African name. *Qibīt-Aššur* 30. appears on fifth place, last of five priests. The other four priests serve Mesopotamian deities (Marduk, Belat-niphi, Ishtar of Nineveh). His Akkadian name, incorporating the name of the main Assyrian god, naturally tells of assimilation. Having said that, he apparently was a driving force in an Assyrian sanctuary to an Egyptian god. For a brief discussion of this individual with regard to Assyrian-Egyptian interaction, see Karlsson 2021b.

***Šarru-lū-dāri* 13.**

The fourth individual of this category is *Šarru-lū-dāri* 13. This individual of masculine gender may be identified as an African on account of institutional affiliation, in his being an Egyptian ruler. *Šarru-lū-dāri* 13., ruler of the Egyptian city of Pelusium, features in state letters and documents and royal inscriptions from Assyria. As for the former source, the actions of *Nikkû*▪ and *Šarru-lū-dāri* 13. are centred on in a query to the sungod (SAA 4 88). A question whether these will attack an envoy of Esarhaddon (*Ša-Nabû-šû*) to Egypt is posed. As for the latter source, the annals of Ashurbanipal (RINAP 5/1 2; 3; 4; 6; 7; 8; 11) also mention *Šarru-lū-dāri* 13. He appears second in a list of 20 Assyrian vassals in Egypt, rulers installed by Esarhaddon and re-installed by Ashurbanipal. *Nikkû*, *Šarru-lū-dāri* 13., and *Pa-qruru*▪ later break their agreement with Ashurbanipal and make overtures to Taharqa, king of Kush. Ashurbanipal's men in Egypt hear of this and have *Nikkû* and *Šarru-lū-dāri* 13. arrested and brought to Nineveh and Ashurbanipal. The Assyrian king takes pity on *Nikkû* and restores him to office, making him a main Assyrian ally in Egypt, while *Šarru-lū-dāri* 13. (in RINAP 5/1 7) is "thro[wn] into confinement (*kīlu*), a place of eternal detainment (*ašar ṣibitti dārî*(?))".[544]

On the basis of the above data, identities, properties, and settings can be identified. *Šarru-lū-dāri* 13. was an Egyptian, a male, an adult, and a member of the elite. He lived in the reigns of Esarhaddon and Ashurbanipal, and he resided in the Egyptian city of Pelusium. The question of how he became integrated into the Neo-Assyrian empire is complex, but it points both to a voluntary and forced process, linked to the varying responses (from submission to rebellion) to Assyrian demands that this individual expressed.[545]

2.2 Likely and possible Africans

The second section brings up likely and possible Africans and their biographic details. Its first subsection focuses on etymology and on likely or possibly African names (2.2.1), while its second subsection deals with people indirectly identifiable as Egyptians, Kushites, or Libyans (2.2.2). In total, 88 individuals will be presented and discussed in this section.

---

[544] Drawing from the text publications and the PNA-entry of H.D. Baker (PNA 3/II, pp. 1248-1249). *Šarru-lū-dāri* 13. is also brought up in Ashurbanipal 118 and 207 (available at http://oracc.org/rinap/Q003817/ and http://oracc.org/rinap/Q007615/ respectively; accessed 2021-08-13).

[545] Baker identifies the name in question as Akkadian, meaning "May the king be eternal!". In contrast to his subsequent rebellion, his (Akkadian) name indicates loyalty to the Assyrian king. Two texts (RINAP 5/1 3; 4) narrate that *Šarru-lū-dāri* 13. alone (without *Nikkû* or *Pa-qruru*) was captured and brought to Assyria. The same texts also say that he alone "plotted evil deeds against the Assyrians". Pelusium (Akk. *Ṣi'nu*, Eg. *Sin*) was a city in the north-eastern part of the Egyptian delta (RGTC 7/2-2, p. 553).

2.2.1 People with likely and possibly African names

The first subsection centres on Africans identifiable on the identification ground etymology, meaning that the language with which a name is written may identify someone as African. 78 individuals will be presented and discussed in this subsection.[546]

Abdi-mašši

The first individual of this category is *Abdi-mašši*. The name of this individual of masculine gender is possibly Egyptian, in the sense that it may contain the Egyptian word element *msi*. *Abdi-mašši* appears in a text (StAT 2 181) from the N31-archive, Assur, and 629 BCE as a witness when *Aššur-gārû'a-nēre* buys the slave woman *Issar-tukallanni* from *Daiān-Marduk*.[547]

On the basis of the above data, the interrogative words who, what, when, and where can be responded to. *Abdi-mašši* may have been an Egyptian, a male, an adult, and a commoner. He lived in the post-Ashurbanipal period, and he appears to have been a resident of the city of Assur. The question of how he ended up in Assyria is difficult to answer, but it is likely that he or older relatives of his came to Assyria forcibly by means of deportation.[548]

Adimasia

The second individual of this category is *Adimasia*. The name of this individual of feminine gender has been classified as possibly Egyptian, although its exact meaning is unknown. *Adimasia* is mentioned in a text (StAT 2 273) from Assur and 636 BCE as a slave woman being sold by *Ṭāb-Bēl* 8., "the Egyptian", to *Adda-dimrī* for 46 shekels of silver.[549]

---

[546] A note on exclusion: the 16 individuals with the name *Ḫarmāku* (R. Mattila, PNA 2/I, pp. 460-461) are not included, due to the likely Akkadian origin of the name and the non-African contexts of the bearers of this name. Mattila appears to be right in claiming that, "there is…no indication that Ḫarmaku/i might be an Egyptian name or that any of the following people were of Egyptian origin", contra E. Edel (1980: 37-40), who sees a link to the name *Ḫur-maḫi* (Eg. *Ḥr-m-ꜣḫt*) attested in Babylonian sources. Following the conclusions in the PNA-entry by R. Mattila and M.P. Streck (PNA 2/I, pp. 453-454), the name *Ḫannî* is not classified as Egyptian (but as West Semitic), contra A. Leahy (1993: 58). *Karme/uni*, listed and classified as possibly Egyptian by H. Ranke (1910: 37) and K. Tallqvist (1914: 112), does not seem to be a personal name.

[547] Drawing from the text publication and a PNAo-entry of H.D. Baker (the name/individual in question is not listed in PNA).

[548] Regarding etymology, the verb *msi* can appear as *mašši* in the cuneiform script (Ranke 1910: 51). Moreover, this individual appears in an "archive of Egyptians". Concerning textual content and context, *Abdi-mašši* is mentioned towards the end of the list of witnesses, which comprises around 20 names. He is without a title, but the titles of other witnesses suggest a military setting. Several people have Egyptian names.

[549] Drawing from the text publication and the PNA-entry of K. Radner (PNA 1/I, p. 53).

On the basis of the above data, identities, properties, and settings can be identified. *Adimasia* may have been an Egyptian, a female, an adult, and a slave. She lived in the later part of the reign of Ashurbanipal, and she seems to have been a resident of the city of Assur. The circumstances leading to this individual being in Assyria are difficult to pin down, but it is likely that she or older relatives of her came to Assyria forcibly through deportation.[550]

Amman-appu

The third individual of this category is *Amman-appu*. The name of this individual of masculine gender can be classified as possibly Egyptian, then meaning "Amun is in the Luxor temple" (Eg. *Imn-m-Ipt*), referring to the Egyptian god Amun. *Amman-appu* appears in a (literary) text (SAA 3 30) from Nineveh and the reign of Ashurbanipal concerning magic against *Bēl-ēṭir*, an enemy of Assyria. The activities of *Amman-appu* are advised against in this context. He may also be the one mentioned (then as *Amman-appi*) in a fragmentary administrative letter (SAA 21 149) from Nineveh and the reign of Ashurbanipal as having written something to someone, with the details unclear due to the broken state of the tablet.[551]

On the basis of the above data, the interrogative words who, what, when, and where can be responded to. *Amman-appu* may have been an Egyptian, a male, an adult, and a member of the elite. He lived in the reign of Ashurbanipal, but his place of residence is unclear. He may have had his base in Egypt, or he may have acted from a vassal state or from Assyria. The question of how he (in some form) became a part of Assyria is difficult to answer, considering the great uncertainties surrounding the identity of this individual. Apparently, he worked against Assyrian interests in some way.[552]

---

550 Regarding etymology, Radner states that the origin of the name is unknown but that it is "possibly Egyptian". Radner presumably centres on the Egyptian textual context and on an analysis that the name in question can not be conclusively tied to another language. Concerning textual content and context, there is no list of witnesses (or any other elaboration other than the date).

551 Drawing from the text publications and the PNA-entries of R. Mattila (PNA 1/I, p. 102) and H.D. Baker and S. Parpola (PNA 2/II, p. 967).

552 Regarding etymology, Mattila sees *Amman-appu* as Elamite, referring to a study by R. Zadok (1984: 11). S. Parpola notes the name "Amun is in the Luxor temple" as well-attested and points to the circumstance that *Bēl-ēṭir* is linked to an Egyptian (*Nummurīja*) in the other text (SAA 3 29) that mentions *Bēl-ēṭir*. For attestations of the name *Imn-m-Ipt* in Assyrian and Egyptian texts, see Ranke 1910: 7; 1935: 27:18, and Tallqvist 1914: 20. As for his name, the Luxor temple was a sanctuary for Amun in Thebes (Shaw and Nicholson 1995: 165). Concerning textual content and context, the role of *Amman-appu* is unclear also in the former, well-preserved text, which contains a passage saying that, "Bibiya, whose abuses are many – A[mmana]ppu gave your *gypsum*, saying: '*Firstly*, his house is dark, *beginning and start*.' He swore by Bel: 'I will not let go until I have fornicated with him'". *Amman-appu* apparently belonged to the elite, in his being linked to state policy and to an important enemy of Assyria.

Amû

The fourth individual of this category is *Amû*. The name of this individual of masculine gender is possibly Egyptian, in the sense that it may contain the Egyptian word element *Imn*, which is the name of the Egyptian god Amun. *Amû* is mentioned in a text (StAT 2 218) from the N31-archive, Assur, and 612 BCE as a witness when *Kuzub-I[ssa]r* borrows something unknown (due to a lacuna) from a certain *Urdu-Aššur*.[553]

On the basis of the above data, identities, properties, and settings can be identified. *Amû* may have been an Egyptian, a male, an adult, and a commoner. He lived in the post-Ashurbanipal period, and he appears to have been a resident of the city of Assur. The circumstances leading to this individual being in Assyria are difficult to pin down, but it is likely that he or older relatives of his came to Assyria forcibly through deportation.[554]

Aptaḫar[...]

The fifth individual of this category is *Aptaḫar[...]*. The name of this individual of masculine gender is possibly Egyptian, in the sense that it may contain the Egyptian word element *Ptḥ*, which is the name of the Egyptian god Ptah. *Aptaḫar[...]* appears in a text (StAT 2 164) from the N31-archive, Assur, and 675 BCE as a witness when *Pabbā'u*▫ gives his daughter (a votaress of Ishtar of Arbela) *Mullissu-ḫammat* to *Awa* (1.), son of *Tap-naḫte*▪ 1., in marriage.[555]

On the basis of the above data, the interrogative words who, what, when, and where can be responded to. *Aptaḫar[...]* may have been an Egyptian, a male, an adult, and a commoner. He lived in the reign of Esarhaddon, and he appears to have been a resident of the city of Assur. The question of how he ended up in Assyria is difficult to answer, but it is likely that he or older relatives of his came to Assyria forcibly by means of deportation.[556]

---

[553] Drawing from the text publication and a PNAo-entry of H.D. Baker (the name/individual in question is not listed in PNA).

[554] Regarding etymology, the name *Imn* can appear as *Amû* in cuneiform, as evidenced in *Amu-rṭēše* (Ranke 1910: 44). Amun is attested as a personal name in the Egyptian onomasticon (Ranke 1935: 26:18). Adding to all this, *Amû* appears in an "archive of Egyptians". Concerning textual content and context, *Amû* is mentioned on fourth place in the list of witnesses, which comprises six names. There are no other Egyptian names in the document.

[555] Drawing from the text publication and a PNAo-entry of H.D. Baker (the name/individual in question is not listed in PNA).

[556] Regarding etymology, the name *Ptḥ* can appear as *(P)taḫ* and similar *Iptiḫ* in cuneiform (Ranke 1910: 50). Numerous names in the Egyptian onomasticon start with this divine name, among them *Ptḥ-ir-di-sw* (Ranke 1935: 138-142). Moreover, this individual appears in an "archive of Egyptians". Concerning textual content and context, this man is mentioned on ninth place in the list of witnesses, which comprises twelve names, several of these Egyptian. He is without a title, but several other witnesses are qualified as priests, implying a cultic setting.

Ata'

The sixth individual of this category is *Ata'*. The name of this individual of masculine gender has been classified as likely Egyptian, although its exact meaning is unknown. *Ata'* is mentioned in a text (StAT 2 184) from the N31-archive, Assur, and the reign of Ashurbanipal or later as giving his sister *Silim-Puṭi-lumur*, a votaress of Ishtar of Arbela, to *Riḫpi-Mūnu*▫ as a wife, with wedding gifts (*zublānû*) and a dowry (*nadunnû*) exchanged.[557]

On the basis of the above data, identities, properties, and settings can be identified. *Ata'* seems to have been an Egyptian, a male, an adult, and a commoner. He lived in the reign of Ashurbanipal or later, and he seems to have been a resident of the city of Assur. The circumstances leading to this individual being in Assyria are difficult to pin down, but it is likely that he or older relatives of his came to Assyria forcibly through deportation.[558]

Attâ-ḫāsi

The seventh individual of this category is *Attâ-ḫāsi*. The name of this individual of feminine gender has been classified as possibly Egyptian, although its exact meaning is unknown. *Attâ-ḫāsi* is mentioned in a text (ND 2315) from Kalhu and 663 BCE as the buyer of a slave woman (whose name is lost) from *Amu-rṭēše*▪ 1. for 30 shekels of silver.[559]

On the basis of the above data, the interrogative words who, what, when, and where can be responded to. *Attâ-ḫāsi* may have been an Egyptian, a female, an adult, and a commoner. She lived in the reign of Ashurbanipal, and she appears to have been a resident of the city of Kalhu. The question of how she ended up in Assyria is difficult to answer, but it is likely that she or older relatives of her came to Assyria forcibly by means of deportation.[560]

---

557 Drawing from the text publication and the PNA-entry of R. Mattila (PNA 1/I, p. 230).

558 Regarding etymology, Mattila states that the name is unknown but that it is "probably Egyptian". The name is brought up also in Ranke 1910: 36 and Tallqvist 1914: 47. Both scholars classify the name as possibly Egyptian. Moreover, this individual appears in an "archive of Egyptians". As for textual content and context, there are around 20 witnesses to this marriage affair. Several of these have Egyptian names. The prominent Egyptian *Lā-turammanni-Aššur* 3.-4. heads the list.

559 Drawing from the description of this text by B. Parker (1954: 40) and the PNA-entry of K. Radner (PNA 1/I, p. 233).

560 Regarding etymology, Radner also claims that the name alternatively may be Semitic and that it (if so) may be related to the name *Mullissu-ḫāṣinat*. In her main interpretation, Radner presumably centres on the Egyptian textual context and on an analysis that the name in question can not be conclusively tied to another language. Concerning textual content and context, Parker states that the names of all (twelve) witnesses are broken. It is noticeable that a woman (in this case *Attâ-ḫāsi*) appears as relatively independent economically.

Daia 1.

The eighth individual of this category is *Daia* 1. The name of this individual of masculine gender has been classified as possibly Egyptian, in the sense that it may contain the Egyptian word element *dyy*. *Daia* 1. appears in a fragmentary text (StAT 2 4) from Assur and 692 BCE as the guarantor when *[...]-naṣapi* and another person (whose name is lost) borrow silver from (probably) the temple of the Assyrian goddess Ishtar of Arbela.[561]

On the basis of the above data, identities, properties, and settings can be identified. *Daia* 1. may have been an Egyptian, a male, an adult, and a commoner. He lived in the reign of Sennacherib, and he seems to have been a resident of the city of Assur. The circumstances leading to this individual being in Assyria are difficult to pin down, but it is likely that he or older relatives of his came to Assyria forcibly through deportation.[562]

Daia 2.

The ninth individual of this category is *Daia* 2. This man appears in a text (*SAAB* 5 25) from Assur and 644 or 625 BCE as a guarantor for the silver which *Nabû-gammuli* owes to *Kanūnāiu*. He may also be the one mentioned in a very fragmentary text (*SAAB* 9 83) from Assur, in which he acts as a witness in a case or transaction which is unclear (due to lacunae). In the former text, *Daia* 2. may be defined as a "master builder" (*etinnu*).[563]

On the basis of the above data, the interrogative words who, what, when, and where can be responded to. *Daia* 2. may have been an Egyptian, a male, an adult, and a member of the elite. He lived in the reign of Ashurbanipal or later, and he appears to have been a resident of the city of Assur. The question of how he ended up in Assyria is difficult to answer, but it is likely that he or older relatives of his came to Assyria forcibly by means of deportation.[564]

---

[561] Drawing from the text publication and the PNA-entry of R. Pruzsinszky (PNA 1/II, p. 367).

[562] Regarding etymology, Pruzsinszky suggests that this name, written ^{m}*da-a-a* or ^{m}*da-a-ia*, is Egyptian or Semitic, citing T. Schneider (1992: 207), among others. It is not clear what Egyptian *dyy* Pruzsinszky speaks of, but Schneider focuses on the name of an Asiatic ruler in a text from New Kingdom Egypt. Schneider brings up an interpretation that is based on a common(?) Semitic word for "hand" (Eg. *d(rt)*), but he himself sees an Ugaritic, Hebrew, and Arabic word for "bird of prey". Alternatively, it may express the Egyptian passive participle *diy*, even though *(r)di* tends to be written with *t* or *ṭ* in cuneiform (Ranke 1910: 55). Names beginning with *(r)di* were quite common in Egypt (Ranke 1935: 396-398). Concerning textual content and context, there are five witnesses to this loan. None of these have an African name.

[563] Drawing from the text publications and the PNA-entry of R. Pruzsinszky (PNA 1/II, p. 367).

[564] The reading "master builder" is proposed by K. Deller (see Fales and Jakob-Rost 1991: 61). F.M. Fales and L. Jakob-Rost (1991) propose the reading Ì.DU$_8$, suggesting that he was a gate guard instead. The reading A.BA, pointing to the scribal profession, is given at Oracc (http://oracc.org/atae/x991025; accessed 2021-08-14). None of the five witnesses in the former document have an

***Daiâ* 1.**

The tenth individual of this category is *Daiâ* 1. The name of this individual of masculine gender has been classified as possibly Egyptian, in the sense that it may contain the Egyptian word element *dyy*. *Daiâ* 1. appears in a text (SAA 6 202) from Nineveh and 680 BCE as a witness when *Mannu-kī-Arbail* buys a vineyard in the city of Kipshuna from the scribe *Balṭāia*.[565]

On the basis of the above data, identities, properties, and settings can be identified. *Daiâ* 1. may have been an Egyptian, a male, an adult, and a commoner. He lived in the reign of Esarhaddon, and he seems to have been a resident of the city of Kipshuna. The circumstances leading to this individual being in Assyria are difficult to pin down, but it is likely that he or older relatives of his came to Assyria forcibly through deportation.[566]

***Daiâ* 2.**

The eleventh individual of this category is *Daiâ* 2. This man appears in a text (SAA 14 97) from Nineveh and 646 BCE as a witness when *Ubbuku* and *Muškēnu-lā-aḫi* lend silver to *Tuqūn-Issar*, "bowmaker of Ashur", against a pledge (the latter's slave *Nabû-nādin-aḫi*).[567]

On the basis of the above data, the interrogative words who, what, when, and where can be responded to. *Daiâ* 2. may have been an Egyptian, a male, an adult, and a commoner. He lived in the reign of Ashurbanipal, and he appears to have been a resident of the city of Nineveh. The question of how he ended up in Assyria is difficult to answer, but it is likely that he or older relatives of his came to Assyria forcibly by means of deportation.[568]

African name. *Daia* 2. appears on fourth place of the five names of witnesses preserved in the latter document. He alone has a (possibly) African name.

565 Drawing from the text publication and the PNA-entry of R. Pruzsinszky (PNA 1/II, p. 367).

566 Regarding etymology, Pruzsinszky suggests that this name, written ^{m}*da-ia-a*, is Egyptian or Semitic, citing T. Schneider (1992: 207), among others. It is not clear what Egyptian *dyy* Pruzsinszky speaks of, but Schneider focuses on the name of an Asiatic ruler in a text from New Kingdom Egypt. Schneider brings up an interpretation that is based on a common(?) Semitic word for "hand" (Eg. *d(rt)*), but he himself sees an Ugaritic, Hebrew, and Arabic word for "bird of prey". Alternatively, it may express the Egyptian passive participle *diy*, even though *(r)di* tends to be written with *t* or *ṭ* in cuneiform (Ranke 1910: 55). Names beginning with *(r)di* were quite common in Egypt (Ranke 1935: 396-398). Concerning textual content and context, *Daiâ* 1. appears as number six of seven witnesses. There is no other African name. Kipshuna was situated north of the Assyrian heartland, despite a reference to "the mina of Carchemish" (RGTC 7/2-1, pp. 343-344).

567 Drawing from the text publication and the PNA-entry of R. Pruzsinszky (PNA 1/II, p. 367).

568 *Daiâ* 2. appears as number four of eight witnesses. There is no other African name in the text.

***Daiâ* 3.**

The twelfth individual of this category is *Daiâ* 3. This man is mentioned in a text (WVDOG 152 I.17) from Assur and 637 BCE as a witness when *Bakuri* and *[Dūrī-Aššur]* appear to agree to exchange agricultural fields with one another.[569]

On the basis of the above data, identities, properties, and settings can be identified. *Daiâ* 3. may have been an Egyptian, a male, an adult, and a commoner. He lived in the reign of Ashurbanipal, and he seems to have been a resident of the city of Assur. The circumstances leading to this individual being in Assyria are difficult to pin down, but it is likely that he or older relatives of his came to Assyria forcibly through deportation.[570]

***Daiâ* (4.)**

The 13th individual of this category is *Daiâ* (4.). This man appears in a text (Edubba 10 28) from Kalhu and 793 or 773 BCE as (along with *Kandilanu* and *Šamaš-na'id*) selling(?) farmland to the "shepherd of the queen" *Ṭāb-aḫūnu* for 100 minas of copper. The group of three is described as from the town Ikamaraia, "palace shepherds under the authority of the chief cook" (*rē'āni ša ekalli ša qāt*(?) *rab nuḫatimmi*).[571]

On the basis of the above data, the interrogative words who, what, when, and where can be responded to. *Daiâ* (4.) may have been an Egyptian, a male, an adult, and a commoner. He lived in the reign of Adad-narari III or Shalmaneser IV, and he appears to have been a resident of the town of Ikamaraia. The question of how he ended up in Assyria is difficult to answer, but it is likely that he or older relatives of his came to Assyria forcibly through deportation.[572]

***Daiaî* (1.)**

The 14th individual of this category is *Daiaî* (1.). The name of this individual of masculine gender has been identified as possibly Egyptian, in the sense that it may contain the Egyptian word element *dyy*. *Daiaî* (1.) appears in a number of texts from Kalhu and the time range of 662-641 BCE as a witness for the local Nabu

---

[569] Drawing from the text publication and the PNA-entry of R. Pruzsinszky (PNA 1/II, p. 367).

[570] *Daiâ* 3. appears as number seven of eight witnesses. There is no other African name in the document, just *Kūsāiu* (10.), meaning "the Kushite". The text in question comes from the archive of *Dūrī-Aššur* (known as Assur 52a), which mentions numerous Egyptians.

[571] Drawing from the text publication and a PNAo-entry of H.D. Baker (the individual in question is not listed in PNA).

[572] There are around 15 witnesses to this affair. None of these have an African name. Obviously, *Daiâ* (4.) was a shepherd (*rē'û*) tied to the local palace and its chief cook. The early date of this tablet is noteworthy, raising further questions regarding how *Daiâ* (4.) came to Assyria. Ikamaraia may have been situated in the Assyrian heartland or in a neighboring region (RGTC 7/2-1, p. 243).

temple when various people (including people of high rank) borrow barley from the temple, namely when the gardener *Bēl-abu-uṣur* and the cupbearer *Nabû-nādin* owe barley (CTN 6 16), when the farmer *Aḫu-lā-amašši* borrows barley (CTN 6 23), when *Nabû-nādin-aḫi* owes barley (CTN 6 20), when *Mušallim-Issar* borrows barley (CTN 6 21), when the forester *Aḫu-erība* owes barley (CTN 6 26), when the gate guard *Arzāni* owes barley (CTN 6 24), when the herald *Dadâ* borrows barley (CTN 6 19), and when *Nabû-turṣanni* owes barley (CTN 6 40). He also witnesses when *Šamaš-šarru-uṣur* buys a house from *Nabû-pî-aḫi-uṣur*, "verger of Nabu" (CTN 6 60). *Daiaî* (1.) is presented as a gate guard (*etû*), probably of the Mesopotamian sanctuary in question.[573]

On the basis of the above data, identities, properties, and settings can be identified. *Daiaî* (1.) may have been an Egyptian, a male, an adult, and a commoner. He lived in the reign of Ashurbanipal, and he seems to have been a resident of the city of Kalhu. The circumstances leading to this individual being in Assyria are difficult to pin down, but it is likely that he or older relatives of his came to Assyria forcibly through deportation.[574]

Daiaî (2.)

The 15th individual of this category is *Daiaî* (2.). This man is mentioned in a text (StAT 3 63) from Assur and 615 BCE as a witness in a lawsuit between *Lā-immašši* and *Adad-milki-ēreš* (a lawsuit initiated by the former) concerning an ox.[575]

On the basis of the above data, the interrogative words who, what, when, and where can be responded to. *Daiaî* (2.) may have been an Egyptian, a male, an adult, and a commoner. He lived in the post-Ashurbanipal period, and he appears to have been a resident of the city of Assur. The question of how he ended up in Assyria is

---

573 Drawing from the text publication and the PNA-entry of R. Pruzsinszky (PNA 1/II, p. 367). There are four more attestations, not brought up in the PNA-entry. These can be found in texts CTN 6 22; 32; 33; 48, with *Daiaî* (1.) acting as a witness for the temple.

574 Regarding etymology, Pruzsinszky suggests that this name, written ^{m}*da-a-a-i*, is Egyptian or Semitic, citing T. Schneider (1992: 207), among others. It is not clear what Egyptian *dyy* Pruzsinszky speaks of, but Schneider focuses on the name of an Asiatic ruler in a text from New Kingdom Egypt. Schneider brings up an interpretation that is based on a common(?) Semitic word for "hand" (Eg. *d(rt)*), but he himself sees an Ugaritic, Hebrew, and Arabic word for "bird of prey". Alternatively, it may express the Egyptian passive participle *diy*, even though *(r)di* tends to be written with *t* or *ṭ* in cuneiform (Ranke 1910: 55). Names beginning with *(r)di* were quite common in Egypt (Ranke 1935: 396-398). Concerning textual content and context, *Daiaî* (1.) appears at the end or in the later part of the lists of witnesses, with the exception of texts CTN 6 22 and 60 where he appears late in the first part. There are no other African names in the documents. His working for the Mesopotamian god Nabu naturally tells of assimilation.

575 Drawing from the text publication and a PNAo-entry of H.D. Baker (the individual in question is not listed in PNA).

difficult to answer, but it is likely that he or older relatives of his came to Assyria forcibly by means of deportation.[576]

Daiaia

The 16th individual of this category is *Daiaia*. The name of this individual of masculine gender has been identified as possibly Egyptian, in the sense that it may contain the Egyptian word element *dyy*. *Daiaia* is mentioned in a text (*SAAB* 9 75) from Assur and 683 BCE as a witness when *Šumma-Aššur* buys a house in Assur from the Assur-based palace manager *Bēl-ana-marruqi*. *Daiaia* is qualified as a foot soldier or outrider (*kallāpu*) in the document in question.[577]

On the basis of the above data, identities, properties, and settings can be identified. *Daiaia* may have been an Egyptian, a male, an adult, and a commoner. He lived in the reign of Sennacherib, and he seems to have been a resident of the city of Assur. The circumstances leading to this individual being in Assyria are difficult to pin down, but it is likely that he or older relatives of his came to Assyria forcibly through deportation.[578]

Din-ḫuru

The 17th individual of this category is *Din-ḫuru*. The name of this individual of masculine gender has been identified as possibly Egyptian, then containing the word element *Ḥr*, which gives the name of the Egyptian god Horus. *Din-ḫuru* is mentioned in a text (CTN 3 41) from Kalhu and 616 BCE as a witness when *Kalbāia* 2. and *Urdu-Mullissu* 10. (of the town Napisina), both with Egyptian patronyms, borrow silver from *Nabû-aḫu-uṣur*.[579]

On the basis of the above data, the interrogative words who, what, when, and where can be responded to. *Din-ḫuru* may have been an Egyptian, a male, an adult, and a commoner. He lived in the post-Ashurbanipal period, and he appears to have been a resident of the town of Napisina. The question of how this individual ended

---

576 There are nine witnesses to this lawsuit, with *Daiaî* (2.) appearing on eighth place, indicating his rank. There does not seem to be any other African name in the document.
577 Drawing from the text publication and the PNA-entry of R. Pruzsinszky (PNA 1/II, p. 367).
578 Regarding etymology, Pruzsinszky suggests that this name, written ᵐ*da-a-a-a-a*, is Egyptian or Semitic, citing T. Schneider (1992: 207), among others. It is not clear what Egyptian *dyy* Pruzsinszky speaks of, but Schneider focuses on the name of an Asiatic ruler in a text from New Kingdom Egypt. Schneider brings up an interpretation that is based on a common(?) Semitic word for "hand" (Eg. *d(rt)*), but he himself sees an Ugaritic, Hebrew, and Arabic word for "bird of prey". Alternatively, it may express the Egyptian passive participle *diy*, even though *(r)di* tends to be written with *t* or *ṭ* in cuneiform (Ranke 1910: 55). Names beginning with *(r)di* were quite common in Egypt (Ranke 1935: 396-398). Concerning textual content and context, there are more than 20 witnesses, with *Daiaia* appearing towards the end. A priest, a palace official, and a "commander-of-fifty" are among the witnesses, of whom only *Daiaia* seems to have a (possibly) African name.
579 Drawing from the text publication and the PNA-entry of R. Mattila (PNA 1/II, p. 385).

up in Assyria is difficult to answer, but it is likely that he or older relatives of his came to Assyria forcibly by means of deportation.[580]

Ḫā-bāštī 1.

The 18th individual of this category is *Ḫā-bāštī* 1. The name of this individual of masculine gender has been identified as possibly Egyptian, then containing the Egyptian word element *Ubasti*, which refers to the Egyptian goddess Bastet. *Ḫā-bāštī* 1. is mentioned in a text (SAA 6 245) from Nineveh and 672 BCE as a witness when *Dannāia* takes land and people as a pledge in a payment for an outstanding silver debt owed by someone, possibly a certain *[...]-ṭaba*, who is qualified as "deputy (governor) of Rasappa".[581]

On the basis of the above data, identities, properties, and settings can be identified. *Ḫā-bāštī* 1. may have been an Egyptian, a male, an adult, and a commoner. He lived in the reign of Esarhaddon, and he seems to have been a resident of western Assyria. The circumstances leading to this individual being in this part of Assyria are difficult to pin down, but it is likely that he or older relatives of his came to Assyria forcibly through deportation.[582]

Ḫā-bāštī 2.

The 19th individual of this category is *Ḫā-bāštī* 2. This man is mentioned in numerous texts from Nineveh and the time range of 679-663 BCE, such as when he acts as a witness when *Pilaqqu-lipirê* borrows a mule from *Mannu-kī-Arbail* (SAA 6 206), when the chariot driver *Rēmanni-Adad* buys five slaves from *Iddāti-Bēl-allak*, *Adad-šarru-uṣur*, and *Šarru-šumu-ukīn* (SAA 6 297), and when someone

---

580 Regarding etymology, Mattila regards the name in question as "possibly including the Egyptian theophoric element Horus". It is possible that the first element of the name expresses the verb *di* and the prepositional phrase *n(.i)* (cf. Ranke 1935: 396:21-397:3). Notably, the textual context is Egyptian. Concerning textual content and context, the names of three witnesses have been preserved. *Din-ḫuru* appears on second place, and the other two witnesses have non-African names.

581 Drawing from the text publication and the PNA-entry made by S. Parpola and K. Radner (PNA 2/I, p. 435).

582 Regarding etymology, Parpola and Radner propose that the name is Akkadian, meaning "the brother is my pride", but also bring up the possibilities that the name may be Aramaic/Hebrew, Arabic, or Phoenician (incorporating an Egyptian divine name). If Phoenician (as proposed by E. Lipiński (1983: 127-132)), the name means "brother of Bastet" (*Aḫ-Ubasti*). The name is brought up also in Tallqvist 1914: 15. Tallqvist translates "my (the) brother is abundance" and classifies it as "evidently foreign". The name of Bastet is normally written *Ubešti* or *Uastu* in cuneiform (Ranke 1910: 47). Concerning textual content and context, six people witness this debt settlement, with *Ḫā-bāštī* 1. appearing as "Habasitema" and on fifth place. None of the other witnesses bear an African name. Judging by toponyms in the text (Rasappa, Carchemish), the geographic setting was western Assyria (see RGTC 7/2-2, pp. 506-509 and 7/1, pp. 70-74 resp.).

whose name is lost purchases land and people from *Ḫaldi-[...]* (SAA 6 269). *Ḫā-bāštī* 2. is qualified as a "chief gatekeeper" (*rab etû*).[583]

On the basis of the above data, the interrogative words who, what, when, and where can be responded to. *Ḫā-bāštī* 2. may have been an Egyptian, a male, an adult, and a member of the elite. He lived in the reigns of Esarhaddon and Ashurbanipal, and he appears to have been a resident of Nineveh. The question of how he ended up in Assyria is difficult to answer, but it is likely that he or older relatives of his came to Assyria forcibly via deportation.[584]

Ḫā-bāštī 3.

The 20th individual of this category is *Ḫā-bāštī* 3. This man is mentioned in a text (SAA 14 27) from Nineveh and 640 BCE as the father of the cohort commander *Aššur-šarru-uṣur*, who appears as a witness when someone whose identity is unclear (due to a lacuna) buys land from *Aḫu-lāmur*, ox fattener of the palace, and(?) *Bēl-gimillu-tēre*.[585]

On the basis of the above data, identities, properties, and settings can be identified. *Ḫā-bāštī* 3. may have been an Egyptian, a male, an adult, and a member of the elite. He lived in the reign of Ashurbanipal, and he seems to have been a resident of the city of Nineveh. The circumstances leading to this individual being in Assyria are difficult to pin down, but it is likely that he or older relatives of his came to Assyria forcibly through deportation.[586]

Ḫaḫpi

The 21st individual of this category is *Ḫaḫpi*. The name of this individual of masculine gender can be classified as possibly Egyptian, in the sense that it may contain the Egyptian word element *Ḥp*, which gives the name of the Egyptian divine Apis bull. *Ḫaḫpi* is mentioned in a text (WVDOG 152 II.7) from the Assur 52b-archive, Assur, and the reign of Ashurbanipal or later as one of the witnesses when *Ḫuru[...]*▪ 2. borrows a sum of silver from *Tap[...]*▫.[587]

---

[583] Drawing from the text publications and the PNA-entry of S. Parpola and K. Radner (PNA 2/I, pp. 435-436). *Ḫā-bāštī* 2. also appears in texts ADD 284; 537; SAA 6 211; 218; 220; 247; 278; 283; 307; 308; 323; 324; 325; 328; 332; 340; 348; 350; SAAS 5 no. 3, all the time in the role of witness.

[584] *Ḫā-bāštī* 2. appears in the middle of the first two lists of witnesses, and as number three of 15 witnesses in the third document. None of the other names in these three documents seem to have an African etymology.

[585] Drawing from the text publication and the PNA-entry made by S. Parpola and K. Radner (PNA 2/I, p. 436).

[586] Seven people witness this land sale. The son of *Ḫā-bāštī* 3. appears on third place. There are no other African names in the document. The fact that he had an officer as a son makes it likely that he belonged to the elite. Following a PNAo-entry by H.D. Baker, the name of the person listed in PNA as *Ḫā-bāštī* 4. should be read *Ḫandisi*, which probably conveys a non-African name.

[587] Drawing from the text publication. *Ḫaḫpi* is not listed in PNA or PNAo.

On the basis of the above data, the interrogative words who, what, when, and where can be responded to. *Ḫaḫpi* may have been an Egyptian, a male, an adult, and a commoner. He lived in the reign of Ashurbanipal or later, and he appears to have been a resident of the city of Assur. The question of how he ended up in Assyria is difficult to answer, but it is likely that he or older relatives of his came to Assyria forcibly by means of deportation.[588]

***Ḫallabēše* 1.**

The 22nd individual of this category is *Ḫallabēše* 1. The name of this individual of masculine gender has been identified as possibly Libyan. *Ḫallabēše* 1. appears in a text (SAA 16 63) from Nineveh and (possibly) the reign of Esarhaddon. This letter-text is directed at the king, and it brings up an accusation against six men and one woman, servants of the governor, about their having committed crimes in Guzana against the Assyrian king. In this context, the anonymous (due to lacunae) writer reports that *Ḫallabēše* 1. and *Bur-Urti*, eunuch and cultic official of the god Baal-Rakkab of the city of Sam'al, have informed him of misdeeds committed by *Tarṣî*, the city scribe of Guzana. *Ḫallabēše* 1. is described as "from Samaria" (*Samirinâiu*) and as "[a servant of] the king" (*[arad] šarri*) in this context.[589]

On the basis of the above data, identities, properties, and settings can be identified. *Ḫallabēše* 1. may have been a Libyan, a male, an adult, and a member of the elite. He lived some time in the seventh century BCE, and he seems to have been a resident of the city of Guzana. The circumstances leading to this individual being in this corner of Assyria are difficult to pin down, but it is likely that he or older relatives of his came to Assyria forcibly via deportation.[590]

---

[588] Regarding etymology, the name of the Apis bull can be written *ḫpi* in cuneiform (Ranke 1910: 56). It is possible that the Egyptian name *Ḫʿi-Ḫpi* (Ranke 1935: 264:16), meaning "Apis shines", may be expressed here (Karlsson 2022c). Notably, this individual appears in an "archive of Egyptians". Concerning textual content and context, the name *Ḫaḫpi* appears as number three of the four names of witnesses that have been preserved. In addition to the names of the creditor and debtor, the list of witnesses contains one clearly Egyptian name and one possibly Egyptian name. In other words, *Ḫaḫpi* features in a clearly Egyptian environment.

[589] Drawing from the text publication and the PNA-entry of R. Mattila (PNA 2/I, p. 443).

[590] Regarding etymology, Mattila arrives at the conclusion that the name is "possibly Libyan", by referring to the work of A. Leahy (1993: 57). The name is brought up also in Tallqvist 1914: 83. Mattila also refers to interpretations which say that the name is Egyptian (conveying *Ḥr-Bs* and the names of the Egyptian god Horus and Egyptian dwarf god Bes) or that it is Phoenician (conveying *ḥlbs*). For the interpretation of *Ḫallabēše* as a Libyan name, see also Leahy 1980 and Draper 2015: 3-4. It may be noted here that *Ḫallabēše* 2.-3. both appear in African textual contexts. Concerning textual content and context, the letter-text in question naturally does not contain a list of witnesses. The ethnonym does not necessarily imply ethnic belonging. It can also (as is likely in this case) indicate previous place of residence. Samerina was the main city of the north-Israelite state Bit-Humri (RGTC 7/1, pp. 209-211).

Ḫallabēše 2.

The 23rd individual of this category is *Ḫallabēše* 2. This man appears in several texts from the archive of *Inurta-šarru-uṣur*, Nineveh, and the reign of Ashurbanipal and later, namely when he acts as a witness when *Puṭi-Athiš*▪ buys the boy *Aḫu-iddina* from the cook and the boy's grandfather *Abdi-Kurri* in a case of adoption (SAA 14 442, dated to 634 BCE), and when *Inurta-šarru-uṣur* 2. lends barley to *Ēdu-šal[lim]* (SAA 14 436). He also appears as the seller of the slave woman *Puṭu-šisi[...]*▪ to *Inurta-šarru-uṣur* 2. for 50 shekels of silver (SAA 14 435, dated to 612 BCE). The same document describes *Ḫallabēše* 2. as a copper smith (*nappāḫ erê*) and as a son of *Illāia*▫. He is also qualified as under the command of the prefect *Abdi-Samsi* 2., who also acts as one of the witnesses.[591]

On the basis of the above data, the interrogative words who, what, when, and where can be responded to. *Ḫallabēše* 2. may have been a Libyan, a male, an adult, and a commoner. He lived in the reign of Ashurbanipal and the following period, and he appears to have been a resident of Nineveh. The question of how he ended up in Assyria is difficult to answer, but it is likely that he or older relatives of his came to Assyria forcibly through deportation.[592]

Ḫallabēše 3.

The 24th individual of this category is *Ḫallabēše* 3. This man appears in a text (StAT 2 177) from the N31-archive, Assur, and 617 BCE as a witness when *Pūnašti*▪ borrows silver from *Kiṣir-Aššur* 45. and *Urdu-Aššur* 5., and in a text (StAT 2 192) from the same archive and city (but from 629 BCE) as the father of *Urdu-Bēlti*, who borrows silver from *Urdu-Aššur* 5.[593]

On the basis of the above data, identities, properties, and settings can be identified. *Ḫallabēše* 3. may have been a Libyan, a male, an adult, and a commoner. He lived in the post-Ashurbanipal period, and he seems to have been a resident of the city of Assur. The circumstances leading to this individual being in Assyria are difficult to pin down, but it is likely that he or older relatives of his came to Assyria forcibly through deportation.[594]

---

[591] Drawing from the text publication and the PNA-entry of R. Mattila (PNA 2/I, p. 443).
[592] Mattila adds that this individual may be identical with *Ḫallabēše* 4. The identification of a *Ḫallabēše* 4. (made by A. Schuster in the same PNA-entry) must be rejected, though. The PNA-entry in question refers to SAA 14 161, r. 12, but the document does not mention a *Ḫallabēše*. The closest is *Ḫašbasnu[...]* on line r. 18. The relevant line (r. 12) does not even contain a name, but summarizes that there are three guarantors of the transaction. *Ḫallabēše* 2. appears on fourth place in the first list of witnesses, which contains around 20 witnesses and several Egyptian names, while he appears on fifth place in the second list of witnesses, which contains eight names and several Egyptian names. *Ḫallabēše* 2. is attested in a clearly African milieu.
[593] Drawing from the text publication and the PNA-entry of R. Mattila (PNA 2/I, p. 443).
[594] This individual and the textual attestations of him are brought up in two PNAo-entries by H.D. Baker, who (without explanation) refers to the name as a "new lemma": *Ḫallabēšu*. Four people

Ḫanabeš

The 25th individual of this category is *Ḫanabeš*. The name of this individual of masculine gender is possibly Libyan. This man is mentioned in a text (StAT 2 53) from Assur and 700 BCE as the owner of a property in Guzana. This property (and the one of *Ribiṣiṣi*) is situated next to a building which is bought by *Qišerāia* from *Sama'*, "the Damascene".[595]

On the basis of the above data, the interrogative words who, what, when, and where can be responded to. *Ḫanabeš* may have been a Libyan, a male, an adult, and a commoner. He lived in the reign of Sennacherib, and he seems to have been a resident of the city of Guzana. The question of how he ended up in this corner of Assyria is difficult to answer, but it is likely that he or older relatives of his came there forcibly by means of deportation.[596]

Ḫana-Ḫūru

The 26th individual of this category is *Ḫana-Ḫūru*. The name of this individual of masculine gender has been identified as likely Egyptian, in the sense that it may contain the Egyptian word element *Ḥr*, which is the name of the Egyptian god Horus. *Ḫana-Ḫūru* appears in a text (SAA 14 102) from Nineveh and 642 BCE as one of the owners (along with *Aḫ-abû* and *Sunāia*) of houses in Nineveh that were situated next to a house bought by *Ḫala-šuri* from *Bir-Attār*.[597]

On the basis of the above data, identities, properties, and settings can be identified. *Ḫana-Ḫūru* seems to have been an Egyptian, a male, an adult, and a commoner. He lived in the reign of Ashurbanipal, and he appears to have been a resident of the city of Nineveh. The circumstances leading to this individual being in Assyria are difficult to pin down, but it is likely that he or older relatives of his came to Assyria forcibly through deportation.[598]

---

witness the loan in text StAT 2 177, with *Ḫallabēše* 3. appearing on second place. One other name is Egyptian, and the prominent Egyptian *Lā-turammanni-Aššur* 3. heads the list. Five people witness the loan in text StAT 2 192. Several witnesses have Egyptian names, and *Lā-turammanni-Aššur* 3. heads the list yet again. *Ḫallabēše* 3. clearly lived in an African milieu.

595 Drawing from the text publication and the PNA-entry of H.D. Baker (PNA 2/I, p. 449).

596 Regarding etymology, Baker does not give any suggestions as to the meaning and etymology of this name but implies that it is linked to *Ḫallabēše*, which is classified as possibly Libyan. C. Draper (2015: 3) equates *Ḫanabeš* with *Ḫallabēše*, which he concludes is a Libyan name. Concerning textual content and context, it may be noted here that the fourth witness of this document is a man referred to as "the Egyptian". Baker describes *Ḫanabeš* as a "landowner in Guzana".

597 Drawing from the text publication and the PNA-entry of H.D. Baker (PNA 2/I, p. 449).

598 Regarding etymology, Baker identifies the first name element as West Semitic and tentatively translates this personal name as "Horus has been merciful". The likely name of this individual obviously refers to a milder side of the falcon-headed god Horus, who was engaged in a battle with Seth over the throne of Egypt (Shaw and Nicholson 1995: 133-134). Concerning textual content and context, there are eight witnesses in the concluding list of witnesses. No other name seems to be of African origin.

Ḫapunapa

The 27th individual of this category is *Ḫapunapa*. The name of this individual of masculine gender can be classified as possibly Egyptian, in the sense that it may contain the Egyptian word elements *Ḥp* (referring to the Egyptian divine Apis bull) and/or *nfr*. *Ḫapunapa* appears in a text (WVDOG 152 II.7) from the Assur 52b-archive, Assur, and the reign of Ashurbanipal or later as one of the witnesses when *Ḫuru[...]*▪ 2. borrows a sum of silver from *Tap[...]*▫.[599]

On the basis of the above data, the interrogative words who, what, when, and where can be responded to. *Ḫapunapa* may have been an Egyptian, a male, an adult, and a commoner. He lived in the reign of Ashurbanipal or later, and he seems to have been a resident of the city of Assur. The question of how this individual ended up in Assyria is difficult to answer, but it is likely that he or older relatives of his came there forcibly by means of deportation.[600]

Ḫašbasnu[...]

The 28th individual of this category is *Ḫašbasnu[...]*. The name of this individual of masculine gender has been classified as possibly Egyptian, although its exact meaning is unknown. *Ḫašbasnu[...]* appears in a text (SAA 14 161) from Nineveh and 623 BCE as a witness for the woman *Niḫti-Eša-rau*▪, who buys *Mullissu-ḫāṣinat* from her father *Nabû-rēḫtu-uṣur* 17. as a wife for her son *Ṣi-ḫû*▪ 4.[601]

On the basis of the above data, identities, properties, and settings can be identified. *Ḫašbasnu[...]* may have been an Egyptian, a male, an adult, and a commoner. He lived in the post-Ashurbanipal period, and he appears to have been a resident of the city of Nineveh. The circumstances leading to this individual being in Assyria are difficult to pin down, but it is likely that he or older relatives of his came to Assyria forcibly through deportation.[602]

---

599 Drawing from the text publication. *Ḫapunapa* is not listed in PNA or PNAo.

600 Regarding etymology, the name of the Apis bull can appear as similar *ḫapi* and *ḫappi'* in cuneiform (Ranke 1910: 56), while the Egyptian adjective *nfr* can appear as *nāpa* and *nap* in cuneiform (Ranke 1910: 53). It is possible that the Egyptian name *Ḥp-nfr* (Ranke 1935: 237:15), meaning "Apis is good/beautiful", is expressed here (Karlsson 2021d). Notably, this individual appears in an "archive of Egyptians". Concerning textual content and context, *Ḫapunapa* appears as number four of four witnesses. The names of the creditor and debtor and the name of one (at least) of the witnesses are Egyptian. All in all, *Ḫapunapa* features in a markedly Egyptian milieu.

601 Drawing from the text publication and the PNA-entry of R. Jas (PNA 2/I, p. 464).

602 Regarding etymology, Jas refers to a study by K. Tallqvist (1914: 87). A. Leahy (1993: 57) reads *Ḫa*-MAŠ-*a* and classifies it as possibly Egyptian. Jas presumably centres on the Egyptian textual context and on an analysis that the name can not be conclusively tied to another language. Concerning textual content and context, 15 people witness this marriage affair, with *Ḫašbasnu[...]* appearing on fifth place. The people involved in the marriage aside, one of the three guarantors and several of the witnesses bear Egyptian names.

Ḫurazuri

The 29th individual of this category is *Ḫurazuri*. The name of this individual of masculine gender can be classified as possibly Egyptian, in the sense that it may contain the Egyptian word element *Ḥr*, which gives the name of the Egyptian god Horus. *Ḫurazuri* appears in a text (WVDOG 152 II.3) from the Assur 52b-archive, Assur, and 640 BCE as a witness when *Puṭu-Paiti*▪ 1. borrows silver from *Zahâ*▫.[603]

On the basis of the above data, the interrogative words who, what, when, and where can be responded to. *Ḫurazuri* may have been an Egyptian, a male, an adult, and a commoner. He lived in the reign of Ashurbanipal, and he appears to have been a resident of the city of Assur. The question of how he ended up in Assyria is difficult to answer, but it is likely that he or older relatives of his came to Assyria forcibly by means of deportation.[604]

Ḫurbianu

The 30th individual of this category is *Ḫurbianu*. The name of this individual of masculine gender can be classified as possibly Egyptian, in the sense that it may contain the Egyptian word element *Ḥr*, which is the name of the Egyptian god Horus. *Ḫurbianu* is mentioned in a text (StAT 2 184) from the N31-archive, Assur, and the reign of Ashurbanipal or later as a son of *Urdibbu* and as one of the witnesses when *Ata'*▫ gives his sister *Silim-Puṭi-lumur*, a votaress of the Assyrian goddess Ishtar of Arbela, to *Riḫpi-Mūnu*▫ as his wife.[605]

On the basis of the above data, identities, properties, and settings can be identified. *Ḫurbianu* may have been an Egyptian, a male, an adult, and a commoner. He lived in the reign of Ashurbanipal or the following period, and he appears to have been a resident of the city of Assur. The circumstances leading to this individual being in Assyria are difficult to pin down, but it is likely that he or older relatives of his came to Assyria forcibly via deportation.[606]

---

603 Drawing from the text publication. *Ḫurazuri* is not listed in PNA or PNAo.

604 Notably, this individual appears in an "archive of Egyptians". *Ḫurazuri* is mentioned both in the list of witnesses on the inner tablet and on the envelope. He features on fourth (of sixth) place in the former text version and on second (of sixth) place in the latter text version. A man with a clearly Egyptian name is listed as a witness in both versions.

605 Drawing from the text publication and a PNAo-entry of H.D. Baker.

606 Regarding etymology, *Ḫurbianu* appears as *Ḫarbiānu* in PNA (R. Mattila, 2/I, p. 459), classified as of unknown meaning and origin. However, the textual context of this individual is Egyptian, and the linguistic element *Ḫur* naturally relates to the Akkadian form of the name Horus (Ranke 1910: 57). Concerning textual content and context, there are more than 20 witnesses to this marriage contract, with *Ḫurbianu* appearing at the end of the list, thus indicating his rank. Several of the witnesses bear Egyptian names. The prominent Egyptians *Lā-turammanni-Aššur* 3.-4. and *Urdu-Aššur* 5. appear on first and third places respectively.

Iašanimu

The 31st individual of this category is *Iašanimu*. The name of this individual of masculine gender has been identified as possibly Egyptian, although a clear connection to an Egyptian word is lacking. *Iašanimu* is mentioned in a text (*SAAB* 9 68) from Assur and 625 BCE as the father of *Lā-turammanni-Aššur* 6., who owes silver to *Dādāia*.[607]

On the basis of the above data, the interrogative words who, what, when, and where can be responded to. *Iašanimu* may have been an Egyptian, a male, an adult, and a commoner. He lived in the post-Ashurbanipal period, and he appears to have been a resident of the city of Assur. The question of how he ended up in Assyria is difficult to answer, but it is likely that he or older relatives of his came to Assyria forcibly by means of deportation.[608]

Iāširu

The 32nd individual of this category is *Iāširu*. The name of this individual of masculine gender can be classified as possibly Egyptian, in the sense that it may contain the Egyptian word element *Wsir*, which refers to the Egyptian god Osiris. *Iāširu* is mentioned in a text (StAT 2 214) from the N31-archive, Assur, and 615 BCE as a witness when *Aššur-[...]-iddina*, *[...]-Issar-[...]*, and *Ubru-Aššur* borrow silver from *[Urdu]-Aššur* 5.[609]

On the basis of the above data, identities, properties, and settings can be identified. *Iāširu* may have been an Egyptian, a male, an adult, and a commoner. He lived in the post-Ashurbanipal period, and he appears to have been a resident of the city of Assur. The circumstances leading to this individual being in Assyria are difficult to pin down, but it is likely that he or older relatives of his came to Assyria forcibly through deportation.[610]

---

[607] Drawing from the text publication and the PNA-entry of E. Frahm (PNA 2/I, p. 494).

[608] Regarding etymology, Frahm suggests that it also is possible that the name is West Semitic, carrying a faulty rendering of the name *Ia-sumu*. He apparently equates the son of *Iašanimu* with the Egyptian *Lā-turammanni-Aššur* 3., but the PNA-entry identifies the son of *Iašanimu* as *Lā-turammanni-Aššur* 6. (R. Pruzsinszky, PNA 2/II, pp. 658-659). Frahm does not specify why he regards *Iašanimu* as possibly Egyptian, other than his pointing to the alleged relation to *Lā-turammanni-Aššur* 3. Of course, it is always possible to propose Egyptian linguistic elements in *Iašanimu*. For example, there are numerous Egyptian names beginning with *Iꜣ* or *Iʿ* (Ranke 1935: 5-7, 11-13). Concerning textual content and context, there are three witnesses to this loan. Two of them are gods(!) (Ashur and Shamash) while the third one is a human being (with an Akkadian name). By contrast, K. Deller, F.M. Fales, and L. Jakob-Rost provide the dates 639/622 BCE.

[609] Drawing from the text publication and a PNAo-entry of H.D. Baker (the name/individual in question is not listed in PNA).

[610] Regarding etymology, Egyptian *Wsir* appears as *Ušīru* in cuneiform (Ranke 1910: 46). Notably, this individual appears in an "archive of Egyptians". Concerning textual content and context, there are ten witnesses to this loan transaction, with *Iāširu* appearing on sixth place. The list contains one more likely Egyptian name.

Illāia

The 33rd individual of this category is *Illāia*. The name of this individual of masculine gender has been identified as likely Egyptian, then containing the Egyptian word *iry*. *Illāia* is mentioned in a text (SAA 14 435) from the archive of *Inurta-šarru-uṣur*, Nineveh, and 612 BCE as the father of the coppersmith *Ḫallabēše*▪ 2., who sells the slave woman *Puṭu-šisi[...]*▪ to *Inurta-šarru-uṣur* 2. for 50 shekels of silver.[611]

On the basis of the above data, the interrogative words who, what, when, and where can be responded to. *Illāia* seems to have been an Egyptian (or Libyan?), a male, an adult, and a commoner. He lived in the post-Ashurbanipal period, and he appears to have been a resident of the city of Nineveh. The question of how he ended up in Assyria is difficult to answer, but it is likely that he or older relatives of his came to Assyria forcibly through deportation.[612]

Kisiri

The 34th individual of this category is *Kisiri*. The name of this individual of masculine gender has been identified as likely Egyptian, although a clear link to an Egyptian word is lacking. *Kisiri* appears in a text (StAT 2 167) from the N31-archive, Assur, and 646 BCE as one of nine or ten men (most of these bearing Egyptian names) who divide an inheritance, in their giving a house to *Tap-naḫte*▪ 3. in lieu of his share. He also appears in a fragmentary text (StAT 3 92) from the same archive and city (but from 613 BCE) as the borrower of a large sum (counted by mina and not by shekel) of silver from *Kiṣir-Aššur* 45.[613]

On the basis of the above data, identities, properties, and settings can be identified. *Kisiri* seems to have been an Egyptian, a male, an adult, and a commoner. He lived in the reign of Ashurbanipal and later, and he appears to have been a resident of the city of Assur. The circumstances leading to this individual being in Assyria are difficult to pin down, but it is likely that he or older relatives of his came to Assyria forcibly through deportation.[614]

---

611 Drawing from the text publication and the PNA-entry of M. Jursa (PNA 2/I, p. 519).

612 Regarding etymology, Jursa refers to a study by A. Leahy (1993: 59). For this name in Egyptian texts, see Ranke 1935: 39:6-7; 41:5-8. The name either means "the one who makes" (41:5-8) or "who is related to" (39:6-7). Notably, this individual appears in an "archive of Egyptians". Concerning textual content and context, there are 13 witnesses to this sale. One of these has an Egyptian name. His son, *Ḫallabēše* 2., is also described as under the command of the prefect *Abdi-Samsi* 2. His family bond with *Ḫallabēše* 2. indicates that *Illāia* was a Libyan as well.

613 Drawing from the text publications, the PNA-entry of P. Charlier and R. Zadok (PNA 2/I, p. 620), and a PNAo-entry of H.D. Baker.

614 Regarding etymology, Charlier and Zadok suggest that if the name is Semitic (instead), the root may be *kšr*, "to be advantageous, proper, suitable". In their main interpretation, they supposedly centre on the solid Egyptian textual context of this individual. Concerning textual content and context, *Kisiri* appears as number six of the inheritance dividers, supposedly indicating his rank. The

***Lābê* (1.)**

The 35th individual of this category is *Lābê* (1.). The meaning of the name of this individual of feminine gender is unclear, but the name has been classified as Egyptian. *Lābê* (1.) is mentioned in a text (WVDOG 152 I.21) from Assur and 617 BCE as a slave woman belonging to the courier *Aššur-mušēzib*, who uses her as a security (*šapartu*) in a loan of leather that involves him and *Dūrī-Aššur*.[615]

On the basis of the above data, the interrogative words who, what, when, and where can be responded to. *Lābê* (1.) may have been an Egyptian, a female, an adult, and a slave. She lived in the post-Ashurbanipal period, and she seems to have been a resident of the city of Assur. The question of how this individual ended up in Assyria is difficult to answer, but it is likely that she or older relatives of her came to Assyria forcibly by means of deportation.[616]

***Lābê* (2.)**

The 36th individual of this category is *Lābê* (2.). This woman is mentioned in a broken text (WVDOG 152 II.10) from the Assur 52b-archive, Assur, and the reign of Ashurbanipal or the following period as (together with *Puṭupašte*▪) involved in a court case (probably concerning an adoption) against *Puṭukiše*▪ regarding the latter's young son *Sabutî*.[617]

On the basis of the above data, identities, properties, and settings can be identified. *Lābê* (2.) may have been an Egyptian, a female, an adult, and a commoner. She lived in the reign of Ashurbanipal or later, and she seems to have been a resident of the city of Assur. The circumstances leading to this individual being in Assyria are difficult to pin down, but it is likely that she or older relatives of her came to Assyria forcibly through deportation.[618]

prominent Egyptians *Urdu-Aššur* 5. and *Lā-turammanni-Aššur* 3. head the list of (six) witnesses, which also includes two possibly Egyptian names. Names of five witnesses are preserved in StAT 3 92. One name is Egyptian, and *Lā-turammanni-Aššur* 3. appears as the third witness.

[615] Drawing from the text publication. *Lābê* is not listed in PNA or PNAo.

[616] Regarding etymology and the identification of the name as Egyptian (but with no further comments), see Radner 2016: 121. Similar *Labâ* is classified as probably West Semitic by H.D. Baker (PNA 2/II, p. 648). In any case, the firm African textual context and the circumstance that the name can not be conclusively tied to another language make it plausible that the name in question is African. Concerning textual content and context, the leather in question appears to be connected to "the household of the chief eunuch". There are eight witnesses to this loan. None of the names of witnesses seem to be African. The text in question comes from the archive of *Dūrī-Aššur* (known as Assur 52a), which mentions numerous Egyptians.

[617] Drawing from the text publication. This name/individual is not listed in PNA or PNAo.

[618] The list of witnesses has not been preserved. The Egyptian context is clear from the facts that the text is part of the Assur 52b-archive and both of the male litigants have Egyptian names.

Lawaḫameḫi

The 37th individual of this category is *Lawaḫameḫi*. The name of this individual of masculine gender has been identified as likely Egyptian, although a clear link to an Egyptian word is lacking. *Lawaḫameḫi* is mentioned in a text (StAT 2 221) from the N31-archive, Assur, and the reign of Ashurbanipal or the following period in relation to *Urdu-Aššur* 5., who places six shekels of silver at the disposal of himself and *Lawaḫameḫi*.[619]

On the basis of the above data, the interrogative words who, what, when, and where can be responded to. *Lawaḫameḫi* seems to have been an Egyptian, a male, an adult, and a commoner. He lived in the reign of Ashurbanipal or later, and he appears to have been a resident of the city of Assur. The question of how he ended up in Assyria is difficult to answer, but it is likely that he or older relatives of his came to Assyria forcibly by means of deportation.[620]

Lulūlu

The 38th individual of this category is *Lulūlu*. The name of this individual of masculine gender has been identified as likely Egyptian, although a clear link to an Egyptian word is lacking. *Lulūlu* is mentioned in a text (StAT 2 167) from the N31-archive, Assur, and 646 BCE as a witness when nine or ten men (most of them having Egyptian names) divide an inheritance, in their giving a house to *Tap-naḫte*▪ 3. in lieu of his share.[621]

On the basis of the above data, identities, properties, and settings can be identified. *Lulūlu* seems to have been an Egyptian, a male, an adult, and a commoner. He lived in the reign of Ashurbanipal, and he appears to have been a resident of the city of Assur. The circumstances leading to this individual being in Assyria are difficult to pin down, but it is likely that he or older relatives of his came to Assyria forcibly through deportation.[622]

Nibḫēa

The 39th individual of this category is *Nibḫēa*. The name of this individual of masculine gender has been identified as likely Egyptian, although a clear link to an

---

619 Drawing from the text publication and the PNA-entry of R. Pruzsinszky (PNA 2/II, p. 659).

620 Regarding etymology, Pruzsinszky presumably centres on the Egyptian textual context and on an analysis that the name can not be conclusively tied to another language. Concerning textual content and context, there are five witnesses to this transaction. None of these have an African name.

621 Drawing from the text publication and the PNA-entry of M. Luukko (PNA 2/II, p. 669).

622 Regarding etymology, Luukko presumably centres on the Egyptian textual context and on an analysis that this name can not be conclusively tied to another language. Concerning textual content and context, *Lulūlu* appears on third place in the list of (six) witnesses. *Urdu-Aššur* 5. and *Lā-turammanni-Aššur* 3. head the list, which includes one more possibly Egyptian name.

Egyptian word is lacking. *Nibḫēa* appears in several texts from the N31-archive and Assur, such as when he acts as a witness when *Urdu-Bēlti*, son of *Ḫallabēše*▫ 3., borrows silver from *Urdu-Aššur* 5. (StAT 2 192, dated to 629 BCE), and when *Lā-turammanni-Aššur* 3., *Ṭāb[...]*, and *Matanaḫte*▪ borrow silver *from Urdu-Aššur* 5. (StAT 2 208, dated to 616 BCE). Along with five other men, he borrows three horses, *iškaru*-tax of the king, from *Urdu-Aššur* 5. (StAT 2 213).[623]

On the basis of the above data, the interrogative words who, what, when, and where can be responded to. *Nibḫēa* seems to have been an Egyptian, a male, an adult, and a commoner. He lived in the post-Ashurbanipal period, and he appears to have been a resident of the city of Assur. The question of how this individual ended up in Assyria is difficult to answer, but it is likely that he or older relatives of his came to Assyria forcibly by means of deportation.[624]

Pabaku

The 40th individual of this category is *Pabaku*. The name of this individual of masculine gender can be classified as possibly Egyptian, in the sense that it may contain the Egyptian word elements *pꜣ* and/or *kꜣ*. *Pabaku* appears in a text (WVDOG 152 II.1) from the Assur 52b-archive, Assur, and 658 BCE as a witness in a silver loan (whose parties are unclear due to lacunae).[625]

On the basis of the above data, identities, properties, and settings can be identified. *Pabaku* may have been an Egyptian, a male, an adult, and a commoner. He lived in the reign of Ashurbanipal, and he appears to have been a resident of the city of Assur. The circumstances leading to this individual being in Assyria are difficult to pin down, but it is likely that he or older relatives of his came to Assyria forcibly through deportation.[626]

---

[623] Drawing from the text publication and the PNA-entry of F.S. Reynolds (PNA 2/II, p. 959).

[624] Regarding etymology, Reynolds presumably centres on the Egyptian textual context and on an analysis that the name in question can not be conclusively tied to another language. It is possible that the Egyptian words *nb* (*nib* in cuneiform) and/or *ḥꜣt* (*ḫē* in cuneiform) may be expressed (Ranke 1910: 52, 56). It should be noted here that V. Donbaz and S. Parpola (2001) read the name as *Nipḫi-Aya* or *Nibḫaya*. Concerning textual content and context, *Nibḫēa* appears last of the five witnesses of the first text and as number five of the six witnesses of the second text. There are other Egyptian names in these two lists. *Lā-turammanni-Aššur* 3. heads the first list. There are four witnesses listed regarding the loan of horses. None of these have an African name. Two of the five men who (along with *Nibḫēa*) borrowed horses have certain or possibly Egyptian names.

[625] Drawing from the text publication. *Pabaku* is not listed in PNA or PNAo.

[626] Regarding etymology, the circumstances that this individual appears in an Egyptian textual context and may contain Egyptian words like *pꜣ* (*pa* in cuneiform) and *kꜣ* (*ku* in cuneiform) (Ranke 1910: 47, 60) support this interpretation. The word element *pꜣ* would convey the definite article *pꜣ*, while the word element *kꜣ* would speak of a concept of the soul in ancient Egypt (Shaw and Nicholson 1995: 146). Following another thread of interpretation, the name *pꜣ-bꜣk*, which means "the servant", is attested in Egyptian texts (Ranke 1935: 104:20). Concerning textual content and context, *Pabaku* heads the list of (three) witnesses, which contains one safely Egyptian name.

Pabbā'u

The 41st individual of this category is *Pabbā'u*. The name of this individual of masculine gender has been identified as likely Egyptian, although its exact meaning is unknown. *Pabbā'u* appears in a text (StAT 2 164) from the N31-archive, Assur, and 675 BCE as giving away his daughter *Mullissu-ḫammat*, a votaress of the Assyrian goddess Ishtar of Arbela, in marriage to *Awa* (1.), son of *Tap-naḫte*▪ 1. The document lists the dowry (*nadunnû*) given by *Pabbā'u* to his daughter. *Pabbā'u* is qualified further as a horse keeper (*mukīl sissê*) of Ishtar of Arbela.[627]

On the basis of the above data, the interrogative words who, what, when, and where can be responded to. *Pabbā'u* seems to have been an Egyptian, a male, an adult, and a commoner. He lived in the reign of Esarhaddon, and he seems to have been a resident of the city of Assur. The question of how he ended up in Assyria is difficult to answer, but it is likely that he or older relatives of his came there forcibly by means of deportation.[628]

Paḫî

The 42nd individual of this category is *Paḫî*. The name of this individual of feminine gender has been identified as likely Egyptian, although its exact meaning is unclear. *Paḫî* appears in a text (SAA 14 155) from Nineveh and 627 BCE as a female slave who is given, together with ten other people and a house, by *Bēl-na'di* to his daughter *Ba'altī-iābatu*.[629]

On the basis of the above data, identities, properties, and settings can be identified. *Paḫî* seems to have been an Egyptian, a female, an adult, and a slave. She lived in the post-Ashurbanipal period, and she appears to have been a resident of the city of Nineveh. The circumstances leading to this individual being in Assyria are difficult to pin down, but it is likely that she or older relatives of her came to Assyria forcibly through deportation.[630]

---

627 Drawing from the text publication and the PNA-entry of C. Ambos (PNA 3/I, p. 977).

628 Regarding etymology, Ambos presumably centres on the Egyptian textual context and on an analysis that the name in question can not be conclusively tied to another language. It is possible that the definite article *pꜣ* (*pa* in cuneiform) forms the initial part of this name (Ranke 1910: 47). Concerning textual content and context, the list of (twelve) witnesses contains several certain and possibly Egyptian names. The Egyptian milieu of this marriage is evident. It is noticeable that Egyptians are associated with the cult of an Assyrian goddess.

629 Drawing from the text publication and the PNA-entry of C. Ambos (PNA 3/I, p. 979).

630 Regarding etymology, Ambos refers to a study by K. Tallqvist (1914: 179). Supposedly, Ambos picks up on the analysis of Tallqvist (who identifies the name as Egyptian). If the initial part of this name is a definite article, feminine *tꜣ* would be expected. Concerning textual content and context, none of the other people given away have an African name, nor any of the nine witnesses.

Pamenapi

The 43rd individual of this category is *Pamenapi*. The name of this individual of masculine gender is possibly Egyptian, in the sense that it may contain the Egyptian word elements *pꜣ* and/or *mn*. *Pamenapi* appears in texts from the N31-archive and Assur, namely when he acts as a witness when nine or ten men (most of them with Egyptian names) give a house to *Tap-naḫte*▪ 3. as his share of an inheritance (StAT 2 167, dated to 646 BCE), and when people (with their names lost) share an inheritance (StAT 2 201, dated to 622 BCE).[631]

On the basis of the above data, the interrogative words who, what, when, and where can be responded to. *Pamenapi* may have been an Egyptian, a male, an adult, and a commoner. He lived in the reign of Ashurbanipal and later, and he seems to have been a resident of the city of Assur. The question of how he ended up in Assyria is difficult to answer, but it is likely that he or older relatives of his came to Assyria forcibly by means of deportation.[632]

Panateḫati

The 44th individual of this category is *Panateḫati*. The name of this individual of masculine gender can be classified as possibly Egyptian, in the sense that it may contain the Egyptian word elements *pꜣ* and/or *nṯr*. *Panateḫati* appears in a text (StAT 3 97) from the N31-archive, Assur, and the reign of Ashurbanipal or later as a witness when *Ḫur-waṣi*▪ 6. and some other people (whose names are not preserved) borrow silver from someone whose name is lacking.[633]

On the basis of the above data, identities, properties, and settings can be identified. *Panateḫati* may have been an Egyptian, a male, an adult, and a commoner. He lived in the reign of Ashurbanipal or later, and he appears to have been a resident of the city of Assur. The circumstances leading to this individual being in Assyria are difficult to pin down, but it is likely that he or older relatives of his came to Assyria forcibly through deportation.[634]

---

[631] Drawing from the text publication. *Pamenapi* is not listed in PNA or PNAo.

[632] Regarding etymology, the verb *mn* appears as *man(a)*, *min*, and *menna* in the cuneiform script (Ranke 1910: 51). Notably, this individual appears in an "archive of Egyptians". Concerning textual content and context, *Pamenapi* appears fourth of the six witnesses of the first text. *Urdu-Aššur* 5. and *Lā-turammanni-Aššur* 3. head the list. He appears seventh of the nine witnesses of the second text. One other name is Egyptian.

[633] Drawing from the text publication and a PNAo-entry of H.D. Baker (the name/individual in question is not listed in PNA).

[634] Regarding etymology, the noun *nṯr* appears as *nāta* and *nūti* in cuneiform (Ranke 1910: 54). There are examples in the Egyptian onomasticon of names beginning with *pꜣ-nṯr* (Ranke 1935: 114:8-9). Notably, this individual appears in an "archive of Egyptians". Concerning textual content and context, out of the four names of witnesses that have been preserved, *Panateḫati* is enumerated on first place. The name directly following his is Libyan.

***Pašî* 1.**

The 45th individual of this category is *Pašî* 1. The name of this individual of masculine gender has been identified as likely Egyptian, although its exact meaning is unclear. *Pašî* 1. is mentioned in a text (SAAS 5 40) from Kalhu and 658 BCE as the payer of a fine (*sartu*) of half a mina of silver to *Gīrî* on behalf of his brother *Agaragara*.[635]

On the basis of the above data, the interrogative words who, what, when, and where can be responded to. *Pašî* 1. seems to have been an Egyptian, a male, an adult, and a commoner. He lived in the reign of Ashurbanipal, and he appears to have been a resident of the city of Kalhu. The question of how he ended up in Assyria is difficult to answer, but it is likely that he or older relatives of his came to Assyria forcibly by means of deportation.[636]

***Pašî* 2.**

The 46th individual of this category is *Pašî* 2. This man is mentioned in a text (*SAAB* 9 98) from Assur and 650 BCE as a witness when *Mannu-kī-aḫḫē* invests a sum of silver in a business venture involving himself, *Nabû-aḫḫē-ballit̩*, and *Limt̩u-rēmūtu*, a group of people referred to as "expedition chiefs" (*bēl ḫarrāni*).[637]

On the basis of the above data, identities, properties, and settings can be identified. *Pašî* 2. seems to have been an Egyptian, a male, an adult, and a commoner. He lived in the reign of Ashurbanipal, and he seems to have been a resident of the city of Assur. The circumstances leading to this individual being in Assyria are difficult to pin down, but it is likely that he or older relatives of his came to Assyria forcibly through deportation.[638]

***Pašî* 3.**

The 47th individual of this category is *Pašî* 3. This man is mentioned in a number of texts from the N31-archive, Assur, and the time range of 646-615 BCE. *Pašî* 3. (along with nine other people, most with Egyptian names) gives a house to *Tap-naḫte*▪ 3. in lieu of his share (StAT 2 167). He acts as a witness in a court case about

---

635 Drawing from the text publication and the PNA-entry of A.M. Bagg (PNA 3/I, p. 992).
636 Regarding etymology, Bagg refers to a study by K. Tallqvist (1914: 180), and brings up the possibility that the name may be Akkadian (if not Egyptian), centred on *pašû*, meaning "to breathe, to fart". Tallqvist simply lists the name. It is possible that the definite article *pꜣ* forms the initial part of this name (Ranke 1910: 47). Several people with this name appear in an "archive of Egyptians". Concerning textual content and context and as for the status of this individual, R. Jas (1996: 62) refers to *Pašî* 1. as a "third party". The context of this obligation is unclear. The names of the other people are clearly not African. The four witnesses to this settlement all have Akkadian names.
637 Drawing from the text publication and the PNA-entry of A.M. Bagg (PNA 3/I, p. 992).
638 This individual appears as the first of six witnesses. None of the other names are African.

six men attacking Egyptian merchants in the house of *Ḫakkubāia* (StAT 2 173-174), and when *Ubru-Aššur* and two other people (whose names are fragmentary) borrow silver from *[Urdu]-Aššur* 5. (StAT 2 214). *Pašî* 3. (and six other people) borrows four horses, *iškaru*-tax of the king, from *Urdu-Aššur* 5. (StAT 2 210), and he (together with at least three other people, whose names are unclear) borrows some horses, *iškaru*-tax of the king, from a certain *Urdu-Aššur* (StAT 2 212). Moreover, *Pašî* 3. features in disposal of a horse, paid for by *Lā-turammanni-Aššur* 3., *Awa* (2.), and *Pi'u*▪ 2. to the servants of the king (StAT 3 87), and he (together with *Ki[...]*) is in disposal of the accounts of *Kiṣir-Aššur* 45. by means of(?) *Bēl-Ḫarran-aplu-uṣur* (StAT 3 93). At the end of the latter text, it is declared that "*Pašî* will assume the responsibility for it (*issu libbi išemme*) (and) pay double". *Pašî* 3. is qualified further as a "cohort commander" (*rab kiṣri*).[639]

On the basis of the above data, the interrogative words who, what, when, and where can be responded to. *Pašî* 3. seems to have been an Egyptian, a male, an adult, and a member of the elite. He lived in the reign of Ashurbanipal and later, and he appears to have been a resident of the city of Assur. The question of how he ended up in Assyria is difficult to answer, but it is likely that he or older relatives of his came to Assyria forcibly by means of deportation.[640]

Pašî 4.

The 48th individual of this category is *Pašî* 4. This man is mentioned in a text (SAA 14 118) from Nineveh and 631 BCE as a witness when *Gīrittu* leases one hectare of a field from *Urdu-Issar* and *Urdu-Aššur*, from the town of Kankanu.[641]

On the basis of the above data, identities, properties, and settings can be identified. *Pašî* 4. seems to have been an Egyptian, a male, an adult, and a commoner. He lived in the reign of Ashurbanipal, and he seems to have been a resident of the town of Kankanu. The circumstances leading to this individual being in Assyria are difficult to pin down, but it is likely that he or older relatives of his came to Assyria forcibly through deportation.[642]

---

[639] Drawing from the text publications, the PNA-entry of A.M. Bagg (PNA 3/I, p. 992), and two PNAo-entries of H.D. Baker.

[640] *Pašî* 3. appears last of the ten people giving away a house. He appears on eighth place (of ten or twelve) and on sixth place (of ten) in the two lists of witnesses. He is mentioned first among the borrowers of horses in StAT 2 210. Especially texts StAT 2 173-174 and StAT 3 87 are rich in Egyptian names. As noted by Bagg, *Pašî* 3. was apparently active in the circle of the prominent Egyptian *Urdu-Aššur* 5.

[641] Drawing from the text publication and the PNA-entry of A.M. Bagg (PNA 3/I, p. 992).

[642] There are 13 witnesses to this lease. *Pašî* 4. appears on sixth place, and there is no further African name. Kankanu may have been a town in the Assyrian heartland (RGTC 7/2-1, p. 286).

Pašî 5.

The 49th individual of this category is *Pašî* 5. This man appears in a text (SAA 14 123) from Nineveh and 630 BCE as a judge who imposes a judgment (*dēnu emēdu*) in a legal dispute brought by *Rēmanni-[...]* against *Malgadi*, whereby *Pašî* 5. orders the defendant to provide men in replacement or else pay a fine in silver.[643]

On the basis of the above data, the interrogative words who, what, when, and where can be responded to. *Pašî* 5. seems to have been an Egyptian, a male, an adult, and a member of the elite. He lived in the post-Ashurbanipal period, and he appears to have been a resident of the city of Nineveh. The question of how he ended up in Assyria is difficult to answer, but it is likely that he or older relatives of his came to Assyria forcibly by means of deportation.[644]

Pašî 6.

The 50th individual of this category is *Pašî* 6. This man appears in a text (SAA 14 114) from Nineveh and 634 BCE as a son of *Ibašši-ilāni* and as the seller of a plot of land in the town of Dayyanu-Adad to *Ṣalmu-aḫḫē*, the king's personal guard, for ten shekels of silver.[645]

On the basis of the above data, identities, properties, and settings can be identified. *Pašî* 6. seems to have been an Egyptian, a male, an adult, and a commoner. He lived in the reign of Ashurbanipal, and he seems to have been a resident of the town of Dayyanu-Adad. The circumstances leading to this individual being in Assyria are difficult to pin down, but it is likely that he or older relatives of his came to Assyria forcibly through deportation.[646]

Pašî 7.

The 51st individual of this category is *Pašî* 7. This man appears in a text (StAT 2 138) from Assur and late in the reign of Ashurbanipal or the following period as a witness when *Nabû-zēru-iddina* buys the slave *[...]ari* from his owner *[...]abu*.[647]

On the basis of the above data, the interrogative words who, what, when, and where can be responded to. *Pašî* 7. seems to have been an Egyptian, a male, an adult, and a commoner. He lived in the reign of Ashurbanipal or later, and he

---

[643] Drawing from the text publication and the PNA-entry of A.M. Bagg (PNA 3/I, p. 992).
[644] The exact status of *Pašî* 5. in this context is unclear, but he was clearly a man of some authority. The title of judge is actually not given in the document. There are no African names in the list of (around 20) witnesses.
[645] Drawing from the text publication and the PNA-entry of A.M. Bagg (PNA 3/I, p. 992).
[646] There are no African names mentioned in the concluding list of witnesses, which contains five names. Dayyanu-Adad may have been a town in the Assyrian heartland or neighbouring regions (RGTC 7/2-1, pp. 18-19).
[647] Drawing from the text publication and the PNA-entry of A.M. Bagg (PNA 3/I, p. 992).

appears to have been a resident of the city of Assur. The question of how he ended up in Assyria is difficult to answer, but it is likely that he or older relatives of his came to Assyria forcibly by means of deportation.[648]

***Pašî* 8.**

The 52nd individual of this category is *Pašî* 8. This man is mentioned in a text (VS 1 95) from the city of Assur and the date of 625 BCE as a witness for an individual named *Urdu-Nanāia*, who buys a slave woman and her daughter.[649]

On the basis of the above data, identities, properties, and settings can be identified. *Pašî* 8. seems to have been an Egyptian, a male, an adult, and a commoner. He lived in the post-Ashurbanipal period, and he seems to have been a resident of the city of Assur. The circumstances leading to this individual being in Assyria are difficult to pin down, but it is likely that he or older relatives of his came to Assyria forcibly through deportation.[650]

***Pašî* 10.**

The 53rd individual of this category is *Pašî* 10. This man is mentioned in numerous texts from Assur in his role as a post-canonical eponym of the year 614 BCE. *Pašî* 10. dates legal documents from Assur (*SAAB* 9 115; 117; StAT 1 36; StAT 2 28; 291; StAT 3 45; 67), as well as administrative texts from the N4-archive and the same city (VAT 8667; 8674; 8681).[651]

On the basis of the above data, the interrogative words who, what, when, and where can be responded to. *Pašî* 10. seems to have been an Egyptian, a male, an adult, and a member of the elite. He lived in the post-Ashurbanipal period, and he seems to have been a resident of the city of Assur. The question of how he ended up in Assyria is difficult to answer, but it is likely that he or older relatives of his came there forcibly by means of deportation.[652]

---

[648] *Pašî* 7. appears on sixth place in the list of (nine) witnesses. His name is the only possibly African name.

[649] Drawing from the text publication and the PNA-entry of A.M. Bagg (PNA 3/I, p. 992).

[650] The list of witnesses in question speaks of eleven people, with *Pašî* 8. appearing on last place. There is no other certain or possibly African name in the document.

[651] Drawing from the text publications, the PNA-entry of A.M. Bagg (PNA 3/I, p. 992), and two PNAo-entries of H.D. Baker. Bagg adds the unpublished text Ass 11682i in this context, following A. Millard (1994: 112).

[652] Judging by his being an eponym, *Pašî* 10. must have been influential in Assyria of the post-Ashurbanipal period. For *Pašî* 9., see subsection 2.1.3.

Patutume

The 54th individual of this category is *Patutume*. The name of this individual of masculine gender can be classified as possibly Egyptian, in the sense that it may contain the Egyptian form *pꜣ-di*. *Patutume* is mentioned in a broken text (WVDOG 152 II.8) from the Assur 52b-archive, Assur, and the reign of Ashurbanipal or later as a witness when *Puṭušu*▪ borrows silver from *Šumma-Nabû*.[653]

On the basis of the above data, identities, properties, and settings can be identified. *Patutume* may have been an Egyptian, a male, an adult, and a commoner. He lived in the reign of Ashurbanipal or later, and he appears to have been a resident of the city of Assur. The circumstances leading to this individual being in Assyria are difficult to pin down, but it is likely that he or older relatives of his came to Assyria forcibly through deportation.[654]

Piluna

The 55th individual of this category is *Piluna*. The name of this individual of masculine gender has been identified as likely Egyptian, although its exact meaning is unclear. *Piluna* is mentioned in texts (StAT 2 216-217) on a tablet and its envelope from the N31-archive, Assur, and 613 BCE as a witness when *Apâ*▫, son of *Apiḫuniawa*▪, borrows silver from *Urdu-Aššur* 5.[655]

On the basis of the above data, the interrogative words who, what, when, and where can be responded to. *Piluna* seems to have been an Egyptian, a male, an adult, and a commoner. He lived in the post-Ashurbanipal period, and he seems to have been a resident of the city of Assur. The question of how he ended up in Assyria is difficult to answer, but it is likely that he or older relatives of his came there forcibly by means of deportation.[656]

---

653 Drawing from the text publication. *Patutume* is not listed in PNA or PNAo.

654 Regarding etymology, this would obviously be a corrupt form of *puṭu*/*puṭi*. For the form *pꜣ-di* in cuneiform, see Ranke 1910: 48. Possibly, this name corresponds to Egyptian *pꜣ-di-Itm*, "given by Atum" (Ranke 1935: 122:15). Notably, this individual appears in an "archive of Egyptians". Concerning textual content and context, *Patutume* appears first of the two names of witnesses that have been preserved, supposedly indicating rank. The other preserved name is not of African origin.

655 Drawing from the text publication and the PNA-entry of R. Pruzsinszky (PNA 3/I, p. 994).

656 Regarding etymology, Pruzsinszky presumably centres on the Egyptian textual context and on an analysis that the name in question can not be conclusively tied to another language. It is possible that *pꜣ* or *pr* form the initial part of this name. The definite article *pꜣ* sometimes appear as *pi* (beside *pa* and *pu*), and the noun *pr* can be manifested as *pi* (beside *pir* and *pu*) in cuneiform (Ranke 1910: 47, 49). Concerning textual content and context, *Piluna* appears last of four witnesses. The other witnesses are *Kiṣir-Aššur* 45. and two people with Egyptian names. *Piluna* clearly lived in an African milieu.

Pilzu

The 56th individual of this category is *Pilzu*. The name of this individual of masculine gender has been identified as likely Egyptian, although its exact meaning is unclear. *Pilzu* appears in a text (StAT 2 229) from the N31-archive, Assur, and the reign of Ashurbanipal or later as a witness when *Šamaš-ibni* redeems his (unnamed) brother from *Urdu-Aššur* 5., settling a lawsuit between him on the one hand and *Ḫuḫamate*, *Urdu-Aššur* 5., and *Sîn-rēšu-išši* on the other.[657]

On the basis of the above data, identities, properties, and settings can be identified. *Pilzu* seems to have been an Egyptian, a male, an adult, and a commoner. He lived in the reign of Ashurbanipal or later, and he appears to have been a resident of the city of Assur. The circumstances leading to this individual being in Assyria are difficult to pin down, but it is likely that he or older relatives of his came to Assyria forcibly through deportation.[658]

Pinaiawa

The 57th individual of this category is *Pinaiawa*. The name of this individual of masculine gender has been identified as likely Egyptian, although its exact meaning is unclear. *Pinaiawa* is mentioned in a text (StAT 2 198) from the N31-archive, Assur, and 623 BCE as a witness concerning a fine for a crime committed by *Bēl-lēšir* in the house of *Urdu-Aššur* 19. He is also a witness in a text (StAT 2 207) from the same archive and city (but from 618 BCE) for *Bābilāiu*, who buys a house in Assur from *Urdu-Aššur*, son of *Puṭi-ḫutapiša*▪. In this context, *Pinaiawa* gives or receives one shekel of silver for the seal of *Bābilāiu* or *Urdu-Aššur*. *Pinaiawa* is qualified as a "commander-of-fifty" (*rab ḫanšê*) and as a superior of *Bābilāiu* or *Urdu-Aššur*, son of *Puṭi-ḫutapiša*.[659]

On the basis of the above data, the interrogative words who, what, when, and where can be responded to. *Pinaiawa* seems to have been an Egyptian, a male, an adult, and a member of the elite. He lived in the post-Ashurbanipal period, and he seems to have been a resident of the city of Assur. The question of how this

---

[657] Drawing from the text publication and the PNA-entry of G. Van Buylaere (PNA 3/I, p. 994).

[658] Regarding etymology, Van Buylaere presumably centres on the Egyptian textual context and on an analysis that the name in question can not be conclusively tied to another language. Again, it is possible that *pꜣ* or *pr* form the initial part of this name. The definite article *pꜣ* sometimes appear as *pi* (beside *pa* and *pu*), and the noun *pr* can be manifested as *pi* (beside *pir* and *pu*) in cuneiform (Ranke 1910: 47, 49). Concerning textual content and context, there are seven witnesses to this redemption of a pledge, with *Pilzu* appearing on third place. One name is safely Egyptian. The one individual who is qualified with a profession is a smith.

[659] Drawing from the text publication and the PNA-entry of R. Pruzsinszky and G. Van Buylaere (PNA 3/I, p. 995).

individual ended up in Assyria is difficult to answer, but it is likely that he or older relatives of his came there forcibly by means of deportation.[660]

Pizešḫurdāia

The 58th individual of this category is *Pizešḫurdāia*. The name of this individual of masculine gender has been identified as likely Egyptian, although its exact meaning is unclear. *Pizešḫurdāia* is mentioned in a text (StAT 2 207) from the N31-archive, Assur, and 618 BCE as one of the witnesses for *Bābilāiu*, who buys a house from *Urdu-Aššur*, son of *Puṭi-ḫutapiša*▪. *Pizešḫurdāia* is qualified further as a chariot driver (*mukīl appāti*).[661]

On the basis of the above data, identities, properties, and settings can be identified. *Pizešḫurdāia* seems to have been an Egyptian, a male, an adult, and a commoner. He lived in the post-Ashurbanipal period, and he appears to have been a resident of the city of Assur. The circumstances leading to this individual being in Assyria are difficult to pin down, but it is likely that he or older relatives of his came to Assyria forcibly through deportation.[662]

Puḫutana

The 59th individual of this category is *Puḫutana*. The name of this individual of masculine gender has been identified as likely Egyptian, although its exact meaning is unclear. *Puḫutana* is mentioned in a text (StAT 2 168) from the N31-archive, Assur, and 645 BCE as the father of *Mannu-kī-Arbail*, who owes 15 shekels of silver to *Ḫūru*▪ 2.[663]

On the basis of the above data, the interrogative words who, what, when, and where can be responded to. *Puḫutana* seems to have been an Egyptian, a male, an adult, and a commoner. He lived in the reign of Ashurbanipal, and he seems to have been a resident of the city of Assur. The question of how he ended up in Assyria is

---

660 Regarding etymology, Pruzsinszky and Van Buylaere presumably centre on the Egyptian textual context and on an analysis that the name can not be conclusively tied to another language. Once again, it is possible that *pꜣ* or *pr* form the initial part of this name. The definite article *pꜣ* sometimes appear as *pi* (beside *pa* and *pu*), and the noun *pr* can be manifested as *pi* (beside *pir* and *pu*) in cuneiform (Ranke 1910: 47, 49). Concerning textual content and context, there are several Egyptian names in the two lists of witnesses, which contain six and 15 names respectively. *Pinaiawa* appears on third and first place respectively in these lists, in this way indicating his high rank. Judging by their professions, numerous witnesses in text StAT 2 207 belonged to the military sphere.

661 Drawing from the text publication and the PNA-entry of G. Van Buylaere (PNA 3/I, p. 998).

662 Regarding etymology, Van Buylaere presumably centres on the Egyptian textual context and on an analysis that the name can not be conclusively tied to another language. Yet again, it is possible that *pꜣ* or *pr* form the initial part of this name. The definite article *pꜣ* sometimes appear as *pi* (beside *pa* and *pu*), and the noun *pr* can be manifested as *pi* (beside *pir* and *pu*) in cuneiform (Ranke 1910: 47, 49). Concerning textual content and context, *Pizešḫurdāia* appears last of 15 witnesses. The list contains several Egyptian names. Numerous witnesses belong to the military sphere.

663 Drawing from the text publication and the PNA-entry of G. Van Buylaere (PNA 3/I, p. 999).

difficult to answer, but it is likely that he or older relatives of his came there forcibly by means of deportation.[664]

Puta[...]

The 60th individual of this category is *Puta[...]*. The name of this individual of masculine gender has been identified as likely Egyptian, although its exact meaning is unclear. *Puta[...]* is mentioned in a text (StAT 2 168) from the N31-archive, Assur, and 645 BCE as a witness when *Mannu-kī-Arbail*, son of *Puḫutana*▫, borrows silver from *Ḫūru*▪ 2.[665]

On the basis of the above data, identities, properties, and settings can be identified. *Puta[...]* seems to have been an Egyptian, a male, an adult, and a commoner. He lived in the reign of Ashurbanipal, and he appears to have been a resident of the city of Assur. The circumstances leading to this individual being in Assyria are difficult to pin down, but it is likely that he or older relatives of his came to Assyria forcibly through deportation.[666]

Puṭi-Mutû

The 61st individual of this category is *Puṭi-Mutû*. The name of this individual of masculine gender has been identified as possibly Egyptian, then containing the Egyptian word elements *pꜣ-di*. *Puṭi-Mutû* is mentioned in a text (*SAAB* 9 90) from Assur and 638 BCE as the lender of eight shekels of silver to *Qītī-mūtī*.[667]

On the basis of the above data, the interrogative words who, what, when, and where can be responded to. *Puṭi-Mutû* may have been an Egyptian, a male, an adult, and a commoner. He lived in the reign of Ashurbanipal, and he seems to have been a resident of the city of Assur. The question of how he ended up in Assyria is difficult to answer, but it is likely that he or older relatives of his came to Assyria forcibly by means of deportation.[668]

---

[664] Regarding etymology, Van Buylaere presumably centres on the Egyptian textual context and on an analysis that this name can not be conclusively tied to another language. It is possible that *pꜣ* forms the initial part of this name. This word element sometimes appear as *pu* (beside *pa* and *pi*) in cuneiform (Ranke 1910: 47). Concerning textual content and context, there are three witnesses to this loan. Two of these names are certain or possibly Egyptian.

[665] Drawing from the text publication and the PNA-entry of M. Weszeli (PNA 3/I, p. 1001).

[666] Regarding etymology, Weszeli suggests that the name may be Akkadian (if not Egyptian). In the main interpretation, Weszeli presumably centres on the Egyptian textual context and on an analysis that the name in question can not be conclusively tied to another language. Supposedly, *Puta[...]* conveys a corrupt form of *puṭu*/*puṭi*, which is derived from Egyptian *pꜣ-di* (Ranke 1910: 48). Concerning textual content and context, there are three witnesses to this loan. Two of these names are certain or possibly Egyptian.

[667] Drawing from the text publication and the PNA-entry of R. Mattila (PNA 3/I, p. 1002).

[668] Regarding etymology, K. Deller, F.M. Fales, and L. Jakob-Rost (1995: 66-67) normalize the name as *Pudimutu(?)*. It is possible that the Egyptian goddess Mut is referred to in this name, although the name of this goddess in cuneiform is not listed by H. Ranke (1910). The name *Pꜣ-di-*

Puṭupiāti

The 62nd individual of this category is *Puṭupiāti*. The name of this individual of masculine gender has been identified as likely Egyptian, although its exact meaning is unclear. *Puṭupiāti* appears in a text (SAA 6 236) from Nineveh and 670 BCE in the context of *Mīnu-aḫṭi-ana-ili* borrowing ten shekels of silver from *Silim-Aššur* for *Puṭupiāti* to have. *Mīnu-aḫṭi-ana-ili* seems to act as a guarantor, making sure that *Silim-Aššur* will have his silver back.[669]

On the basis of the above data, identities, properties, and settings can be identified. *Puṭupiāti* seems to have been an Egyptian, a male, an adult, and a commoner. He lived in the reign of Esarhaddon, and he seems to have been a resident of the city of Nineveh. The circumstances leading to this individual being in Assyria are difficult to pin down, but it is likely that he or older relatives of his came to Assyria forcibly through deportation.[670]

Qišiṣim

The 63rd individual of this category is *Qišiṣim*. The name of this individual of masculine gender has been identified as likely Egyptian, although its exact meaning is unclear. *Qišiṣim* appears in a text (StAT 2 173) from the N31-archive, Assur, and 636 or 625 BCE as a witness in a court case about six men having attacked Egyptian merchants in the house of *Ḫakkubāia*.[671]

On the basis of the above data, the interrogative words who, what, when, and where can be responded to. *Qišiṣim* seems to have been an Egyptian, a male, an adult, and a commoner. He lived in the reign of Ashurbanipal or later, and he seems to have been a resident of the city of Assur. The question of how he ended up in Assyria is difficult to answer, but it is likely that he or older relatives of his came there forcibly by means of deportation.[672]

Mwt is attested in the Egyptian onomasticon (Ranke 1935: 123:17). Mut was the consort of Amun and had Thebes as her main place of worship (Shaw and Nicholson 1995: 193). Concerning textual content and context, there are three witnesses to this loan of silver. All of these have Akkadian names. Deller, Fales, and Jakob-Rost (1995: 66-67) give the date 641 BCE.

669 Drawing from the text publication and the PNA-entry of G. Van Buylaere (PNA 3/I, p. 1003).

670 Regarding etymology, Van Buylaere refers to studies by K. Tallqvist (1914: 183) and H. Ranke (1910: 34, 37). Apparently, Van Buylaere identifies the Egyptian linguistic element *pꜣ-di* (Ranke 1910: 48) as a part of this name. Concerning textual content and context, the list of witnesses contains four names. None of these names are African.

671 Drawing from the text publication and the PNA-entry of H.D. Baker (PNA 3/I, pp. 1015-1016).

672 Regarding etymology, Baker presumably centres on the Egyptian textual context and on an analysis that the name in question can not be conclusively tied to another language. Concerning textual content and context, these six men are described as "thieves" (*sāru*), have non-African names, and one of them is a priest. *Qišiṣim* appears on seventh place in the list of (twelve) witnesses. Several of the witnesses have African names.

Raḫdibi'

The 64th individual of this category is *Raḫdibi'*. The name of this individual of masculine gender has been identified as possibly Egyptian, although its exact meaning is unclear. *Raḫdibi'* appears in a text (StAT 2 180) from the N31-archive, Assur, and 644 or 629 BCE as a witness for *Amu-rṭēše*▪ 3., who buys the woman *Tatašīri*▫ from her husband *Saḫarpunḫu*▫.[673]

On the basis of the above data, identities, properties, and settings can be identified. *Raḫdibi'* may have been an Egyptian, a male, an adult, and a commoner. He lived in the reign of Ashurbanipal or later, and he appears to have been a resident of the city of Assur. The circumstances leading to this individual being in Assyria are difficult to pin down, but it is likely that he or older relatives of his came to Assyria forcibly through deportation.[674]

Rawa

The 65th individual of this category is *Rawa*. The name of this individual of masculine gender has been identified as possibly Egyptian, although its exact meaning is unclear. *Rawa* appears in a text (*Rfdn* 17 12) from Assur and the reign of Ashurbanipal as a witness when *Šamaš-aḫu-uṣur* borrows something unknown (due to lacunae) from *Mannu-kī-Arbail*.[675]

On the basis of the above data, the interrogative words who, what, when, and where can be responded to. *Rawa* may have been an Egyptian, a male, an adult, and a commoner. He lived in the reign of Ashurbanipal, and he seems to have been a resident of the city of Assur. The question of how he ended up in Assyria is difficult to answer, but it is likely that he or older relatives of his came there forcibly by means of deportation.[676]

Riḫpi-Mūnu

The 66th individual of this category is *Riḫpi-Mūnu*. The name of this individual of masculine gender has been identified as possibly Egyptian, then containing the Egyptian word element *Imn*, which is the name of the Egyptian god Amun. *Riḫpi-*

---

673 Drawing from the text publication and the PNA-entry of H. Hunger (PNA 3/I, p. 1028).

674 Regarding etymology, Hunger concludes that the name may be West Semitic (if not Egyptian). In his main interpretation, he presumably centres on the Egyptian textual context and on an analysis that the name can not be conclusively tied to another language. Concerning textual content and context, the names of six witnesses have been preserved, with *Raḫdibi'* appearing last. No other name in the list is of African etymology. V. Donbaz and S. Parpola give the date 644 BCE only.

675 Drawing from the text publication and the PNA-entry of H. Hunger (PNA 3/I, p. 1036).

676 Regarding etymology, Hunger refers to a study by R. Zadok (1998: 22, entry 1.2.11), and brings up the possibility that the name may be Akkadian. There are numerous Egyptian names which may correspond to cuneiform *Rawa* (Ranke 1935: 216-217). Concerning textual content and context, there are four witnesses to this loan, with *Rawa* appearing second. No other name is Egyptian.

Mūnu appears in a text (StAT 2 184) from the N31-archive, Assur, and the reign of Ashurbanipal or later as the husband of *Silim-Puṭi-lumur*, who was a votaress of Ishtar of Arbela and who was given (along with a dowry of silver, furniture, and utensils) in marriage to *Riḫpi-Mūnu* by her brother *Ata'*▫.[677]

On the basis of the above data, identities, properties, and settings can be identified. *Riḫpi-Mūnu* may have been an Egyptian, a male, an adult, and a commoner. He lived in the reign of Ashurbanipal or later, and he seems to have been a resident of the city of Assur. The circumstances leading to this individual being in Assyria are difficult to pin down, but it is likely that he or older relatives of his came to Assyria forcibly through deportation.[678]

Saḫarpunḫu

The 67th individual of this category is *Saḫarpunḫu*. The name of this individual of masculine gender has been identified as likely Egyptian, although its exact meaning is unclear. *Saḫarpunḫu* is mentioned in a text (StAT 2 180) from the N31-archive, Assur, and 644 or 629 BCE as selling his wife *Tatašīri*▫ to *Amu-rṭēše*▪ 3. for half a mina of silver.[679]

On the basis of the above data, the interrogative words who, what, when, and where can be responded to. *Saḫarpunḫu* seems to have been an Egyptian, a male, an adult, and a commoner. He lived in the reign of Ashurbanipal or later, and he seems to have been a resident of the city of Assur. The question of how this individual ended up in Assyria is difficult to answer, but it is likely that he or older relatives of his came there forcibly by means of deportation.[680]

Siḫā'

The 68th individual of this category is *Siḫā'*. The name of this individual of masculine gender has been identified as likely Egyptian, although its exact meaning is unclear. *Siḫā'* appears in a text (StAT 2 167) from the N31-archive, Assur, and 646 BCE as one of nine or ten men (most with Egyptian names) who give a house to *Tap-naḫte*▪ 3. in a case of inheritance, and in a text (StAT 2 208) from the same

---

677 Drawing from the text publication and the PNA-entry of R. Mattila (PNA 3/I, p. 1053).

678 Notably, this individual appears in an "archive of Egyptians". There are around 20 witnesses to this marriage contract. Several of these have Egyptian names. The list is headed by the prominent Egyptian *Lā-turammanni-Aššur* 3.-4. and with the other prominent Egyptians *Urdu-Aššur* 5. and *Kiṣir-Aššur* 45. on third and ninth places respectively.

679 Drawing from the text publication and the PNA-entry of K. Kessler (PNA 3/I, p. 1062).

680 Regarding etymology, Kessler presumably centres on the Egyptian textual context and on an analysis that the name can not be conclusively tied to another language. Concerning textual content and context, there are seven witnesses to this purchase. One name may be Egyptian. The document ends with the assurance that, "Verily *Tataširi* is *not* the wife of th[is] man (*Saḫarpunḫu*)!".

archive and city (but from 616 BCE) as a witness when *Lā-turammanni-Aššur* 3., *Ṭāb[...]*, and *Matanaḫte*▪ borrow silver from *Urdu-Aššur* 5.[681]

On the basis of the above data, identities, properties, and settings can be identified. *Siḫā'* seems to have been an Egyptian, a male, an adult, and a commoner. He lived in the reign of Ashurbanipal and the following period, and he seems to have been a resident of the city of Assur. The circumstances leading to this individual being in Assyria are difficult to pin down, but it is likely that he or older relatives of his came to Assyria forcibly via deportation.[682]

Taḫa'u

The 69th individual of this category is *Taḫa'u*. The name of this individual of masculine gender has been identified as likely Egyptian, although its exact meaning is unclear. *Taḫa'u* appears in a text (StAT 228) from the N31-archive, Assur, and the reign of Ashurbanipal or later as a witness for *Urdu-Aššur* 5., who lends silver to *Šulmu-lušeri*.[683]

On the basis of the above data, the interrogative words who, what, when, and where can be responded to. *Taḫa'u* seems to have been an Egyptian, a male, an adult, and a commoner. He lived in the reign of Ashurbanipal or the following period, and he seems to have been a resident of the city of Assur. The question of how he ended up in Assyria is difficult to answer, but it is likely that he or older relatives of his came there forcibly by means of deportation.[684]

Taia 1.

The 70th individual of this category is *Taia* 1. The name of this individual of masculine gender has been identified as likely Egyptian, although its exact meaning is unclear. *Taia* 1. is mentioned in a text (StAT 2 164) from the N31-archive, Assur, and 675 BCE as the father of *Tutakiḫama*▫, who acts as a witness when *Pabbā'u*▫

---

681 Drawing from the text publication and the PNA-entry of H.D. Baker (PNA 3/I, p. 1108).

682 Regarding etymology, Baker presumably centres on the Egyptian textual context and on an analysis that this name can not be conclusively tied to another language. A link to the Egyptian name *Ṣi-ḫû* is possible, even though *Siḫā'* is not written with an emphatic *s*. For the noun *ḥr* as *ḫā'*, see Ranke 1910: 57. Concerning textual content and context, this man appears on fifth place in the list of house givers and as the fourth of six witnesses, indicating his relative social rank. There are several safely or likely Egyptian names in the two documents. *Urdu-Aššur* 5. heads one of these and *Lā-turammanni-Aššur* 3. the other.

683 Drawing from the text publication and the PNA-entry of D. Schwemer (PNA 3/II, p. 1303).

684 Regarding etymology, Schwemer presumably centres on the Egyptian textual context and on an analysis that the name in question can not be conclusively tied to another language. Concerning textual content and context, there are five witnesses to this loan, with *Taḫa'u* appearing on second place. One further name is of Egyptian origin.

gives away his daughter *Mullissu-ḫammat*, a votaress of Ishtar of Arbela, in marriage to *Awa* (1.), son of *Tap-naḫte*▪ 1.[685]

On the basis of the above data, identities, properties, and settings can be identified. *Taia* 1. seems to have been an Egyptian, a male, an adult, and a commoner. He lived in the reign of Esarhaddon, and he appears to have been a resident of the city of Assur. The circumstances leading to this individual being in Assyria are difficult to pin down, but it is likely that he or older relatives of his came to Assyria forcibly through deportation.[686]

Taia 2.

The 71st individual of this category is *Taia* 2. This man is mentioned in a text (*SAAB* 9 109) from Assur and 615 BCE as one of the witnesses when *Mutaqqin-Aššur* buys the slave *Mannu-kī-ṣābē* from an individual named *Urdu-aḫḫēšu*.[687]

On the basis of the above data, the interrogative words who, what, when, and where can be responded to. *Taia* 2. seems to have been an Egyptian, a male, an adult, and a commoner. He lived in the post-Ashurbanipal period, and he seems to have been a resident of the city of Assur. The question of how he ended up in Assyria is difficult to answer, but it is likely that he or older relatives of his came to Assyria forcibly by means of deportation.[688]

Taia 3.

The 72nd individual of this category is *Taia* 3. This man appears in a text (BATSH 6 60) from Dur-Katlimmu and 637 BCE as a witness when *Šulmu-šarri* buys the slave *Nušku-iddina* from *Nušku-šarru-uṣur*. He (probably) also appears as a witness in a text (BATSH 6 5), wherein *Ša-lā-mašê* lends a sum of silver to *Ilumma-lē'i*.[689]

On the basis of the above data, identities, properties, and settings can be identified. *Taia* 3. seems to have been an Egyptian, a male, an adult, and a commoner. He lived in the reign of Ashurbanipal, and he seems to have been a resident of the city of Dur-Katlimmu. The circumstances leading to this individual

685 Drawing from the text publication and the PNA-entry of D. Schwemer (PNA 3/II, p. 1303).
686 Regarding etymology, Schwemer presumably centres on the Egyptian textual context and on an analysis that the name can not be conclusively tied to another language. Concerning textual content and context, there are twelve witnesses to this marriage deal, with *Tutakiḫama*, son of *Taia*, appearing on sixth place. Several of the witnesses bear Egyptian names and are described as priests.
687 Drawing from the text publication and the PNA-entry of D. Schwemer (PNA 3/II, p. 1303).
688 Schwemer claims that this man is qualified as the father of *Bēssū'a*. However, this patronym is not evident from the text, as published by K. Deller, F.M. Fales, and L. Jakob-Rost (1995: 92-94). There are 17 witnesses to this purchase, with *Taia* 2. appearing on tenth place. There is no other African name. The purchase is made with silver by the mina of Carchemish, thus indicating a partly western setting.
689 Drawing from the text publication and the PNA-entry of D. Schwemer (PNA 3/II, p. 1303).

being in this corner of Assyria are difficult to pin down, but it is likely that he or older relatives of his came to Assyria forcibly via deportation.[690]

Taka'in(?)

The 73rd individual of this category is *Taka'in(?)*. The name of this individual of masculine gender has been identified as likely Egyptian, although its exact meaning is unclear. *Taka'in(?)* appears in a much fragmentary text (SAA 14 309) from Nineveh and (probably) the seventh century BCE as a witness in a loan transaction, whose parties are unclear (due to lacunae).[691]

On the basis of the above data, the interrogative words who, what, when, and where can be responded to. *Taka'in(?)* seems to have been an Egyptian, a male, an adult, and a commoner. He probably lived some time in the seventh century BCE, and he seems to have been a resident of the city of Nineveh. The question of how he ended up in Assyria is difficult to answer, but it is likely that he or older relatives of his came there forcibly by means of deportation.[692]

Tamurtašu

The 74th individual of this category is *Tamurtašu*. The name of this individual of feminine gender has been classified as Egyptian. *Tamurtašu* appears in a text (WVDOG 152 II.2) from the Assur 52b-archive, Assur, and 647 BCE as borrowing five shekels of silver from *Puqulāia*.[693]

On the basis of the above data, identities, properties, and settings can be identified. *Tamurtašu* seems to have been an Egyptian, a female, an adult, and a commoner. She lived in the reign of Ashurbanipal, and she seems to have been a resident of the city of Assur. The circumstances leading to this individual being in Assyria are difficult to pin down, but it is likely that she or older relatives of her came to Assyria forcibly through deportation.[694]

---

690 *Taia* 3. features as number nine of ten and as number five of six in the two lists of witnesses. There are no further African names in the lists in question. It may be noted here that K. Radner (2002) dates the former text to 635 BCE.

691 Drawing from the text publication and the PNA-entry of D. Schwemer (PNA 3/II, p. 1303).

692 Regarding etymology, Schwemer does not specify the basis of his etymological classification, but it may be noted that the name of this individual is mentioned directly after that of the Egyptian *Ḫursisu* in SAA 14 309. Concerning textual content and context, only two lines and the list of witnesses are preserved. The person in question appears second of the five witnesses. The first name of the list conveys an Egyptian name.

693 Drawing from the text publication in question.

694 Regarding etymology and the identification of this name as Egyptian (but with no further comments), see Radner 2016: 121. This name is, however, classified as Akkadian in PNA (S. Parpola, 3/II, p. 1309), meaning "his audience gift". The PNA-entry refers to this very individual. Radner does not specify the basis of her etymological classification, but it is possible that the name in question may incorporate the Egyptian feminine definite article *tꜣ* (Ranke 1910: 60). Notably, this individual appears in an "archive of Egyptians". Concerning textual content and context, there are

Tap[...]

The 75th individual of this category is *Tap[...]*. The preserved part of the name of this individual of masculine gender is likely Egyptian, supposedly pointing to the Egyptian word elements *tȝy.f*. *Tap[...]* appears in a broken text (WVDOG 152 II.7) from the Assur 52b-archive, Assur, and the reign of Ashurbanipal or later as lending four and a half shekels of silver and a fifth shekel of silver to *Ḫuru[...]*▪ (2.).[695]

On the basis of the above data, the interrogative words who, what, when, and where can be responded to. *Tap[...]* seems to have been an Egyptian, a male, an adult, and a commoner. He lived in the reign of Ashurbanipal or later, and he seems to have been a resident of the city of Assur. The question of how he ended up in Assyria is difficult to answer, but it is likely that he or older relatives of his came there forcibly by means of deportation.[696]

Tatašīri

The 76th individual of this category is *Tatašīri*. The name of this individual of feminine gender has been identified as likely Egyptian, although its exact meaning is unclear. *Tatašīri* is mentioned in a text (StAT 2 180) from the N31-archive, Assur, and 644 or 629 BCE as being sold by her husband *Saḫarpunḫu*▫ to *Amu-rṭēše*▪ 3. for half a mina of silver.[697]

On the basis of the above data, identities, properties, and settings can be identified. *Tatašīri* seems to have been an Egyptian, a female, an adult, and a commoner. She lived in the reign of Ashurbanipal or later, and she appears to have been a resident of the city of Assur. The circumstances leading to this individual being in Assyria are difficult to pin down, but it is likely that she or older relatives of her came to Assyria forcibly through deportation.[698]

---

five witnesses to this loan. One of the names is Egyptian. It is noticeable that this (possibly) Egyptian woman apparently could act independently in the public arena.

695 Drawing from the text publication and the PNA-entry of H.D. Baker (PNA 3/II, p. 1311).

696 Regarding etymology and for *tȝy.f* appearing as *tap* in the cuneiform script, see Ranke 1910: 61. Notably, this individual features in an "archive of Egyptians". Concerning textual content and context, there are four witnesses to this loan. Several of the names are safely or likely Egyptian. All in all, *Tap[...]* appears in a solidly Egyptian cultural milieu.

697 Drawing from the text publication and the PNA-entry of N. Vanderroost (PNA 3/II, p. 1321).

698 Regarding etymology, Vanderroost does not specify the basis of the etymological classification, but it is possible that the name may incorporate the Egyptian feminine definite article *tȝ* (Ranke 1910: 60). It may also incorporate the name of the Egyptian god Osiris, written *Ušīru* in cuneiform (Ranke 1910: 46). The name *Tȝ-di(t)-Wsir* is attested in the Egyptian onomasticon (Ranke 1935: 373:1). Notably, this individual appears in an "archive of Egyptians". Concerning textual content and context, there are seven witnesses to this purchase. One of the names of these may be Egyptian.

Tutakiḫama

The 77th individual of this category is *Tutakiḫama*. The name of this individual of masculine gender has been identified as likely Egyptian, although its exact meaning is unclear. *Tutakiḫama* is mentioned in a text (StAT 2 164) from Assur and 675 BCE as a witness when *Pabbā'u*▫ gives away his daughter *Mullissu-ḫammat*, a votaress of Ishtar of Arbela, in marriage to *Awa* (1.), son of *Tap-naḫte*▪ 1. He is qualified further as a son of *Taia*▫ 1.[699]

On the basis of the above data, the interrogative words who, what, when, and where can be responded to. *Tutakiḫama* seems to have been an Egyptian, a male, an adult, and a commoner. He lived in the reign of Esarhaddon, and he seems to have been a resident of the city of Assur. The question of how this individual ended up in Assyria is difficult to answer, but it is likely that he or older relatives of his came to Assyria forcibly by means of deportation.[700]

Zaḫâ

The 78th individual of this category is *Zaḫâ* (or *Ṣa-ḫâ*). The name of this individual of masculine gender can be identified as Egyptian, in the sense that it may contain the Egyptian word element *ḥr*. *Zaḫâ* appears in a text (WVDOG 152 II.3) from the Assur 52b-archive, Assur, and 640 BCE as the lender of five shekels of silver to *Puṭu-Paiti*▪ 1., son of *Puṭu-ḫabišu*▪, and with the woman *Šuḫidinša* held as a pledge in the household of *Zaḫâ*.[701]

On the basis of the above data, identities, properties, and settings can be identified. *Zaḫâ* may have been an Egyptian, a male, an adult, and a commoner. He lived in the reign of Ashurbanipal, and he seems to have been a resident of the city of Assur. The circumstances leading to this individual being in Assyria are difficult to pin down, but it is likely that he or older relatives of his came to Assyria forcibly through deportation.[702]

---

699 Drawing from the text publication and the PNA-entry of M. Groß (PNA 3/II, p. 1337).

700 Regarding etymology, Groß does not specify the basis of her etymological classification. It is possible that the Egyptian words *twt* and/or *ḥm* form parts of this name. For the latter word in cuneiform (appearing as *ḫam*), see Ranke 1910: 56. For names consisting of, or beginning with, *twt* in the Egyptian onomasticon, see Ranke 1935: 379:15-17. Notably, this individual appears in an "archive of Egyptians". Concerning textual content and context, there are twelve witnesses to this marriage deal, with *Tutakiḫama* (qualified by the patronym) appearing on sixth place. Several of the witnesses bear Egyptian names and are qualified as priests.

701 Drawing from the text publication. *Zaḫâ* is not listed in PNA or PNAo.

702 Regarding etymology, an individual with the similar name *Ṣaḫā'* (classified as possibly Aramaic) is included in PNA (M. Luukko, 3/I, p. 1163). Nevertheless, it is plausible to centre on the Egyptian textual context and on an analysis that the name can not be conclusively tied to another language. For the noun *ḥr* in cuneiform (appearing as *ḫā* and *ḫa'*), see Ranke 1910: 57. A link to the Egyptian name *Ṣi-ḫû* is possible, even though the form *Ṣi* rather than the form *Ṣa* would have been expected (to write *Ḏd*). Notably, this individual appears in an "archive of Egyptians". Concerning textual

2.2.2 People indirectly identifiable as Africans

The second subsection deals with Africans identifiable through alternative identification grounds, meaning that textual and onomastic contexts indicate that someone is African. Ten individuals will be presented and discussed in this subsection.

***Abdi-Samsi* 2.**

The first individual of this category is *Abdi-Samsi* 2. This individual of masculine gender can be identified as an Egyptian, on account of various contexts. *Abdi-Samsi* 2. is mentioned in a text (SAA 14 435) from the archive of *Inurta-šarru-uṣur*, Nineveh, and 612 BCE as a witness when *Hallabēše*▫ 2. sells the woman *Puṭu-šisi[...]*▪ to *Inurta-šarru-uṣur* 2. *Abdi-Samsi* 2. here appears as the "prefect" (*šaknu*) of a group of Egyptians based in Nineveh.[703]

On the basis of the above data, the interrogative words who, what, when, and where can be responded to. *Abdi-Samsi* 2. may have been an Egyptian, a male, an adult, and a member of the elite. He lived in the post-Ashurbanipal period, and he seems to have been a resident of the city of Nineveh. The question of how he ended up in Assyria is difficult to answer, but it is likely that he or older relatives of his came there forcibly by means of deportation.[704]

***Awa* (2.)**

The second individual of this category is *Awa* (2.). This individual of masculine gender can be identified as an Egyptian, on account of various contexts. *Awa* (2.) is mentioned in a text (StAT 3 87) from the N31-archive, Assur, and 617 BCE as settling (along with *Lā-turammanni-Aššur* 3. and *Pi'u*▪ 2.) a lawsuit with *Pašî*▫ 3. concerning a horse by paying "the servants of the king" (supposedly some kind of royal officials).[705]

On the basis of the above data, identities, properties, and settings can be identified. *Awa* (2.) seems to have been an Egyptian, a male, an adult, and a commoner. He lived in the post-Ashurbanipal period, and he appears to have been a resident of the city of Assur. The circumstances leading to this individual being

content and context, there are nine (in total) witnesses to this loan transaction. Two of the witnesses have clearly or possibly Egyptian names.

703 Drawing from the text publication and the PNA-entry of F.M. Fales (PNA 1/I, p. 7).

704 Fales identifies the name in question as West Semitic, meaning "servant of Samsi". This purchase is witnessed by 13 people, with *Abdi-Samsi* 2. appearing on second place and being qualified as the prefect of *Ḫallabēše* 2. specifically. One other name of the witnesses is African. The fact that *Abdi-Samsi* 2. is embedded in African contexts makes it likely that also he was an African, despite his West Semitic name.

705 Drawing from the text publication and a PNAo-entry of H.D. Baker.

in Assyria are difficult to pin down, but it is likely that he or older relatives of his came to Assyria forcibly through deportation.[706]

***Inurta-šarru-uṣur* 2.**

The third individual of this category is *Inurta-šarru-uṣur* 2. This individual of masculine gender can be identified as an Egyptian, on account of various contexts. The archive of *Inurta-šarru-uṣur* from Nineveh contains a number of documents (SAA 14 426-456) and has been dated to 669-612 BCE. *Inurta-šarru-uṣur* 2. lends silver or barley to various people, namely when he lends half a mina of silver to *Mannu-kī-Nabû*, "courtier of the House of Succession" (SAA 14 426), when he lends six shekels of silver to *Urdu-Nabû* (SAA 14 429), when he lends an unknown (due to a lacuna) quantity of silver to *Tarība-Is[sar]*, when he lends three homers and three seahs of barley to someone whose name is lost (SAA 14 432), and when he lends an unknown (due to lacunae) quantity of barley to *Ēdu-šal[lim]* (SAA 14 436). He acts as a witness for *Puṭi-Atḫiš*▪ in a case of adoption where the boy *Aḫu-iddina* is sold by his grandfather, the cook *Abdi-Kurra* (SAA 14 442), he buys the slave woman *Puṭu-šisi[...]*▪ from *Ḫallabēše*▫ 2. (SAA 14 435), and he leases a plot of land in the Smiths' Town from the village manager *Ilâ-erība* (SAA 14 434). Furthermore, he lends 220 legs of donkey-mares to *Ilâ-erība* (SAA 14 428), he lends 15 "sta[r-patterned birds]" to *Nabû-[...]* (SAA 14 427), and he is the beneficiary of a fine imposed on *Nabû-šallim-aḫḫē* regarding some donkeys (SAA 14 430). He is qualified further as a "courtier (*mār ekalli*) of the new palace (of Nineveh)".[707]

On the basis of the above data, the interrogative words who, what, when, and where can be responded to. *Inurta-šarru-uṣur* 2. seems to have been an Egyptian, a male, an adult, and a member of the elite. He lived in the reign of Ashurbanipal and later, and he seems to have been a resident of Nineveh. The question of how he ended up in Assyria is difficult to answer, but it is likely that he or older relatives of his came to Assyria forcibly via deportation.[708]

---

[706] In her PNA-entry about this name, Baker likewise implies an Egyptian link (PNA 1/II, p. 433). She also proposes that the name in question is West Semitic, based on a verb meaning "to desire". The other six names (disregarding the eponym name) of the document are Egyptian or reveal an Egyptian (*Lā-turammanni-Aššur* 3.). Also, the text comes from the N31-archive, and the other person named *Awa* (1.) also appears in solidly Egyptian contexts. The fact that *Awa* (2.) is embedded in African contexts makes it likely that also he was an African, despite his possibly West Semitic name.

[707] Drawing from the text publication and the PNA-entry of H.D. Baker (PNA 2/I, p. 556).

[708] Baker identifies the name as Akkadian, meaning "O Ninurta, protect the king!". The text SAA 14 431, brought up by Baker, actually talks of a *Nūr-šarru-uṣur* (a nick-name?). Despite the archive being dated to 669-612 BCE, the (datable) texts included in the PNA-entry just cover the time range of 636-612 BCE. *Inurta-šarru-uṣur* 2. regularly features with people with African names (see e.g. SAA 14 435; 436; 442). Judging by his profession title, the fact that he was a lender, and the circumstance that he appears prominently in the list of witnesses of text SAA 14 442, he must have

***Kiṣir-Aššur* 45.**

The fourth individual of this category is *Kiṣir-Aššur* 45. This individual of masculine gender can be identified as an Egyptian, on account of various contexts. *Kiṣir-Aššur* 45. is mentioned in numerous texts from the N31-archive, Assur, and the time range of 646-613 BCE. Along with *Urdu-Aššur* 5., he is the main protagonist of the N31-archive. Firstly, *Kiṣir-Aššur* 45. features as a party of transactions, often as lending silver or barley. For example, he (along with *Urdu-Aššur* 5.) lends silver to *Pūnašti*▪ (StAT 2 177), and he (again along with *Urdu-[Aššur]* 5.) lends barley to *Lū-šal[im]* and *Nabû-nādin-aḫi* (StAT 2 188). He also buys slaves, such as when he buys the slave woman *Rēmtu-dūrī* from *Addu-pisia* and *Addu-lûkid* (StAT 2 169). He (along with six other men) borrow(s) four horses, *iškaru*-tax of the king, from *Urdu-Aššur* 5. (StAT 2 210-211). Furthermore, *Kiṣir-Aššur* 45. is the beneficiary of a fine imposed on *Aššur-šarru-uṣur* and(?) *Parrūṭu* for a crime committed by these individuals in his house (StAT 2 206). Secondly, *Kiṣir-Aššur* 45. features as a witness, such as when he witnesses when *Mannu-kī-Arbail* borrows silver from *Ḫūru*▪ 2. (StAT 2 168), when *Riḫpi-Mūnu*▫ takes *Silim-Puṭi-lumur*, a sister of *Ata'*▫, as his wife (StAT 2 184), and when *Bābilāiu* buys a house in Assur from *Urdu-Aššur*, son of *Puṭi-ḫutapiša*▪ (StAT 2 207).[709]

On the basis of the above data, identities, properties, and settings can be identified. *Kiṣir-Aššur* 45. seems to have been an Egyptian, a male, an adult, and a member of the elite. He lived in the reign of Ashurbanipal and later, and he seems to have been a resident of the city of Assur. The circumstances leading to this individual being in Assyria are difficult to pin down, but it is likely that he or older relatives of his came to Assyria forcibly through deportation.[710]

---

been an individual of high social status. The fact that he is embedded in African contexts makes it likely that also he was an African, despite his Akkadian name. His personal name, which incorporates the name of a Mesopotamian god, naturally tells of assimilation.

709 Drawing from the text publications, the PNA-entry of H.D. Baker (PNA 2/I, p. 625), and several PNAo-entries of H.D. Baker. *Kiṣir-Aššur* 45. appears as a party of transactions also in StAT 2 178; 183; 186; 187; 224; StAT 3 82; 92; 93; 94. He appears as a witness also in A 1809; StAT 2 173-174; 191; 194; 202; 215; 216-217; 218.

710 Text StAT 3 89 is highly fragmentary, but *Kiṣir-Aššur* 45. seems to play a leading role. Text StAT 2 199 (brought up in the PNA-entry) does not mention *Kiṣir-Aššur* 45. but *Urdu-Aššur* 5. As noted by Baker in a PNAo-entry, the reference to *Kiṣir-Aššur* in text StAT 3 107 can point to anyone of *Kiṣir-Aššur* 45.-49. Baker identifies the name as Akkadian, meaning "host of *Aššur*". *Kiṣir-Aššur* 45. regularly features with people with Egyptian names (see e.g. StAT 2 168 and 184). Judging by the fact that he was a lender (thus in possession of funds), that he was a companion of *Urdu-Aššur* 5., and that he appears prominently in the lists of witnesses of texts (see e.g. StAT 2 215 and 218), he must have been someone of high social status. The fact that he is embedded in African contexts makes it likely that also he was an African, despite his Akkadian name. His personal name, which incorporates the name of the main Assyrian god, naturally tells of assimilation.

Kiṣir-Aššur 46.

The fifth individual of this category is *Kiṣir-Aššur* 46. This individual of masculine gender can be identified as an Egyptian, on account of various contexts. *Kiṣir-Aššur* 46. is mentioned in several texts from the N31-archive and Assur, namely when he acts as a witness when *Kiṣir-Aššur* 45. and *Aššur-seḫa* buy four individuals from *Aššur-šumu-iddina*, *Aššur-aplu-iddin*, and *Zērīja* (StAT 2 183), when *Kiṣir-Aššur* 45. buys the slave woman *Rēmtu-dūrī* from *Adda-pisia* and *Adda-lûkid* (StAT 2 169, dated to 641 BCE), and when *Urdu-Aššur* 5. gives wages to *Aš[šur-...]* and *Aššur-šumu-ka''in* (StAT 2 202, dated to 622 BCE). *Kiṣir-Aššur* 46. is also a witness in a court case regarding six people (with non-African names) having attacked Egyptian merchants in the house of a certain *Ḫakkubāia* (StAT 2 174, dated to 636 or 625 BCE).[711]

On the basis of the above data, the interrogative words who, what, when, and where can be responded to. *Kiṣir-Aššur* 46. seems to have been an Egyptian, a male, an adult, and a commoner. He lived in the reign of Ashurbanipal and the following period, and he seems to have been a resident of the city of Assur. The question of how he ended up in Assyria is difficult to answer, but it is likely that he or older relatives of his came there forcibly via deportation.[712]

Sē'-raḫî 2.

The sixth individual of this category is *Sē'-raḫî* 2. This individual of masculine gender can be identified as an Egyptian, on account of various contexts. He is mentioned in a highly fragmentary text (SAA 16 55) from Nineveh and (probably) the reign of Esarhaddon, which is a letter to the king, seemingly about a legal case that involves *Sē'-raḫî* 2. and one or two groups of people referred to as "the Egyptians" (*Muṣurāiu*).[713]

On the basis of the above data, identities, properties, and settings can be identified. *Sē'-raḫî* 2. may have been an Egyptian, a male, an adult, and a commoner. He probably lived in the reign of Esarhaddon, and he seems to have been a resident of the city of Nineveh. The circumstances leading to this individual being in Assyria are difficult to pin down, but it is likely that he or older relatives of his came to Assyria forcibly through deportation.[714]

---

711 Drawing from the text publication and the PNA-entry of H.D. Baker (PNA 2/I, pp. 625-626).

712 This man appears as number two of nine, three of nine, three(?) of three, and as four of twelve in the lists of witnesses, indicating his rank. In texts StAT 2 174 and 202, he is a witness with his namesake *Kiṣir-Aššur* 45. There are several Egyptian names in the lists, and *Lā-turammanni-Aššur* 3. is brought up repeatedly. The fact that he is embedded in African contexts makes it likely that also he was an African, despite his Akkadian name.

713 Drawing from the text publication and the PNA-entry of F.M. Fales (PNA 3/I, p. 1104).

714 Fales identifies the name as West Semitic, meaning "Se' is benevolent". The ethnonym in question does not seem to be an attribute of *Sē'-raḫî* 2. (there is a break between the name and the

***Sukkāia* 31.**

The seventh individual of this category is *Sukkāia* (or *Sukki-Aya*) 31. This individual of masculine gender can be identified as an Egyptian, on account of various contexts. *Sukkāia* 31. is mentioned in several texts from the N31-archive, Assur, and the time range of 641-614 BCE. He (and a certain *Kiṣir-Aššur*) appear as witnesses in a fragmentary text about *Nabû-[...]* buying three people from *Tardītu-aḫḫē* (KAN 4 23). He also acts as a witness when *Nabû-mētu-balliṭ* sells the female slave *Bānât-Esaggil* to *Kiṣir-Aššur* 45. (StAT 2 178), when the paternal estate of *Lā-turammanni-Aššur* 3. is divided between this man's sons *Ḫut-naḫti*▪ and *Puṭi-Mūnu*▪ 2. (*FNLD* 18), when *Lā-turammanni-Aššur* 3., *Ṭāb[...]*, and *Matanaḫte*▪ borrow silver from *Urdu-Aššur* 5. (StAT 2 208), and (probably also) when the woman *Aḫā[tî]* and her unnamed son are obliged to work for an individual (whose name is lost) as a way of paying a debt (StAT 1 36). The last-mentioned text does not come from the N31-archive (but from the goldsmiths' archive, N33). *Sukkāia* 31. is qualified further as a son of *Nergal-šarru-uṣur*.[715]

On the basis of the above data, the interrogative words who, what, when, and where can be responded to. *Sukkāia* 31. seems to have been an Egyptian, a male, an adult, and a commoner. He lived in the reign of Ashurbanipal and the following period, and he seems to have been a resident of the city of Assur. The question of how he ended up in Assyria is difficult to answer, but it is likely that he or older relatives of his came there forcibly by means of deportation.[716]

***Tallu* 2.**

The eighth individual of this category is *Tallu* 2. This individual of masculine gender can be identified as an Egyptian, on account of various contexts. *Tallu* 2. appears in a text (StAT 3 95) from the N31-archive, Assur, and 658 BCE as a witness when *Ḫapi-maniḫi*▪ borrows silver from *Ḫur-waṣi*▪ 6., in a text (StAT 3 78) from the N31-archive, Assur, and 631 BCE as a witness when *Baṭṭūṭu* borrows silver from *Tap-naḫte*▪ 3., and in a broken text (KAV 189) from the N31-archive

ethnonym). Because of the broken state of the tablet, it is difficult to get a full understanding of the message of the letter, but it seems that *Sē'-raḫî* 2. had sold (without authority?) something to some Egyptians, whom he had ties with. M. Luukko and G. Van Buylaere (2002) names the text on the tablet "petition on behalf of weavers".

715 Drawing from the text publications and the PNA-entry of K. Radner (PNA 3/I, p. 1155).

716 Radner identifies the name as Akkadian, meaning "shrine" or "shrine of Ea". This man appears in the mid-part of the lists of witnesses of the four last-mentioned texts. There are several Egyptian names in the lists, and *Lā-turammanni-Aššur* 3. is brought up repeatedly. The fact that he is embedded in African contexts makes it likely that also he was an African, despite his Akkadian name. His name, which incorporates the name of a Mesopotamian god, naturally tells of assimilation.

and Assur as a witness (along with (other) Egyptians) in a case whose details are unclear, due to the fact that the operative section of the text is completely lost.[717]

On the basis of the above data, identities, properties, and settings can be identified. *Tallu* 2. seems to have been an Egyptian, a male, an adult, and a commoner. He lived in the reign of Ashurbanipal, and he seems to have been a resident of the city of Assur. The circumstances leading to this individual being in Assyria are difficult to pin down, but it is likely that he or older relatives of his came to Assyria forcibly through deportation.[718]

Ulūlāiu 42.

The ninth individual of this category is *Ulūlāiu* 42. This individual of masculine gender can be identified as an Egyptian, on account of various contexts. *Ulūlāiu* 42. is mentioned in a text (SAA 14 161) from Nineveh and 623 BCE as a witness when the woman *Nihti-Eša-rau*▪ buys a wife (with the name *Mullissu-ḫāṣinat*) for her son *Ṣi-ḫû*▪ 4. from the bride's father *Nabû-rēḫtu-uṣur* 17., in a text (SAA 14 433) from the archive of *Inurta-šarru-uṣur*, Nineveh, and 616 BCE as a witness when *Inurta-šarru-uṣur* 2. lends silver to *Tarība-Is[sar]*, and in a text (SAA 14 435) from the archive of *Inurta-šarru-uṣur*, Nineveh, and 612 BCE as a witness when *Inurta-šarru-uṣur* 2. buys the woman *Puṭu-šisi[...]*▪ from *Ḫallabēše*▫ 2.[719]

On the basis of the above data, the interrogative words who, what, when, and where can be responded to. *Ulūlāiu* 42. seems to have been an Egyptian, a male, an adult, and a commoner. He lived in the post-Ashurbanipal period, and he seems to have been a resident of the city of Nineveh. The question of how this individual ended up in Assyria is difficult to answer, but it is likely that he or older relatives of his came there forcibly by means of deportation.[720]

Urdu-Aššur 5.

The tenth individual of this category is *Urdu-Aššur* 5. This individual of masculine gender can be identified as an Egyptian, on account of various contexts. *Urdu-Aššur* 5. appears in numerous texts from the N31-archive, Assur, and the time range of 650-612 BCE. Along with *Kiṣir-Aššur* 45., he is the main protagonist of the N31-

---

[717] Drawing from the text publications and the PNA-entry of R. Mattila (PNA 3/II, p. 1305).

[718] Mattila identifies the name in question as West Semitic, meaning "fox". This man appears as number three of five and as number four of five in the two preserved lists of witnesses. An Egyptian by the name of *Ḫur-waṣi* appears as a witness in text StAT 3 78. The fact that *Tallu* 2. is embedded in African contexts makes it likely that also he was an African, despite his West Semitic name.

[719] Drawing from the text publication and the PNA-entry of K. Radner (PNA 3/II, p. 1377).

[720] Radner identifies the name as Akkadian, meaning "born in *Ulūlu* (= the 6th month)". This man appears as number eleven of 15, two of three, and as five of 13 in the respective lists of witnesses. Texts SAA 14 161 and 435 are rich with African names. The fact that he is embedded in African contexts makes it likely that also he was an African, despite his Akkadian name.

archive. Firstly, *Urdu-Aššur* 5. appears as a party of transactions, often as lending silver, such as when he lends half a mina and five shekels of silver to *Aḫu-dūr-enši* 2., son of *Ḫūru*▪ 2. (StAT 2 191), and when he lends one and a half shekels of silver to *Qibi-[...]* and receives the latter's slave *Puqišu* as security (StAT 2 170). He also lends grain to people, such as when he and *Kiṣir-Aššur* 45. lend five homers of barley to *Qurdi-Issar* and *Abu-lē'i* (StAT 2 187). *Urdu-Aššur* 5. also lends horses, such as when seven men borrow four horses, *iškaru*-tax of the king, from him (StAT 2 210). Also people come to him in the context of debt payments. A court order stipulates that *Nūr-Issar* should send *Amar-Aššur* and another person (whose name is lost) to *Urdu-Aššur* 5. or else go and serve *Urdu-Aššur* 5. himself (StAT 2 165). *Urdu-Aššur* 5. also lends people fish, such as when he lends fish in a vessel to *Bibî* (StAT 2 175). Once, he appears as giving wages to people, namely when he gives five and two-thirds of shekels of silver to *Aš[šur-...]* and *Aššur-šumu-ka''in* for their labour of one month (StAT 2 202). He also receives silver in a case of redemption, namely when *Šamaš-ibni* redeems his brother by paying silver to *Urdu-Aššur* 5., following a lawsuit involving these, *Ḫuḫamate*, and *Sîn-rēšu-išši* (StAT 2 229). Secondly, *Urdu-Aššur* 5. sometimes appears as a witness, such as when he witnesses when *Kiṣir-Aššur* 45. and *Aššur-seḫa* buy four people (StAT 2 183), or when *Ata'*▫ gives his sister *Silim-Puṭi-lumur* in marriage to *Riḫpi-Mūnu*▫ (StAT 2 184). He is qualified further as a "commander-of-fifty" (*rab ḫanšê*).[721]

On the basis of the above data, identities, properties, and settings can be identified. *Urdu-Aššur* 5. seems to have been an Egyptian, a male, an adult, and a member of the elite. He lived in the reign of Ashurbanipal and later, and he seems to have been a resident of the city of Assur. The circumstances leading to this individual being in Assyria are difficult to pin down, but it is likely that he or older relatives of his came to Assyria forcibly through deportation.[722]

---

[721] Drawing from the text publications and the PNA-entry of R. Jas (PNA 3/II, pp. 1399-1400). For more texts on *Urdu-Aššur* 5. as a party of transactions, see StAT 2 171; 177; 185; 192; 194; 195; 197; 199; 203; 208; 209; 214; 215; 216; 217; 219; 221; 223; 225; 226; 228 (silver); 188; 196 (grain); 212; 213 (horses); 166 (people); 222 (fish). Also text StAT 2 167 (not brought up by Jas in his PNA-entry) mentions *Urdu-Aššur* 5. as a witness.

[722] Jas sees the name as Akkadian, meaning "servant of *Aššur*". *Urdu-Aššur* 5. regularly features with people with Egyptian names (see e.g. StAT 2 191; 208). Judging by his profession title, the fact that he was a lender (thus in possession of funds), that he was a companion of *Kiṣir-Aššur* 45., and the fact that he appears prominently in the list of witnesses of texts (see StAT 2 167; 184), he must have been an individual of high social status. As for the status of *Urdu-Aššur* 5. and as concluded by Jas, the title of *Urdu-Aššur* 5. in text StAT 2 212 should probably be read GAL-50 (commander-of-fifty) instead of GAL-MU (chief cook). The fact that he is embedded in African contexts makes it likely that also he was an African, despite his Akkadian name. His personal name, which incorporates the name of the main Assyrian god, naturally tells of assimilation.

2.3 Anonymous Africans

The third section highlights anonymous Africans and their biographic details. These African people appear either individually or as part of a group and are revealed through the use of the Akkadian terms designating Egypt, Kush, and (theoretically) Libya in Neo-Assyrian texts.

The Egyptian(s) 1.

"1 000 troops of Egypt" (*1 000 ṣābē ša Muṣrāiu*) are referred to in a royal inscription of Shalmaneser III (RIMA 3 2) as taking part in a south-western alliance (led by Damascus and Hamath) against Assyria at the battle of Qarqar (situated in Syria) in 853 BCE.

On the basis of the above data, the interrogative words who, what, when, and where can be responded to. The people in question were obviously Egyptians, males, adults, and (largely) commoners. They lived in the reign of Shalmaneser III, and they presumably had their base in Egypt. They were a part of the Neo-Assyrian empire in the sense that they were in direct contact with it, fighting against the Assyrian army.[723]

The Egyptian(s) 2.

"[The people] of Assyria and Egypt" (*[nišē] māt Aššur u māt Muṣur*) are referred to in royal inscriptions of Sargon II (RINAP 2 1; 74) as being arranged to mingle together in order for them to trade with one another, after the Assyrian king in question had opened up a sealed-off harbor district of Egypt in 716 BCE.

On the basis of the above data, identities, properties, and settings can be identified. The people in question were obviously Egyptians (of all sexes, ages, and classes). They lived in the reign of Sargon II, and they obviously stayed in Egypt. They were a part of the Neo-Assyrian empire in the sense that they were in direct contact with it, trading with the Assyrians.[724]

---

[723] The king who dispatched the troops in question was probably Osorkon II of Egypt's 22nd dynasty (Kitchen 1973: 325). The author of the text claims that the alliance in which Egypt formed a part consisted of twelve kings with their forces, and that the alliance was defeated resoundingly. It should be noted here that a minority of scholars does not identify *Muṣrāiu* with Egypt (see e.g. Garelli 1971, contra e.g. Grayson 1996: 23).

[724] Judging by various chronologies, the ruler of (north-eastern) Egypt at this time was the Kushite king Shabaka (Kahn 2001) or Osorkon IV of Egypt's 22nd dynasty (Kitchen 1973). The identity of the harbor district is unknown.

The Kushite(s) 1.

"The king of Meluhha" (*šar māt Meluḫḫa*) is referred to in royal inscriptions of Sargon II (RINAP 2 7; 8) as hearing from afar of the might of Mesopotamian gods, as being overwhelmed by fear of royal radiance or divine brilliance, and as being overcome by terror, with the effect that he extradited Yamani of Ashdod (in 707/706 BCE), who was an Assyrian enemy and who had (initially) found a place of refuge on African soil (in 712 BCE).

On the basis of the above data, the interrogative words who, what, when, and where can be responded to. The person in question was obviously a Kushite, male, adult, and a member of the elite. He lived in the reign of Sargon II, and he obviously resided in Africa. He was a part of the Neo-Assyrian empire in the sense that he was in direct contact with it, co-operating with the Assyrian ruler through his act of extradition.[725]

The Egyptian(s) 3.

"The people of Egypt and the Arabs" (*nišē māt Muṣur u Arabî*) are referred to in a royal inscription of Sargon II (RINAP 2 74) as being overwhelmed by the awesome radiance of the god Ashur, causing their hearts to pound and their arms to become weak. This occurs in the context of Assyrian troops approaching or staying at the borders of Egypt in 716 BCE.

On the basis of the above data, identities, properties, and settings can be identified. The people in question were obviously Egyptians (of all sexes, ages, and classes). They lived in the reign of Sargon II, and they obviously stayed in Egypt. They were a part of the Neo-Assyrian empire in the sense that they were in direct contact with it, anticipating an attack.[726]

The Egyptian(s) 4.

"The vanguard of (the army of) [Egypt]" (*pān ummānāti [māt Muṣri]*) is referred to in a royal inscription of Sargon II (RINAP 2 116) as being defeated by Assyrian troops at the Philistine city of Raphia in 720 BCE, with the insubmissive king of Gaza taken captive in the process.

On the basis of the above data, the interrogative words who, what, when, and where can be responded to. The people in question were obviously Egyptians,

[725] According to the Tang-i Var inscription (RINAP 2 116), the Kushite ruler in question was Shebitku (for a discussion of the evidence, see Kahn 2001). The text contains the narration that Yamani "fled to the (far) edge of Egypt, on the border with the land Meluhha", with Meluhha equated with Kush (Heimpel 1997).

[726] An alliance between Egypt and the Arabs, directed at the Neo-Assyrian state, is imagined here. The passage in question is followed by the afore-mentioned claims of the establishing of a l
and trade opportunities.

males, adults, and (largely) commoners. They lived in the reign of Sargon II, and they presumably had their base in Egypt. They were a part of the Neo-Assyrian empire in the sense that they were in direct contact with it, fighting against the Assyrian army.[727]

The Egyptian(s) and the Kushite(s) 1.

"The kings of Egypt (and) the archers, chariots, (and) horses of the king of the land Meluhha, forces without number" (*šarrāni māt Muṣuri ṣābē qašti narkabāti sisê ša šar māt Meluḫḫa emūqī lā nībi*) are referred to in royal inscriptions of Sennacherib (RINAP 3 4; 15; 16; 17; 21; 22; 23; 46; 140; 142; 165) as in alliance with, and as coming to the aid of, the anti-Assyrian city of Ekron (in the Levant) in the battle at the Philistine city of Eltekeh in 701 BCE.

On the basis of the above data, identities, properties, and settings can be identified. The people in question were obviously Egyptians and Kushites, males, adults, and commoners (and members of the elite). They lived in the reign of Sennacherib, and they presumably had their base in Africa. They were a part of the Neo-Assyrian empire in the sense that they were in direct contact with it, fighting against the Assyrian army.[728]

The Egyptian(s) and the Kushite(s) 2.

"The Egyptian charioteers and princes, together with the charioteers of the king of the land Meluhha" (*bēl narkabāti u mārē šarri Muṣurāiu adi bēl narkabāti ša šar māt Meluḫḫa*) are referred to in royal inscriptions of Sennacherib (RINAP 3 4; 15; 16; 17; 18; 22; 23; 32; 46; 140; 142) as captured alive during the afore-mentioned battle at Eltekeh.

On the basis of the above data, the interrogative words who, what, when, and where can be responded to. The people in question were obviously Egyptians and Kushites, males, adults, and commoners (and members of the elite). They lived in the reign of Sennacherib, and they presumably had their base in Africa. They were a part of the Neo-Assyrian empire in the sense that they were in direct contact with it, fighting against the Assyrian army.[729]

---

727 The king who sent the troops may have been Shabaka (Kahn 2001: 11-12) or Osorkon IV (Kitchen 1973: 375-376). As noted in other texts (RINAP 2 1; 7), the "field-marshal of Egypt", *Rē'e*, lead the troops in battle.

728 Regarding the identity of "the king of the land Meluhha", Shebitku was ruler of Kush (and Egypt) at this time, while the future ruler Taharqa was the one engaged in the actual battle (Kitchen 1973: 383-386; Kahn 2001: 13). According to the royal inscriptions in question, the background to the conflict was a rebellion (supported by Hezekiah, king of Judah) in the Levantine city of Ekron.

729 Regarding the identity of "the king of the land Meluhha", Shebitku was ruler of Kush (and Egypt) at this time, while the future ruler Taharqa was the one engaged in the actual battle (Kitchen 1973: 383-386; Kahn 2001: 13). Apparently, Taharqa managed to escape unfettered.

The Egyptian(s) 5.

"The seed of his father's house (*zēr bīt abīšu*), descendants of earlier kings (*mārē šarri maḫrūte*), ditto; [... of] his house, third-men (*tašlīšu*), charioteers (*ša-narkabti*), ..., [... re]in-[holders] (*mukīl appāti*), archers (*ṣāb qassi*), shield bearers (*(bēl) arīti*), ditto; [...] ..., incantation priests (*āšipu*), dream interpreters (*ḫarṭibu*), [...] veterinarians (*muna''išu*), Egyptian scribes (*ṭupšar Muṣurāiu*), [...], snake-charmers (*mušlaḫḫu*), together with their helpers, ditto; [...], *kāṣiru*-craftsmen, singers (*nuāru*), bakers (*āpiu*?), [...], brewers (*sirāšû*), (together with) their supply managers, ditto; [... clothes] menders (*mugabbû*), hunters (*bā'iru*), leather workers (*aškāpu*), ditto; [...] wheelwrights (*naggār mugerri*), shipwrights (*naggār eleppēti*) [...] of their ..., ditto; [...] iron-[smiths (*nappāḫ parzilli*), (ditto)]" are referred to in a royal inscription of Esarhaddon (RINAP 4 9) as prisoners of war following the conquest of Egypt in 671 BCE.

On the basis of the above data, identities, properties, and settings can be identified. The people in question were obviously Egyptians (of all sexes, ages, and classes). They lived in the reign of Esarhaddon, and they were obviously deported from Egypt. They were a part of the Neo-Assyrian empire in the sense that they were in direct contact with it, being taken as prisoners of war by the Assyrian forces who managed to capture Memphis in 671 BCE.[730]

The Egyptian(s) and the Kushite(s) 3.

"The kings of (Lower) Egypt, Upper Egypt, (and) Kush" (*šarrāni māt Muṣur māt Paturisi māt Kūsi*) are referred to in royal inscriptions of Esarhaddon (RINAP 4 20; 68; 69; 83; 95; 98; 103; 112) as being under the dominion of the Assyrian king. This phrase is part of the titulary of Esarhaddon. The epithet "king of the kings of (Lower) Egypt, Upper Egypt, (and) Kush" was taken by Esarhaddon despite the fact that he never conquered Kush proper.

On the basis of the above data, the interrogative words who, what, when, and where can be responded to. The people in question were obviously Egyptians and Kushites, males, adults, and members of the elite. They lived in the reign of Esarhaddon, and they obviously resided in Africa. They were a part of the Neo-Assyrian empire in the sense that they were in direct contact with it, pictured as being under the dominion of the Assyrian king.[731]

---

[730] The deported people comprise a heterogenous group, consisting of members of the court, soldiers, scholars, performers (including snake-charmers!), craftsmen, and labourers. This passage naturally tells of the great impact the Neo-Assyrian empire had not only on Egypt's political level but also on Egyptian society.

[731] The defeated but not subjugated Kushite king must have been Taharqa. Regarding the identity of the Egyptian kings in question, 20 Egyptian (vassal) kings are enumerated in a royal inscription of Ashurbanipal (RINAP 5/1 11). The epithet gives a rare example of a differentiation of Egypt into Lower and Upper Egypt (Karlsson 2020a).

The Kushite(s) 2.

"Black Meluhhians" (*Meluḫḫē ṣalmūti*) are referred to in a fragmentary royal inscription of Esarhaddon (RINAP 4 35), in the context of a reference to Kush, supposedly conveying an ethnographic remark of some kind.

On the basis of the above data, identities, properties, and settings can be identified. The people in question were obviously Kushites (of all sexes, ages, and classes). They lived in the reign of Esarhaddon, and they obviously stayed in Africa. They were a part of the Neo-Assyrian empire in the sense that they were in direct contact with it, in the context of Esarhaddon and his Egyptian military campaigns.[732]

The Kushite(s) 3.

"The king of Meluhha" (*šar māt Meluḫḫi*) is referred to in royal inscriptions of Esarhaddon (RINAP 4 84; 85; 86), in the context of the titulary of the Assyrian king. Esarhaddon calls himself "the one who defeated the king of Meluhha".

On the basis of the above data, the interrogative words who, what, when, and where can be responded to. The person was obviously a Kushite, male, adult, and a member of the elite. He lived in the reign of Esarhaddon, and he obviously resided in Africa. He was a part of the Neo-Assyrian empire in the sense that he was in direct contact with it, pictured as being pacified by the Assyrian king.[733]

The Kushite(s) 4.

"The kings of the land Gutium, the land Amurru, and Meluhha (Ethiopia), whom I had installed (as rulers) by the command of (the god) Ashur and the goddess Mullissu" (*šarrāni...māt Meluḫḫe ša ina qibīt Aššur u Mullissu ištakkana qātāya*) are referred to in a royal inscription of Ashurbanipal (RINAP 5/1 11), in the context of the Assyrian king speaking of the rebellion of Shamash-shuma-ukin (ruler of Babylonia) and the alliances of this man. Again, the claim that Ashurbanipal had the Kushite king as a vassal is clearly hyperbolic.

On the basis of the above data, identities, properties, and settings can be identified. The person in question was obviously a Kushite, male, adult, and a member of the elite. He lived in the reign of Ashurbanipal, and he obviously resided

---

[732] For ethnographic remarks in Assyrian royal inscriptions, see Zaccagnini 1982. Concerning ethnography and Kush(ites) in the eyes of Assyria(ns), the interpretation of Kipkipi (a place of refuge for Tanutamon) as a derogatory name for the Kushite capital city Napata may be noted (Karlsson 2019).

[733] The defeated but not subjugated Kushite king in question must have been Taharqa. The verb translated as "defeated" (*kamû*, "to bind") conveys the image of a captured enemy.

in Africa. He was a part of the Neo-Assyrian empire in the sense that he was in direct contact with it, pictured as a vassal to the Assyrian king Ashurbanipal.[734]

The Egyptian(s) 6.

"The kings of Egypt, [servants who belonged to] me, together with their boats (and) their forces" (*šarrāni māt Muṣri [ardāni dāgil pānī]ya adi eleppētīšunu emūqīšun*) are referred to in royal inscriptions of Ashurbanipal (RINAP 5/1 2; Ashurbanipal 207) as accompanying Assyrian troops in the latter's move of expelling Taharqa from Egypt in 667 BCE.

On the basis of the above data, the interrogative words who, what, when, and where can be responded to. The people in question were obviously Egyptians, males, adults, and commoners (and members of the elite). They lived in the reign of Ashurbanipal, and they obviously had their base in Egypt. They were a part of the Neo-Assyrian empire in the sense that they were in direct contact with it, fighting alongside Assyria on the battlefield.[735]

The Egyptian(s) 7.

"The emissaries from Egypt, Gaza, Judah, Moab and Ammon" (*ṣīrāni Muṣurāiu…*) are referred to in a letter (SAA 1 110 / SAA 19 159) from the governor *Marduk-rēmanni* to Sargon II as delivering tribute in Kalhu on a certain day. Horses are mentioned in this context.

On the basis of the above data, identities, properties, and settings can be identified. The person in question was obviously an Egyptian, a male, an adult, and a member of the elite. He lived in the reign of Sargon II, and he presumably had his base in Egypt. He was a part of the Neo-Assyrian empire in the sense that he was in direct contact with it, delivering tribute to the Assyrian king in the centre of the Neo-Assyrian state.[736]

---

[734] The defeated but not subjugated Kushite king in question must have been Taharqa. The generic and archaic lands of Gutium and Amurru may represent the eastern and western cardinal points respectively. An Assyrian vassal king in Elam (Humban-nikash II) appears in the same passage.

[735] Regarding the identity of the Egyptian kings in question, 20 Egyptian (vassal) kings are enumerated in a royal inscription of Ashurbanipal (RINAP 5/1 11). The text in question says that the Egyptian kings in question joined Assyrian and Levantine forces on their way to Thebes in southern Egypt, whereto Taharqa had fled. For text Ashurbanipal 207, see http://oracc.org/rinap/Q007615/ (accessed 2021-09-08).

[736] The identity of the king who dispatched the Egyptian emissary to Kalhu is not clear. According to K. Kitchen (1973: 376) and his chronology, the likely candidate is Osorkon IV. *Marduk-rēmanni* 5. was governor of Kalhu under Tiglath-pileser III and Sargon II (R. Mattila, PNA 2/II, p. 721). Horses were both a source of prestige at court and valuable in the military arena (Heidorn 1997).

The Egyptian(s) 8.

"Egyptian troops" (*ṣābē Miṣirāiu*) are referred to in a query (SAA 4 82) to the sun-god which poses the question if Esarhaddon should go with his army to the Philistine city of Ashkelon. The issue whether Egyptian troops will attack him or not is central to this question.

On the basis of the above data, the interrogative words who, what, when, and where can be responded to. The people in question were obviously Egyptians, males, adults, and (largely) commoners. They lived in the reign of Esarhaddon, and they obviously had their base in Egypt. They were a part of the Neo-Assyrian empire in the sense that they were in direct contact with it, potentially opposing Assyrian forces in the Levant.[737]

The Egyptian(s) 9.

"The Egyptians" (*Muṣrāiu*) in general and the Egyptian kings *Nikkû* and *Šarru-lū-dāri* 13. specifically are referred to in a query (SAA 4 88) to the sun-god which poses the question if Esarhaddon's chief eunuch *Ša-Nabû-šû* (who had been sent to Egypt) will be attacked by these African groups and individuals.

On the basis of the above data, identities, properties, and settings can be identified. The people in question were obviously Egyptians, but the generic, unqualified reference hides anything else. They lived in the reign of Esarhaddon, and they obviously stayed in Egypt. They were a part of the Neo-Assyrian empire in the sense that they were in direct contact with it, potentially opposing Assyrian forces in Egypt.[738]

The Egyptian(s) 10.

"The vassals in Egypt" (*salmūti [ša] ina māt Muṣri*) are referred to in a query (SAA 4 88) to the sun-god which poses the question if Esarhaddon's chief eunuch *Ša-Nabû-šû* (who had been dispatched to Egypt) will be attacked by these potentially plotting Africans.

On the basis of the above data, the interrogative words who, what, when, and where can be responded to. The people in question were obviously Egyptians, males, adults, and members of the elite. They lived in the reign of Esarhaddon, and they obviously had their base in Egypt. They were a part of the Neo-Assyrian

---

[737] The king who could have dispatched the troops in question must have been Taharqa. As evident from preserved texts, military campaigns were regularly preceded by omen enquiries (Starr 1990).
[738] Although the reference to "the Egyptians" is generic and unqualified, the textual context indicates that these people belonged to the military. *Ša-Nabû-šû* 5. was appointed c. 671-668 BCE as chief eunuch and functioned as the eponym of 658 BCE (M. Groß, PNA 3/II, pp. 1227-1228).

empire in the sense that they were in direct contact with it, potentially opposing Assyrian forces in Egypt.[739]

The Egyptian(s) and the Kushite(s) 4.

"The Itu'eans and the Elamites, the mounted bowmen, the Hittites, [or] the Gurreans, or the Arameans, [or the Cimmerians, o]r the Philistines, or the Nubians (*Kūsāiu*) (and) the Egyptians (*Muṣrāiu*), or the Shabuqean" are referred to in queries (SAA 4 139; 142; 144; 145) to the sun-god which focus on the issue of potential insurrections against Esarhaddon.

On the basis of the above data, identities, properties, and settings can be identified. The people in question were obviously Africans, but the generic, unqualified reference hides anything else. They lived in the reign of Esarhaddon, and they obviously stayed in Africa. They were a part of the Neo-Assyrian empire in the sense that they were in direct contact with it, potentially opposing Assyrian forces in Egypt or the Levant.[740]

The Kushite(s) 5.

"15 Kushite women" (*15 Kūsāte*) are referred to in a list of female personnel in the palace of Nineveh (SAA 7 24). The Kushite women are listed on second place, after the mention of 36 Aramean women. The totally 140 women are defined as belonging to the father of the crown prince. Several of the women in the list are described as musicians or cultic performers.

On the basis of the above data, the interrogative words who, what, when, and where can be responded to. The people in question were obviously Kushites, females, adults, and (probably) members of the elite. They lived in the reign of Esarhaddon or Ashurbanipal, and they stayed in Nineveh. The question of how they ended up in Assyria is difficult to answer, but it is likely that they or older relatives of theirs came to Assyria forcibly via deportation.[741]

---

739 Regarding the identity of the Egyptian vassals in question, 20 Egyptian (vassal) kings are enumerated in a royal inscription of Ashurbanipal (RINAP 5/1 11). The word *salmūti* derives from a word (*salīmu*) meaning "peace, reconciliation", telling of symbiotic Assyrian-Egyptian relations (CAD S, pp. 100-103).

740 Although the references to "the Egyptians" and "the Kushites" are generic and unqualified, the textual context indicates that these people belonged to the military. The list seems to bring up potential enemies in all points of the compass, thus expressing totality. The list of ethnic groups varies between the four texts, but "the Egyptians" and "the Kushites" are always included (the text passage quoted above comes from SAA 4 142).

741 The Egyptian woman *Amat-Emūni* is one of two women whose names are given. *Amat-Emūni* is listed along with three maids of hers. It is likely that she and her Kushite companions enjoyed relatively high social status. The text is labelled "survey of female singers, etc." in the publication by F.M. Fales and J.N. Postgate (1992).

The Kushite(s) 6.

"The king of Kush" (*šar māt Kūsu*) is referred to in a letter (SAA 10 351) from the scholar *Mār-Issar* to Esarhaddon concerning the interpretation of an omen. According to this interpretation, the rulers of Kush, Tyre, or Mugallu will die (naturally), or the king will take one of these rulers captive, reduce his country, and take the concubines of this man into his possessions.

On the basis of the above data, identities, properties, and settings can be identified. The person in question was obviously a Kushite, male, adult, and a member of the elite. He lived in the reign of Esarhaddon, and he obviously resided in Africa. He was a part of the Neo-Assyrian empire in the sense that he was in direct contact with it, pictured as potentially destined to become subjugated by Assyria and its ruler.[742]

The Egyptian(s) and the Kushite(s) 5.

"The Kushites and Egyptians" (*Kūsāiu Muṣurāiu*) are referred to in a letter (SAA 13 13) from the scribe *Marduk-šallim-aḫḫē* to Esarhaddon or Ashurbanipal concerning the field, seed, and stored grain of theirs in Assur. These agricultural properties seem to have been withheld from the Africans by the scribe, but had now (by the orders of the king) been returned to these.

On the basis of the above data, the interrogative words who, what, when, and where can be responded to. The people in question were obviously Egyptians and Kushites, but the generic, unqualified reference hides anything else. They lived in the reign of Esarhaddon or Ashurbanipal, and they seem to have been residents of Assur (or its surroundings). The question of how they ended up in Assyria is difficult to answer, but it is likely that they or older relatives of theirs came to Assyria forcibly by means of deportation.[743]

The Egyptian(s) 11.

"The Egyptians" (*Muṣurāiu*) are referred to in a letter (SAA 13 144) from the scholar *Nabû-rēši-išši* in Arbela to Esarhaddon or Ashurbanipal, which seems to convey the report of a prophecy. The said scholar seems to claim that the local goddess (Ishtar of Arbela) had questioned why some woodland was given to the Egyptians instead of to the temple.

---

[742] The said Kushite king must have been Taharqa. The last-mentioned punishment signifies the threat of emasculation, in his losing control over his own women (Chapman 2004). *Mār-Issar* 18. was a scholar and an agent of Esarhaddon in Babylonia (H.D. Baker, PNA 2/II, pp. 739-740).

[743] The Africans here appear as working the banks of the Tigris rather than those of the Nile. If the above interpretation concerning the roles of the scribe and the king in this passage is correct, the Assyrian king here appears as the protector of Africans. *Marduk-šallim-aḫḫē* 3. was a scribe and priest of the Ashur temple under Esarhaddon or Ashurbanipal (H.D. Baker, PNA 2/II, p. 726).

On the basis of the above data, identities, properties, and settings can be identified. The people in question were obviously Egyptians, but the generic, unqualified reference hides anything else. They lived in the reign of Esarhaddon or Ashurbanipal, and they seem to have been residents of Arbela. The question of how they ended up in Assyria is difficult to answer, but it is likely that they or older relatives of theirs came to Assyria forcibly via deportation.[744]

The Egyptian(s) 12.

"The Egyptians" (*Muṣurāiu*) are referred to in a highly fragmentary text (SAA 16 55), labelled as a "petition on behalf of weavers". The details of this petition are unclear, but a certain *Sē'-raḫî* 2. and the said Egyptians are mentioned in connection with some stored grain.

On the basis of the above data, the interrogative words who, what, when, and where can be responded to. The people in question were obviously Egyptians, but the generic, unqualified reference hides anything else. They lived in the reign of Esarhaddon, and they seem to have been residents of some Assyrian city or rural area. The question of how they ended up in Assyria is difficult to answer, but it is likely that they or older relatives of theirs came to Assyria forcibly by means of deportation.[745]

The Kushite(s) 7.

"The Kushite girls" (*amāti Kūsāte*) are referred to in a letter (SAA 16 78) from the official *Mannu-kī-Libbāli* to Esarhaddon as having been settled in the royal palace by the writer of the letter and his men. The mention of their settling is made more or less in passing.

On the basis of the above data, identities, properties, and settings can be identified. The people in question were obviously Kushites, females, children(?), and commoners. They lived in the reign of Esarhaddon, and they seem to have been residents of Nineveh. The question of how they ended up in Assyria is difficult to answer, but it is likely that they or older relatives of theirs came to Assyria forcibly by means of deportation.[746]

---

[744] If the above-mentioned interpretation concerning the roles of the priest and the king in this text passage is correct, the Assyrian king here appears as the protector of Africans. Uniquely, Arbela is tied to Africans. *Nabû-rēši-iššì* 6. was a member of the temple personnel in a sanctuary in Arbela (supposedly the Ishtar temple) in the reign of Esarhaddon (M.C. Perroudon, PNA 2/II, p. 864).
[745] The passage is too fragmentary for any firm conclusions. Again, the Africans here appear (in their being connected to grain) as working the banks of the Tigris rather than those of the Nile.
[746] Some inferiority (if not in age) of these female Kushites can be assumed, in light of the qualifying word *amtu*. *Mannu-kī-Libbāli* 2. served as an official in the reign of Esarhaddon (H.D. Baker, PNA 2/II, p. 693).

The Egyptian(s) 13.

"The Egyptians (*Muṣurāiu*) or the Philistines" are referred to in a letter (SAA 19 22) from the Assyrian governor *Qurdi-Aššur-lāmur* to Tiglath-pileser III in the context of restricted trade in the Phoenician cities of Tyre and Sidon. *Qurdi-Aššur-lāmur* writes that he had ordered the local merchants not to sell any timber to the Egyptians or to the Philistines.

On the basis of the above data, the interrogative words who, what, when, and where can be responded to. The people in question were obviously Egyptians, but the generic, unqualified reference hides anything else. They lived in the reign of Tiglath-pileser III, and they presumably had their base in Egypt. They were a part of the Neo-Assyrian empire in the sense that they were in direct contact with it, competing with Assyria in trade matters.[747]

The Egyptian(s) and the Kushite(s) 6.

"Egyptian (scribes)" (*(ṭupšar) Muṣurāiu*) and "Kushites" (*Kūsāiu*) are referred to in a text (NWL 9) from Kalhu and 786 BCE, which lists members of the palace in Kalhu and their wine rations. The former group receives three litres, and the latter group receives six litres.

On the basis of the above data, identities, properties, and settings can be identified. The people in question were obviously Africans, and (partly or wholly) males, adults, and members of the elite. They lived in the reign of Adad-narari III, and they were obviously residents of the city of Kalhu. The question of how they ended up in Assyria is difficult to answer, but it is likely that they or older relatives of theirs came to Assyria forcibly by means of deportation. It can not be excluded, however, that the Egyptian scribes in question, with their special skills, arrived in Assyria as a result of peaceful negotiations between rulers.[748]

[747] The identity of the king behind the targeted Egyptian traders is unknown. According to the chronology of K. Kitchen (1973), it should have been a ruler from the Egyptian delta. D. Kahn (2001: 16-18) identifies the king with the "anti-Assyrian" Tefnakht, and suggests that Tefnakht took control of the delta after the "Kushite ally" Piye (who may have initiated trade relations between Kush and Assyria) had withdrawn to Kush. *Qurdi-Aššur-lāmur* was governor of the Phoenician city of Simirra(?) in the reign of Tiglath-pileser III (G. Van Buylaere, PNA 3/I, pp. 1021-1022). This text highlights the circumstance that also economic issues guided imperial policy. As is commonly known, Phoenicia was famous for its cedar trees and timber.

[748] The Egyptian scribes are listed together with Assyrian and Aramean scribes. The word for scribe is given by the ditto-sign. Considering their higher ration, the Kushite group may have been more numerous. It is unclear what role the Kushite group had. The context suggests that these people were scribes as well, but neither the word for scribe, nor the ditto-sign, are written. Also, it is unclear what script and language these scribes would have mastered.

The Egyptian(s) 14.

"The Egyptian merchants" (*tankarāni Muṣurāiu*) are referred to in a text (StAT 2 173) from the N31-archive, Assur, and 636 or 625 BCE as having entered the house of *Ḫakkubāia* as foreign guests, and as being attacked there by six individuals with non-African names.

On the basis of the above data, the interrogative words who, what, when, and where can be responded to. The people in question were obviously Egyptians, males, adults, and members of the elite. They lived in the reign of Ashurbanipal or later, and they seem to have been residents of the city of Assur. The question of how they ended up in Assyria is difficult to answer, but it is likely that they or older relatives of theirs came to Assyria forcibly via deportation.[749]

The Egyptian(s) 15.

"An Egyptian family" (*qinnu Muṣurāiu*) are referred to in a fragmentary text (StAT 2 253) from Assur and the reign of Ashurbanipal or later, which lists recipients of silver. The following line gives the phrase "they gave him", possibly pointing to the family as part of some transaction.

On the basis of the above data, identities, properties, and settings can be identified. The people in question were obviously Egyptians, and they were (presumably) a group of both men and women, adults and children. A high social status is not readily apparent. The family lived in the reign of Ashurbanipal or later, and they seem to have been residents of the city of Assur. The question of how they ended up in Assyria is difficult to answer, but it is likely that they or older relatives of theirs came to Assyria forcibly by means of deportation.[750]

The Egyptian(s) 16.

"An [Egyptian] merchant" (*tamkār [Muṣurāiu]*) is referred to in a text (StAT 2 271) from Assur and 650 BCE, in which the Egyptian in question sells the woman *Urkittu-[...]* to someone (a male individual) whose name has not been preserved.

On the basis of the above data, the interrogative words who, what, when, and where can be responded to. The person in question was obviously an Egyptian, male, adult, and a member of the elite. He lived in the reign of Ashurbanipal, and he seems to have been a resident of the city of Assur. The question of how he ended

---

[749] The background to this legal case is unclear. It may have been the result of an ethnic conflict and/or a property dispute (Karlsson 2021a). The profession of merchant suggests that these Egyptian individuals enjoyed a privileged social status. There are several people with Egyptian names in the list of witnesses.

[750] The background to the rebursements of silver in this text can not be ascertained. The text comes from the goldsmiths' archive, N33. The document lacks any African name.

up in Assyria is difficult to answer, but it is likely that he or older relatives of his came to Assyria forcibly by means of deportation.[751]

[751] The word "Egyptian" can be reconstructed on the basis of cuneiform traces and scarab seal impressions on the tablet. There are no African names in the list of witnesses of this document.

3. THE EVIDENCE: THE COLLECTIVE LEVEL AND THE DEMOGRAPHIC PERSPECTIVE

This chapter focuses on the gathered evidence in light of the collective level and demographic perspective, meaning that demographic data (hinged on the factors ethnicity, sex/gender, age, class, time and place of living, and mode of integration) are compiled and analysed on the basis of the biographic data collected in the previous chapter. The present chapter has two sections, centred on identities and properties (3.1), responding to who and what, and on settings and circumstances (3.2), responding to when, where, and how. The data on the collective level and demographic perspective are also presented via the tables of subsection 7.1.4.

3.1 Demographics and the African group: identities and properties

The first section discusses the African group on the grounds of identities and properties (responding to who and what). Its subsections deal with the ethnic composition (3.1.1), the sex/gender composition (3.1.2), the age composition (3.1.3), and the class composition (3.1.4) of the African group.

3.1.1 The ethnic composition of the African group

The first subsection centres on the ethnic composition of the African group, discussing from statistics on the relative proportions of the Egyptian, Kushite, and Libyan ethnic groups.

	Egyptian	Kushite	Libyan					
2.1	87.5%	9.7%	2.7%					
2.2	95.5%	0%	4.5%					
2.1+2.2	**89.6%**	**7.2%**	**3.2%**					
2.3	*65.5%*	*34.5%*	*0%*					

As evident from the statistics presented above, the great majority of Africans in Neo-Assyrian texts are Egyptians. Proceeding from the statistics which combine the data on identified and likely/possible Africans, 89.6% of the 345 people in question are Egyptians, 7.2% are Kushites, and 3.2% are Libyans. The differences between the statistics on identified Africans and that on likely/possible Africans are insignificant. Perhaps the absence of any Kushites in the latter group may be noted. The statistics based on anonymous Africans (statistics which should be treated with caution) follow the same pattern, although the proportion of Kushite attestations is significant compared to the proportion of Egyptian attestations.

The finding that the great majority of Africans in Neo-Assyrian texts are Egyptians is to be expected. Egypt was closer to Assyria, the battles took place on Egyptian soil, Egypt had a greater population than Kush and Libya, and so on.[752]

The question is whether the demographic statistics regarding ethnicity differentiate even more, still proceeding from the statistics derived from the combined data on identified and likely/possible Africans?[753] An analysis of the smallest groups of demographic data may be illuminative in this regard.

individual	type	ethnicity	sex	age	class	time	place
Dāri-šarru 2.	2.1.2	**Kushite**	male	adult	upper	Esa/Ash	Ass.
Kūsāiâ 1.	2.1.2	**Kushite**	male	adult	lower	pAsh	Ass.
Kūsāiâ 2.	2.1.2	**Kushite**	male	adult	lower	pAsh	Ass.
Kūsāiu 1.	2.1.2	**Kushite**	male	child	lower	Sar	Ass.
Kūsāiu 2.	2.1.2	**Kushite**	male	adult	lower	Ash	Ass. (N)
Kūsāiu 3.	2.1.2	**Kushite**	male	adult	lower	pAsh	Ass. (As)
Kūsāiu 4.	2.1.2	**Kushite**	male	adult	lower	pAsh	Ass.
Kūsāiu 5.	2.1.2	**Kushite**	male	adult	lower	post-612	Ass.
Kūsāiu 6.	2.1.2	**Kushite**	male	adult	upper	7th c.	Ass. (N)
Kūsāiu (7.)	2.1.2	**Kushite**	male	adult	lower	Ash/pAsh	Ass. (As)
Kūsāiu (8.)	2.1.2	**Kushite**	male	adult	lower	pAsh	Ass. (As)
Kūsāiu (9.)	2.1.2	**Kushite**	male	adult	lower	Ash/pAsh	Ass. (As)
Kūsāiu (10.)	2.1.2	**Kushite**	male	adult	lower	Ash	Ass. (As)
Kusî	2.1.2	**Kushite**	male	adult	upper	8th c.	Ass. (K)
Kūsītu	2.1.2	**Kushite**	female	adult	lower	7th c.	Ass. (N)
Mutakkil-A. 23.	2.1.3	**Kushite**	male	adult	lower	Ash/pAsh	Ass. (As)
Sē'-aqāba 1.	2.1.3	**Kushite**	male	adult	lower	Sar	Ass.
Šabakû	2.1.1	**Kushite**	male	adult	upper	Sar	Africa
Šapataku'	2.1.1	**Kushite**	male	adult	upper	Sar-Sen	Africa
Šēr-manāni	2.1.3	**Kushite**	male	child	lower	Sar	Ass.
Šulmu-šarri 12.	2.1.2	**Kushite**	male	adult	upper	Esa/Ash	Ass.
Tanut-Amani	2.1.1	**Kushite**	male	adult	upper	Ash	Africa
Tarqû	2.1.1	**Kushite**	male	adult	upper	Esa-Ash	Africa
Uš-Anaḫuru	2.1.1	**Kushite**	male	adult	upper	Esa	Ass. (N)
Zabad 4.	2.1.3	**Kushite**	male	adult	lower	pAsh	Ass.

[752] With regard to the issue of population size, B.J. Kemp (1991: 10) has estimated that the population size of Egypt in the late New Kingdom was between four and five million people. As for the Egyptian group, one may assume that a disproportionate share of the Egyptians in Assyria derived from *Lower* Egypt, a region more exposed to Assyrian incursions (Leahy 1993: 62).

[753] By "the combined data on identified and likely/possible Africans", the statistics on ethnicity, sex/gender, age, class, and time and place of living that are given in bold numbers in the tables of this chapter are meant.

individual	type	ethnicity	sex	age	class	time	place
Ḫallabēše 1.	2.2.1	**Libyan**	male	adult	upper	7th c.	Ass.
Ḫallabēše 2.	2.2.1	**Libyan**	male	adult	lower	Ash-pAsh	Ass. (N)
Ḫallabēše 3.	2.2.1	**Libyan**	male	adult	lower	pAsh	Ass. (As)
Ḫanabeš	2.2.1	**Libyan**	male	adult	lower	Sen	Ass.
Lamintu	2.1.1	**Libyan**	male	adult	upper	Esa-Ash	Africa
Susinqu 1.	2.1.1	**Libyan**	male	adult	upper	Sen	Ass. (N)
Susinqu 2.	2.1.1	**Libyan**	male	adult	upper	Esa-Ash	Africa
Takilāti	2.1.1	**Libyan**	male	adult	lower	Ash-pAsh	Ass. (N)
Usilkanu 1.	2.1.1	**Libyan**	male	adult	upper	Sar	Africa
Usilkanu 2.	2.1.1	**Libyan**	male	adult	lower	Ash-pAsh	Ass. (As)
Usilkanu 3.	2.1.1	**Libyan**	male	adult	lower	Ash/pAsh	Ass. (As)

As evident from the statistics presented above, the data concerning the group of (25) Kushites follow the same pattern as the combined data. That said, the circumstance that a relatively low proportion (44%) of Kushites lived in the Assyrian heartland may be noteworthy. The data concerning the group of (eleven) Libyans also follow the same pattern as the combined data. That said, the fact that there are only male and adult Libyans may be noteworthy. It is difficult to say whether any of these minor deviations are meaningful or coincidental.[754]

3.1.2 The sex/gender composition of the African group

The second subsection deals with the sex/gender composition of the African group, proceeding from statistics on the relative proportions of women and men in this group of African individuals.

	male	female	mixed					
2.1	91.8%	8.2%						
2.2	92.0%	8.0%						
2.1+2.2	**91.9%**	**8.1%**						
2.3	*55.2%*	*6.9%*	*37.9%*					

As evident from the statistics presented above, the great majority of Africans in Neo-Assyrian texts are male individuals. Proceeding from the statistics which combine the data on identified and likely/possible Africans, 91.9% of the 345 people in question are male individuals, while 8.1% are female individuals. The differences between the statistics on identified Africans and that on likely/possible

[754] The statistics regarding the Kushite group in percent are as follow: 96% males, 92% adults, 64% lower class, 68% post-conquest era, 44% Assyria proper. The corresponding statistics regarding the Libyan group are as follow: 100% males, 100% adults, 54.5% lower class, 63.6% post-conquest era, 54.5% Assyria proper.

Africans are highly insignificant. The statistics based on anonymous Africans (statistics which should be treated with caution) follow the same pattern, at least if considering the group "mixed" as unfit to include in the calculation.[755]

The finding that the great majority of Africans in Neo-Assyrian texts are male individuals is to be expected, considering the circumstance that ancient Near Eastern societies tended to be male-dominated, or patriarchal, in character.[756]

The question is whether the demographic statistics regarding gender/sex (male/female) differentiate even more, still proceeding from the statistics derived from the combined data on identified and likely/possible Africans? An analysis of the smallest group of demographic data (female) may be illuminative in this regard.

individual	type	ethnicity	sex	age	class	time	place
Adimasia	2.2.1	Egyptian	**female**	adult	slave	Ash	Ass. (As)
Al-ḫapi-mepi	2.1.1	Egyptian	**female**	adult	lower	pAsh	Ass. (N)
Amat-Emūni	2.1.1	Egyptian	**female**	adult	upper	Esa/Ash	Ass. (N)
Apî 1.	2.1.1	Egyptian	**female**	child	slave	pAsh	Ass. (As)
Apî 2.	2.1.1	Egyptian	**female**	adult	lower	pAsh	Ass. (As)
Ašāia	2.1.2	Egyptian	**female**	adult	lower	Ash/pAsh	Ass. (As)
Attâ-ḫāsi	2.2.1	Egyptian	**female**	adult	lower	Ash	Ass. (K)
Bēlet-issē'a 2.	2.1.3	Egyptian	**female**	adult	slave	pAsh	Ass. (As)
Eša-rṭeše	2.1.1	Egyptian	**female**	adult	lower	7th c.	Ass. (N)
Ezibtu 2.	2.1.2	Egyptian	**female**	adult	lower	Ash/pAsh	Ass. (As)
Ispiniša	2.1.2	Egyptian	**female**	adult	lower	Ash/pAsh	Ass. (As)
Karānūtu	2.1.2	Egyptian	**female**	adult	lower	Ash/pAsh	Ass. (As)
Kūsītu	2.1.2	Kushite	**female**	adult	lower	7th c.	Ass. (N)
Lābê (1.)	2.2.1	Egyptian	**female**	adult	slave	pAsh	Ass. (As)
Lābê (2.)	2.2.1	Egyptian	**female**	adult	lower	Ash/pAsh	Ass. (As)
Meia	2.1.1	Egyptian	**female**	adult	lower	7th c.	Ass. (As)
Mullissu-ḫāṣinat	2.1.3	Egyptian	**female**	adult	lower	pAsh	Ass. (N)
Muṣur(ītu) (1.)	2.1.2	Egyptian	**female**	adult	lower	Ash/pAsh	Ass. (As)
Muṣurītu (2.)	2.1.2	Egyptian	**female**	adult	lower	Ash/pAsh	Ass. (As)
Muṣurītu (3.)	2.1.2	Egyptian	**female**	adult	lower	Ash/pAsh	Ass. (As)
Niḫti-Eša-rau	2.1.1	Egyptian	**female**	adult	lower	pAsh	Ass. (N)
Paḫî	2.2.1	Egyptian	**female**	adult	slave	pAsh	Ass. (N)
Puṭu-šisi[...]	2.1.1	Egyptian	**female**	adult	slave	pAsh	Ass. (N)
Tamurtašu	2.2.1	Egyptian	**female**	adult	lower	Ash	Ass. (As)

[755] The term "mixed" draws from unspecific references to the general population, which was (of course) composed of men and women, young and old, high and low, etc.

[756] For studies on (the subordinate status of) women and femininity in the ancient Near East, see Bahrani 2001 and Stol 2016 (particularly pp. 690-691). Also ancient Egypt, which is often referred to as a culture in which women enjoyed a strong position, was a place where men dominated (Robins 1993, particularly pp. 190-191).

Tamūzītu 1.	2.1.2	Egyptian	**female**	adult	lower	Ash/pAsh	Ass. (As)
Tatašīri	2.2.1	Egyptian	**female**	adult	lower	Ash/pAsh	Ass. (As)
Tattapḫa(?)	2.1.1	Egyptian	**female**	adult	lower	Esa/Ash	Ass. (N)
Urkittu-kallat	2.1.2	Egyptian	**female**	adult	lower	Ash/pAsh	Ass. (As)

As evident from the statistics presented above, the data concerning the group of (28) women follow the same pattern as the combined data. That said, the circumstances that a great proportion (96.4%) of women belonged to the lower classes and that all women lived in the Assyrian heartland may be noteworthy. It is difficult to say whether any of these minor deviations are meaningful or coincidental.[757]

3.1.3 The age composition of the African group

The third subsection focuses on the age composition of the African group, discussing from statistics on the relative proportions of adults and minors in this group of African individuals.

	adult	child	mixed				
2.1	98.1%	1.9%					
2.2	100%	0%					
2.1+2.2	**98.6%**	**1.4%**					
2.3	*58.6%*	*3.4%*	*37.9%*				

As evident from the statistics presented above, the great majority of Africans in Neo-Assyrian texts are adult individuals. Proceeding from the statistics which combine the data on identified and likely/possible Africans, 98.6% of the 345 people in question are adult individuals, and 1.4% are individuals of minor age. The differences between the statistics on identified Africans and that on likely/possible Africans are highly insignificant. The statistics based on anonymous Africans (statistics which should be treated with caution) follow the same pattern, at least if considering the group "mixed" as unfit to include in the calculation.

The finding that the great majority of Africans in Neo-Assyrian texts are adult individuals is to be expected, considering the circumstance that ancient Near Eastern societies (like any other society) tend to focus on grown-up individuals.[758]

The question is whether the demographic statistics regarding age (adult/child) differentiate even more, still proceeding from the statistics derived from the

---

757 The statistics regarding the African female group in percent are as follow: 96.4% Egyptians, 96.4% adults, 96.4% lower classes, 89.3% post-conquest era, 100% Assyria proper.

758 For a recent and comprehensive study on children in the ancient Near East, which not the least touches upon the roles and statuses of children in societies, see Henriksen Garroway 2014.

combined data on identified and likely/possible Africans? An analysis of the smallest group of demographic data (child) may be illuminative in this regard.

individual	type	ethnicity	sex	age	class	time	place
Apî 1.	2.1.1	Egyptian	female	**child**	slave	pAsh	Ass. (As)
Kūsāiu 1.	2.1.2	Kushite	male	**child**	lower	Sar	Ass.
Pašî 9.	2.1.3	Egyptian	male	**child**	lower	pAsh	Ass. (As)
Sabutî	2.1.3	Egyptian	male	**child**	lower	Ash/pAsh	Ass. (As)
Šēr-manāni	2.1.3	Kushite	male	**child**	lower	Sar	Ass.

As evident from the statistics presented above, the data concerning the group of (five) children follow the same pattern as the combined data. That said, the circumstance that all children belonged to the lower classes may be noteworthy. It is difficult to say whether this minor deviation is meaningful or coincidental.[759]

3.1.4 The class composition of the African group

The fourth subsection centres on the class composition of the African group, proceeding from statistics on the relative proportions of upper, lower, and slave class members in this group.

The definitions used in this study for the terms that denote classes should be repeated in this context. By "upper class", people qualified as political (rulers), religious (priests), military (officers), and administrative (officials) *leaders*, people who belong to the intelligensia (scholars, scribes, etc.), people who are closely related (in terms of kinship) to individuals of the afore-mentioned groups, and people who are mentioned frequently and prominently in the sources (but without their having labels which indicate social rank) are meant. By "lower class", people not defined as above or as slaves are meant. By "slaves", people who feature as objects of business transactions are meant.

	upper	lower	slave	mixed				
2.1	26.8%	71.6%	1.6%					
2.2	14.8%	81.8%	3.4%					
2.1+2.2	**23.8%**	**74.2%**	**2.0%**					
2.3	*37.9%*	*17.2%*	*0%*	*44.8%*				

As evident from the statistics presented above, the clear majority of Africans in Neo-Assyrian texts belongs to the lower class. Proceeding from the statistics which combine the data on identified and likely/possible Africans, 74.2% of the 345

[759] The statistics regarding the African children group in percent are as follow: 60% Egyptians, 80% males, 100% lower classes, 60% post-conquest era, 60% Assyria proper.

people in question come from the lower class, 23.8% come from the upper class, and 2.0% come from the slave class. The differences between the statistics on identified Africans and that on likely/possible Africans are insignificant. Perhaps the relatively higher proportion of people from the lower class among likely/possible Africans and the relatively higher proportion of people from the upper class among identified Africans may be noted. The statistics based on anonymous Africans (statistics which should be treated with caution) stand out in the sense that the proportion of attestations of individuals from the upper class clearly outnumber those of the lower classes.[760]

The finding that the great majority of Africans in Neo-Assyrian texts belongs to the lower classes is to be expected, considering the circumstance that ancient Near Eastern societies were ruled by elites and were characterized by inequality and naturalized social hierarchies.[761]

The question is whether the demographic statistics regarding class (upper/lower) differentiate even more, still proceeding from the statistics derived from the combined data on identified and likely/possible Africans? An analysis of the smallest group of demographic data (slave class) may be illuminative in this regard.

individual	type	ethnicity	sex	age	class	time	place
Adimasia	2.2.1	Egyptian	female	adult	**slave**	Ash	Ass. (As)
Amman-tanaḫti 2.	2.1.1	Egyptian	male	adult	**slave**	pAsh	Ass. (As)
Apî 1.	2.1.1	Egyptian	female	child	**slave**	pAsh	Ass. (As)
Bēlet-issē'a 2.	2.1.3	Egyptian	female	adult	**slave**	pAsh	Ass. (As)
Lābê (1.)	2.2.1	Egyptian	female	adult	**slave**	pAsh	Ass. (As)
Paḫî	2.2.1	Egyptian	female	adult	**slave**	pAsh	Ass. (N)
Puṭu-šisi[...]	2.1.1	Egyptian	female	adult	**slave**	pAsh	Ass. (N)

As evident from the statistics presented above, the data concerning the group of (seven) slaves largely follow the same pattern as the combined data. That said, the

760 In connection with this discussion on social classes, a few words on professions should be said. More than 30 professions are attested for Africans. These professions can be tied to different sectors of society (administrative, religious, military) and to different levels or kinds of education (intellectual, manual). As for professions and sectors of society, Africans in Neo-Assyrian texts appear (e.g.) as mayor, "son of the palace" (i.e. palace official), "commander-of-fifty", gate guard, priest, and "votaress". As for professions and levels/kinds of education, Africans in Neo-Assyrian texts appear (e.g.) as scribe, "dream interpreter", physician, fuller, weaver, and horse trainer. In other words, the identified and likely/possible Africans in Neo-Assyrian texts had all kinds of occupations. For more on professions and the people in Neo-Assyrian texts, see Baker 2016.

761 For studies on social stratification in ancient Mesopotamia and Egypt, see e.g. Kemp 1991 and Pollock 1999. S. Pollock (1999: 174-185) sees social hierarchy as a fundamental aspect of the (official) ancient Mesopotamian worldview, and B.J. Kemp (1991: 156-157) identifies a "social myth held by the elite" which distinguishes between two social levels: the top bureaucrat and others (apropos the layout of the pyramid city of Kahun). No doubt, both the ancient Mesopotamian and Egyptian societies displayed and promoted social inequality.

circumstances that all slaves were Egyptian and lived in the post-conquest era and in the Assyrian heartland may be noteworthy. It is difficult to say whether any of these minor deviations are meaningful or coincidental. It is definitely noteworthy that only one of the slaves are male. It is difficult to say whether this major deviation is meaningful or coincidental, particularly because the number of people that belonged to the slave class is very small (7 of 345).[762]

3.2 Demographics and the African group: settings and circumstances

The second section discusses the African group based on settings and circumstances (responding to when, where, and how). Its subsections deal with the temporal distribution (3.2.1) and spatial distribution (3.2.2) of the African group, and with the backgrounds to the presence of this group (3.2.3).

3.2.1 The temporal distribution of the African group

The first subsection highlights the temporal distribution of the African group, discussing from statistics on when (time period, reign) the Africans lived within the Neo-Assyrian empire.

	9-8th c.	Sar	Sen	7th c.	Esa	Ash	pAsh	p612
2.1	0.8%	2.9%	3.3%	7.0%	12.6%	33.3%	38.9%	1.2%
2.2	1.1%	0%	3.4%	2.3%	9.7%	42.6%	40.9%	0%
2.1+2.2	**0.9%**	**2.2%**	**3.3%**	**5.8%**	**11.9%**	**35.7%**	**39.4%**	**0.9%**
2.3	*10.3%*	*17.2%*	*6.9%*	*0%*	*43.1%*	*19.0%*	*3.4%*	*0%*

As evident from the statistics presented above, the great majority of Africans in Neo-Assyrian texts lived under Esarhaddon and Ashurbanipal, or in the post-Ashurbanipal period. Proceeding from the statistics which combine the data on identified and likely/possible Africans, 11.9% of the 345 people in question lived in the reign of Esarhaddon, 35.7% lived in the reign of Ashurbanipal, and 39.4% lived in the post-Ashurbanipal period. The differences between the statistics on identified Africans and that on likely/possible Africans are insignificant. The statistics based on anonymous Africans (statistics which should be treated with caution) stand out in the sense that attestations from earlier times are significant.

The finding that the great majority of Africans in Neo-Assyrian texts lived in the post-conquest era (represented by the reigns of Esarhaddon, Ashurbanipal, and the post-Ashurbanipal period) is to be expected, considering the dual and combined

---

762 The statistics regarding the African slave group in percent are as follow: 100% Egyptians, 14.3% males, 85.7% adults, 100% post-conquest era, 100% Assyria proper.

circumstances that Assyrian forces controlled (parts of) Egypt and the Assyrian employment of mass deportations (often along ethno-cultural lines).[763]

The question is whether the demographic statistics regarding time (pre- and post-conquest) differentiate even more, still proceeding from the statistics derived from the combined data on identified and likely/possible Africans? An analysis of the smallest groups of demographic data (9-8th centuries BCE, reigns of Shalmaneser V to Sennacherib) may be illuminative in this regard.

individual	type	ethnicity	sex	age	class	time	place
Abī-Ḫūru 1.	2.1.1	Egyptian	male	adult	lower	**Sen**	Ass. (K)
Daia 1.	2.2.1	Egyptian	male	adult	lower	**Sen**	Ass. (As)
Daiâ (4.)	2.2.1	Egyptian	male	adult	lower	**8th c.**	Ass.
Daiaia	2.2.1	Egyptian	male	adult	lower	**Sen**	Ass. (As)
Ḫanabeš	2.2.1	Libyan	male	adult	lower	**Sen**	Ass.
Ḫur-waṣi 1.	2.1.1	Egyptian	male	adult	lower	**Sen**	Ass. (N)
Ḫur-waṣi 2.	2.1.1	Egyptian	male	adult	lower	**Sen**	Ass. (N)
Ḫur-waṣi (14.)	2.1.1	Egyptian	male	adult	upper	**Shal**	Ass.
Kūsāiu 1.	2.1.2	Kushite	male	child	lower	**Sar**	Ass.
Kusî	2.1.2	Kushite	male	adult	upper	**8th c.**	Ass. (K)
Pir'û	2.1.1	Egyptian	male	adult	upper	**Sar**	Africa
Rasū'	2.1.1	Egyptian	male	adult	lower	**Sen**	Ass. (N)
Ra'û 1.	2.1.1	Egyptian	male	adult	lower	**Sen**	Ass. (As)
Rē'e	2.1.1	Egyptian	male	adult	upper	**Sar**	Africa
Sē'-aqāba 1.	2.1.3	Kushite	male	adult	lower	**Sar**	Ass.
Susinqu 1.	2.1.1	Libyan	male	adult	upper	**Sen**	Ass. (N)
Ṣil-Aššur 2.	2.1.2	Egyptian	male	adult	upper	**Sen**	Ass. (N)
Šabakû	2.1.1	Kushite	male	adult	upper	**Sar**	Africa
Šapataku'	2.1.1	Kushite	male	adult	upper	**Sar-Sen**	Africa
Šēr-manāni	2.1.3	Kushite	male	child	lower	**Sar**	Ass.
Usilkanu 1.	2.1.1	Libyan	male	adult	upper	**Sar**	Africa
Uširiḫiuḫurti	2.1.1	Egyptian	male	adult	lower	**Sen**	Ass.

As evident from the statistics presented above, the data concerning the group of (22) people who lived in the pre-conquest era largely follow the same pattern as the combined data. That said, the circumstance that these people had a relatively low proportion (59.1%) of Egyptians, and the fact that all these people were male individuals may be noteworthy. It is difficult to say whether these minor deviations are meaningful or coincidental. The circumstance that a relatively low proportion

[763] For the phenomenon of mass deportations and the Neo-Assyrian empire, see Oded 1979 and Radner 2012b. According to B. Oded (1979: 19, 22-25, 81), about 80% of Neo-Assyrian deportations took place from the reign of Tiglath-pileser III onwards, and the deportations involved all groups of society (and not just the elite).

(45.5%) of these people lived in Assyria proper is definitely noteworthy. It is difficult to say whether this major deviation is meaningful or coincidental.[764]

3.2.2 The spatial distribution of the African group

The second subsection deals with the spatial distribution of the African group, proceeding from statistics on where (inside/outside Assyria, etc.) in the empire the Africans mentioned in Neo-Assyrian texts lived.

	Assur	*Nineveh*	*Kalhu*	*Arbela*	*provinces*	*Babyl.*	*v. state*	*Africa*
2.1	47.9%	26.5%	3.1%	0%	8.2%	0.8%	1.2%	12.5%
2.2	68.2%	17.0%	4.5%	0%	9.1%	0%	0%	1.1%
2.1+2.2	**53.0%**	**24.1%**	**3.5%**	**0%**	**8.4%**	**0.6%**	**0.9%**	**9.6%**
2.3	*13.8%*	*6.9%*	*3.4%*	*3.4%*	*3.4%*	*0%*	*0%*	*69.0%*

As evident from the statistics presented above, the clear majority of Africans in Neo-Assyrian texts lived in the cities of Assur or Nineveh. Proceeding from the statistics which combine the data on identified and likely/possible Africans, 53.0% of the 345 people lived in Assur, while 24.1% lived in Nineveh. The differences between the statistics on identified Africans and that on likely/possible Africans are fairly insignificant. Perhaps the great proportion of likely/possible Africans in Assur and the high proportion of identified Africans in Africa (mostly Egyptian vassal kings) stand out. The statistics based on anonymous Africans (statistics which should be treated with caution) do not follow the same pattern, especially concerning the much higher proportion of "African Africans".

The finding that the great majority of Africans in Neo-Assyrian texts lived in the Assyrian heartland is to be expected, considering that conquered peoples often were brought to Assyrian proper.[765] The fact that many Africans lived in Nineveh is unsurprising in the light of the status of this city as capital. By contrast, the fact that so many Africans lived in Assur, a city which had lost its former position as the political (beside the religious) capital of Assyria, is less easy to explain. Perhaps it simply happened that someone with the required authority at some point in time decided that the captured Africans should be settled in Assur.[766]

---

[764] The statistics regarding Africans of the pre-conquest era in percent are as follow: 59.1% Egyptians, 100% males, 90.9% adults, 59.1% lower class, 45.5% Assyria proper.

[765] B. Oded (1979: 28) concludes that the main direction of deportations in Neo-Assyrian times was to Assyria proper (delineated by Nineveh in the west, Arbela in the east, and Assur in the south).

[766] The destination for the deportation at least partly depended on the reason(s) behind the deportation. A mass deportation could be made as a punishment, to protect certain peoples, to consolidate the state (with deportees being loyal), to strengthen the army, to gain craftsmen and labourers, to urbanize strategic cities and sites, and to repopulate abandoned and desolate regions for the purpose of agricultural development (Oded 1979: 41-74).

The question is whether the demographic statistics about place (inside/outside Assyria proper) differentiate even more, still proceeding from the statistics of the combined data on identified and likely/possible Africans? An analysis of the smallest groups of demographic data (outside Assyria proper, Africa not included) may be illuminative in this regard.

individual	type	ethnicity	sex	age	class	time	place
Abši-Ešu	2.1.1	Egyptian	male	adult	lower	Ash	**Ass.**
Daiâ 1.	2.2.1	Egyptian	male	adult	lower	Esa	**Ass.**
Daiâ (4.)	2.2.1	Egyptian	male	adult	lower	8th c.	**Ass.**
Dān-Ešu	2.1.1	Egyptian	male	adult	upper	Ash	**Bab.**
Dāri-šarru 2.	2.1.2	Kushite	male	adult	upper	Esa/Ash	**Ass.**
Ḫā-bāštī 1.	2.2.1	Egyptian	male	adult	lower	Esa	**Ass.**
Ḫallabēše 1.	2.2.1	Libyan	male	adult	upper	7th c.	**Ass.**
Ḫanabeš	2.2.1	Libyan	male	adult	lower	Sen	**Ass.**
Ḫur-tibû 2.	2.1.1	Egyptian	male	adult	lower	pAsh	**Ass.**
Ḫur-waṣi 4.	2.1.1	Egyptian	male	adult	upper	Ash	**v. state**
Ḫur-waṣi (14.)	2.1.1	Egyptian	male	adult	upper	Shal	**Ass.**
Issar-dūrī 26.	2.1.3	Egyptian	male	adult	lower	Ash	**Ass.**
Kalbāia 2.	2.1.3	Egyptian	male	adult	lower	pAsh	**Ass.**
Kūsāiâ 1.	2.1.2	Kushite	male	adult	lower	pAsh	**Ass.**
Kūsāiâ 2.	2.1.2	Kushite	male	adult	lower	pAsh	**Ass.**
Kūsāiu 1.	2.1.2	Kushite	male	child	lower	Sar	**Ass.**
Kūsāiu 4.	2.1.2	Kushite	male	adult	lower	pAsh	**Ass.**
Kūsāiu 5.	2.1.2	Kushite	male	adult	lower	post-612	**Ass.**
Lū-šakin 14.	2.1.3	Egyptian	male	adult	lower	Ash	**Ass.**
Muṣurāiu 6.	2.1.2	Egyptian	male	adult	lower	post-612	**Ass.**
Muṣurī	2.1.2	Egyptian	male	adult	upper	Esa-Ash	**v. state**
Pašî 4.	2.2.1	Egyptian	male	adult	lower	Ash	**Ass.**
Pašî 6.	2.2.1	Egyptian	male	adult	lower	Ash	**Ass.**
Pi-san-Eši 2.	2.1.1	Egyptian	male	adult	lower	pAsh	**Ass.**
Sē'-aqāba 1.	2.1.3	Kushite	male	adult	lower	Sar	**Ass.**
Sīn-na'di 27.	2.1.3	Egyptian	male	adult	lower	post-612	**Ass.**
Šarru-lū-dāri 12.	2.1.2	Egyptian	male	adult	upper	Esa	**Bab.**
Šašmâ 1.	2.1.2	Egyptian	male	adult	lower	Ash	**v. state**
Šēr-manāni	2.1.3	Kushite	male	child	lower	Sar	**Ass.**
Šulmu-šarri 12.	2.1.2	Kushite	male	adult	upper	Esa/Ash	**Ass.**
Taia 3.	2.2.1	Egyptian	male	adult	lower	Ash	**Ass.**
Urdu-Mullissu 10.	2.1.3	Egyptian	male	adult	lower	pAsh	**Ass.**
Uširiḫiuḫurti	2.1.1	Egyptian	male	adult	lower	Sen	**Ass.**
Zabad 4.	2.1.3	Kushite	male	adult	lower	pAsh	**Ass.**

As evident from the statistics presented above, the data concerning the group of (34) people who lived outside Assyria proper follow the same pattern as the combined data. That said, the circumstances that these people had a relatively low proportion (64.7%) of Egyptians and that all were male individuals may be noteworthy. It is difficult to say whether any of these minor deviations are meaningful or coincidental. The "African Africans" (33 in number) are all Egyptians, men, adults, members of the elite, and the great majority of them lived in the post-conquest era.[767]

3.2.3 The backgrounds to the presence of the African group

The third subsection centres on the backgrounds to the presence of the African group, identifying and discussing evidence and patterns regarding how Africans became part of Assyria.

As apparent from the preceding chapter, the preserved text corpus does not dwell on the *transition* of African individuals and groups from Africa to western Asia and Assyria. Generally, Africans appear in Assyrian texts as if they had always been part of Assyria. Still, the annals of Sennacherib (e.g. RINAP 3 4) narrate that "Egyptian charioteers and princes and the charioteers of the land of Meluhha" were captured alive during the battle at Eltekeh in 701 BCE. Supposedly, these people were subsequently deported. One document (SAA 11 169) from the reign of Esarhaddon or Ashurbanipal lists "Egyptian deportees and their possessions". An inscription of Esarhaddon (RINAP 4 9) seems to convey a list of people deported from Egypt. The same king narrates that he counted the court of the Kushite king (including the Kushite crown prince) as booty at the fall of Memphis (e.g. RINAP 4 103). The annals of Ashurbanipal speak of "people – male and female" being uprooted at the fall of Thebes (e.g. RINAP 5/1 3).[768]

A basic presumption then is that the great majority of African individuals and groups became part of the Neo-Assyrian empire more or less *by force*. As illustrated by the table in subsection 3.2.1, only 6.4% of the identified and likely/possible Africans combined appear in texts which definitely pre-date the Assyrian conquest of Egypt in 671 BCE. Even then, African prisoners of war following the battles at Qarqar in 853 BCE, Raphia in 720 BCE, and Eltekeh in 701 BCE must be taken into account. Similarly, almost half of the identified and likely/possible Africans combined appear in texts dated to the reigns of Esarhaddon and Ashurbanipal, that is, to a time in which Assyrian forces conducted warfare on Egyptian soil.

Drawing from the combined evidence provided by biographies and Assyrian royal inscriptions, at least four modes of integration (all more or less linked to the use of force) can be distinguished regarding various groups of Africans within the

[767] The statistics regarding Africans outside Assyria proper in percent are as follow: 64.7% Egyptians, 100% males, 94.1% adults, 76.5% lower class, 79.4% post-conquest era. As for the "African Africans", five of these lived in the pre-conquest era. Most of the 33 people are Egyptian vassal kings, notably the 20 rulers enumerated in RINAP 5/1 11.

[768] Conversely, the people of Qirbit, a city in modern-day Iran (RGTC 7/2-2, pp. 494-495), are deported to Egypt following a campaign of Ashurbanipal to the eastern regions (e.g. RINAP 5/1 3).

orbit of the Neo-Assyrian empire, namely the modes or fates of deported, transferred, subjugated, and defeated.

The term "deported" is self-evident. Deportation affected all sections of society, from the commoner to the ruler. The term "transferred" tells of the possible fate of people with prestigious and attractive offices (such as scribes), as they were transferred from an African court to the Assyrian court.[769] The term "subjugated" points to people (such as soldiers, officers, and rulers) who were directly involved in clashes with Assyria and who became Assyrian subjects in this process.[770] The term "defeated" speaks of people (such as soldiers, officers, and rulers) who were directly involved in clashes with Assyria but who did *not* became Assyrian subjects in this process.[771] Naturally, an individual could both be subjugated and deported.[772]

A fifth mode of integration can be distinguished when not focusing on *transition* (from Africa to Asia) or on the use of *force* in the integration process. The term "naturalized" points to African individuals who belonged to the second (or third, etc.) generation of immigrants, in their being born in Assyria and western Asia, and in their having African parents, grandparents, or ancestors. This mode of integration brings to mind the earlier observation about Africans appearing in Assyrian texts "as if they had always been part of Assyria". Undoubtedly, it must have taken some generations for Africans to become established members of Assyrian society and form strong ethnic communities. This group of people, which were integrated by *birth*, probably encompass a significant portion of the Africans of this study.

---

769 The three Egyptian scribes and the three Egyptian dream interpreters in SAA 7 1 (dated to the reign of Esarhaddon or Ashurbanipal) may have been linked to this mode of integration. The same can be said of the Egyptian scribes and "the Kushites" in NWL 9 (dated to 786 BCE). Some scholars suggest that the presence of Kushites in Assyria during the eighth century BCE was the result of initiated trade agreements (centred on horses) between Kush and Assyria (Dalley 1985: 47; Kahn 2001: 16-18).

770 The mayor of Thebes, Mentuemhat, may be an example of an individual subjected to this mode of integration, even though a minority of Assyrian royal inscriptions (e.g. RINAP 5/1 11) suggests that *all* the listed 20 Egyptian vassal kings of RINAP 5/1 11 were deported to Assyria.

771 The "field marshal of Egypt", *Rē'e*, may be an example of an individual subjected to this mode of integration, in his being defeated by Assyrian forces and in his avoiding capture (RINAP 2 1; 7).

772 The king of Memphis and Sais, Necho I, may be an example of an individual subjected to these modes of integration, in his being defeated by the troops of Esarhaddon, and in his being deported to Assyria following a rebellion in the reign of Ashurbanipal. Of course, Necho I was subsequently pardoned and returned to Egypt by Ashurbanipal (see e.g. RINAP 5/1 11).

4. CONCLUSION

This chapter concludes the discussion part of this study. Rather than simply summarizing the results of this study, it reconnects to the discussion in the introduction on integration versus assimilation and on the concepts of Egyptomania and xenophobia (4.1), and places "the Neo-Assyrian experience" of Egypt, Kush, and Libya in a historical context (4.2).

4.1 Africans in the Neo-Assyrian empire: integration and assimilation

The first section deals with the concepts of integration and assimilation with regard to African individuals and groups within the sphere of the Neo-Assyrian empire. It concludes with brief remarks on the relevance of the concepts of Egyptomania and xenophobia in the present context.

As discussed in the introduction, the terms integration and assimilation may signify two different ways to incorporate or be incorporated. Integration represents a softer approach or effect and implies the incorporation of people(s) into a multicultural society and state. Assimilation represents a harder approach or effect and implies the process of acculturation and cultural imperialism with regard to the incorporated people(s). On the basis of the evidence presented in this study, three different, strategic aspects will be examined in order to evaluate whether Africans in Assyria were integrated or assimilated. These aspects are language, religion, and settlement pattern. In other words, the language of personal names, divine names incorporated into personal names, and the settlement pattern of the African group will be highlighted.

A clear mapping of the evidence is essential in order to evaluate integration and assimilation on the basis of the language of personal names and divine names in personal names. In the two tables below, identified Africans (of section 2.1) and people identifiable as Africans (of subsection 2.2.2) whose names contain *both* African and non-African linguistic elements (first table) or whose names contain *entirely* non-African linguistic elements (second table) are listed. The names of non-African deities or spirits are marked in bold letters.[773]

individual	type	ethnicity	sex	age	class	time	place
Abdi-Mūnu	2.1.1	Egyptian	male	adult	lower	pAsh	Ass. (As)
Abī-Ḫūru 1.	2.1.1	Egyptian	male	adult	lower	Sen	Ass. (K)

[773] Personal names that convey ethnonyms (*Muṣurāiu*, *Kūsāiu*, etc.) are not included in the tables. Although these names are classified as Akkadian, Aramaic, or West Semitic in the PNA-entries (Lipiński, 2/I, pp. 642-643; Hunger, 2/I, pp. 643-644; Jursa, 2/II, p. 772), they are after all derived from names of African lands. Regarding the selection of names for analysis, only personal names that generally are well-understood (hence those of 2.1 and 2.2.2) are examined.

Abī-Ḫūru 2.	2.1.1	Egyptian	male	adult	lower	pAsh	Ass. (N)
Amān-išme	2.1.1	Egyptian	male	adult	lower	pAsh	Ass. (As)
Amat-Emūni	2.1.1	Egyptian	female	adult	upper	Esa/Ash	Ass. (N)
Dān-Ešu	2.1.1	Egyptian	male	adult	upper	Ash	Bab.
Šē'i-Ēši	2.1.1	Egyptian	male	adult	lower	pAsh	Ass. (N)
Šumma-Ēši	2.1.1	Egyptian	male	adult	upper	Ash	Ass. (As)

individual	type	ethnicity	sex	age	class	time	place
*Abdi-**Samsi*** 2.	2.2.2	Egyptian	male	adult	upper	pAsh	Ass. (N)
Aḫu-dūr-enši 2.	2.1.3	Egyptian	male	adult	lower	pAsh	Ass. (As)
***Aššur**-dūrī* (6.)	2.1.3	Egyptian	male	adult	lower	Ash/pAsh	Ass. (As)
Awa (1.)	2.1.3	Egyptian	male	adult	lower	Esa	Ass. (As)
Awa (2.)	2.2.2	Egyptian	male	adult	lower	pAsh	Ass. (As)
Barīku 8.	2.1.3	Egyptian	male	adult	lower	Ash	Ass. (As)
***Bēlet**-issē'a* 2.	2.1.3	Egyptian	female	adult	slave	pAsh	Ass. (As)
*Bur-**Kūbi***	2.1.2	Egyptian	male	adult	lower	pAsh	Ass. (As)
Dāri-šarru 2.	2.1.2	Kushite	male	adult	upper	Esa/Ash	Ass.
Ezibtu 2.	2.1.2	Egyptian	female	adult	lower	Ash/pAsh	Ass. (As)
***Gula**-ēṭir* 3.	2.1.3	Egyptian	male	adult	lower	7th c.	Ass. (As)
***Inurta**-šarru-uṣur* 2.	2.2.2	Egyptian	male	adult	upper	Ash-pAsh	Ass. (N)
***Issar**-dūrī* 26.	2.1.3	Egyptian	male	adult	lower	Ash	Ass.
*Kalb**āia*** 2.	2.1.3	Egyptian	male	adult	lower	pAsh	Ass.
Karānūtu	2.1.2	Egyptian	female	adult	lower	Ash/pAsh	Ass. (As)
*Kiṣir-**Aššur*** 45.	2.2.2	Egyptian	male	adult	upper	Ash-pAsh	Ass. (As)
*Kiṣir-**Aššur*** 46.	2.2.2	Egyptian	male	adult	lower	Ash-pAsh	Ass. (As)
*Kiṣir-**Aššur*** (66.)	2.1.2	Egyptian	male	adult	lower	Ash/pAsh	Ass. (As)
*Lā-turam.-**Aššur*** 3.	2.1.3	Egyptian	male	adult	upper	Ash-pAsh	Ass. (As)
Lū-šakin 14.	2.1.3	Egyptian	male	adult	lower	Ash	Ass.
Mannu-kī-Nīnua 13.	2.1.2	Egyptian	male	adult	lower	Ash	Ass. (K)
Menas(s)ê 3.	2.1.2	Egyptian	male	adult	lower	pAsh	Ass. (As)
***Mullissu**-ḫāṣinat*	2.1.3	Egyptian	female	adult	lower	pAsh	Ass. (N)
*Mutakkil-**Aššur*** 23.	2.1.3	Kushite	male	adult	lower	Ash/pAsh	Ass. (As)
***Nabû**-rēḫtu-uṣur* 17.	2.1.3	Egyptian	male	adult	lower	pAsh	Ass. (N)
***Nabû**-šēzibanni* 12.	2.1.4	Egyptian	male	adult	upper	Esa-Ash	Africa
Nādinu (26.)	2.1.3	Egyptian	male	adult	lower	Ash/pAsh	Ass. (As)
*Qibīt-**Aššur*** 30.	2.1.4	Egyptian	male	adult	upper	Ash	Ass. (As)
*Qīš**āia*** 2.	2.1.2	Egyptian	male	adult	lower	pAsh	Ass. (As)
*Rīb**āia*** 11.	2.1.3	Egyptian	male	adult	lower	7th c.	Ass. (As)
***Sē'**-aqāba* 1.	2.1.3	Kushite	male	adult	lower	Sar	Ass.
***Sē'**-raḫi* 2.	2.2.2	Egyptian	male	adult	lower	Esa	Ass. (N)
***Sīn**-na'di* 27.	2.1.3	Egyptian	male	adult	lower	post-612	Ass.
*Sukk**āia*** 31.	2.2.2	Egyptian	male	adult	lower	Ash-pAsh	Ass. (As)
*Sukk**āia*** 43.	2.1.3	Egyptian	male	adult	lower	Ash/pAsh	Ass. (As)
*Ṣil-**Aššur*** 2.	2.1.2	Egyptian	male	adult	upper	Sen	Ass. (N)
Šarru-lū-dāri 12.	2.1.2	Egyptian	male	adult	upper	Esa	Bab.

Šarru-lū-dāri 13.	2.1.4	Egyptian	male	adult	upper	Esa-Ash	Africa
Šarru-lū-dāri 33.	2.1.3	Egyptian	male	adult	lower	7th c.	Ass. (As)
Šašmâ 1.	2.1.2	Egyptian	male	adult	lower	Ash	v. state
***Šēr**-manāni*	2.1.3	Kushite	male	child	lower	Sar	Ass.
Šulmu-šarri 12.	2.1.2	Kushite	male	adult	upper	Esa/Ash	Ass.
Ta'lâ 5.	2.1.2	Egyptian	male	adult	lower	Ash/pAsh	Ass. (As)
Tallu 2.	2.2.2	Egyptian	male	adult	lower	Ash	Ass. (As)
Tamūzītu 1.	2.1.2	Egyptian	female	adult	lower	Ash/pAsh	Ass. (As)
Tarḫursi 2.	2.1.3	Egyptian	male	adult	lower	pAsh	Ass. (As)
*Ṭāb-**Bēl*** 7.	2.1.3	Egyptian	male	adult	lower	pAsh	Ass. (As)
*Ṭāb-**Bēl*** 8.	2.1.2	Egyptian	male	adult	lower	Ash	Ass. (As)
*Ubru-**Mullissu***	2.1.3	Egyptian	male	adult	lower	pAsh	Ass. (N)
Ubrūtu 4.	2.1.3	Egyptian	male	adult	lower	Ash/pAsh	Ass. (As)
Ulūlāiu 42.	2.2.2	Egyptian	male	adult	lower	pAsh	Ass. (N)
*Urdu-**Aššur*** 5.	2.2.2	Egyptian	male	adult	upper	Ash-pAsh	Ass. (As)
*Urdu-**Aššur*** 7.	2.1.3	Egyptian	male	adult	lower	pAsh	Ass. (As)
*Urdu-**Mullissu*** 10.	2.1.3	Egyptian	male	adult	lower	pAsh	Ass.
*Urdu-**Nabû*** 13.	2.1.3	Egyptian	male	adult	lower	Ash/pAsh	Ass. (As)
*Urdu-**Nanāia*** 20.	2.1.3	Egyptian	male	adult	lower	Ash/pAsh	Ass. (As)
***Urkittu**-kallat*	2.1.2	Egyptian	female	adult	lower	Ash/pAsh	Ass. (As)
Zabad 4.	2.1.3	Kushite	male	adult	lower	pAsh	Ass.

The two tables above include eight Africans with personal names that contain both African and non-African linguistic elements and 58 Africans with names that contain only non-African linguistic elements. In other words, a quarter (24.7%) of the identified and identifiable Africans have names with non-African linguistic elements. Considering this circumstance and the fact that a significant number of Africans are bound to lay hidden behind Semitic personal names,[774] the proportion of Africans with non-African names is substantial. Unsurprisingly, the foreign linguistic elements in question are generally Akkadian or Aramaic.[775] These two languages were the most important ones in the Neo-Assyrian empire. In terms of dominant language, an "Aramaization of Assyria" can be detected (Tadmor 1982).

The two tables include 36 Africans with personal names that contain names of Mesopotamian deities or West Semitic deities or spirits. In other words, 13.5% of the identified and identifiable Africans have names which relate to foreign supernatural beings. Considering the presumption that the adoption of foreign theonyms was (more or less) stigmatic, and the fact that a significant number of Africans with names that mention non-African supernatural beings are bound to lay

---

[774] Of course, not all Africans with foreign names will be revealed by Africans ethnonyms, family relations, or institutional affiliations.

[775] With the exception of *Tarḫursi* 2., whose name may be Anatolian, according to the interpretation of R. Pruzsinszky (PNA 3/II, p. 1316).

hidden behind Semitic personal names, the proportion of Africans with names that speak of foreign supernatural beings is not insignificant. The Mesopotamian deities employed to name Africans are the gods Ashur, Ea, (N)inurta, Nabu, Sin, and the goddesses Aia, Gula, Ishtar, Mullissu, and Nanaia.[776] The West Semitic deities or spirits *Kūbi*, *Samsi*, *Sē'*, *Šašm*, and *Šēr* are called upon in names of African individuals.[777]

Regarding the settlement pattern in relation to integration or assimilation, this study shows that there were African, or Egyptian, communities in the Assyrian heartland. Egyptian communities can be identified at least in documents from Assur and Nineveh.

Consider, for example, the following document (SAA 6 142) from Nineveh and 692 BCE, which centres on the purchase of a house in Nineveh by the Egyptian man *Ṣil-Aššur* 2. The translation of the document, given below, follows that of T. Kwasman and S. Parpola (1991).

> Fingernail of Šarru-lu-dari,
> fingernail of Atar-suru,
> fingernail of Amat-Su'la, wife of Bel-duri, shield-bearing 'third man,'
> owners of the house being sold.
>
> A built house with its beams, doors and a yard in Nineveh, adjoining the house of Mannu-ki-ahhe, the house of Ilu-issiya, and the street — Ṣilli-Aššur, Egyptian scribe, has contracted and bought it for one mina of silver (by the mina) of the king from Šarru-lu-dari, Atar-suru and Amat-Su'la, the wife of Bel-duri. The money is paid completely. That house is purchased and acquired. Any revocation, lawsuit, or litigation is void. Whoever in the future, at any time, whether these men (or anyone else), seeks a lawsuit and litigation against Ṣilli-Aššur, shall pay 10 minas of silver.
>
> Witness Šusanqu, the king's brother-in-law.
> Witness Hur-waṣi, 'third man.'
> Witness Rasu', chief boatman.
> Witness Nabû-duru-uṣur, (horse) raiser.
> Witness Hur-waṣi, chief boatman.
> Witness Sin-šarru-uṣur. Witness Zitt[i].
> Month Sivan (III), 16th day, eponym year of Zazaya, governor of Arpad.

---

776 In addition, *Bēl* and *Bēlet* probably refer to Mesopotamian deities, and *Urkittu* should be a reference to Ishtar. According to the work by J. Black and A. Green (1992: 40, 128-129, 132-133), *Bēl* refers to Marduk and *Bēlet(-ilī)* to Mesopotamian mother- and birth goddesses. Ishtar had the city of Uruk as one of her main places of worship (Black and Green 1992: 108-109).

777 Regarding *Kūbi*, *Samsi*, *Sē'*, *Šašm*, and *Šēr*, the respective PNA-entries (Baker, 1/II, p. 354; 3/II, p. 1264; Fales 1/I, p. 7; 3/I, pp. 1098, 1104; Weszeli and Zadok, 3/II, p. 1253) state that they are part of West Semitic personal names, and that they express theonyms or appear as agents in relation to the name bearer, clearly indicating that these were regarded as supernatural beings. *Samsi* may be the West Semitic form of the Mesopotamian sun-god Shamash. The name *Abdi-Samsi* is written with the divine determinative (*MZL*, sign 10) in front of the second element in SAA 14 30.

Witness Šamaš-kenu-uṣur.
Witness Mituru. Witness Nabû-šumu-iddina.

Apart from the buyer himself, who is qualified as an "Egyptian scribe" (*ṭupšar Muṣurāiu*), the list of witnesses mentions four people with African names, namely *Susinqu* 1., *Ḫur-waṣi* 1., *Rasū'*, and *Ḫur-waṣi* 2. These four individuals also head the list of witnesses. In other words, already in the reign of Sennacherib and firmly in the pre-conquest era, it is possible to distinguish an Egyptian community in the Assyrian heartland, in this case in Nineveh. From Nineveh and the *post*-conquest era, there is the archive of *Inurta-šarru-uṣur*, an "archive of Egyptians".

Consider also, for example, the following document (StAT 2 167) from Assur and 646 BCE, which centres on the transfer of a house in Assur to the Egyptian man *Tap-naḫte* 3. The translation of the document, given below, follows that of V. Donbaz and S. Parpola (2001).

> Seal of Paw[aya], seal of Re'uni, ditto of Amehi, ditto of Ametanahte, ditto of Siha', ditto of Kisiri, ditto of Batunahte, ditto of Butanahte, ditto of Kiṣir-šarruti from Tua (and of) Pašî.
>
> A house of 6 seahs in front of the *ekiri* house — they have given it to Tapnahte in lieu of his share. Whoever contravenes, shall pay five minas of silver to Tapnahte. May Aššur, Šamaš and Nabû be his prosecutors.
>
> Witness Urdu-Aššur, commander-of-fifty.
> Witness La-turammanni-Aššur,
> Witness Lululu,
> Witness Pamenapi,
> Witness Unamâ,
> Witness Ni[...]*da*hi.
> Month Ab (V), [30th] day, eponym year of Nabû-šar-ahhe[šu].

There are individuals with African names both among the transaction parties and witnesses. The benificiary, *Tap-naḫte* 3., has an Egyptian name, most of the conveyers of the house (*Ameḫi*, *Amman-tanaḫti* 1., *Batu-naḫti*, *Butanaḫte*, *Kisiri*, *Pašî* 3., *Siḫā'*) have clearly or likely/possibly Egyptian names, and several of the witnesses (*Lulūlu*, *Pamenapi*) bear likely or possibly Egyptian names. Moreover, the prominent Egyptians *Lā-turammanni-Aššur* 3. and *Urdu-Aššur* 5. function as witnesses. The text belongs to the N31-archive, an "archive of Egyptians". As already noted, in addition to this archive, also archive Assur 52b can be considered as an archive of Egyptians from Assur.

To summarize this discussion on integration or assimilation with regard to Egyptians, Kushites, and Libyans in the Neo-Assyrian empire, the results are ambiguous. The significant proportion of Africans with personal names that contain non-African linguistic elements or the names of non-African supernatural beings points to assimilation, while the settlement pattern (as revealed by the preserved text corpus) show the existence of strong African, or Egyptian, communities in the Assyrian heartland and therefore rather points to the process of integration. Apparently, Africans in Assyria simultaneously included and excluded foreign elements, in a complex process which speaks both of surrender and resistance in a foreign environment. Not least, it points to the concept of ethnicity as being fluid and dynamic, and constantly (re-)negotiated.

An Egyptomania on the part of the ethnic majority group is not readily apparent, at least not if Egyptians are expected to have an elevated status in Assyrian society. It is true, however, that the above-mentioned presence of Egyptian scholars (*ḫarṭibu*) and scribes (*ṭupšarru*) in Assyria can be seen as evidence of a kind of Egyptomania, at least at the Assyrian court. Certainly, the Egyptian population in Assyria does not appear to have been particularly oppressed, judging by their maintained, native cultural markers and their participation in Assyrian society. Xenophobia on the part of the ethnic minority group is not readily apparent either, especially considering the phenomenon of Egyptians and Kushites adopting foreign linguistic elements and foreign divine names in their personal names. On the contrary, it is easy to get the impression that the African group in Assyria aimed for inclusion (and thus survival) in an alien environment. The discrepancy between highly ideological royal inscriptions and pragmatic, down-to-earth archival texts comes across yet again.

4.2 African-Mesopotamian relations: the Neo-Assyrian experience

The second section places "the Neo-Assyrian experience" of Africa in a historical context, examining the periods before, during, and after Assyrian rule. The intensity (frequent/infrequent) and nature (equal/unequal) of African-Mesopotamian relations are highlighted in this concluding discussion.

Prior to the Neo-Assyrian period, the contacts between Egypt and Mesopotamia appear to have been relatively infrequent and largely based on equality. Earlier scholars often discuss Mesopotamian influence on early Egypt, some even suggesting that a north-eastern "dynastic race" invaded Egypt and introduced "civilization" at the end of prehistoric Egypt (see e.g. Emery 1961). This view has been modified substantially over the last decades. Although Mesopotamian cultural influence is duly recognized, the internal development and inner dynamics of the early Egyptian state are now the focal points (see e.g. Teeter 2011).

Much later, in the early Middle Assyrian period, the king of Assyria initiated diplomatic contacts with New Kingdom Egypt, seeking entry into the brotherhood of Near Eastern kings. If anything, Assyria appears as an upstart in relation to established and powerful Egypt. In the late Middle Assyrian period, an Assyrian ruler (Ashur-bel-kala) claims to have received exotic gifts from an anonymous "king of Egypt" (*šar māt Muṣre*). Although the Assyrian king apparently sought to present this gift as "tribute", implying a relationship along the lines of superiority/subordination, the goods transfer in question was probably merely of a voluntary, diplomatic kind (Kuhrt 1997: 350-352, 361).

In the Neo-Assyrian period, contacts between Egypt and Mesopotamia became more frequent, and the relationship turned clearly asymmetric (in terms of power balance), with the Neo-Assyrian state closing in on the Egyptian rulers and Kushite kings.[778] Finally, in 671 BCE, the Neo-Assyrian army entered Egypt and annexed Lower Egypt to the Neo-Assyrian empire. 20 Egyptian rulers, from the delta in the north to Thebes in the south, became vassals to the Assyrian king. A few years later, in 664-663 BCE, Assyrian forces marched into Upper Egypt, sacked the city of Thebes, and managed to pacify the Kushite state and to quell the ambitions of the Kushite kings to rule over Egypt (Kuhrt 1997: 634-638).

A profound change in the relationship between Egypt and Mesopotamia had now occurred, with relations being more frequent and essentially one-sided. A foreign administration was imposed on Egypt, and many Egyptians, Kushites, and Libyans were deported to the heartland of the Neo-Assyrian empire. Of course, Egypt had experienced foreign domination before (notably during the Hyksos), but the entry of the Neo-Assyrian empire on the scene presented something markedly different. At the ideological level, the strong and proud Egyptian civilization had been challenged, and the Egyptians had become subjects of a state ruled by "Asiatics".[779] No wonder then that, in the words of W. Helck (2005: 151-152), "there are no monuments from the time of Assyrian rule in Egypt, nor did those who fought against this control, such as Tanutamen and Montuemhat, the ruler of Thebes, mention their Assyrian overlords in texts. Only in later texts did the Assyrians emerge as sworn enemies. This suggests that Assyrian rule in Egypt was seen as an abnormal period and was therefore dealt with in a customary Egyptian fashion, by concealment."[780] In other words, the Assyrian phase of Egyptian history presented a trauma, at least on the ideological level.

The Assyrian grip on Egypt gradually loosened following the second Egyptian campaign of Ashurbanipal in 664-663 BCE. By 656 BCE, Psammetichus I, a former Assyrian vassal in Egypt, had managed to gain control both of the north, pushing back Assyrian claims, and the south, pushing back Kushite claims. Egypt was now unified and independent, entering the Saite period, often referred to as a renaissance of Egyptian culture (Kuhrt 1997: 636-646).

This development hardly affected those Africans who had once been deported to Assyria, thriving Egyptian communities of the late seventh century BCE, evidenced in the various "archives of Egyptians" from Assur and Nineveh. The downfall of the Neo-Assyrian empire, including the conquest of Assur by the

---

[778] Regarding the early Neo-Assyrian period, contacts between Assyria and Egypt were sparse, judging by the preserved Assyrian royal inscriptions. Shalmaneser III claims to have defeated Egyptian troops in the battle at Qarqar and to have received "tribute" (*maddattu*) from Egypt. Concerning the reigns of Tiglath-pileser III, Sargon II, and Sennacherib, contacts between Assyria and Egypt (and Kush) were more frequent. Assyrian royal inscriptions paint the picture of Egyptian tribute and of Assyrian victories in the battles of Raphia in 720 BCE (against Egypt) and Eltekeh in 701 BCE (against Egypt and Kush) (Kuhrt 1997: 488, 499).

[779] Ancient Egypt is often regarded as inward-looking and ethno-centric, as well as having the worldview according to which foreigners (including "Asiatics") were part of a chaotic periphery and signified the hostile "Nine Bows" (*psḏt-pḏwt*) (Loprieno 1988; Assmann 1990).

[780] For the "later texts" in question, see the overview by K. Ryholt (2004) of Demotic literature pertaining to the Assyrian (re-)conquest of Egypt.

Medes in 614 BCE and the conquest of Nineveh by a Babylonian-Median coalition in 612 BCE must have affected the exiled Africans much more. Even though a fraction of the Africans in Assyria may have managed to return to Egypt in the turmoil, the vast majority of Africans living in Assyria are likely to have been killed or taken as prisoners of war by the Babylonian and Median troops that invaded the Assyrian heartland. Tellingly, individuals with Egyptian names subsequently appear in texts from the Neo-Babylonian state.[781] One chapter in the relationship between the ancient Egyptian and Mesopotamian civilizations had ended and another had begun.

[781] Still, a significant proportion of the "Babylonian Egyptians" must have arrived in southern Mesopotamia after battles between Egyptian and Babylonian forces in/near Egypt and in the Levant. For discussions of Egyptians in Babylonia, see Wiseman 1966; Hackl and Jursa 2015. For a list of Egyptian names attested in Neo-Babylonian (and Persian) texts, see Ranke 1910: 38-42.

5. BIBLIOGRAPHY

Ahmad, A.Y. 1996. "The Archive of Aššur-mātu-taqqin found in the new town of Aššur and dated mainly by post-canonical eponyms". *Al-Rafidan* 17: 207-288.

Ahmad, A.Y. and Postgate, J.N. 2007. *Archives from the Domestic Wing of the North-West Palace at Kalhu/Nimrud.* Edubba 10. London: NABU Publications.

Al-Asil, N. 1955. "News and Correspondence". *Sumer* 11: 129-132.

Albright, W.F. 1956. "Further Synchronisms between Egypt and Asia in the Period 935-685 BC". *Bulletin of the American Schools of Oriental Research* 141: 23-27.

Assmann, J. 1990. *Ma'at. Gerechtigkeit und Unsterblichkeit im Alten Ägypten*. Munich: Verlag C.H. Beck.

Bagg, A.M. 2007. *Die Orts- und Gewässernamen der neuassyrischen Zeit, Teil 1: Die Levante*. Répertoire Géographique des Textes Cunéiformes 7/1. Wiesbaden: Dr. Ludwig Reichert Verlag.

— 2011. *Die Assyrer und das Westland. Studien zur historischen Geographie und Herrschaftspraxis in der Levante im 1 Jt. v. u. Z.* Orientalia Lovaniensia Analecta 216. Leuven, Paris, and Walpole: Peeters.

— 2017. *Die Orts- und Gewässernamen der neuassyrischen Zeit, Teil 2: Zentralassyrien und benachbarte Gebiete, Ägypten und die arabische Halbinsel*. Répertoire Géographique des Textes Cunéiformes 7/2. Wiesbaden: Dr. Ludwig Reichert Verlag.

Bahrani, Z. 2001. *Women of Babylon: Gender and Representation in Ancient Mesopotamia*. London and New York: Routledge.

Baines, J. 1996. "Contextualizing Egyptian Representations of Society and Ethnicity". Pp. 339-384 in *The Study of the Ancient Near East in the Twenty-First Century*, eds. J. Cooper and G. Schwartz. The William Foxwell Albright Centennial Conference. Winona Lake: Eisenbrauns.

Baker, H.D. (ed.) 2000. *The Prosopography of the Neo-Assyrian Empire, Volume 2, Part 1: H-K*. Helsinki: Neo-Assyrian Text Corpus Project.

— 2001. *The Prosopography of the Neo-Assyrian Empire, Volume 2, Part 2: L-N*. Helsinki: Neo-Assyrian Text Corpus Project.

— 2002. *The Prosopography of the Neo-Assyrian Empire, Volume 3, Part 1: P-Ṣ*. Helsinki: Neo-Assyrian Text Corpus Project.

— 2011. *The Prosopography of the Neo-Assyrian Empire, Volume 3, Part 2: Š-Z*. Helsinki: Neo-Assyrian Text Corpus Project.

— 2016. *The Prosopography of the Neo-Assyrian Empire, Volume 4, Part 1: Neo-Assyrian Specialists: Crafts, Offices, and Other Professional Designations*. Helsinki: Neo-Assyrian Text Corpus Project.

Barth, F. 1969. *Ethnic Groups and Boundaries: The Social Organization of Culture Difference*. London: George Allen and Unwin.

Bilabel, F. and Grohmann, A. 1927. *Geschichte Vorderasiens und Ägyptens vom 16. Jahrhundert v. Chr. bis auf die Neuzeit*. Heidelberg: C. Winter.

Black, J. and Green, A. 1992. *Gods, Demons and Symbols of Ancient Mesopotamia: An Illustrated Dictionary*. London: British Museum Press.

Borger, R. 1960. "Das Ende des ägyptischen Feldherrn Sib'e = So'". *Journal of Near Eastern Studies* 19: 49-53.

— 2003. *Mesopotamisches Zeichenlexikon*. Alter Orient und Altes Testament 305. Münster: Ugarit-Verlag.

Brunner, H. 1952-53. "Ein assyrisches Relief mit einer ägyptischen Festung". *Archiv für Orientforschung* 16: 253-262.

Budka, J. 2000. "Die Beziehungen Ägyptens zu Vorderasien im 4. Jahrtausende v. Chr.". *Kemet* 9: 18-20.

Chandra, K. 2012. *Constructivist Theories of Ethnic Politics*. New York: Oxford University Press.

Chapman, C.R. 2004. *The Gendered Language of Warfare in the Israelite-Assyrian Encounter*. Harvard Semitic Monographs 62. Winona Lake: Eisenbrauns.

de Clercq, M. 1888. *Collection de Clercq: Catalogue Methodique et Raisonné – Antiquités Assyriennes*. Paris: Ernest Leroux.

Cohen, E.S. 1992. *Egyptianization and Acculturation Hypothesis: An Investigation of the Pan-Grave, Kerman and C-Group Material Cultures in Egypt and the Sudan during the Second Intermediate Period and Eighteenth Dynasty*. PhD dissertation, Yale University.

Cohen, G.N. and Westbrook, R. (eds.) 2000. *Amarna Diplomacy: The Beginnings of International Relations*. Baltimore: Johns Hopkins University Press.

Cole, S.W. and Machinist, P. 1998. *Letters from Assyrian and Babylonian Priests to Kings Esarhaddon and Assurbanipal*. State Archives of Assyria 13. Helsinki: Neo-Assyrian Text Corpus Project.

Collon, D. 1995. *Ancient Near Eastern Art*. London: British Museum Press.

Dalley, S. 1985. "Foreign Chariotry and Cavalry in the Armies of Tiglath-pileser III and Sargon II". *Iraq* 47: 31-48.

Dalley, S. and Postgate, J.N. 1984. *The Tablets from Fort Shalmaneser*. Cuneiform Texts from Nimrud 3. London: British Institute for the Study of Iraq.

Delitzsch, F. 1907. *Vorderasiatische Schriftdenkmäler der Königlichen Museen zu Berlin, Hefte 1*. Leipzig: J.C. Hinrichs.

Deller, K. 1985. "Köche und Küche des Aššur-Tempels". *Baghdader Mitteilungen* 16: 347-376.

Deller, K., Fales, F.M., and Jakob-Rost, L. 1995. "Neo-Assyrian Texts from Assur Private Archives, Part 2". *State Archives of Assyria Bulletin* 9.

Derry, D.E. 1956. "The Dynastic Race in Egypt". *Journal of Egyptian Archaeology* 42: 80-85.

Dietrich, M. 1975a. "Assyrien und Ägypten". *Lexikon der Ägyptologie* 1: 498-499.

— 1975b. "Babylonien und Ägypten". *Lexikon der Ägyptologie* 1: 592-593.

Donbaz, V. and Parpola, S. 2001. *Neo-Assyrian Legal Texts in Istanbul*. Studien zu den Assur-Texten 2. Saarbrücken: Saarbrücker Druckerei und Verlag.

Draper, C. 2015. "Two Libyan Names in a Seventh Century Sale Document from Assur". *Journal of Ancient Egyptian Interconnections* 7/2: 1-15.

Edel, E. 1980. *Neue Deutungen keilschriftlicher Umschreibungen ägyptischer Wörter und Personennamen*. Österreichische Akademie der Wissenschaften; Philosophisch-historische Klasse 375. Vienna: Verlag der Österreichische Akademie der Wissenschaften.

Elat, M. 1978. "The Economic Relations of the Neo-Assyrian Empire with Egypt". *Journal of the American Oriental Society* 98: 20-34.

Emery, W.B. 1961. *Archaic Egypt*. Harmondsworth: Penguin Books.

Erman, A. and Grapow, H. 1926-1961. *Wörterbuch der ägyptischen Sprache*. Berlin: Akademie-Verlag.

Faist, B. 2007. *Alltagstexte aus neuassyrischen Archiven und Bibliotheken der Stadt Assur*. Studien zu den Assur-Texten 3. Wiesbaden: Harrassowitz.
— 2010. *Neuassyrische Rechtsurkunden, IV*. Wissenschaftliche Veröffentlichungen der Deutschen Orient-Gesellschaft 132. Wiesbaden: Harrassowitz.
Fales, F.M. 1979. "A List of Assyrian and West Semitic Women's Names". *Iraq* 41: 55-73.
— 1981. "A Literary Code in Assyrian Royal Inscriptions: The Case of Ashurbanipal's Egyptian Campaigns". Pp. 169-202 in *Assyrian Royal Inscriptions: New Horizons*, ed. F.M. Fales. Orientis antiqui collectio 17. Rome: Isitituto per l'Oriente.
— 1983. "Studies on Neo-Assyrian Texts II: 'Deeds and Documents' from the British Museum". *Zeitschrift für Assyriologie und Vorderasiatische Archäologie* 73: 232-254.
Fales, F.M. and Jakob-Rost, L. 1991. "Neo-Assyrian Texts from Assur: Private Archives in the Vorderasiatisches Museum of Berlin, Part 1". *State Archives of Assyria Bulletin* 5.
Fales, F.M. and Postgate, J.N. 1992. *Imperial Administrative Records, Part I: Palace and Temple Administration*. State Archives of Assyria 7. Helsinki: Neo-Assyrian Text Corpus Project.
— 1995. *Imperial Administrative Records, Part II: Provincial and Military Administration*. State Archives of Assyria 11. Helsinki: Neo-Assyrian Text Corpus Project.
Fecht, G. 1958. "Zu den Namen ägyptischer Fürsten und Städte in den Annalen des Assurbanipal und der Chronik des Assarhaddon". *Mitteilungen des deutschen archäologischen Instituts, Abteilung Kairo* 16: 112-119.
Feldman, M.H. 2004. "Nineveh to Thebes and Back: Art and Politics between Assyria and Egypt in the Seventh Century BCE". *Iraq* 66: 141-150.
Frahm, E. 2010. "Hochverrat in Assur". Pp. 89-139 in *Assur-Forschungen*, eds. S.M. Maul and N. Heeßel. Wiesbaden: Harrassowitz.
— 2011. "Die Inschriftenreste auf den Obeliskenfragmenten aus Assur". Pp. 59-75 in J. Orlamünde, *Die Obeliskenfragmenten aus Assur*. Wissenschaftliche Veröffentlichungen der Deutschen Orient-Gesellschaft 135. Wiesbaden: Harrassowitz.
Frame, G. 2021. *The Royal Inscriptions of Sargon II, King of Assyria (721-705 BCE)*. Royal Inscriptions of the Neo-Assyrian Period 2. Philadelphia: University of Pennsylvania Press.
Friedrich, J., Meyer, G.R., Ungnad, A., and Weidner, E.F. 1940. *Die Inschriften vom Tell-Halaf: Keilschrifttexte und aramäische Urkunden aus einer assyrischen Provinzhaupstadt*. Archiv für Orientforschung, Beiheft 6. Berlin: Im Selbstverlage des Herausgebers.
Gardiner, A.H. 1961. *Egypt of the Pharaohs: An Introduction*. Oxford: Clarendon Press.
Garelli, P. 1971. "Nouveau coup d'oeil sur Muṣur". Pp. 37-48 in *Festschrift A. Dupont-Sommer*, eds. A. Caquout and M. Philonenko. Paris: Libraire d'Amerique et d'Orient Adrien.
Gelb, I.J. et al. 1956-2010. *The Assyrian Dictionary of the Oriental Institute of the University of Chicago*. Chicago: Oriental Institute of the University of Chicago.
Giveon, R. 1972. "An Egyptian Official at Gezer?". *Israel Exploration Journal* 22: 143-144.
Gordon, A. 2001. "Foreigners". Pp. 544-548 in *The Oxford Encyclopedia of Ancient Egypt, II*, ed. D. Redford. Oxford and New York: Oxford University Press.
Grayson A.K. 1996. *Assyrian Rulers of the Early First Millennium BC II (858-745 BC)*. Royal Inscriptions of Mesopotamia, Assyrian Periods 3. Toronto, Buffalo, and London: University of Toronto Press.
Grayson, A.K. and Novotny, J. 2012, 2014. *The Royal Inscriptions of Sennacherib, King of Assyria (704-681 BC)*. Royal Inscriptions of the Neo-Assyrian Period 3. Winona Lake: Eisenbrauns.

Hackl, J. and Jursa, M. 2015. "Egyptians in Babylonia in the Neo-Babylonian and Achaemenid Periods". Pp. 157-180 in *Exile and Return: The Babylonian Context*, eds. J. Stökl and C. Waerzeggers. Berlin: Walter de Gruyter.

Heidorn, L.A. 1997. "The Horses of Kush". *Journal of Near Eastern Studies* 56: 105-114.

Heimpel, W. 1997. "Meluḫḫa". *Reallexikon der Assyriologie und Vorderasiatischen Archäologie* 8: 53-55.

Helck, W. 1977. "Fremdvölkerdarstellung". *Lexikon der Ägyptologie* 2: 315-321.

— 2005. "Assyrians". Pp. 150-152 in *Encyclopedia of the Archaeology of Ancient Egypt*, ed. K.A. Bard. London: Routledge.

Henriksen Garroway, K. 2014. *Children in the Ancient Near Eastern Household*. Explorations in Ancient Near Eastern Civilizations 3. Winona Lake: Eisenbrauns.

Herbordt, S., Mattila, R., Parker, B., Postgate, J.N., and Wiseman, D.J. 2019. *Documents from the Nabu Temple and from Private Houses*. Cuneiform Texts from Nimrud 6. London: British Institute for the Study of Iraq.

Herrmann, G. and Laidlaw, S. 2013. *Ivories from Rooms SW 11/12 and T10 Fort Shalmaneser*. Ivories from Nimrud 7. London: British Institute for the Study of Iraq.

Huber, I. 2006. "Von Affenwärtern, Schlangenbeschwörern und Palastmanagern: Ägypter im Mesopotamien des ersten vorchristlichen Jahrtausends". Pp. 303-329 in *Altertum und Mittelmeerraum*, eds. R. Rollinger and B. Truschnegg. Stuttgart: Franz Steiner Verlag.

Ismail, B.K. and Postgate, J.N. 1993. *Texts from Nineveh*. Texts in the Iraq Museum 11. Baghdad: Directorate General of Antiquities.

Jacobsen, T. 1939. *Cuneiform texts in the National Museum, Copenhagen*. Copenhagen: C.T. Thomsens bogtrykkeri.

Jas, R. 1996. *Neo-Assyrian Judicial Procedures*. State Archives of Assyria Studies 5. Helsinki: Neo-Assyrian Text Corpus Project.

Johns, C.H.W. 1898-1923. *Assyrian Deeds and Documents*. London: George Bell and Sons.

Kaelin, O. 1999. *Ein assyrisches Bildexperiment nach ägyptischem Vorbild. Zur Planung und Ausführung der "Schlacht am Ulai"*. Münster: Ugarit-Verlag.

Kahn, D. 2001. "The Inscription of King Sargon II at Tang-i Var and the Chronology of Dynasty 25". *Orientalia* 70/1: 1-18.

— 2006. "The Assyrian Invasions of Egypt (673-663 BC) and the Final Expulsion of the Kushites". *Studien zur altägyptischen Kultur* 34: 251-267.

— 2018. "Nebuchadnezzar and Egypt: An Update on Egyptian Monuments". *Hebrew Bible and Ancient Israel* 7: 63-76.

Kalvelagen, R. Katz, D., and van Soldt, W.H. (eds.). 2005. *Ethnicity in Ancient Mesopotamia: Papers Read at the 48th Rencontre Assyriologique Internationale, Leiden 1-4 July 2002*. PIHANS 102. Leiden: Nederlands Instituut voor het Nabije Oosten.

Kantor, H.J. 1952. "Further Evidence for Early Mesopotamian Relations with Egypt". *Journal of Near Eastern Studies* 11: 239-250.

Karlsson, M. 2016. *Relations of Power in Early Neo-Assyrian State Ideology*. Studies in Ancient Near Eastern Records 10. Boston and Berlin: Walter de Gruyter.

— 2018. "Egypt and Kush in Neo-Assyrian State Letters and Documents". *State Archives of Assyria Bulletin* 24: 37-61.

— 2019. "'The City of the kipkip-Speech'? Kipkipi in Ashurbanipal's Inscriptions". *Der Antike Sudan. Mitteilungen der Sudanarchäologischen Gesellschaft zu Berlin* 30: 175-179.

— 2020a. "Upper Egypt in Neo-Assyrian Official Inscriptions: A Case Study in Neo-Assyrian Imperial Ideology". *Journal of Ancient Egyptian Interconnections* 27: 51-69.

— 2020b. "Egypt and Kush in Neo-Assyrian Royal Inscriptions". *Res Antiquae* 17: 165-188.
— 2021a. "The Legal Case of StAT 2 173-174: Ethnic Conflict or Property Dispute?". *Nouvelles assyriologiques brèves et utilitaires* 2021-3: 207-208 (no. 88).
— 2021b. "A Sanctuary of Horus in Assyria?". *Göttinger Miszellen* 264: 15-18.
— 2021c. "Representations of Asia(tics) in Kushite Royal Inscriptions". *Res Antiquae* 18: 183-204.
— 2021d. "*Ḫapunapa*: A new Egyptian name in cuneiform?". *Nouvelles assyriologiques brèves et utilitaires* 2021-4: 272-273 (no. 116).
— 2022a. "*Ḫapi-maniḫi*: A new Egyptian name in cuneiform?". *Nouvelles assyriologiques brèves et utilitaires* 2022-1: 53-54 (no. 27).
— 2022b. "Musuri ('the Egyptian'), King of Moab". *Journal of Ancient Egyptian Interconnections* 33: 20-26.
— 2022c. "*Ḫaḫpi*: A new Egyptian name in cuneiform?" (forthcoming).
Karmel Thomason, A. 2004. "From Sennacherib's Bronzes to Taharqa's Feet: Conceptions of the Material World at Nineveh". *Iraq* 66: 151-162.
Kemp, B.J. 1991. *Ancient Egypt: Anatomy of a Civilization*. London and New York: Routledge.
King, L.W. 1914. "Some New Examples of Egyptian Influence at Nineveh". *Journal of Egyptian Archaeology* 1: 107-109, 237-240.
Kinnier Wilson, J.V. 1972. *The Nimrud Wine Lists: A Study of Men and Administration at the Assyrian Capital in the Eighth Century, B.C.* Cuneiform Texts from Nimrud 1. London: British School of Archaeology in Iraq.
Kitchen, K.A. 1973. *The Third Intermediate Period in Egypt (1100-650 B.C.)*. Warminster: Aris & Phillips.
Kuhrt, A. 1997. *The Ancient Near East c. 3000-330 BC.* Routledge History of the Ancient World. London and New York: Routledge.
Kwasman, T. and Parpola, S. 1991. *Legal Transactions of the Royal Court of Nineveh, Part I: Tiglath-Pileser III through Esarhaddon*. State Archives of Assyria 6. Helsinki: Neo-Assyrian Text Corpus Project.
Layard, A.H. 1853. *A Second Series of the Monuments of Nineveh*. London: John Murray.
Leahy, A. 1979. "Nespamedu, 'King of Thinis'". *Göttinger Miszellen* 35: 31-39.
— 1980. "'Harwa' and 'Harbes'". *Chronique d'Égypte* 55: 43-63.
— 1983. "The Proper Name *Pišanḫuru*". *Göttinger Miszellen* 62: 37-48.
— 1985. "The Libyan Period in Egypt: An Essay in Interpretation". *Libyan Studies* 16: 51-65.
— 1993. "The Egyptian Names". Pp. 56-62 in Ismail and Postgate 1993.
Leclant, J. 1961. *Montouemhat, quatrième prophète d'Amon, prince de la Ville*. Bibliothèque d'étude 35. Cairo: IFAO.
Leichty, E. 2011. *The Royal Inscriptions of Esarhaddon, King of Assyria (680-669 BC)*. Royal Inscriptions of the Neo-Assyrian Period 4. Winona Lake: Eisenbrauns.
Lipiński, E. 1972. "The Egyptian-Babylonian War of the Winter 601-600 B.C.". *Annali dell'istituto universitario orientali di Napoli* 22: 235-241.
— 1983. "Les Phéniciens à Ninive au temps des Sargonides: Ahoubasti, portier en chef". Pp. 125-134 in *Atti del I Congresso Internazionale di Studi Fenici e Punici 1*, ed. P. Bartoloni. Rome: Consiglio Nazionale delle Richerche.
Liverani, M. 1988. *Antico Oriente. Storia, società, economia*. Rome and Bari: Laterza.

— 2001 [1990]. *Prestige and Interest: International Relations in the Ancient Near East, 1600-1100 BC*. Studies in Diplomacy. Basingstoke and New York: Palgrave Macmillan.
Livingstone, A. 1989. *Court Poetry and Literary Miscellanea*. State Archives of Assyria 3. Helsinki: Neo-Assyrian Text Corpus Project.
Loprieno, A. 1988. *Topos und Mimesis. Zum Ausländer in der ägyptischen Literatur*. Ägyptologische Abhandlungen 48. Wiesbaden: Harrassowitz.
Luukko, M. 2012. *The Correspondence of Tiglath-Pileser III and Sargon II*. State Archives of Assyria 19. Helsinki: Neo-Assyrian Text Corpus Project.
Luukko, M. and Van Buylaere, G. 2002. *The Political Correspondence of Esarhaddon*. State Archives of Assyria 16. Helsinki: Neo-Assyrian Text Corpus Project.
Lüddeckens, E., Brunsch, W., Thissen, H.-J., Wittmann, G., and Zauzich, K.-T. 1980-2000. *Demotisches Namenbuch*. Wiesbaden: Reichert.
Macalister, R.A.S. 1912. *The Excavation of Gezer, I-III*. London: Committee of the Palestine Exploration Fund.
Machinist, P. 1993. "Assyrians on Assyria in the First Millennium B.C.". Pp. 77-104 in *Anfänge politischen Denkens in der Antike*, ed. K. Raaflaub. Schriften des historischen Kollegs. Kolloquien 24. Munich: Oldenbourg Verlag.
Mariette, A. 1872. *Monuments divers recueillis en Egypt et en Nubie*. Paris: A. Franck.
Matić, U. 2020. *Ethnic Identities in the Land of the Pharaohs: Past and Present Approaches in Egyptology*. Ancient Egypt in Context. Cambridge: Cambridge University Press.
Mattila, R. 2002. *Legal Transactions of the Royal Court of Nineveh, Part II: Assurbanipal through Sîn-šarru-iškun*. State Archives of Assyria 14. Helsinki: Neo-Assyrian Text Corpus Project.
Miglus, P.A., Radner, K., and Stępniowski, F.M (eds.). 2016. *Ausgrabungen in Assur: Wohnquartiere in der Weststadt, Teil I*. Wissenschaftliche Veröffentlichungen der Deutschen Orient-Gesellschaft 152. Wiesbaden: Harrassowitz.
Millard, A. 1994. *The Eponyms of the Assyrian Empire 910-612 BC*. Helsinki: Neo-Assyrian Text Corpus Project.
Moorey, P.R.S. 1987. "On Tracking Cultural Transfers in Prehistory: The Case of Egypt and Lower Mesopotamia in the Fourth Millennium BC". Pp. 36-46 in *Centre and Periphery in the Ancient World*, eds. M. Rowlands, M.T. Larsen, and K. Kristiansen. Cambridge: Cambridge University Press.
Moran, W.L. 1992. *The Amarna Letters*. Baltimore: Johns Hopkins University Press.
Morkot, R.G. 2000. *The Black Pharaohs: Egypt's Nubian Rulers*. London: Rubicon Press.
Na'aman, N. and Zadok, R. 2000. "Assyrian Deportations to the Province of Samerina in the Light of Two Cuneiform Tablets from Tel Hadid". *Tel Aviv* 27: 159-188.
Novotny, J. and Jeffers, J. 2018. *The Royal Inscriptions of Ashurbanipal (668-631 BC), Aššur-etel-ilāni (630-627 BC), and Sîn-šarra-iškun (626-612 BCE), Kings of Assyria*. Royal Inscriptions of the Neo-Assyrian Period 5/1. Philadelphia: University of Philadelphia Press.
O'Connor, D. 1990. "The Nature of the Tjemhu (Libyan) Society in the Later New Kingdom". Pp. 29-113 in *Libya and Egypt: c 1300-750 BC*, ed. A. Leahy. London: School of Oriental and African Studies.
Oded, B. 1979. *Mass deportations and deportees in the Neo-Assyrian Empire*. Wiesbaden: Dr. Ludwig Reichert Verlag.
Onasch, H.-U. 1994. *Die assyrischen Eroberungen Ägyptens*. Ägypten und Altes Testament 27. Wiesbaden: Harrassowitz.

Osing, J. 1978. "Zu einigen ägyptischen Namen in keilschriftlicher Umschreibung". *Göttinger Miszellen* 27: 37-41.
Parker, B. 1954. "The Nimrud Tablets, 1952: Business Documents". *Iraq* 16: 29-58.
Parpola, S. 1970. *Neo-Assyrian Toponyms*. Alter Orient und Altes Testament 6. Neukirchen Vluyn and Kevelaer: Neukirchener Verlag and Butzon & Bercker.
— 1979. *Cuneiform Texts from Babylonian Tablets in the British Museum: Neo-Assyrian Letters from the Kuyunjik Collection*. Cuneiform Texts from Babylonian Tablets in the British Museum 53. London: Trustees of the British Museum.
— 1987. *The Correspondence of Sargon II, Part I: Letters from Assyria and the West*. State Archives of Assyria 1. Helsinki: Neo-Assyrian Text Corpus Project.
— 1993. *Letters from Assyrian and Babylonian Scholars*. State Archives of Assyria 10. Helsinki: Neo-Assyrian Text Corpus Project.
— 2018. *The Correspondence of Assurbanipal, Part I: Letters from Assyria, Babylonia, and Vassal States*. State Archives of Assyria 21. Helsinki: Neo-Assyrian Text Corpus Project.
Pedersén, O. 1986. *Archives and Libraries in the City of Assur: A Survey of the Material from the German Excavations, Part 2*. Studia Semitica Upsaliensia 8. Uppsala: Uppsala University.
— 1998. *Archives and Libraries in the Ancient Near East*. Bethesda: CDL Press.
Pedersén, O. and Troy, L. 1993. "Egyptians in Nineveh". *Nouvelles assyriologiques brèves et utilitaires* 1993-2: 39 (no. 48).
Peiser, F.E. 1905. "Ein neuer assyrischer Kontrakt". *Orientalische Literaturzeitung* 8: 130-133.
Petrie, F. 1939. *The Making of Egypt*. London: Sheldon Press.
Piepkorn, A.C. 1933. *Historical Prism Inscriptions of Ashurbanipal*. Assyriological Studies 5. Chicago: University of Chicago Press.
Pollock, S. 1999. *Ancient Mesopotamia*. Case Studies in Early Societies 1. Cambridge: Cambridge University Press.
Postgate, J.N. 1976. *Fifty Neo-Assyrian Legal Documents*. Warminster: Aris & Phillips.
Quirke, S. 1992. *Ancient Egyptian Religion*. London: British Museum Press.
Radner, K. (ed.) 1998. *The Prosopography of the Neo-Assyrian Empire, Volume 1, Part 1: A*. Helsinki: Neo-Assyrian Text Corpus Project.
— 1999 (ed.). *The Prosopography of the Neo-Assyrian Empire, Volume 1, Part 2: B-G*. Helsinki: Neo-Assyrian Text Corpus Project.
Radner, K. 1999. *Ein neuassyrisches Privatarchiv der Tempelgoldschmiede von Assur*. Studien zu den Assur-Texten 1. Saarbrücken: Saarbrücker Druckerei und Verlag.
— 2002. *Die neuassyrischen Texte aus Tall Šāḫ Ḥamad. Mit Beiträgen von Wolfgang Röllig zu den aramäischen Beischriften*. Berichte der Ausgrabung Tell Schech Hamad 6. Berlin: Dietrich Reimer Verlag.
— 2009. "The Assyrian King and His Scholars: The Syro-Anatolian and Egyptian Schools". Pp. 221-238 in *Of God(s), Trees, Kings, and Scholars: Neo-Assyrian and Related Studies in Honour of Simo Parpola*, eds. M. Luukko, S. Svärd, and R. Mattila. Studia Orientalia 106. Helsinki: Finnish Oriental Society.
— 2012a. "After Eltekeh: Royal Hostages from Egypt at the Assyrian Court". Pp. 471-479 in *Stories of Long Ago: Festschrift for M.D. Roaf*, eds. H.D. Baker, K. Kaniuth, and A. Otto. Alter Orient und Altes Testament 397. Münster: Ugarit-Verlag.
— 2012b. "Mass deportation: the Assyrian resettlement policy". *Assyrian Empire Builders*. http://www.ucl.ac.uk/sargon/essentials/governors/massdeportation/ (accessed 2021-09-

28).
— 2015. "A Neo-Assyrian Slave Sale Contract of 725 BC from the Peshdar Plain and the Location of the Palace Herald's Province". *Zeitschrift für Assyriologie und Vorderasiatische Archäologie* 105: 192-197.
— 2016. "Die beiden neuassyrischen Privatarchive". Pp. 79-133 in Miglus, Radner, and Stępniowski (eds.) 2016.
Ranke, H. 1910. *Keilschriftliches Material zur altägyptischen Vokalisation*. Berlin: Verlag G. Reimer.
— 1911. "Zur keilschriftlichen Umschreibung ägyptischer Eigennamen". *Zeitschrift für ägyptische Sprache und Altertumskunde* 48: 112.
— 1935. *Die ägyptischen Personennamen, I*. Glückstadt: J.J. Augustin.
— 1952. *Die ägyptischen Personennamen, II*. Glückstadt/Hamburg and Locust Valley: J.J. Augustin.
Reade, J.E. 2002. "The Ziggurat and Temples of Nimrud". *Iraq* 64: 135-216.
Riggs, C. and Baines, J. 2012. "Ethnicity". *UCLA Encyclopedia of Egyptology*. http://digital2.library.ucla.edu/viewItem.do?ark=21198/zz002bpmfm (accessed 2021-12-05).
Ritner, R. 2009. "Fragmentation and Re-Integration in the Third Intermediate Period". Pp. 327-340 in *The Libyan Period in Egypt*, eds. G. Broekman, R. Demarée, and O. Kaper. Leiden: Nederlands Instituut voor het Nabije Oosten.
Robins, G. 1993. *Women in Ancient Egypt*. London: British Museum Press.
Röllig, W. 1997. "Mişir, Mizru, Muṣur, Muṣri III, Muzir". *Reallexikon der Assyriologie und vorderasiatischen Archäologie* 8: 264-269.
Ryholt, K. 2004. "The Assyrian Invasion of Egypt in Egyptian Literary Tradition: A Survey of the Narrative Source Material". Pp. 483-510 in *Assyria and Beyond*, ed. J.G. Dercksen. Leiden: Nederlands Instituut voor het Nabije Oosten.
Schneider, T. 1992. *Asiatische Personennamen in ägyptischen Quellen des Neuen Reiches*. Orbis biblicus et orientalis 114. Freiburg and Göttingen: Universitätsverlag Freiburg and Vandenhoeck & Ruprecht.
Schroeder, O. 1920. *Keilschrifttexte aus Assur verschiedenen Inhalts*. Wissenschaftliche Veröffentlichungen der Deutschen Orient-Gesellschaft 35. Leipzig: J.C. Hinrichs.
Shaw, I. and Nicholson, P. 1995. *British Museum Dictionary of Ancient Egypt*. London: British Museum Press.
Smith, A.D. 1986. *The Ethnic Origins of Nations*. Oxford: Blackwell.
Spalinger, A. 1974. "Esarhaddon and Egypt: An Analysis of the First Invasion of Egypt". *Orientalia* 43: 295-326.
— 1977. "Egypt and Babylonia: A Survey (c. 620 BC-550 BC)". *Studien zur altägyptischen Kultur* 5: 221-244.
Spieckermann, H. 1982. *Juda unter Assur in der Sargonidenzeit*. Forschungen zur Religion und Literatur des Alten und Neuen Testaments 129. Göttingen: Vandenhoeck & Ruprecht.
Stamm, J.J. 1939. *Die akkadische Namensgebung*. Leipzig: Hinrichs.
Starr, I. 1990. *Queries to the Sungod: Divination and Politics in Sargonid Assyria*. State Archives of Assyria 4. Helsinki: Neo-Assyrian Text Corpus Project.
Steindorff, G. 1890. "Die keilschriftliche Wiedergabe ägyptischer Eigennamen". *Beiträge zur Assyriologie und semitischen Sprachwissenschaft* 1: 330-361, 593-612.
Stol, M. 2016. *Women in the Ancient Near East*. Boston and Berlin: Walter de Gruyter.
Struve, W. 1927. "Ein Ägypter – Schwiegersohn des Sanherib". *Zeitschrift für ägyptische Sprache und Altertumskunde* 62: 66.

Tadmor, H. 1982. “The Aramaization of Assyria”. Pp. 449-470 in *Mesopotamien und seine Nachbarn. Politische und kulturelle Wechselbeziehungen im alten Vorderasien vom 4. bis 1 Jahrtausend v. Chr*, eds. H.-J. Nissen and J. Renger. Berliner Beiträge zum Vorderen Orient 1. Berlin: Dietrich Reimer Verlag.
Tallqvist, K. 1914. *Assyrian Personal Names*. Acta Societatis Scientiarum Fennicae 43. Helsinki: Finnish Academy of Sciences.
Teeter, E. (ed.) 2011. *Before the Pyramids: The Origins of Egyptian Civilization*. Oriental Institute Museum Publications 33. Chicago: University of Chicago Press.
Török, L. 1997. *The Kingdom of Kush: Handbook of the Napatan-Meroitic Civilization*. Handbook of Oriental Studies, Section 1: The Near and Middle East 31. Leiden: Brill.
Van De Mieroop, M. 2016. *A History of the Ancient Near East ca. 3000-323 BC*. Blackwell History of the Ancient World. Chichester: Wiley Blackwell.
Vittmann, G. 1984. “Zu einigen keilschriftlichen Umschreibungen ägyptischer Personennamen”. *Göttinger Miszellen* 70: 65-66.
Vogt, E. 1957. “Die neubabylonische Chronik über die Schlacht bei Karkemisch und die Einnahme von Jerusalem”. *Vetus Testamentum* 4: 67-96.
Wengrow, D. 2011. “The Invention of Writing in Egypt”. Pp. 99-103 in Teeter (ed.) 2011.
Wiseman, D.J. 1966. “Some Egyptians in Babylonia”. *Iraq* 28: 154-158.
Yoyotte, J. 1952. “Quelque toponymes égyptiens mentionnés dans les ‘Annales d’Assurbanipal’ (Rm. I, 101-105)”. *Revue d’Assyriologie et Archéologie Orientale* 46: 212-214.
— 1960. “Anthroponymes d’origine libyenne dans les documents égyptiens”. *Comptes rendus du groupe linguistique d’études chamito-sèmitiques* 8: 22-24.
Zaccagnini, C. 1982. “The Enemy in the Neo-Assyrian Royal Inscriptions: The ‘Ethnographic’ Description”. Pp. 409-424 in *Mesopotamien und seine Nachbarn. Politische und kulturelle Wechselbeziehungen im alten Vorderasien vom 4. bis 1. Jahrtausend v. Chr*, eds. H.-J. Nissen and J. Renger. Berliner Beiträge zum Vorderen Orient 1. Berlin: Dietrich Reimer Verlag.
Zadok, R. 1977a. *On West Semites in Babylonia during the Chaldean and Achaemenian Periods: An Onomastic Study*. Jerusalem: H. J. & Z. Wanaarta.
— 1977b. “On Some Egyptians in First Millennium Mesopotamia”. *Göttinger Miszellen* 26: 63-68.
— 1984. *The Elamite Onomasticon*. Naples: Istituto universitario orientale.
— 1997. “The Ethno-Linguistic Composition of Assyria Proper in the 9th-7th Centuries BC”. Pp. 209-216 in *Assyrien im Wandel der Zeiten*, eds. H. Waetzoldt and H. Hauptmann. Heidelberg: Heidelberger Orientverlag.
— 1998. “West Semitic Names in Neo-Assyrian Sources”. *Nouvelles assyriologique brèves et utilitaires* 1998-1: 21-23 (no. 20).
— 2010. “Anatolians in Neo-Assyrian Documents”. Pp. 411-439 in *Pax Hethitica*, eds. Y. Cohen, A. Gilan, and J.L. Miller. Studien zu den Boğazköy-Texten 51. Wiesbaden: Harrassowitz Verlag.
— 2018. “An Egyptian in Kurdistan”. *Nouvelles assyriologique brèves et utilitaires* 2018-1: 51-53 (no. 30).
Zeidler, J. 1994. “Einige neue keilschriftliche Entsprechungen ägyptischer Personennamen: Zu weiteren Namen in Jacobsen, CTNMC Nr. 68”. *Die Welt des Orients* 43: 36-56.

6. ILLUSTRATIONS

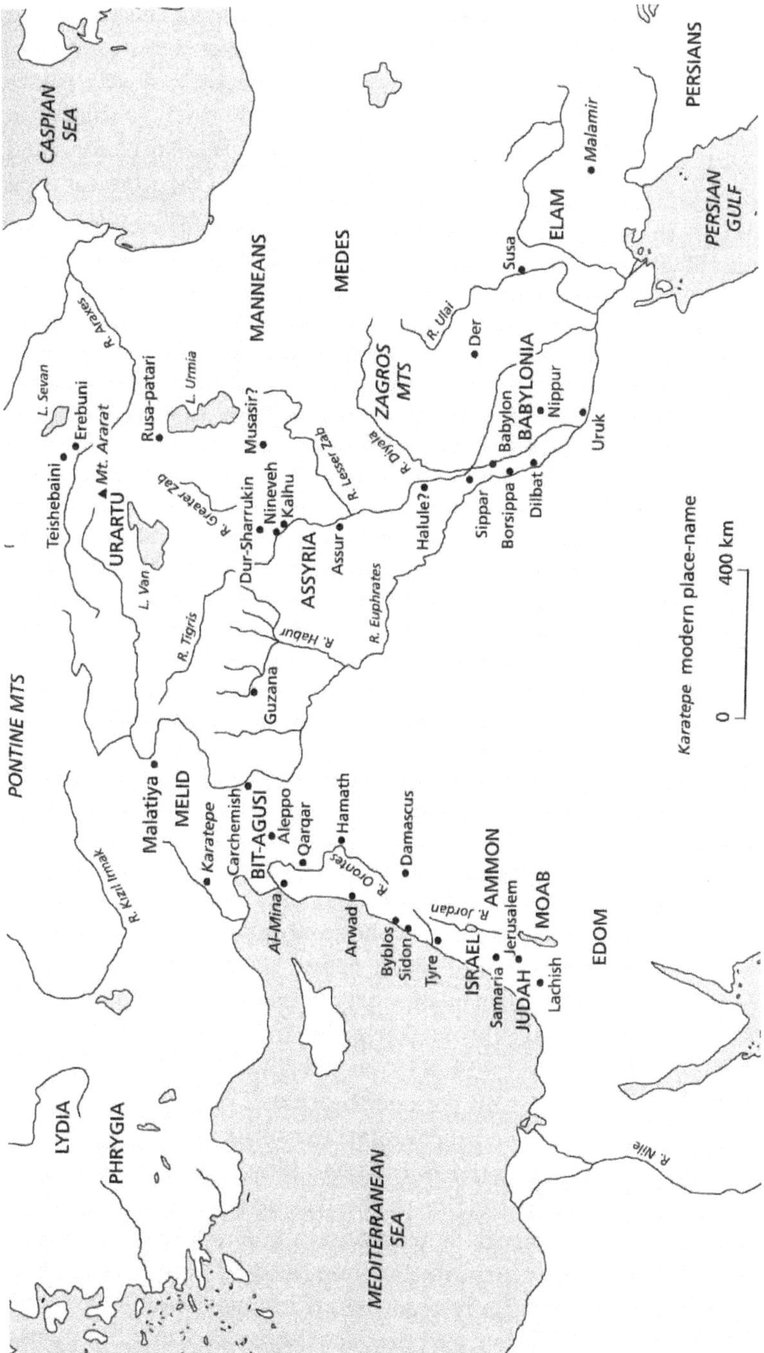

Fig. 1: Map of the ancient Near East (in the early first millennium BCE). After Van De Mieroop 2016: 225, map 11.1.

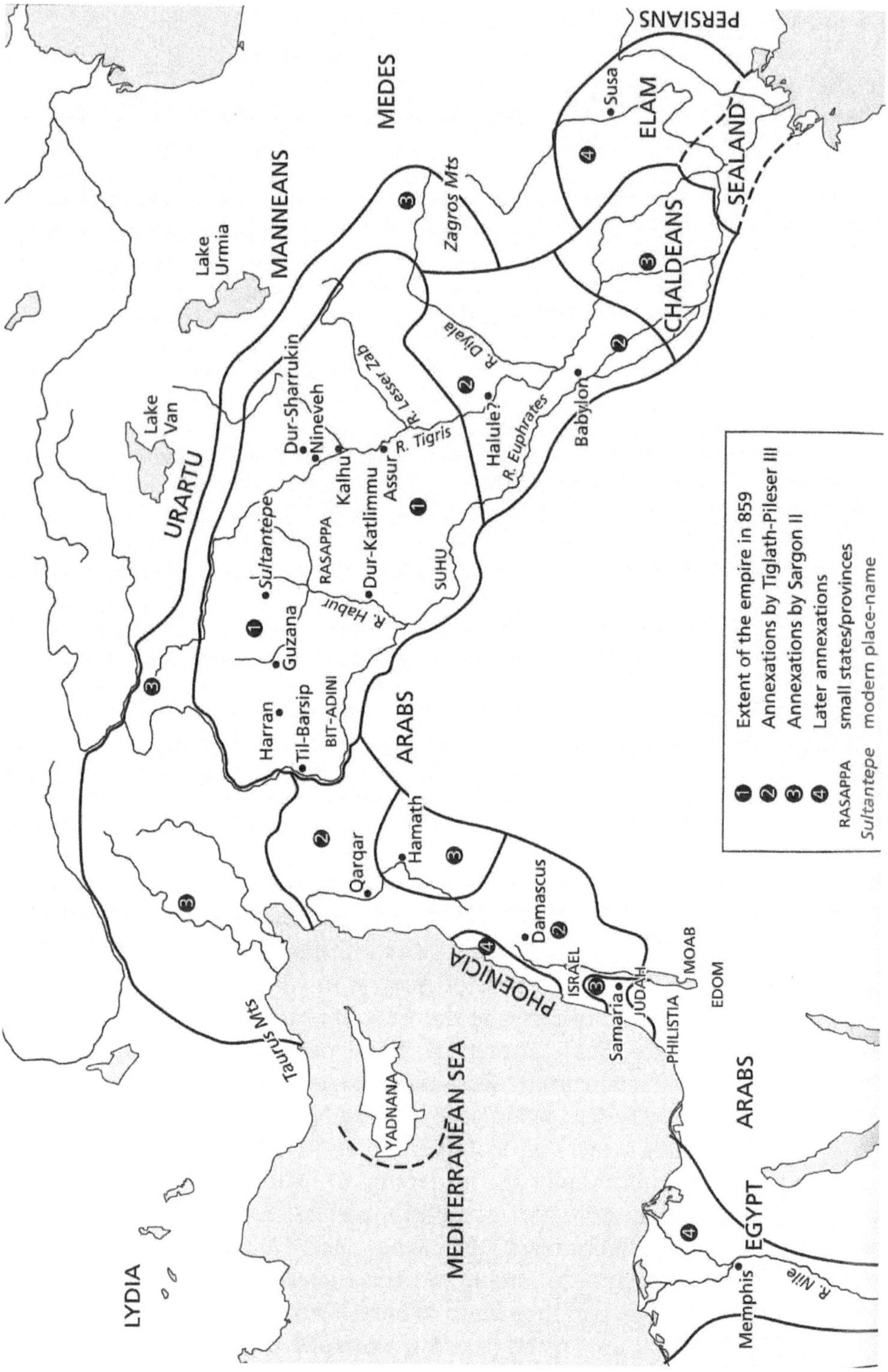

Fig. 2: The expansion of the Neo-Assyrian empire. After Liverani 1988: 793 (as adapted in Van De Mieroop 2016: 258, map 12.1).

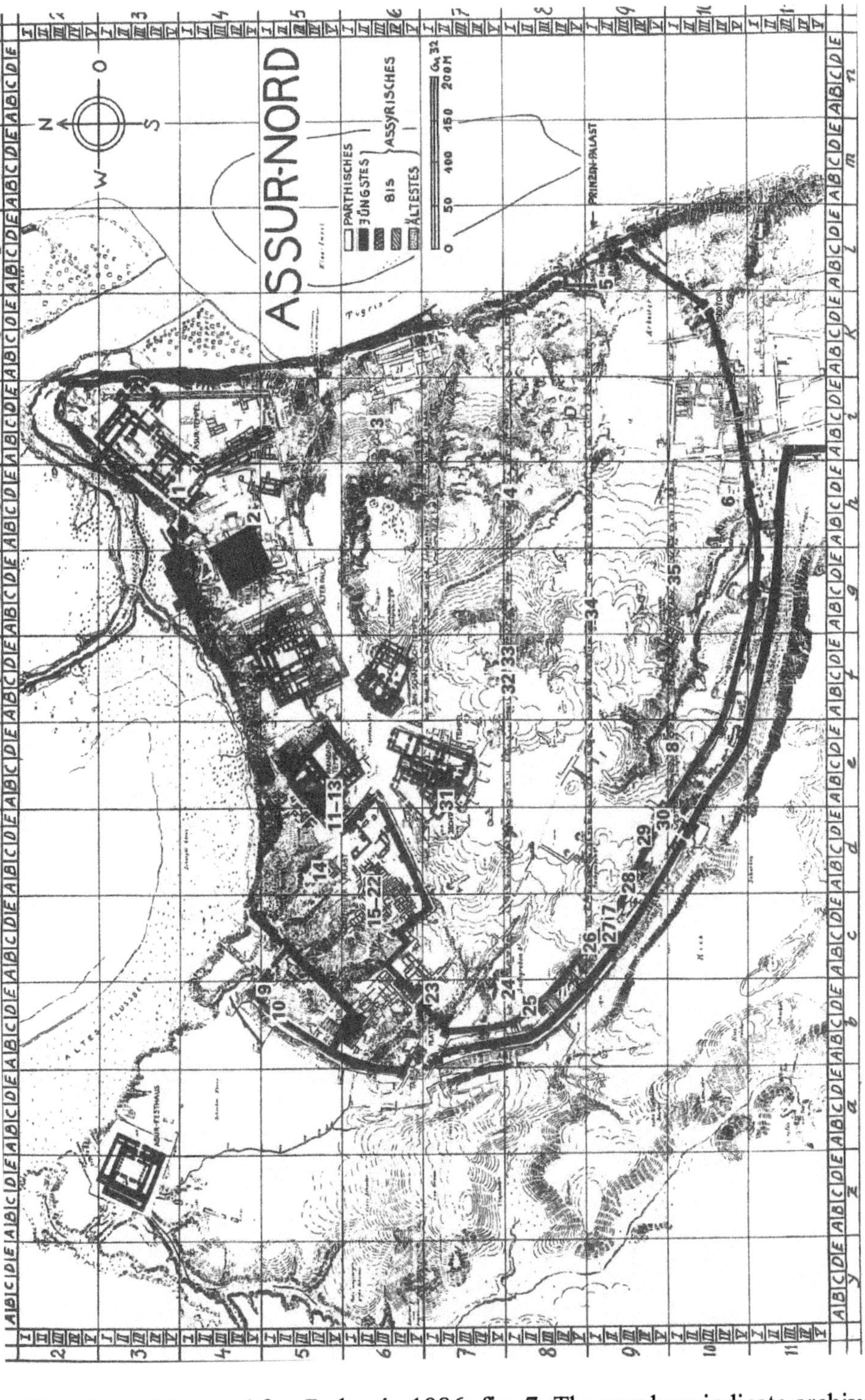

Fig. 3: City plan of Assur. After Pedersén 1986: fig. 7. The numbers indicate archives and libraries, as classified by O. Pedersén. N31 signifies an "archive of Egyptians". Assur 52b – another archive of Egyptians – was excavated just to the south of N31.

Fig. 4: Victory stele of Esarhaddon. Esarhaddon, with a Phoenician ruler and a Kushite ruler or crown prince at his feet. After Leichty 2011: 183, fig. 5.

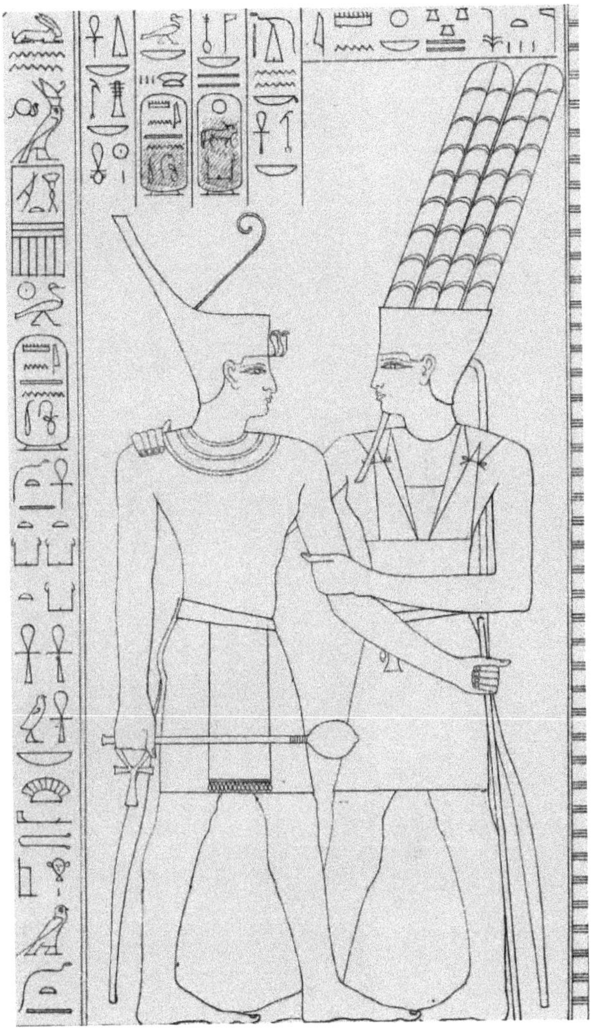

Fig. 5 (left): Wall relief showing Taharqa and Isis. The Kushite king Taharqa, wearing the Atef crown, is embraced by the Egyptian goddess Isis. After Mariette 1872: pl. 79.

Fig. 6 (right): Wall relief showing Tanutamon and Amun. The Kushite king Tanutamon, wearing the Lower Egyptian crown, is embraced by the Egyptian god Amun. After Mariette 1872: pl. 80.

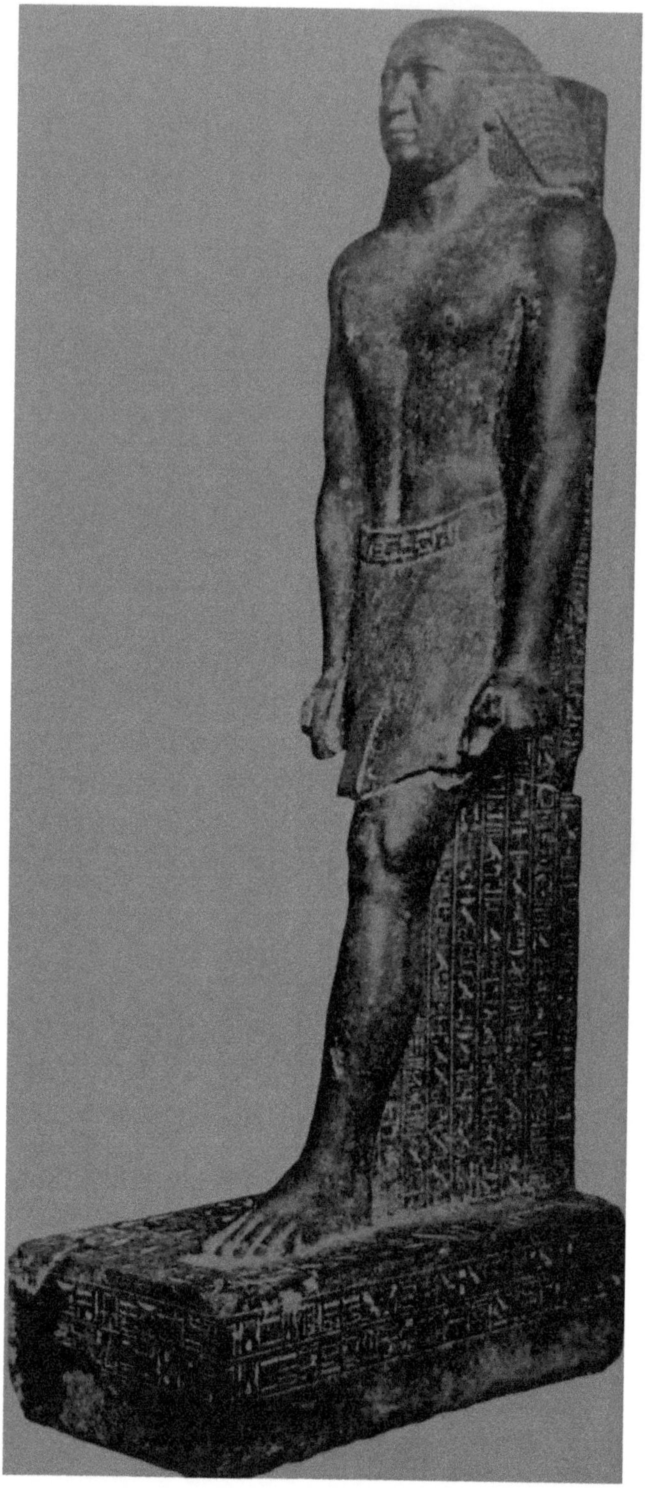

Fig. 7: Statue of Mentuemhat. The fourth prophet of Amun and mayor of Thebes, Mentuemhat, depicted in a striding pose. After Leclant 1961: pl. 1.

Fig. 8: Wall relief showing Assyrian attack on Egypt. Assyrian forces besiege an Egyptian city, take prisoners of war, and appear next to a row of deported people. After Brunner 1952-53: 256, Abb. 1.

Fig. 9 (above): Glazed tile showing an Egyptian. The dead or fatally injured man has fallen into a watercourse, with the image being a part of an Assyrian-Egyptian battle scene. After Layard 1853: pl. 53:1.

Fig. 10 (below): Glazed tile showing a group of Egyptians. A row of captives, with the image being a part of an Assyrian-Egyptian battle scene. After Layard 1853: pl. 54:7.

Fig. 11 (above): Ivory panel from Assyria showing Egyptian king(s). Egyptian king(s) with sceptres and jugs flank(s) a stylized tree. After Herrmann and Laidlaw 2013: 34, fig. 64.

Fig. 12 (below): Cylinder seal with cuneiform and Egyptian figures. An Egyptian ruler(?) flanked by two Egyptian gods. After de Clercq 1888: pl. xxxv, fig. 386.

7. APPENDICES AND INDICES

7.1 Appendices

7.1.1 Identified Africans

The table below lists the identified Africans and their biographic data discussed above. Preciser identification ground is indicated in the column "type" and the numbers in this column refer to subsections in this book. The remaining columns focus on identities, properties, and settings, and respond to the interrogative words who, what, when, and where. As for the interrogative word where, the classification "Ass." usually includes information on city of residence. Circumstances and the interrogative word how are focused on and responded to elsewhere.[782]

individual	**type**	**ethnicity**	**sex**	**age**	**class**	**time**	**place**
Abdi-Mūnu	2.1.1	Egyptian	male	adult	lower	pAsh	Ass. (As)
Abī-Ḫūru 1.	2.1.1	Egyptian	male	adult	lower	Sen	Ass. (K)
Abī-Ḫūru 2.	2.1.1	Egyptian	male	adult	lower	pAsh	Ass. (N)
Abši-Ešu	2.1.1	Egyptian	male	adult	lower	Ash	Ass.
Aḫu-dūr-enši 2.	2.1.3	Egyptian	male	adult	lower	pAsh	Ass. (As)
Aḫūru	2.1.1	Egyptian	male	adult	lower	Ash-pAsh	Ass. (As)
Al-ḫapi-mepi	2.1.1	Egyptian	female	adult	lower	pAsh	Ass. (N)
Amān-išme	2.1.1	Egyptian	male	adult	lower	pAsh	Ass. (As)
Amat-Emūni	2.1.1	Egyptian	female	adult	upper	Esa/Ash	Ass. (N)
Ameḫi	2.1.1	Egyptian	male	adult	lower	Ash	Ass. (As)
Amman-tanaḫti 1.	2.1.1	Egyptian	male	adult	lower	Ash	Ass. (As)
Amman-tanaḫti 2.	2.1.1	Egyptian	male	adult	slave	pAsh	Ass. (As)
Amu-rṭēše 1.	2.1.1	Egyptian	male	adult	lower	Ash	Ass. (K)
Amu-rṭēše 2.	2.1.1	Egyptian	male	adult	lower	pAsh	Ass. (N)
Amu-rṭēše 3.	2.1.1	Egyptian	male	adult	upper	Ash-pAsh	Ass. (As)
Apâ	2.1.3	Egyptian	male	adult	lower	7th c.	Ass. (As)
Apî 1.	2.1.1	Egyptian	female	child	slave	pAsh	Ass. (As)
Apî 2.	2.1.1	Egyptian	female	adult	lower	pAsh	Ass. (As)
Apiḫuniawa	2.1.1	Egyptian	male	adult	lower	7th c.	Ass. (As)
Aṣê	2.1.1	Egyptian	male	adult	lower	pAsh	Ass. (N)
Ašāia	2.1.2	Egyptian	female	adult	lower	Ash/pAsh	Ass. (As)

[782] The following abbreviations apply: (As) = Assur, Ash = Ashurbanipal, Ass. = Assyria, Bab. = Babylonia, Esa = Esarhaddon, (K) = Kalhu, (N) = Nineveh, pAsh = post-Ashurbanipal period, Sar = Sargon II, Sen = Sennacherib, Shal = Shalmaneser V.

Aššur-dūrī (6.)	2.1.3	Egyptian	male	adult	lower	Ash/pAsh	Ass. (As)
Ati'	2.1.1	Egyptian	male	adult	lower	pAsh	Ass. (N)
Aṭû	2.1.1	Egyptian	male	adult	lower	7th c.	Ass. (As)
Awa (1.)	2.1.3	Egyptian	male	adult	lower	Esa	Ass. (As)
Bakkî	2.1.1	Egyptian	male	adult	lower	pAsh	Ass. (As)
Barīku 8.	2.1.3	Egyptian	male	adult	lower	Ash	Ass. (As)
Batu-naḫti	2.1.1	Egyptian	male	adult	lower	Ash	Ass. (As)
Bēlet-issē'a 2.	2.1.3	Egyptian	female	adult	slave	pAsh	Ass. (As)
Bukunanni'pi 1.	2.1.1	Egyptian	male	adult	upper	Esa-Ash	Africa
Bukunanni'pi 2.	2.1.1	Egyptian	male	adult	upper	Esa-Ash	Africa
Bukurninip	2.1.1	Egyptian	male	adult	upper	Esa-Ash	Africa
Bur-Kūbi	2.1.2	Egyptian	male	adult	lower	pAsh	Ass. (As)
Butanaḫte	2.1.1	Egyptian	male	adult	lower	Ash	Ass. (As)
Butinaḫ	2.1.1	Egyptian	male	adult	lower	pAsh	Ass. (As)
Dān-Ešu	2.1.1	Egyptian	male	adult	upper	Ash	Bab.
Dāri-šarru 2.	2.1.2	Kushite	male	adult	upper	Esa/Ash	Ass.
Eptimu-rṭešu	2.1.1	Egyptian	male	adult	upper	Esa-Ash	Africa
Ēšâ	2.1.1	Egyptian	male	adult	lower	7th c.	Ass. (As)
Eša-rṭeše	2.1.1	Egyptian	female	adult	lower	7th c.	Ass. (N)
Ezibtu 2.	2.1.2	Egyptian	female	adult	lower	Ash/pAsh	Ass. (As)
Gula-ēṭir 3.	2.1.3	Egyptian	male	adult	lower	7th c.	Ass. (As)
[...]gurši	2.1.4	Egyptian	male	adult	upper	Esa/Ash	Ass. (N)
Ḫapi-maniḫi	2.1.1	Egyptian	male	adult	lower	Ash	Ass. (As)
Ḫapi-nāu	2.1.1	Egyptian	male	adult	lower	pAsh	Ass. (As)
Ḫaqu-nēši	2.1.1	Egyptian	male	adult	lower	pAsh	Ass. (N)
Ḫasâ	2.1.1	Egyptian	male	adult	lower	Ash	Ass. (N)
Ḫatpi-Ašte	2.1.1	Egyptian	male	adult	lower	pAsh	Ass. (As)
Ḫatpi-Mūnu	2.1.1	Egyptian	male	adult	lower	Ash	Ass. (N)
Ḫatpi-Napi	2.1.1	Egyptian	male	adult	lower	pAsh	Ass. (As)
Ḫipirrāu	2.1.1	Egyptian	male	adult	lower	Esa	Ass. (As)
Ḫuddāia 4.	2.1.3	Egyptian	male	adult	lower	Ash	Ass. (N)
Ḫursisu	2.1.1	Egyptian	male	adult	lower	7th c.	Ass. (N)
Ḫur-šia	2.1.1	Egyptian	male	adult	lower	pAsh	Ass. (As)
Ḫur-ši-Ēšu 1.	2.1.1	Egyptian	male	adult	upper	Esa-Ash	Africa
Ḫur-ši-Ēšu 2.	2.1.1	Egyptian	male	adult	upper	Esa-Ash	Ass. (N)
Ḫur-ši-Ēšu 3.	2.1.1	Egyptian	male	adult	lower	Ash	Ass. (N)
Ḫur-tibû 1.	2.1.1	Egyptian	male	adult	lower	7th c.	Ass. (N)
Ḫur-tibû 2.	2.1.1	Egyptian	male	adult	lower	pAsh	Ass.
Ḫūru 1.	2.1.1	Egyptian	male	adult	upper	Esa	Ass. (N)
Ḫūru 2.	2.1.1	Egyptian	male	adult	upper	Ash-pAsh	Ass. (As)
Ḫūru 3.	2.1.1	Egyptian	male	adult	lower	pAsh	Ass. (As)
Ḫūru-[...] (1.)	2.1.1	Egyptian	male	adult	lower	7th c.	Ass. (N)
Ḫūru-[...] (2.)	2.1.1	Egyptian	male	adult	lower	Ash	Ass. (As)
Ḫur-waṣi 1.	2.1.1	Egyptian	male	adult	lower	Sen	Ass. (N)
Ḫur-waṣi 2.	2.1.1	Egyptian	male	adult	lower	Sen	Ass. (N)

Ḫur-waṣi 3.	2.1.1	Egyptian	male	adult	upper	Esa	Ass. (N)
Ḫur-waṣi 4.	2.1.1	Egyptian	male	adult	upper	Ash	v. state
Ḫur-waṣi 5.	2.1.1	Egyptian	male	adult	lower	Ash/pAsh	Ass. (N)
Ḫur-waṣi 6.	2.1.1	Egyptian	male	adult	upper	Ash-pAsh	Ass. (As)
Ḫur-waṣi 7.	2.1.1	Egyptian	male	adult	lower	pAsh	Ass. (As)
Ḫur-waṣi 8.	2.1.1	Egyptian	male	adult	lower	pAsh	Ass. (As)
Ḫur-waṣi 9.	2.1.1	Egyptian	male	adult	lower	Ash/pAsh	Ass. (As)
Ḫur-waṣi 10.	2.1.1	Egyptian	male	adult	upper	pAsh	Ass. (As)
Ḫur-waṣi 11.	2.1.1	Egyptian	male	adult	lower	pAsh	Ass. (As)
Ḫur-waṣi (12.)	2.1.1	Egyptian	male	adult	lower	pAsh	Ass. (As)
Ḫur-waṣi (13.)	2.1.1	Egyptian	male	adult	upper	pAsh	Ass. (As)
Ḫur-waṣi (14.)	2.1.1	Egyptian	male	adult	upper	Shal	Ass.
Ḫuṭ-naḫti	2.1.1	Egyptian	male	adult	upper	pAsh	Ass. (As)
Ispiniša	2.1.2	Egyptian	female	adult	lower	Ash/pAsh	Ass. (As)
Issar-dūrī 26.	2.1.3	Egyptian	male	adult	lower	Ash	Ass.
Išpimāṭu	2.1.1	Egyptian	male	adult	upper	Esa-Ash	Africa
Kalbāia 2.	2.1.3	Egyptian	male	adult	lower	pAsh	Ass.
Karānūtu	2.1.2	Egyptian	female	adult	lower	Ash/pAsh	Ass. (As)
Kiṣir-Aššur (66.)	2.1.2	Egyptian	male	adult	lower	Ash/pAsh	Ass. (As)
Kurarâ	2.1.1	Egyptian	male	adult	lower	7th c.	Ass. (N)
Kūsāiâ 1.	2.1.2	Kushite	male	adult	lower	pAsh	Ass.
Kūsāiâ 2.	2.1.2	Kushite	male	adult	lower	pAsh	Ass.
Kūsāiu 1.	2.1.2	Kushite	male	child	lower	Sar	Ass.
Kūsāiu 2.	2.1.2	Kushite	male	adult	lower	Ash	Ass. (N)
Kūsāiu 3.	2.1.2	Kushite	male	adult	lower	pAsh	Ass. (As)
Kūsāiu 4.	2.1.2	Kushite	male	adult	lower	pAsh	Ass.
Kūsāiu 5.	2.1.2	Kushite	male	adult	lower	post-612	Ass.
Kūsāiu 6.	2.1.2	Kushite	male	adult	upper	7th c.	Ass. (N)
Kūsāiu (7.)	2.1.2	Kushite	male	adult	lower	Ash/pAsh	Ass. (As)
Kūsāiu (8.)	2.1.2	Kushite	male	adult	lower	pAsh	Ass. (As)
Kūsāiu (9.)	2.1.2	Kushite	male	adult	lower	Ash/pAsh	Ass. (As)
Kūsāiu (10.)	2.1.2	Kushite	male	adult	lower	Ash	Ass. (As)
Kusî	2.1.2	Kushite	male	adult	upper	8th c.	Ass. (K)
Kūsītu	2.1.2	Kushite	female	adult	lower	7th c.	Ass. (N)
Lamintu	2.1.1	Libyan	male	adult	upper	Esa-Ash	Africa
Lā-turammanni-Aššur 3.-4.	2.1.3	Egyptian	male	adult	upper	Ash-pAsh	Ass. (As)
Lū-šakin 14.	2.1.3	Egyptian	male	adult	lower	Ash	Ass.
Mannu-kī-Nīnua 13.	2.1.2	Egyptian	male	adult	lower	Ash	Ass. (K)
Manti-me-ḫē	2.1.1	Egyptian	male	adult	upper	Esa-Ash	Africa
Matanaḫte	2.1.1	Egyptian	male	adult	lower	pAsh	Ass. (As)
Meia	2.1.1	Egyptian	female	adult	lower	7th c.	Ass. (As)
Menas(s)ê 3.	2.1.2	Egyptian	male	adult	lower	pAsh	Ass. (As)
Mullissu-ḫāṣinat	2.1.3	Egyptian	female	adult	lower	pAsh	Ass. (N)
Muṣurāiu 1.	2.1.2	Egyptian	male	adult	upper	Esa	Ass. (N)
Muṣurāiu 2.	2.1.2	Egyptian	male	adult	lower	Ash	Ass. (N)

Muṣurāiu 3.	2.1.2	Egyptian	male	adult	lower	pAsh	Ass. (K)
Muṣurāiu 4.	2.1.2	Egyptian	male	adult	lower	pAsh	Ass. (As)
Muṣurāiu 5.	2.1.2	Egyptian	male	adult	lower	7th c.	Ass. (As)
Muṣurāiu 6.	2.1.2	Egyptian	male	adult	lower	post-612	Ass.
Muṣurī	2.1.2	Egyptian	male	adult	upper	Esa-Ash	v. state
Muṣur(ītu) (1.)	2.1.2	Egyptian	female	adult	lower	Ash/pAsh	Ass. (As)
Muṣurītu (2.)	2.1.2	Egyptian	female	adult	lower	Ash/pAsh	Ass. (As)
Muṣurītu (3.)	2.1.2	Egyptian	female	adult	lower	Ash/pAsh	Ass. (As)
Mutakkil-Aššur 23.	2.1.3	Kushite	male	adult	lower	Ash/pAsh	Ass. (As)
Nabareu	2.1.1	Egyptian	male	adult	lower	Ash/pAsh	Ass. (As)
Nabû-rēḫtu-uṣur 17.	2.1.3	Egyptian	male	adult	lower	pAsh	Ass. (N)
Nabû-šēzibanni 12.	2.1.4	Egyptian	male	adult	upper	Esa-Ash	Africa
Nādinu (26.)	2.1.3	Egyptian	male	adult	lower	Ash/pAsh	Ass. (As)
Naḫkê	2.1.1	Egyptian	male	adult	upper	Esa-Ash	Africa
Naḫti-ḫuru-ansini	2.1.1	Egyptian	male	adult	upper	Esa-Ash	Africa
Nibiḫis (1.)	2.1.1	Egyptian	male	adult	lower	pAsh	Ass. (As)
Nibiḫis (2.)	2.1.1	Egyptian	male	adult	lower	pAsh	Ass. (As)
Niḫarā'u	2.1.1	Egyptian	male	adult	upper	Esa	Ass. (N)
Niḫti-Eša-rau	2.1.1	Egyptian	female	adult	lower	pAsh	Ass. (N)
Nikkû	2.1.1	Egyptian	male	adult	upper	Esa-Ash	Africa
Nummurīja	2.1.1	Egyptian	male	adult	upper	Ash	Africa
Pa-qruru	2.1.1	Egyptian	male	adult	upper	Esa-Ash	Africa
Pašî 9.	2.1.3	Egyptian	male	child	lower	pAsh	Ass. (As)
Pīlušu	2.1.1	Egyptian	male	adult	lower	pAsh	Ass. (As)
Pīnapi	2.1.1	Egyptian	male	adult	lower	Ash	Ass. (As)
Pir'û	2.1.1	Egyptian	male	adult	upper	Sar	Africa
Pi-san-Eši 1.	2.1.1	Egyptian	male	adult	upper	Ash	Ass. (N)
Pi-san-Eši 2.	2.1.1	Egyptian	male	adult	lower	pAsh	Ass.
Pi-san-Eši 3.	2.1.1	Egyptian	male	adult	lower	pAsh	Ass. (N)
Pišamelki	2.1.1	Egyptian	male	adult	upper	Esa-Ash	Africa
Pi-šan-Ḫuru	2.1.1	Egyptian	male	adult	upper	Esa-Ash	Africa
Pi'u 1.	2.1.1	Egyptian	male	adult	upper	pAsh	Ass. (K)
Pi'u 2.	2.1.1	Egyptian	male	adult	lower	pAsh	Ass. (As)
Pūiama	2.1.1	Egyptian	male	adult	upper	Esa-Ash	Africa
Pūlušu	2.1.1	Egyptian	male	adult	lower	pAsh	Ass. (As)
Pūnašti	2.1.1	Egyptian	male	adult	lower	pAsh	Ass. (As)
Puṭi[...] (1.)	2.1.1	Egyptian	male	adult	lower	Ash	Ass. (As)
Puṭi[...] (2.)	2.1.1	Egyptian	male	adult	upper	Esa	Africa
Puṭi-Atḫiš	2.1.1	Egyptian	male	adult	lower	Ash	Ass. (N)
Puṭi-Bina[...]	2.1.1	Egyptian	male	adult	lower	Ash	Ass. (As)
Puṭi-Eše	2.1.1	Egyptian	male	adult	lower	pAsh	Ass. (N)
Puṭi-Ḫūru	2.1.1	Egyptian	male	adult	lower	Esa/Ash	Ass. (N)
Puṭi-ḫutapiša	2.1.1	Egyptian	male	adult	lower	pAsh	Ass. (As)
Puṭi-Māni	2.1.1	Egyptian	male	adult	lower	Esa/Ash	Ass. (N)
Puṭi-Mūnu 1.	2.1.1	Egyptian	male	adult	lower	Ash	Ass. (As)

Puṭi-Mūnu 2.	2.1.1	Egyptian	male	adult	upper	pAsh	Ass. (As)
Puṭi-Nūnu	2.1.1	Egyptian	male	adult	lower	pAsh	Ass. (As)
Puṭiše 1.	2.1.1	Egyptian	male	adult	upper	Ash-pAsh	Ass. (N)
Puṭiše 2.	2.1.1	Egyptian	male	adult	lower	Ash	Ass. (As)
Puṭiše 3.	2.1.1	Egyptian	male	adult	lower	pAsh	Ass. (As)
Puṭi-Šīri 1.	2.1.1	Egyptian	male	adult	upper	Esa	Ass. (N)
Puṭi-Šīri 2.	2.1.1	Egyptian	male	adult	lower	Esa/Ash	Ass. (N)
Puṭi-Šīri 3.	2.1.1	Egyptian	male	adult	lower	Ash/pAsh	Ass. (K)
Puṭi-Šīri 4.	2.1.1	Egyptian	male	adult	lower	pAsh	Ass. (As)
Puṭi-Šīri 5.	2.1.1	Egyptian	male	adult	lower	pAsh	Ass. (As)
Puṭi-Šīri 6.	2.1.1	Egyptian	male	adult	lower	7th c.	Ass. (N)
Puṭu-Bāšti 1.	2.1.1	Egyptian	male	adult	upper	Esa-Ash	Africa
Puṭu-Bāšti 2.	2.1.1	Egyptian	male	adult	lower	Ash	Ass. (As)
Puṭu-Bāšti 3.	2.1.1	Egyptian	male	adult	lower	Ash/pAsh	Ass. (As)
Puṭubikišu	2.1.1	Egyptian	male	adult	lower	Ash	Ass. (As)
Puṭubišu	2.1.1	Egyptian	male	adult	lower	Ash/pAsh	Ass. (As)
Puṭu-ḫabišu	2.1.1	Egyptian	male	adult	lower	Ash	Ass. (As)
Puṭukiše	2.1.1	Egyptian	male	adult	lower	Ash/pAsh	Ass. (As)
Puṭu-Meḫēši 1.	2.1.1	Egyptian	male	adult	lower	pAsh	Ass. (N)
Puṭu-Meḫēši 2.	2.1.1	Egyptian	male	adult	lower	pAsh	Ass. (N)
Puṭupašte	2.1.1	Egyptian	male	adult	lower	Ash/pAsh	Ass. (As)
Puṭu-Paiti 1.	2.1.1	Egyptian	male	adult	lower	Ash	Ass. (As)
Puṭu-Paiti 2.	2.1.1	Egyptian	male	adult	lower	pAsh	Ass. (N)
Puṭu-šisi[...]	2.1.1	Egyptian	female	adult	slave	pAsh	Ass. (N)
Puṭušu	2.1.1	Egyptian	male	adult	lower	Ash/pAsh	Ass. (As)
Putu-zutaḫa	2.1.1	Egyptian	male	adult	lower	Ash	Ass. (As)
Puṭu-[...]	2.1.1	Egyptian	male	adult	lower	Ash	Ass. (N)
Qašḫamete	2.1.1	Egyptian	male	adult	lower	Ash-pAsh	Ass. (As)
Qibīt-Aššur 30.	2.1.4	Egyptian	male	adult	upper	Ash	Ass. (As)
Qīšāia 2.	2.1.2	Egyptian	male	adult	lower	pAsh	Ass. (As)
Quni-Ḫūru	2.1.1	Egyptian	male	adult	lower	pAsh	Ass. (N)
Raḫpau 1.	2.1.1	Egyptian	male	adult	lower	Esa	Ass. (As)
Raḫpau 2.	2.1.1	Egyptian	male	adult	upper	pAsh	Ass. (As)
Ra'sî	2.1.1	Egyptian	male	adult	upper	Esa/Ash	Ass. (N)
Rasū'	2.1.1	Egyptian	male	adult	lower	Sen	Ass. (N)
Ra'û 1.	2.1.1	Egyptian	male	adult	lower	Sen	Ass. (As)
Ra'û 2.	2.1.1	Egyptian	male	adult	lower	Ash	Ass. (As)
Ra'û 3.	2.1.1	Egyptian	male	adult	lower	Ash	Ass. (N)
Ra'û 4.	2.1.1	Egyptian	male	adult	lower	Ash/pAsh	Ass. (As)
Ra'û 5.	2.1.1	Egyptian	male	adult	lower	7th c.	Ass. (N)
Rē'e	2.1.1	Egyptian	male	adult	upper	Sar	Africa
Rībāia 11.	2.1.3	Egyptian	male	adult	lower	7th c.	Ass. (As)
Ri-m-pi-aue	2.1.1	Egyptian	male	adult	lower	Ash/pAsh	Ass. (As)
Sabutî	2.1.3	Egyptian	male	child	lower	Ash/pAsh	Ass. (As)
Sa-ḫpi-māu	2.1.1	Egyptian	male	adult	lower	pAsh	Ass. (N)

Sē'-aqāba 1.	2.1.3	Kushite	male	adult	lower	Sar	Ass.
Sīn-na'di 27.	2.1.3	Egyptian	male	adult	lower	post-612	Ass.
Sukkāia 43.	2.1.3	Egyptian	male	adult	lower	Ash/pAsh	Ass. (As)
Susinqu 1.	2.1.1	Libyan	male	adult	upper	Sen	Ass. (N)
Susinqu 2.	2.1.1	Libyan	male	adult	upper	Esa-Ash	Africa
Ṣi-ḫû 1.	2.1.1	Egyptian	male	adult	upper	Esa-Ash	Africa
Ṣi-ḫû 2.	2.1.1	Egyptian	male	adult	upper	Esa/Ash	Ass. (N)
Ṣi-ḫû 3.	2.1.1	Egyptian	male	adult	lower	Esa/Ash	Ass. (N)
Ṣi-ḫû 4.	2.1.1	Egyptian	male	adult	lower	pAsh	Ass. (N)
Ṣi-Ḫuru 1.	2.1.1	Egyptian	male	adult	upper	Esa/Ash	Ass. (N)
Ṣi-Ḫuru 2.	2.1.1	Egyptian	male	adult	upper	Esa	Africa
Ṣil-Aššur 2.	2.1.2	Egyptian	male	adult	upper	Sen	Ass. (N)
Ṣumaššeri	2.1.1	Egyptian	male	adult	lower	Esa/Ash	Ass. (N)
Šabakû	2.1.1	Kushite	male	adult	upper	Sar	Africa
Šapataku'	2.1.1	Kushite	male	adult	upper	Sar-Sen	Africa
Šarru-lū-dāri 12.	2.1.2	Egyptian	male	adult	upper	Esa	Bab.
Šarru-lū-dāri 13.	2.1.4	Egyptian	male	adult	upper	Esa-Ash	Africa
Šarru-lū-dāri 33.	2.1.3	Egyptian	male	adult	lower	7th c.	Ass. (As)
Šašmâ 1.	2.1.2	Egyptian	male	adult	lower	Ash	v. state
Šē'i-Ēši	2.1.1	Egyptian	male	adult	lower	pAsh	Ass. (N)
Šēr-manāni	2.1.3	Kushite	male	child	lower	Sar	Ass.
Šulmu-šarri 12.	2.1.2	Kushite	male	adult	upper	Esa/Ash	Ass.
Šumma-Ēši	2.1.1	Egyptian	male	adult	upper	Ash	Ass. (As)
Taḫ-arṭiše 1.	2.1.1	Egyptian	male	adult	lower	pAsh	Ass. (As)
Taḫ-arṭiše 2.	2.1.1	Egyptian	male	adult	lower	pAsh	Ass. (N)
Takilāti	2.1.1	Libyan	male	adult	lower	Ash-pAsh	Ass. (N)
Ta'lâ 5.	2.1.2	Egyptian	male	adult	lower	Ash/pAsh	Ass. (As)
Tamūzītu 1.	2.1.2	Egyptian	female	adult	lower	Ash/pAsh	Ass. (As)
Tanut-Amani	2.1.1	Kushite	male	adult	upper	Ash	Africa
Tap-naḫte 1.	2.1.1	Egyptian	male	adult	lower	Esa	Ass. (As)
Tap-naḫte 2.	2.1.1	Egyptian	male	adult	upper	Esa-Ash	Africa
Tap-naḫte 3.	2.1.1	Egyptian	male	adult	lower	Ash	Ass. (As)
Tap-naḫte 4.	2.1.1	Egyptian	male	adult	lower	Ash	Ass. (As)
Tarḫursi 2.	2.1.3	Egyptian	male	adult	lower	pAsh	Ass. (As)
Tarqû	2.1.1	Kushite	male	adult	upper	Esa-Ash	Africa
Tattapḫa(?)	2.1.1	Egyptian	female	adult	lower	Esa/Ash	Ass. (N)
Ṭāb-Bēl 7.	2.1.3	Egyptian	male	adult	lower	pAsh	Ass. (As)
Ṭāb-Bēl 8.	2.1.2	Egyptian	male	adult	lower	Ash	Ass. (As)
Ubru-Mullissu	2.1.3	Egyptian	male	adult	lower	pAsh	Ass. (N)
Ubrūtu 4.	2.1.3	Egyptian	male	adult	lower	Ash/pAsh	Ass. (As)
Unamunu	2.1.1	Egyptian	male	adult	upper	Esa-Ash	Africa
Urdu-Aššur 7.	2.1.3	Egyptian	male	adult	lower	pAsh	Ass. (As)
Urdu-Mullissu 10.	2.1.3	Egyptian	male	adult	lower	pAsh	Ass.
Urdu-Nabû 13.	2.1.3	Egyptian	male	adult	lower	Ash/pAsh	Ass. (As)
Urdu-Nanāia 20.	2.1.3	Egyptian	male	adult	lower	Ash/pAsh	Ass. (As)

Urkittu-kallat	2.1.2	Egyptian	female	adult	lower	Ash/pAsh	Ass. (As)
Usilkanu 1.	2.1.1	Libyan	male	adult	upper	Sar	Africa
Usilkanu 2.	2.1.1	Libyan	male	adult	lower	Ash/pAsh	Ass. (As)
Usilkanu 3.	2.1.1	Libyan	male	adult	lower	Ash/pAsh	Ass. (As)
Usta-Ḫuru	2.1.1	Egyptian	male	adult	lower	pAsh	Ass. (K)
Uṣi-Ḫanša	2.1.1	Egyptian	male	adult	lower	Esa/Ash	Ass. (N)
Uš-Anaḫuru	2.1.1	Kushite	male	adult	upper	Esa	Ass. (N)
Uširiḫiuḫurti	2.1.1	Egyptian	male	adult	lower	Sen	Ass.
Uta-Ḫūru	2.1.1	Egyptian	male	adult	lower	Ash	Ass. (N)
Zabad 4.	2.1.3	Kushite	male	adult	lower	pAsh	Ass.
Zateubatte	2.1.2	Egyptian	male	adult	lower	pAsh	Ass. (As)

7.1.2 Likely and possible Africans

The table presented below lists the likely and possible Africans and their biographic data discussed above. Preciser identification ground is indicated in the column "type" and the numbers in this column refer to subsections in this book. The remaining columns focus on identities, properties, and settings, and respond to the interrogative words who, what, when, and where. As for where, the classification "Ass." usually includes information on city of residence. Circumstances and the interrogative word how are focused on and responded to elsewhere.[783]

individual	**type**	**ethnicity**	**sex**	**age**	**class**	**time**	**place**
Abdi-mašši	2.2.1	Egyptian	male	adult	lower	pAsh	Ass. (As)
Abdi-Samsi 2.	2.2.2	Egyptian	male	adult	upper	pAsh	Ass. (N)
Adimasia	2.2.1	Egyptian	female	adult	slave	Ash	Ass. (As)
Amman-appu	2.2.1	Egyptian	male	adult	upper	Ash	Africa
Amû	2.2.1	Egyptian	male	adult	lower	pAsh	Ass. (As)
Aptaḫar[...]	2.2.1	Egyptian	male	adult	lower	Esa	Ass. (As)
Ata'	2.2.1	Egyptian	male	adult	lower	Ash/pAsh	Ass. (As)
Attâ-ḫāsi	2.2.1	Egyptian	female	adult	lower	Ash	Ass. (K)
Awa (2.)	2.2.2	Egyptian	male	adult	lower	pAsh	Ass. (As)
Daia 1.	2.2.1	Egyptian	male	adult	lower	Sen	Ass. (As)
Daia 2.	2.2.1	Egyptian	male	adult	upper	Ash/pAsh	Ass. (As)
Daiâ 1.	2.2.1	Egyptian	male	adult	lower	Esa	Ass.
Daiâ 2.	2.2.1	Egyptian	male	adult	lower	Ash	Ass. (N)
Daiâ 3.	2.2.1	Egyptian	male	adult	lower	Ash	Ass. (As)
Daiâ (4.)	2.2.1	Egyptian	male	adult	lower	8th c.	Ass.
Daiaî (1.)	2.2.1	Egyptian	male	adult	lower	Ash	Ass. (K)

[783] The following abbreviations apply: (As) = Assur, Ash = Ashurbanipal, Ass. = Assyria, Esa = Esarhaddon, (K) = Kalhu, (N) = Nineveh, pAsh = post-Ashurbanipal period, Sen = Sennacherib.

Daiaî (2.)	2.2.1	Egyptian	male	adult	lower	pAsh	Ass. (As)
Daiaia	2.2.1	Egyptian	male	adult	lower	Sen	Ass. (As)
Din-ḫuru	2.2.1	Egyptian	male	adult	lower	pAsh	Ass. (K)
Ḫā-bāštī 1.	2.2.1	Egyptian	male	adult	lower	Esa	Ass.
Ḫā-bāštī 2.	2.2.1	Egyptian	male	adult	upper	Esa-Ash	Ass. (N)
Ḫā-bāštī 3.	2.2.1	Egyptian	male	adult	upper	Ash	Ass. (N)
Ḫaḫpi	2.2.1	Egyptian	male	adult	lower	Ash/pAsh	Ass. (As)
Ḫallabēše 1.	2.2.1	Libyan	male	adult	upper	7th c.	Ass.
Ḫallabēše 2.	2.2.1	Libyan	male	adult	lower	Ash-pAsh	Ass. (N)
Ḫallabēše 3.	2.2.1	Libyan	male	adult	lower	pAsh	Ass. (As)
Ḫanabeš	2.2.1	Libyan	male	adult	lower	Sen	Ass.
Ḫana-Ḫūru	2.2.1	Egyptian	male	adult	lower	Ash	Ass. (N)
Ḫapunapa	2.2.1	Egyptian	male	adult	lower	Ash/pAsh	Ass. (As)
Ḫašbasnu[...]	2.2.1	Egyptian	male	adult	lower	pAsh	Ass. (N)
Ḫurazuri	2.2.1	Egyptian	male	adult	lower	Ash	Ass. (As)
Ḫurbianu	2.2.1	Egyptian	male	adult	lower	Ash/pAsh	Ass. (As)
Iašanimu	2.2.1	Egyptian	male	adult	lower	pAsh	Ass. (As)
Iāširu	2.2.1	Egyptian	male	adult	lower	pAsh	Ass. (As)
Illāia	2.2.1	Egyptian	male	adult	lower	pAsh	Ass. (N)
Inurta-šarru-uṣur 2.	2.2.2	Egyptian	male	adult	upper	Ash-pAsh	Ass. (N)
Kisiri	2.2.1	Egyptian	male	adult	lower	Ash-pAsh	Ass. (As)
Kiṣir-Aššur 45.	2.2.2	Egyptian	male	adult	upper	Ash-pAsh	Ass. (As)
Kiṣir-Aššur 46.	2.2.2	Egyptian	male	adult	lower	Ash-pAsh	Ass. (As)
Lābê (1.)	2.2.1	Egyptian	female	adult	slave	pAsh	Ass. (As)
Lābê (2.)	2.2.1	Egyptian	female	adult	lower	Ash/pAsh	Ass. (As)
Lawaḫameḫi	2.2.1	Egyptian	male	adult	lower	Ash/pAsh	Ass. (As)
Lulūlu	2.2.1	Egyptian	male	adult	lower	Ash	Ass. (As)
Nibḫēa	2.2.1	Egyptian	male	adult	lower	pAsh	Ass. (As)
Pabaku	2.2.1	Egyptian	male	adult	lower	Ash	Ass. (As)
Pabbā'u	2.2.1	Egyptian	male	adult	lower	Esa	Ass. (As)
Paḫî	2.2.1	Egyptian	female	adult	slave	pAsh	Ass. (N)
Pamenapi	2.2.1	Egyptian	male	adult	lower	Ash-pAsh	Ass. (As)
Panateḫati	2.2.1	Egyptian	male	adult	lower	Ash/pAsh	Ass. (As)
Pašî 1.	2.2.1	Egyptian	male	adult	lower	Ash	Ass. (K)
Pašî 2.	2.2.1	Egyptian	male	adult	lower	Ash	Ass. (As)
Pašî 3.	2.2.1	Egyptian	male	adult	upper	Ash-pAsh	Ass. (As)
Pašî 4.	2.2.1	Egyptian	male	adult	lower	Ash	Ass.
Pašî 5.	2.2.1	Egyptian	male	adult	upper	pAsh	Ass. (N)
Pašî 6.	2.2.1	Egyptian	male	adult	lower	Ash	Ass.
Pašî 7.	2.2.1	Egyptian	male	adult	lower	Ash/pAsh	Ass. (As)
Pašî 8.	2.2.1	Egyptian	male	adult	lower	pAsh	Ass. (As)
Pašî 10.	2.2.1	Egyptian	male	adult	upper	pAsh	Ass. (As)
Patutume	2.2.1	Egyptian	male	adult	lower	Ash/pAsh	Ass. (As)
Piluna	2.2.1	Egyptian	male	adult	lower	pAsh	Ass. (As)
Pilzu	2.2.1	Egyptian	male	adult	lower	Ash/pAsh	Ass. (As)

Pinaiawa	2.2.1	Egyptian	male	adult	upper	pAsh	Ass. (As)
Pizešḫurdāia	2.2.1	Egyptian	male	adult	lower	pAsh	Ass. (As)
Puḫutana	2.2.1	Egyptian	male	adult	lower	Ash	Ass. (As)
Puta[...]	2.2.1	Egyptian	male	adult	lower	Ash	Ass. (As)
Puṭi-Mutû	2.2.1	Egyptian	male	adult	lower	Ash	Ass. (As)
Puṭupiāti	2.2.1	Egyptian	male	adult	lower	Esa	Ass. (N)
Qišiṣim	2.2.1	Egyptian	male	adult	lower	Ash/pAsh	Ass. (As)
Raḫdibi'	2.2.1	Egyptian	male	adult	lower	Ash/pAsh	Ass. (As)
Rawa	2.2.1	Egyptian	male	adult	lower	Ash	Ass. (As)
Riḫpi-Mūnu	2.2.1	Egyptian	male	adult	lower	Ash/pAsh	Ass. (As)
Saḫarpunḫu	2.2.1	Egyptian	male	adult	lower	Ash/pAsh	Ass. (As)
Sē'-raḫî 2.	2.2.2	Egyptian	male	adult	lower	Esa	Ass. (N)
Siḫā'	2.2.1	Egyptian	male	adult	lower	Ash-pAsh	Ass. (As)
Sukkāia 31.	2.2.2	Egyptian	male	adult	lower	Ash-pAsh	Ass. (As)
Taḫa'u	2.2.1	Egyptian	male	adult	lower	Ash/pAsh	Ass. (As)
Taia 1.	2.2.1	Egyptian	male	adult	lower	Esa	Ass. (As)
Taia 2.	2.2.1	Egyptian	male	adult	lower	pAsh	Ass. (As)
Taia 3.	2.2.1	Egyptian	male	adult	lower	Ash	Ass.
Taka'in(?)	2.2.1	Egyptian	male	adult	lower	7th c.	Ass. (N)
Tallu 2.	2.2.2	Egyptian	male	adult	lower	Ash	Ass. (As)
Tamurtašu	2.2.1	Egyptian	female	adult	lower	Ash	Ass. (As)
Tap[...]	2.2.1	Egyptian	male	adult	lower	Ash/pAsh	Ass. (As)
Tatašīri	2.2.1	Egyptian	female	adult	lower	Ash/pAsh	Ass. (As)
Tutakiḫama	2.2.1	Egyptian	male	adult	lower	Esa	Ass. (As)
Ulūlāiu 42.	2.2.2	Egyptian	male	adult	lower	pAsh	Ass. (N)
Urdu-Aššur 5.	2.2.2	Egyptian	male	adult	upper	Ash-pAsh	Ass. (As)
Zaḫâ	2.2.1	Egyptian	male	adult	lower	Ash	Ass. (As)

7.1.3 Anonymous Africans

The table presented below lists the anonymous Africans and their biographic data discussed above. Preciser identification ground is indicated in the column "type" and the numbers in this column refer to section(s) in this book. The remaining columns focus on identities, properties, and settings, and respond to the interrogative words who, what, when, and where. As for where, the classification "Ass." may include information on city of residence. The classification "mixed" is employed for unqualified ethnonym references in the plural. Circumstances and the interrogative word how are focused on and responded to elsewhere.[784]

[784] The following abbreviations apply: Ada = Adad-narari III, (Ar) = Arbela, (As) = Assur, Ash = Ashurbanipal, Ass. = Assyria, Esa = Esarhaddon, (K) = Kalhu, (N) = Nineveh, pAsh = post-Ashurbanipal period, Sar = Sargon II, Sen = Sennacherib, Sha = Shalmaneser III, Tig = Tiglath-pileser III.

people	type	sex	age	class	time	place
the Egyptian(s) 1.	2.3	male	adult	lower	Sha	Africa
the Egyptian(s) 2.	2.3	mixed	mixed	mixed	Sar	Africa
the Kushite(s) 1.	2.3	male	adult	upper	Sar	Africa
the Egyptian(s) 3.	2.3	mixed	mixed	mixed	Sar	Africa
the Egyptian(s) 4.	2.3	male	adult	lower	Sar	Africa
the Egyptian(s) and the Kushite(s) 1.	2.3	male	adult	mixed	Sen	Africa
the Egyptian(s) and the Kushite(s) 2.	2.3	male	adult	mixed	Sen	Africa
the Egyptian(s) 5.	2.3	mixed	mixed	mixed	Esa	Africa
the Egyptian(s) and the Kushite(s) 3.	2.3	male	adult	upper	Esa	Africa
the Kushite(s) 2.	2.3	mixed	mixed	mixed	Esa	Africa
the Kushite(s) 3.	2.3	male	adult	upper	Esa	Africa
the Kushite(s) 4.	2.3	male	adult	upper	Ash	Africa
the Egyptian(s) 6.	2.3	male	adult	mixed	Ash	Africa
the Egyptian(s) 7.	2.3	male	adult	upper	Sar	Africa
the Egyptian(s) 8.	2.3	male	adult	lower	Esa	Africa
the Egyptian(s) 9.	2.3	mixed	mixed	mixed	Esa	Africa
the Egyptian(s) 10.	2.3	male	adult	upper	Esa	Africa
the Egyptian(s) and the Kushite(s) 4.	2.3	mixed	mixed	mixed	Esa	Africa
the Kushite(s) 5.	2.3	female	adult	upper	Esa/Ash	Ass. (N)
the Kushite(s) 6.	2.3	male	adult	upper	Esa	Africa
the Egyptian(s) and the Kushite(s) 5.	2.3	mixed	mixed	mixed	Esa/Ash	Ass. (As)
the Egyptian(s) 11.	2.3	mixed	mixed	mixed	Esa/Ash	Ass. (Ar)
the Egyptian(s) 12.	2.3	mixed	mixed	mixed	Esa	Ass.
the Kushite(s) 7.	2.3	female	child	lower	Esa	Ass. (N)
the Egyptian(s) 13.	2.3	mixed	mixed	mixed	Tig	Africa
the Egyptian(s) and the Kushite(s) 6.	2.3	male	adult	upper	Ada	Ass. (K)
the Egyptian(s) 14.	2.3	male	adult	upper	Ash/pAsh	Ass. (As)
the Egyptian(s) 15.	2.3	mixed	mixed	lower	Ash/pAsh	Ass. (As)
the Egyptian(s) 16.	2.3	male	adult	upper	Ash	Ass. (As)

7.1.4 Demographic statistics

The tables below present demographic statistics, compiled on the basis of the gathered, individual biographic data about ethnicity, sex, age, class, time period, and place of residence of the groups of identified Africans (257 people), likely/possible Africans (88 people), and (29) attestations of anonymous Africans (both individuals and groups). Circumstances and the interrogative word how are focused on and responded to elsewhere.[785]

[785] The following abbreviations apply: Ash = Ashurbanipal, Esa = Esarhaddon, pAsh = post-Ashurbanipal period, p612 = post-612 period, Sar = Sargon II, Sen = Sennacherib. The term "provinces" corresponds to the code "Ass." in tables 7.1.1-3. The abbreviations "Babyl." and "v. state" stand for Babylonia and vassal state

A) identified Africans

	Egyptian	Kushite	Libyan					
ethnicity	87.5%	9.7%	2.7%					
	male	*female*						
sex	*91.8%*	*8.2%*						
	adult	child						
age	98.1%	1.9%						
	upper	*lower*	*slave*					
class	*26.8%*	*71.6%*	*1.6%*					
	9-8th c.	Sar	Sen	7th c.	Esa	Ash	pAsh	p612
time	0.8%	2.9%	3.3%	7.0%	12.6%	33.3%	38.9%	1.2%
	Assur	*Nineveh*	*Kalhu*	*Arbela*	*provinces*	*Babyl.*	*v. state*	*Africa*
place	*47.9%*	*26.5%*	*3.1%*	*0%*	*8.2%*	*0.8%*	*1.2%*	*12.5%*

B) likely and possible Africans

	Egyptian	Kushite	Libyan					
ethnicity	95.5%	0%	4.5%					
	male	*female*						
sex	*92.0%*	*8.0%*						
	adult	child						
age	100%	0%						
	upper	*lower*	*slave*					
class	*14.8%*	*81.8%*	*3.4%*					
	9-8th c.	Sar	Sen	7th c.	Esa	Ash	pAsh	p612
time	1.1%	0%	3.4%	2.3%	9.7%	42.6%	40.9%	0%
	Assur	*Nineveh*	*Kalhu*	*Arbela*	*provinces*	*Babyl.*	*v. state*	*Africa*
place	*68.2%*	*17.0%*	*4.5%*	*0%*	*9.1%*	*0%*	*0%*	*1.1%*

C) identified + likely and possible Africans

	Egyptian	Kushite	Libyan					
ethnicity	89.6%	7.2%	3.2%					
	male	*female*						
sex	*91.9%*	*8.1%*						
	adult	child						
age	98.6%	1.4%						
	upper	*lower*	*slave*					
class	*23.8%*	*74.2%*	*2.0%*					

respectively. The term "mixed" draws from table 7.1.3 and points to a heterogenous (in terms of sex, age, class, etc.) group of people. In the compilation of statistics, dates like Esa-Ash (or Esa/Ash) were treated as half Esarhaddon, half Ashurbanipal, with 0.5 points apportioned to each reign. The same logic was used with regard to (e.g.) "the Egyptian(s) and the Kushite(s) 1." from table 7.1.3.

	9-8th c.	Sar	Sen	7th c.	Esa	Ash	pAsh	p612
time	0.9%	2.2%	3.3%	5.8%	11.9%	35.7%	39.4%	0.9%
	Assur	*Nineveh*	*Kalhu*	*Arbela*	*provinces*	*Babyl.*	*v. state*	*Africa*
place	*53.0%*	*24.1%*	*3.5%*	*0%*	*8.4%*	*0.6%*	*0.9%*	*9.6%*

D) anonymous Africans

	Egyptian	Kushite	Libyan					
ethnicity	65.5%	34.5%	0%					
	male	*female*		*mixed*				
sex	*55.2%*	*6.9%*		*37.9%*				
	adult	child		mixed				
age	58.6%	3.4%		37.9%				
	upper	*lower*	*slave*	*mixed*				
class	*37.9%*	*17.2%*	*0%*	*44.8%*				
	9-8th c.	Sar	Sen	7th c.	Esa	Ash	pAsh	p612
time	10.3%	17.2%	6.9%	0%	43.1%	19.0%	3.4%	0%
	Assur	*Nineveh*	*Kalhu*	*Arbela*	*provinces*	*Babyl.*	*v. state*	*Africa*
place	*13.8%*	*6.9%*	*3.4%*	*3.4%*	*3.4%*	*0%*	*0%*	*69.0%*

7.1.5 Egyptian names and words in cuneiform

In the context of identifying Africans in Neo-Assyrian texts, the list given below is a methodological tool. It is a revised version of the "Verzeichnis der in keilschriftlicher Umschreibung erhaltenen ägyptischen Worte und Eigennamen" (Ranke 1910: 43-62).[786]

hieroglyphs	**cuneiform**	**meaning**	**context**	**period**
ꜣs(t)	*Ēšu/Eš/Ēši'*	Isis	*Ḫarsiyaēšu*	ass, nb
ỉb	*ība/ībi*	heart	*Ḫatḫ(a)rība*	ass
Ip(t)	*Appa/Appi*	Luxor	*Aman'appa*	mb
Imn	*Amāna/Amānu/Aman/ Amūnu/Amanē*	Amun	*Unamūnu*	mb, ass, nb
Imn-ỉỉr-di-sw	*Amurtēše*	PN		ass
Imn-[m-]Ip(t)	*Aman'appa*	PN		mb
Imn-mš	*Amanmaš(š)a*	PN		mb
Imn-nsw-tꜣwy	*M(i)ustū*	Amun-king-of-2-lands	*Paṭm(i)ustū*	nb

786 The most important revised element is the inclusion of words and names with direct links between hieroglyph and cuneiform forms in "Liste I-III" (Ranke 1910: 7-42) but excluded from the above-mentioned list (Ranke 1910: 43-62). These words and names are marked with asterixes in the list presented below. The abbreviations follow those in Ranke's study, namely PN: personal name, RN(KN): royal name, ass: Assyrian period, mb: Middle Babylonian period, nb: Neo-Babylonian or Persian period. For source references, see Ranke 1910: 7-42.

Imn-ḥtp(w)	*Amanḫatpi*	PN		mb
Imn-tꜣf-nḫt	*Amūnutapunaḫti*	PN		nb
In(w)	*Āna/Ūnu*	Heliopolis		mb, ass
ỉr(ỉ)	*ar*	to make	*Iptiḫarṭēšu*	ass, nb
ỉry	*era*	in relation to	*Naptera*	mb
ỉkn	*akunu*	*ỉkn*-vessel		mb
ỉ(t)rw	*yaru*	flood	*Yaru'ū*	ass
*I(t)rw-ꜥꜣ**	*Yaru'ū*	Nile river		ass
ỉdḥw	*aṭḫū*	marshes	*Naṭḫū*	ass
ꜥꜣ	*'ū/'ā/'a*	great	*Yaru'ū*	ass, nb
Wꜣḏy(t)	*Waṣu*	Wadyet	*Ṣuwaṣu*	ass
wꜥw	*wēḫi/wēḫu/wēḫ/ wē(')a/wē(')u/wē*	official		mb
wpwty	*uputi*	messenger		mb
wn	*un*	to be	*Unamūnu*	ass
Wn-Imn	*Unamūnu*	PN		ass
wr	*wīra/wīri/wēra/wēri*	great	*Pawīra*	mb
wrs	*urušša*	headrest		mb
Wsỉrỉ	*Ušīru*	Osiris	*Pušīru*	ass
wsr	*waš*	strong	*Wašmu'ari'a*	mb
Wsr-mꜣꜥ(t)-Rꜥ	*Wašmu'ari'a*	RN		mb
wḏꜣ	*uṣi*	healthy	*Uṣiḫanša*	ass
Wḏꜣ-Ḫnsw	*Uṣiḫanša*	PN		ass
bꜣ	*bi*	ram	*Binṭēṭi*	ass
Bꜣst(t)	*Ubešti/Uastu*	Bastet	*Puṭubešti*	ass, nb
bꜣk	*buk(k)u*	servant	*Bukkuna(n)ni'ipi*	ass
Bꜣk-n(y)-nỉf(w)	*Bukkuna(n)ni'ipi*	PN		ass
Bꜣk-n(y)-rnf	*Bukurninip*	PN		ass
bꜣ(t)	*bū*	tree	*Ḫartibū*	ass
bỉty	*ibya*	king of Lower Egypt	*ỉnsỉbya*	mb
pꜣ	*pa/pi/pu*	the	*Paḳruru*	mb, ass
pꜣ[-n]	*p(a)*	who belongs to…	*Pamūnu*	nb
*Pꜣ-[n-]Imn**	*Pamūnu*	PN		nb
Pꜣ-wr	*Pawīra*	PN		mb
(Pꜣ-)bꜣ-nb-ḏḏ(t)	*P/Binṭēṭi*	Mendes		ass
*Pꜣ-Rꜥ-m-ḥ(b)**	*Pari'amaḫu*	PN		mb
Pꜣ-ḥm-nṯr	*Paḥamnāta*	PN		mb
Pꜣ-ḫr(y)	*Paḫura*	PN		mb
Pꜣ-š(rỉ)-n-Ḥr	*Pišanḫūru*	PN		ass
Pꜣ-ḳrr	*Paḳrūru*	PN		ass
pꜣ-dỉ	*puṭ(u)/puṭi/paṭ(a)*	who is given by…	*Puṭupaiti*	ass, nb
Pꜣ-dỉ-ꜣs(t)	*Paṭ(a)'ēši'*	PN		nb
Pꜣ-dỉ-Imn-nsw-tꜣwy	*Paṭm(i)ustū*	PN		nb
Pꜣ-dỉ-Bꜣst(t)	*Puṭubešti*	PN		ass, nb
Pꜣ-dỉ-mꜣḥsꜣ	*Puṭumḫēšu*	PN		ass

Pȝ-di-ny-ȝs(t)	*Paṭan(i)'ēši'*	PN		nb
Pȝ-di-Nfr-tm	*Paṭniptēmu*	PN		nb
*Pȝ-di-Ḥr**	*Puṭiḫūru*	PN		ass
pr	*pir/pi/pu*	house	*pir'ū*	ass
pr-ʿȝ	*pir'u/pir'ū*	great house		ass
Pr-Wsiri	*Pušīru*	Per-Osiris		ass
Pr-nb	*Punūbu*	Per-nub		ass
*Pr-Ḥwtḥr-nbt-pr-kȝt**	*Piḫattiḫūrunpikī*	Trenuthis		ass
Pr-Spd	*Pišapti/Pišaptu*	Per-Sopdu		ass
*Pr-Spdw-ʿȝ**	*Pišapṭi'ā*	Per-Sopdu-aa		ass
pḥty	*paḫita*	strength	*Minpaḫitarī'a*	mb
Psmṯk	*Pišamelki/Pisamiski*	RN/PN		ass, nb
Ptḥ	*(P)taḫ/Taḫ/Iptiḫ*	Ptah	*Iptiḫarṭēšu*	mb, ass
Ptḥ-iir-di-sw	*Iptiḫarṭēšu*	PN		ass
*Ptḥ-mʿy**	*Taḫmaya*	PN		mb
Ptḥ-ms	*Taḫmašši*	PN		mb
m	*ma/me*	in	*Mantimeḫē*	mb, ass
mȝi-ḥsȝ	*mḫēšu*	wild lion	*Puṭumḫēšu*	ass
mȝʿ(t)	*mu'uwa/mū'a/mu'a/ muwa/mū/mu*	truth	*Minmu'arī'a*	mb
*Mʿy**	*Māya*	PN		mb
(i)m.w	*māu*	therein	*Saḫpimāu*	ass
mn	*man(a)/min/menna*	to endure	*Manaḫpirya*	mb, nb
*Mn-pḥty-Rʿ**	*Minpaḫitarī'a*	RN		mb
*Mn-mȝʿ(t)-Rʿ**	*Minmu'arī'a*	RN		mb
Mn-nfr	*Mempi/Mimpi/Membi*	Memphis		ass, nb
Mn-ḫpr-Rʿ	*Manaḫpirya*	RN		mb
Mnṯw	*Manti*	Monthu	*Mantimeḫē*	ass
Mnṯw-m-ḥȝ(t)	*Mantimeḫē*	PN		ass
mʿy	*māi*	beloved	*Māiamāna*	mb
*Mʿy-Imn**	*Mā'iamāna*	PN		mb
*mhn**	*maḫan*	*mhn*-vessel		mb
ms(i)	*mašši/maš(š)a/maše*	to beget	*Ḫāramašši*	mb
mdw	*māṭu*	staff	*Išpimāṭu*	ass
mḏkt	*maziḳda*	*mḏkt*-vessel		mb
nȝ	*an/n(a)*	the	*Naḫtiḫūruansēni*	ass
Nȝ-ʿȝ-ȝs(t)	*Na'a'ēsi'*	PN		nb
n.i	*n(i)*	to me	*Paṭan(i)ēsi'*	nb
N/niw(t)	*N/ni'i*	Thebes/city		ass
n(y)	*na*	of	*Bukkuna(n)ni'ipi*	mb, ass
nb	*nib*	lord	*Nibmu'ari'a*	mb
nb	*nūbu*	gold	*Punūbu*	ass
Nb-mȝʿ(t)-Rʿ	*Nibmu'ari'a*	RN		mb
nf	*ni'ipi*	breath	*Bukkuna(n)ni'ipi*	ass
nfr	*nāp(a)/nap/nip*	good (m.)	*Ri'anāp(a)*	mb, nb

*Nfr-ḫprw-Rʿ**	*Naphu'ururīya*	RN		mb
nfrt	*napt*	good (f.)	*Naptera*	mb
Nfrt-iry	*Naptera*	PN		mb
Nfr-tm	*Niptēmu*	Nefertum	*Paṭniptēmu*	nb
nms(t)	*namša*	*nms(t)*-vessel		mb
nḫt	*naḫti/naḫtu/niḫti*	to be strong	*Naḫtiḫūruansēni*	ass
nḫt	*naḫti*	strength	*Tapnaḫti*	ass, nb
Nḫt-ȝs(t)-irw	*Niḫti'ešarau*	PN		ass
Nḫt-Ḥp	*Naḫtuḫappi'*	PN		nb
Nḫt-Ḥr-nȝ-šnw	*Naḫtiḫūruansēni*	PN		ass
(n)s	*iš*	belonging to…	*Išpimāṭu*	ass
nsw(t)	*nši*	king of Upper Egypt	*Ḫininši*	ass
*nsw(t)-bit(y)**	*insibya*	king of Egypt		mb
Ns-pȝ-mdw	*Išpimāṭu*	PN		ass
Nkȝw	*Nik(k)ū*	RN		ass
nṯr	*nāta/nūti*	god	*Paḫnūti*	mb, ass
Rʿ	*Rī'a/Rīya/Ri'a/Riya*	Re	*Minmuarī(')a*	mb
Rʿ-ms-sw	*Ri'amašēša*	RN		mb
Rʿ-nfr	*Ri'anāp(a)*	PN		mb
(i)r.w	*arau*	against it	*Niḫarau*	ass
rn	*rīn*	name	*Bukurninip*	ass
rhd(t)	*raḫta*	*rhd(t)*-vessel		mb
rḫ	*ruḫi*	acquaintance		mb
rsy	*rēsi*	southern	*Paturēsi*	ass
rdi	*ṭē/tai*	to give	*Iptiḫarṭēšu*	ass, nb
ḥȝ(t)	*ḫē*	front	*Mantimeḫē*	ass
*Ḥwy**	*Ḫā'i*	PN		mb
ḥw(t)	*ḫi/ḫa/ḫatti*	house	*Ḫatḫ(a)rība*	mb, ass
Ḥw(t)-Ḥr(w)	*Ḫattiḫūru*	Hathor	*Piḫattiḫūrunpikī*	ass
Ḥw(t)-kȝ-Ptḥ	*Hiku(p)taḫ*	Memphis		mb
Ḥw(t)-tȝ-ḥry-ib	*Ḫatḫarība/Ḫatḫirībi*	Athribis		ass
Ḥp	*Ḫpi/Ḫappi'/Ḫapi*	Hapi	*Saḫpimāu*	ass, nb
Ḥp-mn	*Ḫapimenna*	PN		nb
ḥm	*ḫam*	servant	*Paḫamnāta*	mb
ḥm-nṯr	*ḫamnāta/ḫanāte*	priest	*Paḫamnāta*	mb
Ḥnn-nsw(t)	*Ḫininši*	Herakleopolis		ass
ḥr	*'iḫ*	on	*ku'iḫku*	mb
ḥr	*ḫā/ḫa'*	face	*Ṣiḫā*	ass, nb
Ḥr(i)	*Ḫūru*	PN		ass
Ḥr(w)	*Ḫāra/Ḫūru/Ḫar*	Horus	*Naḫtiḫūruansēni*	mb, ass
Ḥr-ms(w)	*Ḫāramašši*	PN		mb
Ḥr-sȝ-ȝs(t)	*Ḫarsiyaēšu*	PN		ass
Ḥr-[n]-tȝ-bȝ(t)	*Ḫartibū*	PN		ass
ḥsy	*ḫasaya*	praised		ass
ḥtp	*ḫatpi*	to be satisfied	*Amanḫatpi*	mb

ḫpr	*(a)ḫpir*	to become (sg.)	*Manaḫpirya*	mb
ḫprw	*ḫu'uru/ḫuru/ḫur'i/ [ḫu]ra/ḫur/ḫū*	to become (pl.)	*Napḫu'ururī[ya]*	mb
Ḫmnw	*Ḫ(i)mūni*	Hermopolis		ass
Ḫnsw	*Ḫanša*	Khonsu	*Uṣiḫanša*	ass
ḫr(y)	*ḫura*	Syrian	*Paḫura*	mb
sꜣ	*siya*	son	*Ḫarsiyaēšu*	ass
Sꜣ(w)	*Saya*	Sais		ass
Sꜣwt(i)	*Šiyāutu*	Asyut		ass
sw	*ša/šu/še/si*	he/him	*Iptiḫarṭēšu*	mb, ass, nb
Spdw	*Šapṭi/Šapṭu*	Sopdu	*Pišapṭi'ā*	ass
stp	*šatep*	chosen	*Šatepnarī'a*	mb
Stp-n(y)-Rʿ	*Šatepnarī'a*	RN		mb
šwbt	*šu'ibda*	*šwbt*-vessel		mb
Šbk	*Šabakū*	RN		ass
šn(w)	*sēni*	tree(s)	*Naḫtiḫūruansēni*	ass
šri	*ša*	child	*Pišanḫūru*	ass
šrdn	*šerdanu/šerdani*	*šrdn*-people		mb
Ššnḳ	*Susinḳu*	PN		ass
ḳrr(w)	*ḳrūru*	frog	*Paḳrūru*	ass
kꜣ	*kū/ku*	soul	*zabnakū*	mb
kꜣ-ḥr-kꜣ	*ku(i)'iḫku*	*kꜣ-ḥr-kꜣ*-vessel		mb
K(ꜣ)š	*Kāši/Kūsi/Kūsu/Kūšu*	Kush		mb, ass, nb
kꜣ(t)	*kī*	cow?	*Piḫattiḫūrunpikī*	ass
*kb**	*kūpa*	*kb*-vessel		mb
kṯ(n)	*kuzi/guzi*	charioteer		mb
tꜣ	*ti/t(a)*	the	*Ḫartibū*	ass, nb
tꜣ[-n]	*ta*	who belongs to…	*Taḫē...*	nb
tꜣ	*tu*	land	*Paturēsi*	ass
tꜣwy	*tū*	two lands	*Paṭm(i)ustū*	nb
Tꜣf-nḫt	*Tapnaḫti*	PN		ass
Tiy	*Teye*	RN		mb
tm	*tēmu*	to be complete	*Niptēmu*	nb
Thrḳ	*Tarḳū*	RN		ass
ṯꜣ(i)	*sa/si*	to take	*Sa(i)ḫpimāu*	ass
*ṯꜣb-n(y)-kꜣ**	*zabnāku*	*ṯꜣb-n(y)-kꜣ*-vessel		mb
*Ṯꜣ-Ḥp-imw**	*Saḫpimāu*	PN		ass
Ṯb-nṯr	*Zabnūti*	Sebennytos		ass
*ds**	*ṭaši*	*ds*-vessel		mb
Ḏʿn(t)	*Ṣa'anu/Ṣi'inu*	Tanis/Pelusium		ass
Ḏḥwty	*T(i)ḫut*	Thoth	*T(i)ḫutartais*	nb
Ḏḥwty-iir-di-sw	*T(i)ḫut'artais*	PN		nb
ḏd	*ṣi*	say	*Ṣiḫā*	ass, nb
Ḏd-Wꜣḏy(t)	*Ṣuwaṣu*	PN		ass
Ḏd-ḥr	*Ṣiḫā*	PN		ass, nb

ḏd(t)	*ṭēṭi*	stability	*Binṭēṭi*	ass

7.2 Indices

7.2.1 Deities

deity	page(s)
Aia	116
Amun	4, 13-14, 16-19, 31, 47, 65, 91, 95-96, 98, 140-141, 170, 172, 234-235
Anukis	31
Apis	16, 29, 78, 83-84, 150, 153
Ashur	44, 83, 89, 94, 96, 155, 186, 190, 194, 215
Atum	166
Baal-Rakkab	150
Bastet	70-71, 74, 148-149
Bel	119, 133, 215
Belat-niphi	138
Belet	123, 215
Bes	151
Ea	125, 129, 131, 215
Gula	124, 215
Hathor	14, 32
Horus	14f, 27, 33f, 36-39, 49f, 52, 56, 58f, 64, 78, 86f, 97, 100, 148, 151, 153, 155
Ishtar/Urkittu	16, 32, 64, 74, 92, 120, 122, 138, 142-143, 155, 160, 172, 174, 177, 194, 215
Isis	15, 26-28, 33-34, 51-52, 56, 63, 89-90, 234
Khonsu	98
Kūbi	101, 215
Mahes	73-74
Marduk	70, 89, 138, 215
Min	65
Month	47
Mullissu	127, 133, 135, 190, 215
Mut	98, 170
Nabu	89, 128, 131, 137-138, 215
Nanaia	136, 215
Nefertem	27
Ninurta	180, 215
Nun	66
Onuris	98-99
Osiris	15, 27, 39, 68, 99, 156, 177
Ptah	16, 27, 90, 142
Ra	53, 71, 79, 83
Sakhmet	74

Satis	30-31
Sē'	130, 215
Seth	39, 52, 78, 153
Shamash/*Samsi*	4, 52, 94, 155, 179, 191-192, 215
Sin	131, 215
Šašm	118, 215
Šēr	132, 215

7.2.2 People

Individual	**page(s)**
Abdâ	117
Abdi-Kurra	30, 35, 62, 67, 77, 99, 180
Abdi-maššī	140
Abdi-Mūnu	13, 212
Abdi-Samsi 2.	151, 156, 179, 213
Abdūnu	91
Abī-erība	40
Abī-Ḫūru 1.	14, 207, 212
Abī-Ḫūru 2.	14-15, 213
Abši-Ešu	15, 124, 126, 209
Abu-dūrī	103, 135
Abu-lē'i	41, 184
Abu-lēšir	106, 136
Adad-milki-ēreš	147
Adad-milki-ilā'ī	106, 136
Adad-narari III	146, 196
Adad-rapa	56
Adad-šarru-uṣur	149
Adda-dimrī	140
Adda-lûkidi	77
Adda-pisia	77, 181
Addî	124
Adimasia	119, 140, 202, 205
Agaragara	162
Aḫ-abû	80, 153
Aḫāt-abīša	91
Aḫā[tî]	37, 182
Aḫātī-ṭābat	112, 124
Aḫu-dūr-enši 2.	36, 121, 184, 213
Aḫu-erība	146
Aḫū'a-erība	103, 135
Aḫu-iddina	30, 35, 62, 66, 77, 99, 179
Aḫu-lā-amašši	146
Aḫu-lāmur	149

Bukurninip	25
Bur-Kūbi	101, 213
Bur-Urti	150
Butanaḫte	25-26, 216
Butinaḫ	26
Dadâ	146
Dādāia	155
Daia 1.	144, 207
Daia 2.	144
Daiâ 1.	145, 209
Daiâ 2.	145
Daiâ 3.	146
Daiâ (4.)	146, 207, 209
Daiaî (1.)	146-147
Daiaî (2.)	147-148
Daiaia	148, 207
Daiān-Marduk	31, 44, 54, 101, 140
Dān-Ešu	26-27, 209, 213
Dannāia	148
Dāri-šarru 2.	102, 118, 200, 209, 213
Dauskunu	97
Din-ḫuru	148
Dūrī-Aššur	3, 100, 102f, 109, 113, 115f, 119, 127f, 131, 134, 136, 145, 157f
Dūr-mākî-Ninurta	97
Ēdu-šal[lim]	14, 63, 67, 151, 179
Epšanni-Issar	90
Eptimu-rṭešu	27
Esarhaddon	9, 11-12, 17, 24-25, 27...
Ēšâ	28
Eša-rṭeše	28, 202
Ezibtu 2.	102, 202, 213
Gīr-Hâ	56-57
Gīrî	162
Gīrittu	164
Gula-ēṭir 3.	48, 124, 129, 213
[...]gurši	79, 85, 137
Gyges	57
Ḫā-bāštī 1.	149, 209
Ḫā-bāštī 2.	149-150
Ḫā-bāštī 3.	150
Ḫabil-kēnu	100, 131
Ḫaḫpi	150-151
Ḫakkubāia	36, 71, 163, 171, 181, 196
Ḫala-šuri	153
Ḫallabēše 1.	151, 201, 209

Ḫur-waṣi 7.	41, 44
Ḫur-waṣi 8.	41-44, 132
Ḫur-waṣi 9.	41-44
Ḫur-waṣi 10.	41-44
Ḫur-waṣi 11.	41-44
Ḫur-waṣi (12.)	43-44
Ḫur-waṣi (13.)	44
Ḫur-waṣi (14.)	44-45, 207, 209
Ḫuṭ-naḫti	23, 29, 36, 40, 45, 54, 59, 67, 90, 125, 182
Iadī'-Iāu	65, 71
Ia-sumu	155
Iašanimu	156
Iāširu	156
Ibašši-ilāni	164
Iddāti-Bēl-allak	149
Idrāia	67
Ilā-ēdiš	13
Ilâ-erība	180
[Il-ḫ]azi	112
Illāia	151, 156
Ilu-issīya	215
Ilumma-lē'i	175
Indî	41, 55, 63, 94
Inurta-ballissu	87
Inurta-šarru-uṣur 2.	4, 14, 35, 62-63, 67, 76, 151, 156, 179-181, 183, 213
Ispiniša	103, 202
Issar-dūrī 26.	15, 125-126, 209, 213
Issar-šumu-iddina	59
Issar-tukallanni	31, 44, 54, 101, 140
Išpimāṭu	45-46
It'amar	55
Kablā	44
Kalbāia 2.	35, 57, 125, 135, 148, 209, 213
Kamabānu	56
Kandilanu	145
Kanūnāiu	128, 144
Kapī[ru]	15
Karānūtu	103, 115, 202, 213
Kisiri	157, 216
Kiṣir-Aššur 45.	15, 21, 23, 32, 36-37…181…
Kiṣir-Aššur 46.	182, 213
Kiṣir-Aššur (66.)	104, 135, 213
Kiṣir-Issar	118
Kiṣir-Nabû	100, 102, 114, 119, 128, 135
Kiṣir-šarrūti	216

Kurarâ	46
Kurilītu	72
Kūsāiâ 1.	104-105, 200, 209
Kūsāiâ 2.	105, 200, 209
Kūsāiu 1.	105, 130, 132, 200, 204, 207, 209
Kūsāiu 2.	106, 200
Kūsāiu 3.	106, 108, 127, 200
Kūsāiu 4.	107, 136, 200, 209
Kūsāiu 5.	107, 200, 209
Kūsāiu 6.	108, 200
Kūsāiu (7.)	108, 200
Kūsāiu (8.)	108-109, 200
Kūsāiu (9.)	109, 127, 200
Kūsāiu (10.)	109-110, 145, 200
Kusasu	118
Kusî	110, 200, 207
Kūsītu	110-111, 200, 202
Kuzub-I[ssa]r	141
Lābê (1.)	157, 202, 205
Lābê (2.)	158, 202
Lā-immašši	147
Lamintu	46-47, 201
Lamkiat(?)	59
Lā-turammanni-Aššur 3.-4.	16, 18, 20, 23-24, 26…126…
Lawaḫameḫi	158
Limṭu-rēmūtu	163
Lulūlu	159, 216
Luqu	91
Lū-šakin 14.	15, 124, 127, 209, 213
Lū-šal[im]	180
Malgadi	164
Mannu-kī-Adad	110
Mannu-kī-aḫḫē	163, 215
Mannu-kī-Arbail	31, 36, 40, 81, 144, 149, 169, 172, 180
Mannu-kī-Aššur	106, 125, 136
Mannu-kī-Ešarra	67
Mannu-kī-ilī	13
Mannu-kī-Libbāli	195
Mannu-kī-māt-Aššur	57, 78
Mannu-kī-Nabû	179
Mannu-kī-Nīnua 13.	111, 213
Mannu-kī-ṣābē	174
Manti-me-ḫē	47
Marduk-erība	40
Marduk-rēmanni	191

Pašî 3.	37, 59, 163-164, 179, 216
Pašî 4.	164, 209
Pašî 5.	165
Pašî 6.	165, 209
Pašî 7.	165-166
Pašî 8.	166
Pašî 9.	20-21, 129, 133, 166, 204
Pašî 10.	166
Patutume	167
Paw[aya]	216
Pilaqqu-lipirê	149
Piluna	167
Pīlušu	54-55, 60
Pilzu	168
Pinaiawa	168-169
Pīnapi	55
Pir'û	55-56, 207
Pi-san-Eši 1.	56
Pi-san-Eši 2.	35, 57, 125, 135, 209
Pi-san-Eši 3.	57
Pišamelki	12, 47, 57-58, 137, 218
Pi-šan-Ḫuru	58
Pi'u 1.	59
Pi'u 2.	37, 59, 90, 163, 179
Piye	47, 195
Pizešḫurdāia	169
Psammetichus I	12, 47, 57-58, 137, 218
Puglu	87
Puḫutana	169
Pūiama	60
Pūlušu	60
Pūnašti	15, 61, 125, 152, 180
Puqišu	184
Puqulāya	61
Puta[...]	169
Puṭi[...] (1.)	61
Puṭi[...] (2.)	62
Puṭi-Atḫiš	30, 35, 62, 66, 77, 99, 151, 179
Puṭi-Bina[...]	40, 55, 63, 93
Puṭi-Eše	16, 63, 67, 74
Puṭi-Ḫūru	64
Puṭi-ḫutapiša	26, 32, 41-42, 64, 79, 101, 116, 120, 132, 134, 168, 181
Puṭi-Māni	65
Puṭi-Mūnu 1.	65
Puṭi-Mūnu 2.	18, 20-21, 23, 29, 36, 40, 45, 54, 59, 66-67, 70, 79, 90, 123, 125

Ummanigash	27
Unabi	15, 60
Unamâ	216
Unamunu	96
Urdu-aḫḫēšu	174
Urdu-Aia	105
Urdu-Aššur	141, 163
Urdu-Aššur 5.	15, 18, 20-21, 23-24, 36-37…185…
Urdu-Aššur 7.	32, 41-42, 64, 79, 101, 116, 120, 132, 135, 168, 214
Urdu-Bēlti	41, 54, 90, 159
Urdu-Issar	164
Urdu-Mullissu 10.	35, 57, 125, 135, 148, 210, 214
Urdu-Nabû	97, 179
Urdu-Nabû 13.	103, 135, 214
Urdu-Nanāia	165
Urdu-Nanāia 20.	119, 136, 214
Urdu-Nanāia 21.	136
Urkittu-[…]	197
Urkittu-kallat	120, 202, 214
Usilkanu 1.	96-97, 201, 207
Usilkanu 2.	97
Usilkanu 3.	97-98
Usta-Ḫuru	98
Uṣi-Ḫanša	98
Uš-Anaḫuru	99, 200
Uširiḫiuḫurti	99, 207, 210
Uta-Ḫūru	100
Yamani	11, 89, 186
Zabad 4.	106, 136-137, 201, 210, 214
Zab[i?…]	111
Zaḫâ	73, 75-76, 154, 178
Zamunu(?)	37, 66, 70
Zateubatte	120-121
Zazaya	216
Zērî	138
Zērīja	181
Zēru-ukīn	107
Zitt[i]	216

7.2.3 Places

toponym	**page(s)**
Abydos	46
Ahni	24
Amarna/Akhetaton	1, 10-11, 53

Phoenicia	195
Pishapdia	50
Punubu	93
Qarqar	185, 211, 218
Qirbit	209
Raphia	83, 187, 211, 218
Rasappa	102, 118, 148-149
Sais	52-54, 58, 211
Sam'al	150
Samaria	150
Sebennytos	34
Sidon	195
Simirra	195
Sinai	8
Siut	85
Tanis	56, 70-71, 83, 96
Taremu	74
Tel Hadid	117-118
Thebes	12, 14, 47, 92, 94-95, 98, 141, 170, 190, 210-211, 218
Thinis	45
Tigris	7
Trenuthis	27
Tyre	94, 111, 193, 195
Uruk	10, 120, 215
Yanibir-suhuri	105, 130
Zagros	88

7.2.4 Texts

text	**page(s)**
A 1809	126, 181
ADD 284	149
ADD 537	149
Ashurbanipal 72	94
Ashurbanipal 73	94
Ashurbanipal 117	94
Ashurbanipal 118	52, 54, 58, 94, 138
Ashurbanipal 119	94
Ashurbanipal 121	92, 94
Ashurbanipal 122	92, 94
Ashurbanipal 196	94
Ashurbanipal 197	92, 94
Ashurbanipal 207	52, 54, 92, 137-138, 190
BagM 16 31	126
BATSH 6 3	107

RINAP 2 63	96
RINAP 2 74	186
RINAP 2 82	56, 96
RINAP 2 116	88, 186-187
RINAP 3 4	187-188, 210
RINAP 3 15	187-188
RINAP 3 16	187-188
RINAP 3 17	187-188
RINAP 3 18	188
RINAP 3 21	187
RINAP 3 22	187-188
RINAP 3 23	187-188
RINAP 3 32	188
RINAP 3 46	187-188
RINAP 3 140	187-188
RINAP 3 142	187-188
RINAP 3 165	187
RINAP 4 1	114
RINAP 4 5	114
RINAP 4 8	94
RINAP 4 9	36, 39, 62, 87, 188, 210
RINAP 4 15	94
RINAP 4 20	189
RINAP 4 34	94
RINAP 4 35	189
RINAP 4 38	94
RINAP 4 39	94
RINAP 4 60	94-95
RINAP 4 68	189
RINAP 4 69	189
RINAP 4 83	189
RINAP 4 84	189
RINAP 4 85	189
RINAP 4 86	189
RINAP 4 95	189
RINAP 4 98	9, 94, 98, 189
RINAP 4 103	94, 98, 189
RINAP 4 112	189
RINAP 5/1 2	52, 54, 94, 138, 190
RINAP 5/1 3	92, 94, 138-139, 210
RINAP 5/1 4	92, 94, 138-139
RINAP 5/1 6	49, 52, 54, 58, 92, 94, 114, 137-138
RINAP 5/1 7	49, 51, 54, 94, 138
RINAP 5/1 8	52, 54, 94, 138
RINAP 5/1 9	92

RINAP 5/1 11	24, 27, 34, 45-47, 49-51, 54, 57-58, 60, 70, 84-85, 88, 92-94, 137-138, 189-190, 192, 210-211
RINAP 5/1 15	94
SAA 1 110	191
SAA 3 29	53, 141
SAA 3 30	140
SAA 4 82	191
SAA 4 84	94
SAA 4 88	52, 138, 191
SAA 4 130	94
SAA 4 139	192
SAA 4 142	192
SAA 4 144	192
SAA 4 145	192
SAA 6 142	39, 84, 116, 215
SAA 6 202	144
SAA 6 206	149
SAA 6 211	149
SAA 6 218	149
SAA 6 220	149
SAA 6 236	170
SAA 6 245	148
SAA 6 247	149
SAA 6 269	149
SAA 6 278	149
SAA 6 283	149
SAA 6 297	149
SAA 6 307	149
SAA 6 308	149
SAA 6 311	15, 124, 126
SAA 6 323	149
SAA 6 324	149
SAA 6 325	149
SAA 6 328	149
SAA 6 332	149
SAA 6 340	149
SAA 6 348	149
SAA 6 350	149
SAA 7 1	36, 39, 51, 79, 85-87, 136, 211
SAA 7 2	86-87
SAA 7 5	68
SAA 7 9	34
SAA 7 24	193
SAA 7 30	107
SAA 7 47	101-102, 118

SAA 7 48	101
SAA 10 112	117
SAA 10 351	193
SAA 11 169	28, 35, 37, 46, 64-65, 68, 86, 88, 95, 98, 210
SAA 11 201	105, 130, 132
SAA 13 13	193
SAA 13 144	194
SAA 14 16	112, 124
SAA 14 19	124
SAA 14 26	91
SAA 14 27	149
SAA 14 29	105
SAA 14 30	215
SAA 14 91	56
SAA 14 97	145
SAA 14 102	153
SAA 14 110	105
SAA 14 114	164
SAA 14 118	164
SAA 14 119	31, 81
SAA 14 120	31, 81
SAA 14 123	164
SAA 14 154	91
SAA 14 155	161
SAA 14 161	19, 22, 51, 73, 75, 83, 86, 127, 133, 151, 154, 183-184
SAA 14 171	57
SAA 14 244	82
SAA 14 309	33, 175
SAA 14 427	180
SAA 14 428	180
SAA 14 429	179
SAA 14 430	67
SAA 14 432	179
SAA 14 433	183
SAA 14 434	67, 180
SAA 14 435	63, 75, 151, 156, 178, 180, 184
SAA 14 436	14, 63-64, 67, 151, 179-180
SAA 14 442	30, 34, 62, 67, 77, 99, 151, 180
SAA 14 443	16, 22, 63, 74
SAA 14 445	67
SAA 14 446	22, 30, 89, 91
SAA 14 449	63
SAA 14 450	63
SAA 16 50	111
SAA 16 55	182

StAT 2 178	36-37, 41, 101, 126, 181-182
StAT 2 179	43
StAT 2 180	20, 171-172, 177
StAT 2 181	30, 43, 54, 101, 139
StAT 2 183	126, 180-181, 184
StAT 2 184	36-37, 41-42, 54-55, 83, 122, 126, 142, 155, 172, 181, 184-185
StAT 2 185	184
StAT 2 186	180
StAT 2 187	41, 180, 184
StAT 2 188	180, 184
StAT 2 191	36-37, 121, 126, 180, 184-185
StAT 2 192	41, 54, 90, 126, 152, 159, 184
StAT 2 194	66, 180, 184
StAT 2 195	54, 184
StAT 2 196	184
StAT 2 197	77-78, 184
StAT 2 198	41, 44, 50, 167
StAT 2 199	181, 184
StAT 2 201	43, 161
StAT 2 202	180-181, 184
StAT 2 203	184
StAT 2 204	20, 33
StAT 2 206	180
StAT 2 207	26, 32, 41-42, 64, 79, 101, 116, 132, 134, 168, 181
StAT 2 208	47, 126, 159, 173, 182, 184-185
StAT 2 209	55, 125, 184
StAT 2 210	41, 163, 180, 184
StAT 2 211	41, 54, 126, 180
StAT 2 212	163, 184-185
StAT 2 213	20, 36-37, 159, 184
StAT 2 214	156, 163, 184
StAT 2 215	180-181, 184
StAT 2 216	21, 41, 121, 166, 180, 184
StAT 2 217	21, 23, 41, 121, 166, 180, 184
StAT 2 218	141, 180
StAT 2 219	184
StAT 2 221	158, 184
StAT 2 222	184
StAT 2 223	184
StAT 2 224	180
StAT 2 225	54, 184
StAT 2 226	184
StAT 2 228	48, 184
StAT 2 229	41, 167, 184
StAT 2 231	126

WVDOG 152 I.37	103, 112, 131
WVDOG 152 I.38	100, 102, 120, 131
WVDOG 152 I.39	100, 128
WVDOG 152 I.41	102-103, 131
WVDOG 152 I.42	131
WVDOG 152 I.43	103, 128
WVDOG 152 I.47	109
WVDOG 152 I.48	131
WVDOG 152 I.52	131
WVDOG 152 I.56	100, 103, 115, 128
WVDOG 152 I.57	100
WVDOG 152 I.58	103, 115, 134
WVDOG 152 I.59	100
WVDOG 152 I.68	102, 131
WVDOG 152 II.1	72, 160
WVDOG 152 II.2	61, 176
WVDOG 152 II.3	72, 75-76, 154, 178
WVDOG 152 II.6	72
WVDOG 152 II.7	38, 61, 150, 153, 176
WVDOG 152 II.8	76, 166
WVDOG 152 II.9	103, 135
WVDOG 152 II.10	73-74, 121, 129, 158
WVDOG 152 II.11	131
YBC 11382	117
ZA 73 11	3, 65, 71
ZA 105	44

7.2.5 Egyptian words

word	**meaning**	**page(s)**
ꜣw	length	80
ꜣḫt	horizon	139
=i	my	18, 148
iꜣwt	old age	78
imy-r	overseer	47
ir	make	19, 27-28, 46, 78, 90, 142, 156
iry	related to	156
ity	sovereign	75
id	deaf	23
ym	sea	60
ꜥꜣ	great	55
ꜥnḫ	life	49
ꜥr	bring	16
=w	them	32, 49, 51, 83
wiꜣ	bark	83

sn	brother	56, 58
sḫmt	woman	77
st	her	28
šnw	tree	49
šry	son	56, 58
ḳi	young	77
ḳn	strong	78
ḳrr	frog	54
kꜣ	soul	46, 52-53, 160
tꜣ	the	35, 95, 161, 176-177
tꜣy	this	18, 92, 176
twt	image	177
ṯꜣ	seize	83
ṯꜣty	vizier	46
(r)di	give	19, 27-28, 61-68, 70-77, 90, 142-144, 147-148, 166, 169-170, 177
d(rt)	hand	143-144, 147
ḏd	say	39, 85-86, 173, 178

PUBLICATIONS OF THE FOUNDATION FOR FINNISH ASSYRIOLOGICAL RESEARCH

No. 1: Pirjo Lapinkivi, *The Neo-Assyrian Myth of Ištar's Descent and Resurrection* (= State Archives of Assyria Cuneiform Texts, Vol. VI). Helsinki, 2010.

No. 2: Amar Annus and Alan Lenzi, *Ludlul bēl nēmeqi: The Standard Babylonian Poem of the Righteous Sufferer* (= State Archives of Assyria Cuneiform Texts, Vol. VII). Helsinki, 2010.

No. 3: Selim Adali, *The Scourge of God: The Ummanmanda and Its Significance in the First Millennium BC* (= State Archives of Assyria Studies, Vol. XX). Helsinki, 2011.

No. 4: Heather D. Baker (ed.), *The Prosopography of the Neo-Assyrian Empire,* Volume 3, Part II. Helsinki, 2011.

No. 5: Sherry Lou Macgregor, *Beyond Hearth and Home: Women in the Public Sphere in Neo-Assyrian Society* (= State Archives of Assyria Studies, Vol. XXI). Helsinki, 2012.

No. 6: Mikko Luukko, *The Correspondence of Tiglath-Pileser III from Calah/Nimrud* (= State Archives of Assyria, Vol. XIX). Helsinki, 2013.

No. 7: Rumen Kolev, *The Babylonian Astrolabe: The Calendar of Creation* (= State Archives of Assyria Studies, Vol. XXII). Helsinki, 2013.

No. 8: Mikko Luukko and Simonetta Ponchia, *The Standard Babylonian Myth of Nergal and Ereškigal* (= State Archives of Assyria Cuneiform Texts, Vol. VIII). Helsinki, 2013.

No. 9: Takayoshi Oshima, *The Babylonian Theodicy* (= State Archives of Assyria Cuneiform Texts, Vol. IX). Helsinki, 2013.

No. 10: Heather D. Baker, *Neo-Assyrian Specialists: Crafts, Offices and other Professional Designations* (= Prosopography of the Neo-Assyrian Empire, Volume 4, Part I). Helsinki, 2017.

No. 11: Jamie Novotny, *Selected Royal Inscriptions of Assurbanipal: L3, L4, LET, Prism I, Prism T, and Related Texts* (= State Archives of Assyria Cuneiform Texts, Vol. X). Helsinki, 2014.

No. 12: Saana Svärd, *Women and Power in Neo-Assyrian Palaces* (= State Archives of Assyria Studies, Vol. XXIII). Helsinki, 2015.

No. 13: Simo Parpola, *Assyrian Royal Rituals and Cultic Texts* (= State Archives of Assyria, Vol. XX). Helsinki, 2017.

No. 14: Tzvi Abusch, *The Anti-Witchcraft Series Maqlû: A Student Edition and Selected Commentary* (= State Archives of Assyria Cuneiform Texts, Vol. XI). Helsinki, 2015.

No. 15: Amar Annus, *The Overturned Boat: Intertextuality of the Adapa Myth and Exorcist Literature* (= State Archives of Assyria Studies, Vol. XXIV). Helsinki, 2016.

No. 16/1-3: Simo Parpola, *Etymological Dictionary of the Sumerian Language I-III*. Helsinki, 2016, 2022.

No. 17: Vladimir Sazonov, *Die assyrischen Königstitel und –epitheta vom Anfang bis Tukulti-Ninurta I. und seinen Nachfolgern* (= State Archives of Assyria Studies, Vol. XXV). Helsinki, 2016.

No. 18: Baruch Ottervanger, *The Tale of the Poor Man of Nippur* (= State Archives of Assyria Cuneiform Texts, Vol. XII). Helsinki, 2016.

No. 19: Mattias Karlsson, *Alterity in Ancient Assyria* (= State Archives of Assyria Studies, Vol. XXVI). Helsinki, 2017.

No. 20: Simo Parpola, *The Correspondence of Assurbanipal, Part I; Letters from Assyria, Babylonia, and Vassal States* (= State Archives of Assyria, Vol. XXI). Helsinki, 2018.

No. 21: Jérôme Pace, *Mythopoëia, ou l'art de forger les « mythes »* (= State Archives of Assyria Studies, Vol. XXVII). Helsinki, 2018.

No. 22: Shigeo Yamada (ed.), *Neo-Assyrian Sources in Context: Thematic Studies on Texts, History, and Culture* (= State Archives of Assyria Studies, Vol. XXVIII). Helsinki, 2019.

No. 23: G.B. Lanfranchi, R. Mattila and R. Rollinger (eds.), *Writing Neo-Assyrian History: Sources, Problems, and Approaches* (= State Archives of Assyria Studies, Vol. XXIX). Helsinki, 2019.

No. 24: Johannes Bach, *Untersuchungen zur transtextuellen Poetik assyrischer herrschaftlich-narrativer Texte* (= State Archives of Assyria Studies, Vol. XXX). Helsinki, 2020.

No. 25: Mattias Karlsson, *From the Nile to the Tigris: African Individuals and Groups in Texts from the Neo-Assyrian Empire* (= State Archives of Assyria Studies, Vol. XXXI). Helsinki, 2022.